THE YALE EDITIONS OF

The Private Papers
of James Boswell

PRIDE AND NEGLIGENCE

The History of the

Boswell Papers

BY

FREDERICK A. POTTLE

STERLING PROFESSOR OF ENGLISH EMERITUS

YALE UNIVERSITY

McGraw-Hill Book Company

NEW YORK   TORONTO   LONDON

Thomas H. Quinn, Michael Hennelly, and Carolyn Cott were the editors of this book. Christine Aulicino was the designer. Teresa F. Leaden supervised the production. It was set in Garamond by Photo-Data, Inc.
Printed and bound by R.R. Donnelley & Sons, Inc.

Library of Congress Cataloging in Publication Data

Pottle, Frederick Albert
    The history of the Boswell papers.

    (The Yale editions of the private papers of James Boswell)
    Includes bibliographical references and index.
    1. Boswell, James, 1740–1795—Archives.   I. Title. II. Series: Yale editions of the private papers of James Boswell.
PR3325.P617 1980   828'.609   80–14710
1 2 3 4 5 6 7 8 9 RRD RRD 80987654321

PR
3325
.P617
1982

The preparation of *Pride and Negligence: The History of the Boswell Papers* was generously supported by the Research Program of the National Endowment for the Humanities. We are also deeply grateful for timely gifts of matching funds from the Andrew W. Mellon Foundation and the following individuals.

PATRONS

Curtis Carroll Davis   William Peyton May

Wilmarth S. Lewis   Warren H. Smith

FRIENDS

Richard N. Berry   Jean and Maurice Jacobs

Charles Beecher Hogan   Arthur M. Kaplan

Mary Hyde   Nonna and René Wellek

Margaret H. Wimsatt

The Yale Editions of the Private Papers of James Boswell consists of two independent but parallel series. One, the "research" edition, gives a complete text of Boswell's journals, notes, and memoranda, of his correspondence, and of the *Life of Johnson* from the original manuscript. It preserves the spelling and capitalization of the original documents, and is provided with extensive scholarly annotation. A large group of editors is engaged in this comprehensive undertaking. The first three volumes of at least thirty appeared in 1966, 1969, and 1976 respectively. The other series, the reading or "trade" edition, selects from the total mass of papers those portions that appear likely to be of general interest and presents them in modern spelling and with appropriate annotation. The publishers have also issued limited de luxe printings of some of the trade volumes, with extra illustrations and special editorial matter, but neither the trade volumes nor the de luxe printings include matter from Boswell's archives that will not appear in the research edition.

The present volume is a hybrid. It was planned many years ago to accompany and introduce Marion S. Pottle's *Catalogue* of the Boswell papers at Yale.

CONTENTS

ACKNOWLEDGEMENTS

This book was completed in an earlier form more than twenty years ago, and I fear that my memory as to who helped me then is very imperfect. Harriet Chidester certainly typed and retyped various drafts, and I had advice for revision from Frederick W. Hilles and Herman W. Liebert (Editorial Committee) and Robert F. Metzdorf (Secretary to the Committee). As for the later recasting and expansion, my memory is clearer. Caterina Kazemzadeh retyped the manuscript, which had become an untidy mixture of pencilled manuscript copy and typed pages scrawled with pencilled corrections. Much of the research and verification was delegated to Rachel McClellan and Carolyn M. Gould. Maura D. Shaw Tantillo and Carolyn Cott styled the final copy for the printer. Frank Brady, Herman W. Liebert, and Irma S. Lustig of the Editorial Committee read and criticized the finished copy for the printer. Alan S. Bell and Mary Hyde of the Advisory Committee read copy or proofs and returned valuable suggestions, as did also Heyward Isham. In my "Prologue" (p. 1) I acknowledge the great generosity of Heyward and Jonathan Isham in lending me for extended periods many of their father's papers that touch upon this history.

Myrtle Baird and Dr. Jean Munro looked up various matters for me in the Scottish Record Office and elsewhere in Edinburgh. Dr. Francis H. W. Sheppard, General Editor, Survey of London, found and sent us copies of Euphemia Boswell's will and directed us further to the National Register of Archives (Scotland), Edinburgh, where Dr. Peter Anderson, Senior Research Assistant, turned up evidence of William George Adam's continuing kindness to Euphemia.

Marlene Demarque compiled the index.

I leave to my "Prologue" to detail my extensive and pervasive debt to David Buchanan.

Sterling Library,   FREDERICK A. POTTLE
Yale University
16 February 1981

CUE TITLES AND ABBREVIATIONS

A: See *Catalogue* in the present list.

BP: *The Private Papers of James Boswell from Malahide Castle, in the Collection of Lt.-Col. Ralph Heyward Isham,* ed. Geoffrey Scott and F. A. Pottle, 18 vols., 1928–1934. Index vol., 1937.

C: See *Catalogue* in the present list.

Catalogue: M. S. Pottle, C. C. Abbott, and F. A. Pottle, forthcoming *Catalogue of the Papers of James Boswell at Yale University.* Each item is assigned an individual number in one of seven categories: A (e.g. A 20) = accounts; C (e.g. C 45) = correspondence, all letters not by Boswell; J (e.g. J 55) = journal by Boswell; L (e.g. L 25) = letters by Boswell; Lg (e.g. Lg 3) = legal papers; M (e.g. M 5) = manuscripts by Boswell not accounts, journal, or letters; and P (e.g. P 60) = printed pieces.

DNB: *The Dictionary of National Biography from the Earliest Times to 1900,* ed. Sir Leslie Stephen and Sir Sidney Lee, various printings.

Earlier Years: F. A. Pottle, *James Boswell: The Earlier Years, 1740–1769,* 1966.

Fac. Adv.: Sir Francis J. Grant, *The Faculty of Advocates in Scotland, 1532–1943,* 1944. (Scottish Record Society, part 145.)

Fettercairn Papers: Papers in the collection of Mrs. Peter Somervell, now deposited in the National Library of Scotland. Photocopies at Yale.

Gent. Mag.: *The Gentleman's Magazine,* 1731–1907.

IFC: Isham's Fettercairn Correspondence. Correspondence, 1936–49, between the late Lt.-Col. Ralph H. Isham and his solicitors, Denton Hall and Burgin of London and Steedman Ramage and Co., W. S., Edinburgh. Isham's own communications are drafts or copies. Lent by Heyward and Jonathan T. Isham for the preparation of *Pride and Negligence: The History of the Boswell Papers.*

IFP: Correspondence and other personal papers of Lt.-Col. Ralph H. Isham, now in the custody of his son Jonathan T. Isham at New Canaan, Connecticut. Isham's own communications are drafts or copies. Generally cited as from David Buchanan, TA.

ILP: Isham Legal Papers, David Buchanan's designation for papers or copies of papers in the archives of Steedman Ramage and Co. or in the Isham family papers, or in both. My ILT is included in his ILP, but his ILP contains papers not in the Isham Legal Papers lent to me. Always cited as from TA.

ILT: Isham Legal Transcripts. Typed transcripts of legal documents made for Isham for use in the Fettercairn Cause. Lent by Heyward and Jonathan T. Isham.

ILT: List A: Transcripts made in 1936 by or for Steedman Ramage and Co. from documents then in the hands of Scott Moncrieff and Trail, W. S., Edinburgh, at that time solicitors for the sixth Lord Talbot de Malahide. At the time of the death of Joyce, Lady Talbot de Malahide (1 July 1980), these documents, belonging to her, were either in her house of Abbeylea, Ballybrack, Co. Dublin, Eire, or in the hands of David Shaw and Co., solicitors, Ayr, Scotland. Lent by Heyward and Jonathan T. Isham.

ILT: List B: Transcripts made by Denton Hall and Burgin from documents lent directly to Colonel Isham by the sixth Lord Talbot de Malahide, as per inventory, 17 March 1937. At the time of the death of Joyce, Lady Talbot de Malahide (1 July 1980), these documents, belonging to her, were either in her house of Abbeylea, Ballybrack, Co. Dublin, Eire, or in the hands of David Shaw and Co., solicitors, Ayr, Scotland. Lent by Heyward and Jonathan T. Isham.

ILT: List C: Transcripts made by Denton Hall and Burgin and Steedman Ramage and Co., from printed legal documents, or documents in public registry. Lent by Heyward and Jonathan T. Isham.

ITC: Isham's Talbot Correspondence. Correspondence, 1926–49 between Isham, the sixth Lord Talbot de Malahide, Joyce, Lady Talbot de Malahide, and others concerning the Boswell papers at Malahide Castle. Isham's own communications are drafts or copies. Lent by Heyward and Jonathan T. Isham.

J: See *Catalogue* in the present list.

L: See *Catalogue* in the present list.

Letters JB: *Letters of James Boswell*, ed. C. B. Tinker, 2 vols., 1924.

Letters SJ: *The Letters of Samuel Johnson, with Mrs. Thrale's Genuine Letters to Him*, ed. R. W. Chapman, 3 vols., 1952.

Lg: See *Catalogue* in the present list.

Life: James Boswell, *The Life of Samuel Johnson*, originally published in 2 vols., 1791. Reference by volume and page is to the edition of G. B. Hill, revised by L. F. Powell, 6 vols., 1934–1964.

Lit. Car.: F. A. Pottle, *The Literary Career of James Boswell*, 1929; reprinted 1965, 1967.

Lond. Chron.: *The London Chronicle*, 1757 + . (The title varies, but is *The London Chronicle* throughout the volumes to which I make reference.)

M: See *Catalogue* in the present list.

OED: *Oxford English Dictionary*.

P: See *Catalogue* in the present list.

P.C.C.: Prerogative Court of Canterbury.

Reg. B. of C. and S.: Registered in the Books of Council and Session, Register House, Edinburgh. "Dur[ie]" and "Mack[enzie]" indicate the office.

Sat. Rev. Lit.: *Saturday Review (of Literature)*, New York, 1924–1951.

Scots Mag.: *The Scots Magazine*, 1739–1817.

TA: David Buchanan, *The Treasure of Auchinleck*, 1974.

TFP: Talbot Family Papers, being correspondence and other papers in the possession of Joyce, Lady Talbot de Malahide at the time of her death. Lord and Lady Talbot's own communications are drafts or copies. Always cited as from TA.

TLS: *Times Literary Supplement*, London

PROLOGUE

THE STORY OF THE RECOVERY of the Boswell papers is interesting enough to be told in detail and important enough to be subjected to periodic revision. The appearance of Marion S. Pottle's comprehensive *Catalogue of the Papers of James Boswell at Yale University* would seem to justify the correcting and extending of a narrative which I published almost thirty years ago in the *de luxe* edition of *Boswell's London Journal*.[1] I hope that besides introducing the *Catalogue* it will also be found readable as a book in its own right.

The original plan of the Editorial Committee of the Yale Editions indeed called for publication of Catalogue and extended History together twenty years ago, before any other of the volumes of the Research Edition; and I began my revision of the History in 1958 in accordance with that plan. The history I had published in 1951 had been written with hardly any knowledge of the evidence which had been collected and fitted together by Colonel Isham's lawyers in the Fettercairn litigation (1936–48). I had, I fear, assumed that the arguments in that case consisted almost entirely of abstract legal principles neither compelling nor useful to an historian. But when Colonel Isham's sons, Heyward and Jonathan T. Isham, responding generously to the plea of the Committee to lend me whatever matter they had which might be helpful, deposited in the Yale Library the mass of legal transcripts which

---

[1] *Boswell's London Journal, 1762–1763, together with Journal of My Jaunt. Harvest 1762*, William Heinemann, Ltd., 1951. Three significant studies had appeared earlier: (1) Geoffrey Scott's "General Introduction" to the first volume of *Private Papers of James Boswell from Malahide Castle in the Collection of Lt.-Colonel Ralph Heyward Isham*, 1928; (2) my "Preface" to *The Private Papers of James Boswell from Malahide Castle in the Collection of Lt.-Colonel Ralph Heyward Isham: A Catalogue*, by Frederick A. Pottle and Marion S. Pottle, 1931; (3) "Boswell's Archives", by R. W. Chapman, in *Essays and Studies by Members of the English Association*, xvii. 1931 (pub. 1932).

the lawyers had assembled, I found my views of the History quite revolutionized. I had not known that James Boswell's debts were so large; I had not known that his children had to resort to arbitration to resolve the ambiguities of his will; I had not known that his elder son's debts were so huge that the creditors of his personal estate were fain to settle for only ten shillings in the pound. The Isham brothers also greatly extended my knowledge of events by putting in my hands the file of their father's correspondence with Lord and Lady Talbot de Malahide. Problems raised by that correspondence caused me to write to many other people who were in a position to give direct testimony.

My narrative was completed for publication in the spring of 1960, and was submitted for comment to Lady Talbot de Malahide, to Heyward and Jonathan Isham, and to various members of the Advisory Board, including Donald F. Hyde. On 10 March 1962, Mr. and Mrs. Hyde and the Isham brothers met in New Haven with the Editorial Committee and requested that the scope and style of the History be reconsidered. Instead of a diachronical history of the papers from 1795, they wished a narrative focused on Colonel Isham's character and achievement; they felt that the behaviour of the late R. W. Chapman in the Fettercairn episode should be more fully scrutinized; and they thought the handling throughout should be more dramatic and lively. It was agreed that publication should be postponed till they could submit an alternative narrative for my consideration. Hyde then asked David Buchanan, W. S., partner in the Edinburgh firm of Steedman Ramage and Co., to compile a record of the legal aspects of the story. (Buchanan's father, E. P. Buchanan, also a partner of Steedman Ramage and Co., had managed Isham's case in the Fettercairn litigation before the Court of Session in Edinburgh.)[2] David Buchanan, however, soon became deeply interested in the story as a whole, went far beyond Hyde's commission, and ended by producing a full and extended account, which was submitted to the Editorial Committee eight years after the meeting which authorized it. Hyde had meantime died (1966).

On 27 October 1970, writing for the Editorial Committee, I informed Mrs. Hyde that because of fundamental differences of scope, organization, and tone, it did not appear feasible to merge David Buchanan's account with mine, and that, as a massive and coherent study in its own right, it merited independent publication. David Buchanan has accordingly published his account,[3] and I am now publishing mine.

The circumstances of the case complicate the usual etiquette of acknowledgement. David Buchanan, as he kindly states, had my manuscript before him from the first, and with my permission used it as freely as though it had been a published book. Though he has preceded me in publication, I shall not think it necessary to

---

[2]To prevent confusion in what follows, I have thought it wise to use specific style (E. P. Buchanan, David Buchanan) wherever either is mentioned.

[3]*The Treasure of Auchinleck*, 1974.

acknowledge debt to him for matter that stood substantially in its present form before he began work on his book. He collected a great deal of evidence that I did not have, and I have revised my narrative accordingly. I have ended by taking more from him than he took from me. I have tried to acknowledge the evidence and ideas that I really had from him, but I am uncomfortably aware that my indebtedness has not been fully stated. One improves one's work in all kinds of minute and subtle ways after reading a parallel study by a vigorous and sometimes opposed mind. And my debt has not been confined to the text of David Buchanan's book. I read his drafts and his proofs, and we carried on a correspondence, voluminous on both sides, in which we argued contested points and attempted to resolve our differences. He has also read the present book in typescript and has sent me extended comments on it.

Though this history deals mainly with the papers of the Biographer of Johnson, it will not be amiss to remind the reader at the outset that the Boswell papers at Yale are in fact what remains of the papers of a landed family founded in 1504. The papers of the sixteenth-century Boswells of Auchinleck are comparatively few and are mainly of the charter sort; indeed, it was not till the latter half of the seventeenth century that Auchinleck began to acquire archives of general historical interest. Anna Hamilton, wife of David Boswell, the sixth laird, was sister to Sir David Hamilton, Kt., physician to Queen Anne: he wrote her many pious letters which went into the Auchinleck archives. The seventh laird, Old James Boswell (as we call him to distinguish him from his more famous grandson), betook himself to a profession and a town life through at least half of each year. An advocate with one of the largest practices at the Scots bar, he married the youngest daughter of the second Earl of Kincardine, and through that marriage acquired interesting and valuable Bruce papers: letters of Lord Kincardine, of his Dutch countess Veronica van Aerssen van Sommelsdyck, and of some of her noble relations. Old James himself wrote and preserved a diary and expense account covering his years of study at the University of Leiden. The eighth laird, Boswell's father, a judge, antiquary, and classical scholar, formed a fine library of books at Auchinleck and systematically extended the archives. The tenth laird, Boswell's son, left a large deposit of personal papers, and there are also at Yale many from the time of the later heirs to the estate. Mrs. Pottle's *Catalogue* deals fully with the papers of the Biographer and selectively with those of Old James Boswell, Lord Auchinleck, Sir Alexander Boswell, and Sir James Boswell; the other documents in the collection have been inventoried at Yale, but must wait for a published catalogue.

PUZZLES
AT THE OUTSET

IN ORDER TO UNDERSTAND the nature of the motley heap of documents
which it is the purpose of the *Catalogue* to describe, one needs to know something
about the motives which caused—better say, drove—James Boswell to make that
extraordinary collection. Some of those motives are obvious and could be assumed.
He was, to begin with, a collector in the ordinary sense of the word. The fine library
of books at Auchinleck, as I have said, was formed principally by his father and
his elder son, but he made intelligent additions to it. He went more or less
systematically about the business of getting famous living men to write him autograph letters, and was distressed if the letters were mechanically imperfect. "I
beg you may put John Wilkes at the end of your letters," he wrote to one of his
favourite correspondents, "that they may not look like unsigned Title Deeds." He
was proud of adding to his collection things like the manuscript of Allan Ramsay's
Gentle Shepherd which Ramsay himself had presented to the Countess of Eglinton,
to whom the piece was dedicated.

And he was an earnest if fitful antiquary. He spent hours on end in the Laigh
Parliament House reading the records of the Privy Council of Scotland and making
extracts. He studied the Registers of Baptisms of the city of Edinburgh from 1700,
taking notes on the people he knew. He carried on an antiquarian correspondence
with Lord Hailes, and hunted out answers for problems which Hailes sent him. He
was a literary historian (does not the *Life of Johnson* exhibit "a view of literature and
literary men in Great-Britain, for near half a century"?) and was always on the
lookout for the manuscript stuff from which the liveliest part of literary history is
written. He begged or simply made off with interesting papers belonging to other
people when he found them lying about and thought they were not likely to be

preserved. He referred more than once—pompously but not inaccurately—to his "Archives at Auchinleck".

These traits are important and must not be overlooked, but by themselves they are not enough to account for Boswell's papers. The ones that count for more are a passion for being known, a hunger for self-analysis and for good advice, a sheer disinterested love of the varieties of human nature, and a compulsion to extend life by a written record.

Boswell was an egoist and an exhibitionist. The fear that his wavering flame would be overcome by the darkness of contemporary unconcern or of future forgetfulness was with him an obsession. He cheerfully admitted that if Dr. Kippis, who referred to him in print as "the ingenious, worthy, and well-known author of the Account of Corsica", "had ransacked Johnson's Dictionary for epithets to please Mr. Boswell he could not have done more for him. . . . *Virum volitare per ora* has allways been Mr. Boswell's ambition." Like others not unknown to fame, he thought bad publicity better than none. There can be no doubt that in seeking out the great he was impelled by a wish to be talked about, to ensure himself of present and future notice by connecting his name with those of as many famous men as possible. Would not the world, after reviewing his epistolary correspondence, see that Sir John Hawkins had been malevolent in referring to him as if he were quite unknown?

To any one who has not lived long and intimately with Boswell, this passion for being widely known will seem not only the surface trait which he presents most consistently to the public but actually the most significant of his urges. There are in fact some that go deeper; or at least it is possible to get below the passion for being known and talked of and to see it in more fundamental terms. Boswell combined overweening ambition with an unusual amount of self-doubt and vacillation. His exhibitionism was at least partly compensatory. He was always analyzing himself unfavourably and always seeking out great men—Johnson, Rousseau, Voltaire, Paoli—in the hope that they could infuse into him something of their own strength of character. One of his reasons for keeping a journal was to record the good advice of those whom he had elected to be his mentors.

Finally, and most important, he had an enormous and disinterested zest for living. He relished every variety of human nature, but he was especially a connoisseur of articulate greatness. Conversational wit and wisdom were for him a passion and a feeling. Yet the feast was not complete, the experience not really lived through, until he had got it written down. "I should live no more than I can record," he once wrote, "as one should not have more corn growing than one can get in." Hence his ideal of an extended confessional journal of high literary finish for every day of his life. He fell far short of his ideal, but he probably did manage to write more private journal of real literary excellence than anybody else has ever done. Where the fully written journal fails, he has often left condensed journals and diaries. The great journal, with its subsidiary diaries and notes, is the frame of reference for all the rest. To use Wordsworth's figure (Wordsworth would not have approved), it is the cathedral to which the other papers are cells, oratories, and sepulchral recesses.

Wordsworth kept *The Prelude* in manuscript during his lifetime, but gave permission for it to be published immediately after his death. It is not necessary to make Boswell's journal another *Prelude* in order to continue the comparison usefully. Wordsworth wished the story of the growth of his own mind to be given to the world, but felt that it would be embarrassing and in bad taste to publish it himself. He wished also to save his wife and children from embarrassment after he was gone. Consequently, though he had told them all about his illegitimate daughter, he contented himself in *The Prelude* with the uneasy mystification of Vaudracour and Julia. Surely, if he had been writing for 1950 instead of 1850, he would have given in the poem a straightforward account of his brief and passionate encounter with Annette Vallon—or at least as much of an account as was relevant to the story of his education as a poet. Boswell was not inhibited by scruples as to bad taste and was not embarrassed by general public disclosures concerning his own character. He not only wished to be talked about; he also had a kind of strange feeling as if he wished nothing to be secret that concerned himself. But he had a very natural wish to have it in his own power to control the disclosures. Any thought of his private records falling into the hands of strangers filled him with horror, and on at least one occasion he expressed a clear conviction that a full publication of his journals in his children's lifetimes would be undesirable for their sakes. He put the journals in the archives and probably hoped they would some day be published in full—say, about 1950. He probably hoped that selective publication would be possible sooner. When, in his will, he left power to three of his intimate friends to publish at discretion from his papers, specifically mentioning manuscripts of his own composition, it may have been with the wistful thought that his friends could do for his great autobiography what Wordsworth personally was to do for his. He certainly did not think a full publication immediately feasible. And it is probable that his main object in appointing literary executors was not the extended publication of the journal at all.

Boswell drew his will on 28 May 1785, ten years before his death. Though it was this document alone that governed the disposition of his papers, its terms become clearer when one realizes that his provisions for the care of his family and the distribution of his property after his death are contained in not one but several documents, the will being the fourth in the series. On 7 August 1776 he had joined with his father in executing a deed of entail which made it unnecessary, and indeed out of his power, to determine further the inheritance of the ancestral landed estate. Auchinleck, on his own death, would go automatically to his eldest son. What the entail did leave him power to do was to burden the estate with provisions for his wife and the children who did not succeed. And the entail did not affect his own personal estate, which, at the time he drew the will, included not only lands he had himself purchased, but also the library, furniture, and plate ("the effects" at Auchinleck)—and the archives.

On 4 January 1780 he nominated his wife and Sir William Forbes tutors and curators of his children, expressing a wish that all his children should be partly educated in England, and that any of his sons who should show a disposition for learning should be kept some years at the University of Oxford. "And I hope they will be brought up with an attachment to Auchinleck the seat of their ancestors." A codicil added to the document four days later merely limited the legal responsibilities of the guardians. He succeeded to the estate on 30 August 1782.

On 19 March 1785, just before setting off for London on a jaunt which he knew would be protracted, he made the provision for his wife and children (other than Alexander) which the entail permitted, appointing to his wife the liferent of certain "locality" lands in the Auchinleck estate, should he predecease her, and charging the estate with annuities for James, Veronica, Euphemia, and Elizabeth. Then, in London, on 28 May 1785, being, as he says, "under the apprehension of some danger to my life, which however may prove a false alarm", he drew what he calls his last will and testament.

In the will, he appointed his wife and Sir William Forbes to be his executors, with provision that if either predeceased him the survivor should serve alone. He attempted to ensure that two treasured family heirlooms, the ebony cabinet and the silver-gilt dressing-plate of his great-grandmother Veronica, Countess of Kincardine, should always remain in the family, by disponing them to the successive heirs of entail of Auchinleck, with a provision that any heir who should alienate them should forfeit £1,000. He left all the lands he held in fee simple (that is, the lands he had purchased himself) to the heirs of entail, subject to the payment of his debts, requiring the first heir, within six months of succeeding, to put these lands under the Auchinleck entail. He left his brother Thomas David £100 to purchase a piece of plate and his brother John fifty guineas to purchase a ring "or whatever other thing he may like best to keep for my sake". He bequeathed gold mourning-rings to ten named friends. He left his overseer James Bruce and his housekeeper Mrs. Bell Bruce small annuities and other benefits. He granted favourable leases to several of his tenants at Auchinleck whose families had possessed their farms for many generations. Since the remaining provisions present the principal problem addressed by this narrative, they had better be given in his own words.

> Furthermore as my late honoured Father made a very curious collection of the
> Classicks and other Books which it is desireable should be preserved for ever in the
> Family of Auchinleck I do by these presents dispone to the successive heirs of entail
> of the Barony of Auchinleck ⟨the⟩¹ greek and latin Books, as also all Manuscripts of

---

¹The holograph original is a single folio leaf, written on both sides. The upper left-hand corner of the recto has been torn off, with consequent mutilation of the ends of the first four lines on the verso. The word at the end of the second line is missing without trace. A copy certified by T. D. Boswell ("Compared and found to agree with the original this copy has been immediately sealed up. London 25 May 1795") reads "the" with no mention of a lacuna (ILT: List A). The lacuna was noted when the will was copied into the Register Volume of the Books of Council and Session at some date very soon after 7 Aug. 1795.

whatever kind lying in the House of Auchinleck under the same conditions and under the same forfeiture as I have mentioned with regard to the Ebony Cabinet and dressing Plate. And all my other moveable Estate or executry, I leave equally among my younger children the furniture in the House of Auchinleck to be valued by two sworn Appraisers and the Heir to keep it at that value and pay the same to my younger children, excepting however all my pictures which I dispone to the said successive heirs of entail under the same conditions and forfeiture as above mentioned and excepting also the furniture in my house at Edinburgh which I bequeath to my dear Wife. . . . And I hereby leave to the said Sir William Forbes the Reverend Mr. Temple and Edmund Malone Esquire all my Manuscripts of my own composition and all my letters from various persons to be published for the benefit of my younger children as they shall decide that is to say they are to have a discretionary power to publish more or less.

A codicil added two days later is of great interest to a biographer but contains nothing that affects this narrative. Of crucial importance for our present purpose, however, is a second and final codicil added on 22 December of the same year:

Having entire confidence in the discretion honour and talents of my friend Edmund Malone Esqr. I, in case of my death leave to him the care of all my Collection of Papers and Letters and Memorandums for writing the Life of Dr. Johnson in token whereof I now deliver to the said Edmond Malone Esqr. the key of my Bureau in the house of General Paoli in which Bureau he will find the key of a drawer belonging to it in which are several parcels of the said materials, as also the key of a Trunk belonging to me which is at Mr. Dilly's in which Trunk are many volumes of a Journal or Diary kept by me, from which a variety of passages concerning Dr. Johnson may be excerpted I trust that he will not divulge any thing he may find in the said Volumes which ought to be concealed and as I have already by my Will left what profits may arise from the publication of any of my papers, to my younger children I depend on my friends attention to their interest in what is hereby committed to him.

If we combine this codicil with Boswell's statement that he drew his will under the apprehension of some danger to his life, we shall have a better notion of what was his principal purpose in appointing literary executors. His apprehensions rose from his having just published a feverish pamphlet (*Letter to the People of Scotland,* 1785) containing a good deal of outspoken criticism of Henry Dundas, the political boss of Scotland. He feared that Dundas might call him out and shoot him. When he named the three literary trustees, it is most likely that his main concern was for his Johnsonian materials. To put his journal, or his correspondence with the great, or his projected memoirs of Lord Kames, or his travels on the Continent, in shape for publication would have required many hours of skilled and devoted editorial labour, and he could not confidently predict that any of these works would make money. As for his projected memoirs of Johnson, he was in no doubt at all. Only Boswell himself could have produced the *Life of Johnson* as we know it, but any intelligent editor could have prepared for the press the manuscript account of the tour to the Hebrides with Johnson, and could have gone on to compile from the other papers a highly saleable book of Johnsonian letters and conversations. And

Boswell knew it. In the previous December, on the day after he heard the news of Johnson's death, he had received a letter from his publisher, Dilly, asking him if he could have a biography of four hundred pages ready in six weeks. He had already told Dilly that he intended to take his time with the biography, but having satisfied himself that the Hebridean journal would make a publishable book by itself, he had resolved to take advantage of the great current interest in Johnsoniana by bringing out that portion of his saga immediately. As soon as he could manage it, he had gone down to London to revise the manuscript and see it through the press. But he had allowed himself to be distracted by dissipation and diverted into the Dundas business, and had hardly got started on the revision when the publication of the pamphlet put him under apprehension of danger to his life. Under the circumstances, he could not help thinking with dismay of the commercial value, not only of the Hebridean journal if once it could be got into the printer's hands, but also of everything else in his collection bearing on Johnson. And he could not help thinking either of the scanty provision his previous settlements had made for his younger children. (In 1785 all his children were young: the oldest twelve, the youngest five.)[2]

The apprehension did prove a false alarm. Dundas did not call him out, and was perhaps less annoyed by the *Letter to the People of Scotland* than Boswell had hoped he would be. Boswell published the Hebridean journal without mishap. And the encouragement and expert assistance which he received from Malone during the preparation of that book caused him to modify his literary trust. After the *Journal of a Tour to the Hebrides* had been published, he added the codicil quoted above, entrusting to Malone singly his materials for a life of Johnson. The last sentence of the codicil surely makes clear that he never intended that his journal should be printed in its entirety by his literary executors.

The codicil became inoperative when Boswell completed the *Life of Johnson* himself in 1791, but he made no further changes in the will. This cannot confidently be attributed to negligence, for we know that he did review his settlements twice after that time. On 12 October 1791 (the *Life* had appeared in May) he nominated Thomas David Boswell guardian to the children in place of Mrs. Boswell, who had died in 1789, and on the same day directed that his daughters' annuities should not be cut on marriage as stipulated in the settlement of March 1785.[3] Then on 3 March 1795, at a meeting of The Club (the document is witnessed by the Duke of Leeds, Lord Macartney, Lord Palmerston, and Sir William Scott), he gave effect to an enthusiastic declaration made many years before that his daughter Veronica should have £500 of additional fortune because at the age of four months she had shown fondness for Dr. Johnson. This was only a little over two months before his

---

[2]"Younger", as it appears in Boswell's settlements, is technical: it means "all my children except my heir". In point of fact two of his daughters were older than the elder son, Alexander. In what follows I have sometimes used the term myself for the sake of brevity.

[3]See above, p. 8.

death. All the settlements except the entail were completely in his own hand and were obviously of his own devising. It would have saved a good deal of trouble later if he had enlisted the services of some lawyer with more practice in drawing such documents.

It is not difficult to find reasons for his retaining the provision for literary executors. He still had in mind to publish the book of his travels on the Continent, and may have thought it prudent to provide for the completion of that work if he should die with it unfinished. The review of the journal which he had made in writing the *Life* may have confirmed him in thinking that somebody could make a book out of his vast autobiographical record. At any rate, when he died on 19 May 1795, Forbes, Malone, and Temple found themselves entrusted with the task of reviewing his papers and deciding whether any further publication should be made.

Since it was afterwards alleged that the entire business of the trust was administered by Forbes,[4] it is important to record that all three literary executors took their trust seriously. It is true that they never met all together to discuss their course of action (Forbes lived in Edinburgh, Malone in London, and Temple near Penryn, Cornwall), but Temple did meet with Malone, and Forbes attempted to secure joint decision by long, careful letters to Malone and Temple. Malone and Forbes both went through a large part of the papers, and arrangements would undoubtedly have been made for Temple to read in them as extensively as he chose if he had not died within fifteen months of Boswell.

The papers were numerous and were partly at Auchinleck and partly in London. The journals, especially, had been removed from Scotland because Boswell needed them in writing the *Life,* and had never returned them. Docketing on some of the letters now at Yale appears to indicate that Alexander Boswell collected the papers in London. Forbes certainly trusted Alexander, with whom he was associated as executor and guardian, to sort out those at Auchinleck. Alexander (who was then only nineteen) reported on 8 July 1795 that the appraisers had already done their work at Auchinleck and that the cattle had been sold. He promised within a few days to bring in to Edinburgh "all letters that can possibly concern litterary Subjects" in order that Forbes might "chuse such as are fit for publication".[5] If he was as selective as this sounds, it is possible that some of Boswell's papers that we now consider important remained at Auchinleck during all the vicissitudes next to be described.

Forbes, though fully recognizing Temple's right to be consulted, at first went into specifics only with Malone, no doubt because Malone already had access to a

---

[4]Below, p. 57.

[5]In an earlier letter to Forbes he had written, "I cannot think of parting with an old favourite Cow of my Mothers aged 15—nor my Fathers old Horse now of little use being about 24 years old. He was bred here and my Father determined that he should run about for his life—These therefore I shall take the liberty of buying at the Sale" (24 June 1795, Fettercairn Papers). See *Life* iv. 248, 250.

large part of the papers. On 14 August 1795—three months after Boswell's death—
he wrote to Malone as follows:

> Mr. Boswell has left with me a large parcel of his Fathers letters and papers; being
> a part of that Collection, with the charge of examining which Our late worthy friend,
> by his will, has honoured Mr. Temple, and you, and me: A task, this, it must be
> owned of very considerable delicacy.—Yet, I think we may lay down to ourselves
> certain Canons or principles, by which to judge whether any, or what part of the papers
> may be proper for publication. . . .
>
> I am busily employed in perusing the whole, which, as soon as I have gone thro'
> them, I shall pack up in a Box and forward to you by the Waggon; and in the same
> manner, when you have perused those letters and papers that are in the house in London,
> I shall be much obliged to you to take the trouble of forwarding them to me by the
> same mode of conveyance. They shall be afterwards carefully returned to you.

Forbes's letter went unanswered for more than eight months. Malone's excuses,
partially conveyed through James Boswell the younger, were that he was out of
town on a five-months' bout of research when Forbes's letter arrived; that delivery
of the letter was delayed even after his return; and that in any case his eyes were
not in condition for more manuscript work till towards the end of December. He
read in Boswell's papers then, but postponed reply while he wrote and published
his book exposing the Ireland forgeries. It was not until 25 April 1796 that he
finally got to his answer.

> I never think without regret of our late worthy and most kind friend, and of the
> manner in which by his own imprudence he in fact threw away his life. . . .
>
> I have carefully examined all his papers, but I do not find any thing intended or
> proper for publication. He had meditated a Life of Lord Kaims, for which materials
> were collected, but nothing written. His Journals are extremely curious, and at some
> future period, I mean eight or ten years hence, his second son, who is a very promising
> young man, when his education is finished, and his mind more mature, might I think
> make an entertaining work out of them, sifting and garbelling them properly; for in
> the freedom of his heart, he put down many things both of himself and others that
> should not appear. They are very numerous, for he continued to journalise till the year
> 1794, though latterly less copiously and with less vivacity than formerly.—As these
> Journals are the only MSS. of any value that he has left, and their loss would be
> irretrievable, I would submit to you, Sir, whether it would not be more prudent to
> let them remain here than run the risk of their transmission to Scotland, as probably
> business or pleasure may draw you hither ere long, when you can have an opportunity
> of examining them all. I have looked into some of them, and always with pleasure,
> but it was so mixed with melancholy at reviewing scenes in many of which I was myself
> engaged, that several of them have been still unexamined.—There are some letters and
> minutes concerning Voltaire, Rousseau, and other celebrated men, while he was abroad,
> that would render some little account of his travels curious: but that must also be
> hereafter the work of his son James.

Though Malone does not say so, he had already been in touch with Temple, who had called on him in London on 2 July, just before Malone departed for Oxford. Temple reported the meeting in a letter to Forbes written on 27 April 1796, that is, almost simultaneously with the letter of Malone's just cited. Temple acknowledges "the memorial of our ever to be lamented Friend" (the gold mourning-ring specified in Boswell's will), and says he is very desirous of the honour of Forbes's acquaintance and correspondence, which surely indicates that if he had had any letters from Forbes up to that time, they had been official, brief, and impersonal. Temple devotes the greater part of his letter to a request that all his letters to Boswell and all Boswell's letters to himself found among Boswell's papers be ultimately given to him in accordance with an agreement of his and Boswell's that the survivor should be put in possession of the whole correspondence. The part of the letter touching directly on the literary trust ran as follows:

> When I saw Mr. Malone and Mr. Langton in London in October last, I had some conversation with them respecting his Papers (not with them together, but separately) and it was doubted whether it would be better to select and publish them while his parts and talents were fresh in every one's memory, or to wait till his sons were of age. Various intentions and purposes are mentioned to me in his Letters, but I fear he made little progress in any of them. Probably much interesting matter may be picked out of his Journals, but regard to living names may make great caution necessary in the use of them.

Forbes acceded to Malone's eminently sensible suggestion, already knowing that Temple was, to say the least, not eager for immediate publication. He wrote to Malone on 30 June 1796:

> I much approve of your idea of our doing nothing in regard to the publication of any of our late much regarded friend's papers at present; but rather to wait till his second son be of an age fit for selecting such of them as may be proper for the publick eye.—Of those which were brought to me from Auchinleck-house, I have read a considerable part; but find them to consist almost entirely of letters from his private friends, by no means fit for the press, but highly valuable and interesting to his family; as they contain the most striking memorials of the high degree of estimation in which he was held by as numerous and respectable a Circle of Acquaintance, as almost any private Gentleman, I believe, could boast of.—Besides these, there is one and but one Journal of a Circuit.[6]—After I have gone thro' the whole, I will carefully send them to you, in order that the papers may be altogether.—His journals are, indeed, exceedingly Curious, for it was a faculty he possessed and had Cultivated far beyond any man I ever knew. He used occasionally, during our uninterrupted intercourse while he resided in Edinburgh, to favour me with a perusal of these; and they ever afforded me a rich entertainment.—I therefore look forward with great expectation to my having

---

[6] I think this means, "Besides the letters, there is one and but one journal: it is a journal of a circuit."

the opportunity of seeing those now in your possession.—Altho I have no immediate, I may rather say, scarcely a remote view of being in London, I cannot urge you to send them to me, if you are impressed with any idea, that they would be exposed to danger by the way; Altho I do not myself entertain the smallest doubt of their arriving here very safely, if packt in a Box and sent by the Waggon.

A few days afterwards he wrote to Temple, no doubt relaying Malone's suggestion. The letter is not known to exist, but Temple recorded its receipt in his diary: "Tuesday 19th [July 1796] . . . Recd. a long letter from Sir Wm. Forbes respecting my dear Boswell's Letters and Papers." He died less than a month later, without casting his vote, so far as is known. But since he had said of what was for him the most sensitive portion of the papers (his correspondence with Boswell), "I am ready to concur in whatever may be thought for the good of the Family", there is no reason to suppose that he would have dissented from the judgement of his colleagues.

In the summer of 1796 young James Boswell was seventeen years old. He was his father's favourite and had much of his father's temperament and literary tastes. But the reason for leaving the decision to him was surely not, as has been suggested, that Alexander had scant sympathy with his father's literary reputation. (I shall return to this charge later on.) It was partly because Malone and Forbes had decided to shift to younger and less burdened shoulders the task of editing that any publication would require, and James appeared better fitted for this task than Alexander. It was mainly, however, because James would share the profits resulting from publication and Alexander would not.

Though the surviving letters of Forbes and Malone are by no means explicit as to what happened next, they do indicate that Forbes's programme was followed: that Forbes sent Malone the papers in his hands, and that Malone later sent the united collection to Forbes in Scotland. The papers had presumably left London some time before May 1799, the date of publication of the third edition of the *Life,* for Malone in that edition queried the accuracy of the text of a letter from Johnson to Bennet Langton, adding, "but the original letter not being now in Mr. Langton's hands, the errour (if it be one) cannot be corrected". Langton had informed him that Boswell had not given the letter back. We do not know why a search in Scotland was impossible or not feasible, but Malone would hardly have written as he did if Boswell's papers were still where he could search them himself. That he believed all the papers to have been returned to Scotland by this date is further indicated by a letter which Alexander Boswell wrote to Forbes on 5 June 1799: "I called on Mr. Malone today He knows of no more journals he however means to search and write to you soon." It would be most interesting to know what portion or portions of the journal Forbes thought to be missing—perhaps some of the leaves (still missing) which Boswell used as printer's copy for the *Life?*

Five years later, when Malone was seeing the fourth edition of the *Life* through the press, he asked Forbes to consult the original manuscripts of five letters of Johnson that Boswell had printed in whole or in part, and to verify readings which seemed to him suspicious. The detail is so complicated that much of it must be relegated to a back note, but the main points to be inferred from the correspondence that ensued seem to be as follows: Malone thought Forbes should have in his hands a letter from Johnson to an unnamed correspondent which Boswell had described as being in his own "large and various collection of [Johnson's] writings"; he thought Forbes should also have a letter from Johnson to Lucy Porter which Miss Porter's executor had informed him Boswell had never returned. He was not sure that Forbes would have three letters to Boswell which he wished consulted. He could naturally give Forbes no lead for running down the letter to the unnamed correspondent, but he thought the one to Lucy Porter would be found at the proper place in the manuscript of the *Life*. As for the letters to Boswell, "I apprehend he kept all Dr. Johnson's letters to himself in one bundle, and arranged in the order of time; and this bundle must be either in your possession or at Auchinleck." He also asked Forbes to keep an eye out for three documents which Boswell in the *Life* said he had deposited in the British Museum or the Bodleian Library, though he had in fact not done so. One puzzling feature of his queries is that though in his first letter (3 March 1804) he had asked Forbes to hunt out *three* letters from Johnson to Boswell, two months later he wrote as though he had never mentioned more than *one*. This is annoying, for one of the letters thus eliminated is crucial to our narrative, as will presently appear. The best explanation probably is that before Forbes's report on his search arrived, the printer had reached the three letters in question and Malone had had to settle the textual problems without help from the manuscripts. His procedure was on the whole conservative. Of his three suspected misreadings, he found one to be a simple corruption of the third edition and corrected it silently. A second, which occurred in a line of Sidney quoted by Johnson, he emended from Sidney's text, explaining in a footnote what he had done. The third, for which he had no external authority, he allowed to stand without change or comment. The letter he continued to ask about was that containing the line from Sidney. He was naturally more concerned to have confirmation of the emendation he had actually made than of the one he had not ventured.

Forbes's reports on his search are all untraced, and Malone's allusions do not enable us to reconstruct them with certainty. In particular, we cannot quite conclude from the negative evidence of the fourth edition of the *Life* that Forbes never turned up any of the eight documents Malone inquired about. He *may* have found some of them after the fourth edition was all in print, and his report *may* have been overlooked or forgotten when the copy for the fifth edition was prepared. But my own guess is that he replied that the papers were in complete disorder and that the finding of any particular document meant piecemeal sorting, which, without luck, might consume days; that he had spent several fruitless hours at the task, but could not be sure that the papers in question might not be somewhere in the mass.

Malone's reference to Auchinleck may be merely a general conclusion: since no papers remained in London, anything not in Forbes's hands must have somehow or other got to Auchinleck in Boswell's lifetime and must have been overlooked or deliberately retained when Alexander turned over the papers to Forbes. I suspect, however, that it is limited: he thought Boswell might well have placed in some special repository at Auchinleck the precious bundle containing Johnson's letters to himself. I do not think that he thought that any papers had been sent to Auchinleck since Boswell's death. We may safely conclude that all the papers brought to Forbes from Auchinleck and all the papers found in Boswell's house in London were in Forbes's hands from about 1797 to 1806. They remained there because Forbes was the senior literary executor and had better provision than Malone for storing papers; because the suggested ten years that were to elapse before James Boswell the younger was to survey the collection would extend to 1806; perhaps most important of all, because Forbes was the executor of the estate, and it was not till 1805 that he received judicial instruction as to how he was to distribute the personal or "moveable" property.

Boswell's settlements had proved to be inaccurate, ambiguous, and contradictory. Indeed, the only articles that gave the executor no trouble were those providing memorials for Boswell's brothers and a group of his friends. Good samples of the ambiguities of the will are furnished in the portion quoted above, pp. 8–9. Did Boswell intend to give the heirs of entail the entire "collection of the Classicks and other Books" at Auchinleck or only "the greek and latin Books"? Did he mean to give the same heirs "all my pictures" or merely all the pictures "in the House of Auchinleck"? (It made a difference, for his pictures by Reynolds of Johnson and himself were both in the house in London.) The most troublesome article, however, was the one which directed that the unentailed lands should go to the heir, but "after payment of my debts" and under a requirement of entailing the lands within six months. At the time of his death, Boswell held a considerable amount of landed property in fee simple. He had himself purchased the lands of Dalblair, of Willockshill, of Foardmouth, and of Knockroon, and had been given by his father a valuable dwelling-house in Edinburgh. But he had mortgaged the lands for at least two-thirds of their sale value and the house for more than it was now worth, and his other debts were large. A memorial drawn up shortly after his death by his cousin Robert Boswell for the five children and their tutors estimates the total debts at nearly £12,000, £5,870 of this amount being "heritable", that is, secured by the landed property. Assuming that "all my debts" meant literally all debts against the estate, Alexander was asked to pay nearly £12,000 and to receive funds estimated at about £9,000. But of the real estate, which represented the greater part of the funds, he could sell no part to meet the debts; rather, he had to entail it all and thereafter receive only rental from it. Two eminent advocates to whom he submitted a memorial advised him to abandon his father's heritage altogether and to represent him only as heir of entail, or at least to have only so much connexion with the heritage as to bring it to a judicial sale with the consent of the creditors. Alexander consequently put in motion a "process of sale and ranking", which required an action of the Court of Session, and therefore was not the sort of thing that could be done in a hurry. The properties were sold on 21 November 1798 and 22 May 1799. Alexander bought in Knockroon and Willockshill, but let the small property of Foardmouth and the large property of Dalblair go. This would have broken his father's heart, for Dalblair was the property which gave him his first territorial designation. It looks also in retrospect as though Dalblair was undervalued. It realized only £2,369 at the judicial sale, but in 1862 sold for £17,300, having by that time been surveyed and found to be rich in minerals.

The debts proved to have been underestimated, but the lands sold for more than had been expected, so that the total picture of Boswell's personal affairs turned out to be less gloomy than had been thought. After realizing nearly all the funds and paying nearly all the bills, Sir William Forbes, on 26 November 1801, found himself with a balance on hand of £2,103. 8s. 6d. The question now was, who had title to this surplus? If the provisions of the original settlements had been unclear, they were now rendered doubly uncertain by the fact that Alexander had had some of them set aside by judicial action. Furthermore, unfortunate antagonisms had developed among the heirs. Veronica had died on 26 September 1795, only four months after her father, of shockingly rapid consumption, her illness precipitated, it was said, by over-exertion in nursing her father, particularly by strains incurred in attempting to lift him in bed. James adored Alexander and, if he had stood by himself, would never have opposed Alexander in anything. But Euphemia, who attained her majority just at the time of her father's death, was strong-willed, independent, and incurably extravagant. She bought expensive and unsuitable attire and entertained lavishly, taking especial delight in private musicals. Her sole continuing provision under Boswell's settlements was an annuity of £100 a year, but at the time of his death she was already secretly in debt, and before the end of the year had to turn over to Forbes a sheaf of personal bills totalling £107. 10s. 10d. In 1801, at Auchinleck, where she had been living since 1796, she had to inform Forbes that she had run herself deeply in debt a second time, partly by lavish purchase of household supplies, partly by ordering clothes from a distance. When Alexander (as she believed, at his wife's insistence) let her know that it would not be unpleasing to him if she lived elsewhere, she took lodgings in Edinburgh and later in London, and as "Miss Boswell of Auchinleck" lived more in the style of a laird than of an annuitant. Always desperate (indeed, justly afraid of being incarcerated) because of her debts, she was not likely to overlook any opportunity of picking up sums of money however small. Alexander felt disgraced by her and allowed her letters to lie unopened.

Elizabeth, Boswell's "English" daughter, not quite fifteen at the time of his death, was not a good scholar, hated her school, and left it for good in 1797, when she went to live at Auchinleck with Euphemia, Alexander before his marriage (26 November 1799) being only occasionally in residence. In the summer of 1798 she fell violently in love with her second cousin, William Boswell, Robert Boswell's eldest son, and the pair of them, she eighteen and he a year and a half older, importuned Alexander for instant marriage. Alexander had previously been fond of William, but he treated his suit as in the highest degree preposterous and ridiculous, not primarily because his sister was too young to marry, nor even because she was in such a bad state of health (during 1798–99 she nearly died of an illness that seemed ominously like Veronica's), but because he thought she was marrying beneath her station and condemning herself to a life of squalid penury. He finally gave in with a completely bad grace, and was not mollified when Robert Boswell gave his son a marriage settlement guaranteeing him an income of £500 a year— a very considerable commitment, for William was still a student and did not pass advocate till the following July. After Elizabeth married in 1799, Alexander and James, so far as I can discover, never visited, spoke to, or wrote to her again.

Alexander himself, as will be evident, was far from faultless. Handsome, spirited, likeable, eminently sane, he was also imperious, impatient of opposition, and unforgiving. Worse, he was as extravagant and in his handling of money basically as irresponsible as Euphemia. He did not spend money foolishly, but he spent in a handsome fashion much more money than was his to spend. Sir William repeatedly offered to settle his affairs in such a way that by assigning a portion of his rents to pay interest and gradually extinguish his debts, he could from the first have £1,000 a year clear to live on. Unlike his three predecessors in the estate, Alexander had no professional earnings to eke out his rents, but he insisted from the first on living in a more lavish manner than they, making extensive improvements, living part of each year in Edinburgh and London, finally setting up a private printing-press and running for Parliament. Sir William had all along not only been confident that Boswell's estate would cover his debts and his legacies, but he had even continued to hope that there might be a surplus. He was keenly aware of the problems that might arise in dividing the surplus if there was one, and had hoped that Alexander would resolve the differences between himself and the other heirs by promptly paying in the considerable sums he owed the executry, and by timely offers of composition with the other heirs on matters of real perplexity. But Alexander never had any money except when he had just borrowed some, he showed temper when Euphemia asked legitimate questions, and by letting matters drift without yielding any points, he made sure that they would never be settled without legal action. When, in 1801, Euphemia indicated that she was going to press for her rights to their full extent, Sir William informed Alexander that resort to the court or to arbitration would be necessary.

No evidence as to Elizabeth's attitude has appeared. Her husband, as by law provided, represented her interest. I do not get the impression that William Boswell was grasping or vindictive, but he was a lawyer, and it would have been inhuman to expect him not to abet Euphemia and not to press his wife's claims firmly.

In November 1802, Sir William and the Boswells referred the case for arbitration to the Rt. Hon. Charles Hope, Lord Advocate. James, Euphemia, and Elizabeth were represented by a legal agent and by counsel, as was also Alexander.

The younger children, through their lawyers, submitted a long written statement of their claims, to which Alexander (also through his lawyers) made written answer with extended presentation of his own counter-claims. From time to time Hope sent the parties brief written statements of opinions he had reached, and they (again through their lawyers) returned written replies. Hope also heard their counsel viva voce. On 19 March 1804 he pronounced an interim decreet arbitral, to which the parties returned long written answers; on 7 February 1805 he pronounced a final decreet. The final decreet corrected or amplified the interim decreet, but did not repeat the findings which Hope still considered satisfactory.

By his will Boswell put all his personal manuscripts in the hands of trustees to be published for the benefit of his younger children if the trustees should decide that such publication was appropriate. The only other provision in his settlements which could have any bearing on the destination of his personal papers on his death also occurs in the will, some sentences earlier. Since the passage is a double crux, I shall venture to present it again:

> Furthermore as my late honoured Father made a very curious collection of the Classicks and other Books which it is desireable should be preserved for ever in the Family of Auchinleck I do by these presents dispone to the successive heirs of entail of the Barony of Auchinleck ⟨the⟩ greek and latin Books, as also all Manuscripts of whatever kind lying in the House of Auchinleck under the same conditions and under the same forfeiture as I have mentioned with regard to the Ebony Cabinet and dressing Plate.

The phrase "all Manuscripts of whatever kind lying in the House of Auchinleck" is so capacious and express that a judge at any time charged with the responsibility of awarding property in accordance with it would probably consider it safer to assume that Boswell wrote a basically illogical sentence than that he meant by it something different from what he clearly seems to say. As an historian and biographer, I should choose the reverse assumption. Taken in context, I have never been able to convince myself that by "Manuscripts of whatever kind" Boswell was referring to his own personal papers at all. I have always found Boswell eminently logical. When he writes hastily he may write obscurely, but he does not commit glaring *non sequiturs*. It is simply not like him to say that he is disponing his own private papers to the heirs of entail because his father had made a choice collection of classics and other books which ought to be preserved for ever at Auchinleck. What he is disponing should in logic be something that *Lord Auchinleck* had collected. If his sentence were expanded enough to remove the obscurity, I think it would read something like this: "Because my late father made a collection of Greek and Latin classics and other books so choice that it ought always to remain at Auchinleck, I dispone to the heirs of entail the most significant portion of that collection, namely, the Greek and Latin books and the manuscript books, whatever language they happen to be written in. I should like to dispone the entire library in the same way, but I have to think of making provision for my younger children, and I shall therefore allow the rest of the books to fall into the executry, hoping, however, that my heir will purchase them and dispone them similarly." Like other distinguished libraries of the time, Lord Auchinleck's contained a great many manuscript books. In the Sotheby Sale "of the Selected Portion of the Celebrated Auchinleck Library formed by the late Lord Auchinleck", 23–25 June 1893, I count over eighty manuscript volumes, some in Latin, some in Greek, some in French, some even in Dutch, but the great majority in English.

Whom did Boswell wish to inherit his private papers? Undoubtedly, in my opinion, his heir, Alexander, and the succeeding heirs of entail. How, then, did he think Alexander was going to get those papers? It sounds odd in speaking of a lawyer, but I concur with David Buchanan in thinking that he felt that no formal deed was necessary to achieve that end. There was an extensive archive of family papers at Auchinleck, going back to the early sixteenth century and earlier, but I would venture to guess that none of the lairds of Auchinleck had ever inherited the family papers by specific bequest. It had simply been taken for granted by everybody concerned that the archives went from heir to heir and stayed in Auchinleck House. Before Boswell's time, the family papers were not the sort of thing one could put much of a cash value on. If they fell technically into an executry or residuary estate destined away from the heir, the parties concerned, I think, unwittingly or consciously abandoned them to him. We naturally now think of Boswell's private papers as having an enormous cash value, but that view would not have obtained in 1785 when the will was drawn. Boswell did make formal provision for profits arising from *publication* of the papers, and probably thought that by that act he had done all he needed to do.

Any one who wishes to get the proper perspective on this matter should read the full texts of Hope's interim and final decreets. Findings concerning annuities occupied far more space in the documents than the findings on the executry and the bequests to the heir. The share of each of the younger children in the executry after the debts were paid was a modest lump sum, never to be repeated, but annuities ran for life. The annuities all together could not exceed one fourth of the free rents of Auchinleck, and it made a great difference what date was set for defining the base rental. I shall not go into further detail in this matter but shall report merely that Hope's decreet establishing the base rental as of 1795 increased James's annuity to roughly £210 per annum and his sisters' to roughly £140 each.

Alexander claimed that the heritable estate should be subject only to the bonds on it and that he should have the sum (about £1,700) remaining from the sale of the lands after the bonded debt had been paid. He further claimed that his declining to take up the lands and entail them under the terms of his father's will did not void the specific bequests to himself as heir of entail, and that he should consequently receive the ebony cabinet, the dressing-plate, the books, and the pictures. The younger children claimed that the entire net proceeds from the sale of the lands should be applied to the debts, and that since Alexander had defeated the purpose of the will by causing the lands to be sold, he had abandoned his right to all the specific bequests, and that these objects consequently became part of the general movable estate or executry, and hence devolved to themselves.

> They claim the Ebony Cabinet Dressing Plate, Greek and Latin [books] and Manuscripts at Auchinleck. . . . The Memorialists also claim all their Fathers other Books of whatever description not included under the term Greek and Latin [and] manuscripts, lying at Auchinleck. . . . They also claim all his letters and Copies of letters and Manuscripts not lying at Auchinleck, at the time of his death. . . .

Hope ruled that the lands were liable for the whole debts to the full sum realized and that the executry was liable only secondarily; that the entail of his own lands which Boswell had intended was defeated by the burdens he himself had put on the properties, not by Alexander's repudiating the settlement.

> BUT in other respects I FIND that the said Mr. James Boswells Trust Deed must have effect,—*so* that the said Alexander Boswell will take as an Heir loom (as the English call it) the Ebony Cabinet and Dressing Plate, and also the Greek and Latin Books at Auchinleck, belonging to his said Father, FIND that all the other Books wherever situated, at Mr. Boswell's death, fall to belong to the Younger Children, but that the said Alexander Boswell is entitled to have them, if he pleases, at a Valuation, FURTHER FIND that all the Medals, Coins and Moveable property of whatever description, and wherever situated, and also the Pictures in London, must go to the Younger Children.

The reader who has struggled through the argument so far will at once protest a curious discrepancy. Hope says that apart from matters connected with annuities, the sale of Boswell's lands, and the question as to how far his heritable property was burdened with his personal debts, "the said Mr. James Boswells Trust Deed" (that is, his will) "must have effect"; and he apparently begins to enumerate the "Heir looms" which Alexander will still receive: the ebony cabinet, the dressing-plate, the Greek and Latin books at Auchinleck. We expect him to continue, "the manuscripts" (however he defines that term), and "the pictures". But in fact he omits all mention of manuscripts, and he awards the pictures only by implication: "the Pictures in London must go to the Younger Children".

David Buchanan thinks the failure to award the manuscripts can only have been an oversight.

> There was no reason to differentiate the manuscripts at Auchinleck from the Greek and Latin books at Auchinleck. All were part and parcel of the same bequest and subject to the same terms and conditions. If the arbiter awarded the Greek and Latin books to Alexander, he must also have meant him to have the manuscripts.

In view of the amount of written communication between the parties, it seems surprising that an oversight of this magnitude should have been allowed to pass, especially as it occurred in the interim decreet. A review of the correspondence (nearly all of it seems to have been preserved) persuades me however that an oversight was indeed possible. Since Hope early in the proceedings announced his intention of awarding the "heirlooms" to Alexander, it was up to Alexander's lawyers, not to those of the younger children, to inform Hope in the clearest and most emphatic manner where they thought his language, proposed or formally adopted, failed to express the meaning they understood to be agreed upon. Alexander's lawyers continued to mention manuscripts and pictures ("[Mr. Boswell] also Entails all *Greek* and *Latin* Books, and Manuscripts . . .—he also dispones *all* his *pictures* to his heirs of Entail"), but they never wrote, "With all submission, should not the Honble. Arbiter award manuscripts to the heir as well as Greek and Latin books? Should he not *expressly* award the pictures to the heir?" On 3 March 1804 (about two weeks before Hope issued the interim decreet) a meeting of "Mr. Farquharson Accomptant", the agents, and William Boswell occurred. Hope had asked the parties whether they wished him to fix principles only or principles "applied by an Accomptant . . . so as that the Decreet Arbitral may be made special as to sums", and they had chosen the latter arrangement. Alexander was directed to produce fourteen pieces of information. Production No. 10 read as follows:

> Mr. Davidson to inquire of Mr. Boswell, whether he is to avail himself of the Advocates intended Decreet Arbitral respecting all the late Mr. Boswells books; and if he does not, then he must deliver up to the Executor all the books whatever, with the exception of the Greek and Latin books and manuscripts which were lying in the house of Auchinleck, at the time of the late Mr. James Boswells death.

The relevant passage in Hope's original notes, sent to the parties as far back as June 1803, had read as follows:

> But in other respects I am clear that the Trust deed must have effect—so that the heir will take as an heir loom (as the English call it) the Ebony Cabinet and Dressing Plate and Books—
> As to what books it is certainly doubtful. The Preamble of the Clause points at all the Books collected by Lord Auchinleck, but the dispositive clause seems to be limited to Greek and Latin—
> I think the parties as their Fathers intention seems so doubtful ought to settle the matter—Thus—Let the heir have the books paying *half* their apprised value by some person skilled in their value.

On Alexander's protest, Hope later (February 1804) made a new proposal: that Alexander should take the Greek and Latin books, "all other Books to belong to the Executors, but Heir to have them if he pleases, at a valuation". In neither case did he make any mention of manuscripts, though the lawyers on both sides in their meeting of 3 March 1804 understood that his "intended Decreet" would specify them. When Hope's clerk drafted the relevant portion of the decreet, he copied the original notes with no significant change till he got to "Dressing Plate and", after which he incorporated the new matter as to Greek and Latin books and Alexander's right to purchase the other books at a valuation. Still no mention of manuscripts.

Though I consider it possible that Hope's failure to award the manuscripts was an oversight, I should prefer another solution if the legal experts think it tenable. The manuscripts were not the only item Hope failed to award: he said that the pictures in London should go to the younger children, but he nowhere said who was to get the pictures at Auchinleck. (Alexander certainly retained them.) I suggest that when he says that in other respects the provisions of the will should be followed, he means just that: "When I have not ruled otherwise, follow the provisions of the will." It was not necessary, I propose, for him to award the pictures: Boswell's will had done it in an acceptable fashion. It was not necessary for him to list all five "heirlooms" (ebony cabinet, dressing-plate, Greek and Latin books, manuscripts, pictures); his list is exemplary not enumerative. With regard to manuscripts, he confirmed the designation of the will, whatever that was.

The settlement of Boswell's estate was by no means wound up by the pronouncement of the final decreet arbitral. The will had given Alexander the right to purchase the furniture in Auchinleck House at a valuation by sworn appraisers, and this appraisal (which set a value of £576. 8s. 2d., exclusive of books, pictures, silver, and liquors) had been on hand since July 1795. Hope had also extended Alexander's right of purchase to the books at Auchinleck other than those disponed to him as heir of entail, and this valuation (£97) had been made or was going forward. But there were many other problems. There were books in Boswell's London house and in the house in St. Andrew Square, Edinburgh. There remained also at Auchinleck many articles from Boswell's time which would be classified as furniture and effects that the appraisers had not valued. They had not listed, let alone valued, the contents of the ebony cabinet, apparently assuming that the contents went to Alexander with the cabinet. Some of these articles (coins and medals, impressions of antique gems by Tassie, miniature portraits, a diamond ring) were of considerable value. The appraisers listed but did not value some articles they considered worthless ("A parcel of Lumber") or not Boswell's property ("A Harpsichord/Miss Boswell's"). A more interesting group in this second category consisted of a considerable quantity of table-linen and china which they apparently thought should be reserved for the heir, though Boswell had given no direction to that effect ("18 Table Napkins with David Boswell and Ann Hamilton wove in"; "2 Table cloths and 26 Napkins. E. B. 34 with the Boswell and Bruce's Crests wrought in the middle of the Napkins"; "A Table cloth and 12 Napkins. E. E. 43 with the Boswell and Erskine's Crests wove in the corner"; "A sett of Tea China with the Arms of the Family"). Besides these, the younger children claimed the value of the wines and spirits which Alexander had found at Auchinleck when he took over after his father's death, and of a whole series of petty articles which they believed they remembered from their childhood and youth, concerning which the inventory was silent. It still remained necessary for Alexander to come to an agreement to turn these articles over to the younger children or to purchase them at a negotiated price. These negotiations occupied the greater part of a year.

After her crisis of 1801, Euphemia made no appeal to her family though she continued to live far beyond her means, presumably getting credit by exaggerated report of her expectations from the executry. Just before the final decreet was pronounced, however, she had to inform them that she was reduced to extremity. She was threatened with immediate distraint of her furniture; she had run up an enormous hairdresser's bill; she was under arrestment for £50 to a Mr. William Coulter ("I suppose for stockings!" Alexander wrote indignantly, "infatuated creature!"); another arrestment for £127 had come in. She wanted James to let her draw his share of the division of the executry; she even proposed taking over for her present use the money set aside to fund Mrs. Bruce's annuity.[7] Alexander, who reported "that in less than four Years she had spent all her share of the Executry and the value of her Annuity making her expenditure about £700 a year", thought her situation hopeless, and was disposed to let her extricate herself from her scrape by selling all or part of her annuity; if her creditors would agree, he said he would pay annually such sum as she would set apart from her annuity to pay her debts, and would continue to pay it even if she died before the debts were discharged. On 27 March 1805 she assigned her claim on the executry funds to David Wemyss, W.S., "in trust for behoof of herself and her creditors". The creditors allowed her to retain £50 from her annuity for her own use.

William Boswell and Wemyss of course did not want to receive physical possession of a miscellaneous collection of second-hand household effects; they wished to get as large an offer for the entire lot of appraised and unappraised movables as Alexander could be persuaded to make. The list they submitted was excessively detailed ("Beautiful Wax fruits"; "Forreign Shells"; "Forreign Birds"; "Snakes in bottles"), showing, as David Buchanan says, that "they were ready to haggle over every item". They proposed a grand total of £400. Alexander's solicitor, Harry Davidson, got this reduced to £300, plus two Indian gongs and a diamond ring which the younger children were to sell for themselves. On 9 and 13 December 1805 Sir William Forbes gave formal effect to Hope's findings and obtained his own discharge as executor in an official document as puzzling in what it says as Hope's decreet was in what it omitted:

> Provided and Declared that this present Disposition and Assignation shall not be held to convey to the said Disponees and Assignees . . . the Manuscripts and Letters left by the said deceased James Boswell to the care of [   ] Temple and [   ] Malone Esquires and of me the said Sir William Forbes with discretionary powers to us to publish more or less of them for behoof of his younger children which manuscripts and Letters shall be held to remain in the same situation as before granting these presents notwithstanding thereof.

Forbes had no judicial powers. As executor of Boswell's personal estate, he was under obligation to turn over to the heirs, as designated by the arbiter, whatever

---

[7] See above, p. 8.

remained of Boswell's personal property after all his debts had been paid, at the same time receiving from the heirs a discharge from his responsibilities as executor. His responsibility as regards Boswell's personal papers was twofold. As executor of the estate, he held legal title to these papers, of course only for the purpose of delivering them to the beneficiary entitled. As literary executor, without in any way holding title to the documents, he was burdened with the trust of deciding what part, if any, should be published for the benefit of Euphemia, James, and Elizabeth. The papers were at the time in his keeping in Edinburgh, and it was convenient to let them stay there till the literary trust had been completed. Forbes understandably wished to dispense with the legal formality of putting the papers physically into Alexander's hands at Auchinleck as Alexander's property, only to have immediately to demand them back again for the purposes of the literary trust.

It seems to have been the intent of the arbitration of 1805 to resolve all matters relating to the executry and to enable the administration of the estate to be completed. It would have been possible, I am told,[8] for firm title to pass to Alexander without his being put in physical possession of the corpus, provided that he knew of the arrangement and agreed to it, as he no doubt would have been willing to do. But Forbes (or the lawyer's clerk who drew his disposition and assignation) went beyond the needs of the situation, and (as indicated by the word "convey") withheld title to the papers from Alexander, and in effect continued Forbes as executor of the estate in that one area. So far as I can see, he died in office and was discharged only informally, though probably effectively, when his son sent the papers back after his death to Alexander.

On 21 and 31 December 1805 the younger children granted Alexander a complete discharge from any claims they might have had against their father's books, wherever located; all table-linen not formerly valued; plates, prints, coins and medals of every description, etc., etc., "and in general all and every other article and articles as well not mentioned in the foresaid enumeration as therein specified in and about said house of Auchinleck to which we or any of us have right or any manner of claim whatsoever". "Again," said David Buchanan, "there was no specific reference to the papers."

> The parties seem to have side-stepped the issue because they regarded the papers as being in a special category and never really attempted to analyse the legal rights of ownership. An attitude such as this would explain the exclusion of the papers from the assignation granted by Forbes. An alternative explanation [advanced by lawyers in our own century] was that the general clause in the assignation by the "younger children", although limited to articles "in and about the said house of Auchinleck", was wide enough to carry to Alexander any right they might have had to the papers. The papers, or most of them, were not at Auchinleck at this date, but they had only been temporarily removed for perusal by the literary executors and Auchinleck was their proper home.

---

[8]David Buchanan and I have corresponded at length on this problem, which he calls "very curious" (TA, p. 199). He is not, however, to be held as approving my conclusions.

On 10 November 1806 Forbes died, aged only sixty-seven. James by that time had not made his examination of the papers.

Our sole information as to the conclusion of the trust comes from a letter that Malone wrote to Euphemia Boswell on 4 May 1809. The formality and sharpness of its tone probably indicate that she had addressed him peremptorily, as she had earlier addressed Forbes; certainly they reflect a disapproval of her behaviour that Malone shared with her brothers. About the time she went to London, apparently, she had begun signing herself "Euphemia Bte. Boswell", the mysterious "Bte.", on Alexander's scornful testimony, standing for "Botetourte". The barony of Botetourt, in abeyance for nearly four hundred years, had been revived in 1764 by Norborne Berkeley, subsequently Governor of Virginia.[9] In abeyance again when he died in 1770, it was confirmed in 1803 to the Duke of Beaufort, the Governor's nephew. Euphemia may have been coyly hinting at relationship with the Botetourt line, a relationship that must have been very remote, if it existed at all, or (more probably) was devising an aristocratic *nom de plume,* her notion now being to support herself by writing and composing. She actually eked out her £50 by sending begging letters to all the Boswell connexion, attacking Alexander wildly and spitefully, and representing herself as oppressed and neglected by her family.

Foley Place [London] May 4, 1809

Dear Madam,

To your first letter there was no date of time, nor any denotation of place; so that an answer could not be easily given: however, I should have answered such parts of it as I could read before now,[10] but for some unexpected avocations;—having learned your address from your brother.—You are, I conceive, under some mistake with respect to your father's papers. I was not his Executor; but to the best of my recollection he desired, in his will, that no use should be made of them without the consent of Sir Wm. Forbes and myself. They were put into my hands by Sir William; and after an inspection, I was clearly of opinion that they contained nothing fit for the press. I afterwards returned them to Sir William Forbes; and since his death, a large parcel of them was sent from Scotland to London for the inspection and consideration of your brother, James; who, after examining them, clearly co-incided with me, respecting the impropriety of printing any part of them. They are now deposited at Auchinleck; in which repository, I trust, they will be suffered to remain in peace. I am, Madam, your most humble and obedient Servant,

Edmond Malone

The clear implication of this is that Forbes died with the literary trust undischarged and with the papers still in his hands. He was no doubt very busy during a good part of 1806 with his life of Beattie, which was published in June of that

---

[9]Botetourt died in Virginia and is buried in Williamsburg. One of the counties of Virginia is named for him.

[10]Euphemia Boswell's later hand is perhaps the most baffling of all those represented in the Boswell Papers at Yale.

year, but there are really no good grounds for accusing him of negligence. Nor does it appear that James Boswell the younger was guilty of serious procrastination. The ten years which had been proposed for the finishing of his education and the maturing of his mind were a round number, and can certainly be stretched to include a few months of grace. Forbes was only sixty-seven when he died, and his death may have been without warning. What is more surprising is Malone's statement that he himself disapproved of printing any of the papers, for that had not been at all the tone of his report to Forbes in June 1796. According to his own admission, he had not then read all the journals, and fuller reading may have caused him to change his mind. Perhaps he had been influenced by Forbes, who left slips in the journal indicating that he had found some passages "exceptionable" and others "reprehensible"; perhaps James had convinced him of the impropriety of any publication, though in writing to Euphemia he thought it prudent to present the decision as primarily his own. At any rate, Malone caused at least some of the papers to be sent down to London for James to read. It was Malone's belief that all of them were then sent to Auchinleck. In this he was certainly mistaken.

CHAPTER II

JOHNSON'S PORTRAIT

LEAVES

AUCHINLECK

THE EVIDENCE WE HAVE as to the return of the papers to Auchinleck shows that they came back at intervals in at least three separate parcels. The earliest indication that some of them had arrived home is perhaps a letter to Alexander from Alexander Fraser Tytler, Lord Woodhouselee, dated 27 June 1808. Wood-houselee, who had published a life of Lord Kames in 1807 and was seeking additions for a second edition, wrote on that date to Alexander, requesting sight of the materials Boswell had collected for the same purpose, and Alexander acknowledged possession.[1] Malone clearly thought Boswell's papers relating to the *Life of Johnson* were at Auchinleck by 28 September 1808. On that date, being engaged in preparing copy for the sixth edition of the *Life of Johnson,* he wrote to James then at Auchinleck, as he had earlier written to Sir William Forbes, asking him to hunt out the originals of six letters of Johnson and verify readings of which he was suspicious. If James searched, he searched to little purpose, as is shown by a letter to him from Alexander, 21 March 1809: "Another Trunk has arrived from Sir William Forbes it contains some of the Manuscript of the Life, but I was much disappointed at not finding one Letter of Johnsons for it is Strange not to have one Specimen of his handwriting at Auchinleck." Alexander must have received at least one more parcel of papers after this, for though the Auchinleck deposit, as held at Malahide in the twentieth century, contained no autograph *letters* of Johnson's except a single one-line message to Boswell, easily overlooked because Boswell had overwritten it heavily with journal notes, it did contain several conspicuous specimens of Johnson's *handwriting.* And on 4 May 1809, as we have seen, Malone stated to Euphemia his belief that the

---

[1] I shall return later in this chapter to this successful early appeal by a qualified scholar to see and print from Boswell's private papers. Here I cite it merely as evidence as to where the papers were in June 1808.

papers (surely he meant *all* of them) were "now deposited at Auchinleck". He died on 26 April 1812.

It is at least doubtful that James Boswell the younger did return to Auchinleck all the papers that were sent to London for his inspection; certainly if he did return them, he got some of them back from the archives later. When he died suddenly in 1822 at the age of forty-three, his affairs proved to be in such disorder that a judicial sale of his fine library for the benefit of his creditors was ordered. The printed catalogue of this sale listed nearly a score of lots that had formed part of his father's papers. Besides a number of Johnson manuscripts (many of them autograph) which had been among the materials that Boswell had assembled for writing the *Life,* the sale included the manuscript of Boswell's *Boswelliana* (an extensive collection of anecdotes and witty sayings in most of which Boswell himself had figured), the probably much less extensive manuscript of Boswell's "Dictionary of the Scottish Language", and a miscellaneous and annoyingly undercatalogued lot consisting of proofs of the first edition of the *Life* and "loose Papers, Letters, and Memoranda" also relating to the *Life.* No other manuscripts by Boswell are specified, but the descriptions of a number of lots are ominously vague, and at least nine uncatalogued "bundles" were auctioned at the end of the sale. This sale of the younger James Boswell's library was the first known leak from the archives, and it was probably much more considerable than the printed catalogue indicates. A large manuscript collection of verses by Boswell came to the Bodleian Library in the bequest of Francis Douce, who died in 1834. Nothing is known of its previous history, but the sale of 1825 seems the most plausible avenue of exit from the archives. Since James Boswell the younger had inherited Malone's papers, the sale also included many of Malone's correspondences. In the supplement to the edition of the *Life of Johnson,* 1835, commonly called "Croker's second", John Wright printed extracts from nine important letters from Boswell to Malone, the originals of which were then in the collection of William Upcott, antiquary and collector. These probably came to Upcott, directly or indirectly, from the Boswell sale of 1825. Yet the great majority of Boswell's letters to Malone, as well as various private papers of James Boswell the younger, later turned up in the Boswell archives. Clearly, before the sale somebody had put to one side a mass of papers which the Boswell family at Auchinleck wished to keep. It is not hard to guess who made the division or why his sorting was imperfect.

Alexander Boswell, Boswell's elder son, was laird from 1795 to 1822. Sir Walter Scott says that he was very proud and thought that his father had lowered himself by attendance on Johnson and by writing his life; that he disliked any allusion to the book or to Johnson himself, and had banished Reynolds's portrait of Johnson from the drawing-room at Auchinleck. The last charge, indeed, Scott made on hearsay, but he vouched personally for the rest. One must take this testimony very seriously. Scott's characterizations of people whom he knew only from books and records undoubtedly need to be used with some caution ("I only put a cocked hat on their heads, and stick a cane into their hands—to make them fit for going into company"). But he was only four years older than Alexander Boswell and was his friend. Their many common interests—Tory politics, antiquarianism, authorship, book-collecting, volunteer cavalry—should have enabled him to make a report on Alexander's attitudes as accurate as it was perceptive. One cannot convincingly argue that Alexander's many attractive qualities prove Scott wrong. Granted that Alexander was cultured, brave, magnanimous; granted that he got the best part of his education at Eton; granted that he was twice elected M.P. for an English constituency; granted that he knew several of Johnson's friends intimately; granted that he was a lover of scholarship and of literature—indeed, was an author himself—he could still have shown a narrow, bitter, and violent streak of family pride. He *was* a very proud man; he *did* disown a sister because he thought her guilty of marrying beneath her station. Alexander's character, in short, like that of most real human beings, was capable of harbouring great contradictions. In deciding how he felt about his father and his father's book, we must be cautious of inferences and must try to stick to established fact. When we take that stance, we see at once that the most troublesome part of Scott's testimony is almost certainly inference. He *observed* Alexander's behaviour—his gestures, facial expression, tone of voice—when Johnson or the *Life of Johnson* was discussed, but surely Alexander never told him *why* he showed displeasure on such occasions. Scott was told that Reynolds's portrait was no longer hung in the drawing-room at Auchinleck; that it had been *"banished"* was his inference or his informant's. We have in several of Alexander's private letters to James clear indication that he did not resent his father's deference to Johnson or his making a life of Johnson the main labour of his life. One of these letters has already been quoted. If Alexander's aim was to suppress all visible signs of Johnson at Auchinleck, why should he have lamented that he had no specimens of Johnson's handwriting?[1a] Why should he have asked James to recommend the best edition of Johnson's works ("There is not a Copy in the Library")? Another of the letters reduces the "banishment" of Johnson's portrait to a difficult choice in the use of wall space. The picture *was* taken down in 1810, along with every other picture at Auchinleck, in a comprehensive bout of authentication, cleaning, and rearrangement. Alexander's report to James (volunteered and not in the least defensive) was that he wished to rehang the Johnson, but because of its size had been unable to find a place for it that suited him.

Alexander's private letters, like those of the other Boswell children, show deep and abiding affection for Boswell. I remember only one criticism, and that halfjocular: he thought Boswell a poor judge of painting.[2] He admired his father's skill

---

[1a]Above, p. 28.

[2]"The *authenticated* ones [pictures at Auchinleck] are to be replaced [i.e. rehung] the *spurious* removed. Of these I am glad to say there are but few. It was a vile trick of so *honest* a man to shake our belief by adopting daubs" (Alexander Boswell to James Boswell the younger, 2 June 1810, C 272.3).

in recording conversation, and he took pride in his fame as the biographer of Johnson.[3]

But he was a proud—indeed, as I have said, an imperious—man, and it implies no inconsistency to say that he would have disliked the allusions to the *Life* and to Johnson that most people made in his presence. Those of us in the present day who like and admire Boswell dislike most of the bantering clichés concerning him that we encounter and we try to avoid any but serious and informed discussion. Macaulay had not yet written his essay, but Peter Pindar, Gifford, and especially the Collings-Rowlandson caricatures had already made Boswell a stereotype of fatuity to those who had not known him or read his book. Alexander knew on the contrary that his father was characterized by bright, brisk intelligence; and he knew that his father's willingness to let Johnson maul him in order to obtain memorable sayings implied no willingness to allow people generally to walk over him. Alexander knew, but he no doubt found it intolerable that any one should ignorantly show condescension to the memory of the ninth laird of Auchinleck. And perhaps he found even more trying the areas in which condescension was just, areas in which Boswell was fair game for ridicule. There are indeed such areas. Sir Walter Scott had them in mind when he wittily remarked that "Boswells book though one of the most entertaining in the world is not just what one would wish a near relation to have written."[4] Boswell was outspokenly vain; he asserted a right to behave both like an ancient gentleman and like a buffoon; he was sometimes pompous; he marred a masterpiece of great art by intrusions of his own seldom memorable judgements in politics and religion. It would not have been strange if Alexander had become sore as to his father's genuine weaknesses, nor that he should have preferred a tactic of silence, accompanied by some gesture of displeasure, to constant defence. He would have been averse to further exposure of such weaknesses of his father and would have heartily concurred in Malone's wish that Boswell's private papers should rest in peace for some time.

The literary trust created by Boswell's will presumably remained extant though dormant till Malone, the last of the literary trustees, died in 1812. After that all questions of publication would legally have been for Alexander to decide. The

---

[3]"A few days ago I read the Life of Doctor Johnson which I know not if I ever read with care before. Although Johnsons conversation from the marked manner must have been more easily retained in the memory than that of the generality of men which neither has the point nor strength of sentiment which his possess'd yet I cannot but wonder at my Fathers talent for recording which he had in an eminent degree" (Alexander Boswell to Sir William Forbes, 19 Apr. 1799, Fettercairn Papers). "I had last night a Letter from Dr. Brewster who conducts the Edinburgh Encyclopaedia wishing me to furnish materials for a Life of my father for that work and a request that I should write the article: for both I am unqualified. At the same time I am so convinced of the propriety of our doing our endeavours to give *him* in proper colours in a work of such consequence that I have no doubt you will immediately to prevent such accounts as have hitherto appeared give your earnest exertion and best aid" (Alexander Boswell to James Boswell the younger, 20 Feb. 1811, C 272.6).

[4]See below, p. 41.

problem of the legal rights of the younger children, however, is going to come up for discussion again, and in preparation for that discussion I shall pause here to carry their story forward to 1836.

Veronica, as has been reported, died unmarried shortly after her father, on 26 September 1795. Elizabeth also died young, on 1 January 1814, leaving three sons and a daughter. James the younger died unmarried on 24 February 1822. I shall have more to say of his death later. Euphemia never married. She lived at Auchinleck from 1796 to 1801, in Edinburgh from 1801 to 1805, and then went to London, where she hung loose upon society, making efforts to support herself as a writer and musical composer. She was most of the time in desperate straits because of her debts, and wrote urgent begging letters to her father's friends and to various great personages of the day, representing herself as cruelly neglected and repressed by her family. Dr. Charles Rogers, who seems to have had access to papers not reported since his time, says that she "entreated pecuniary aid" from Lord Chancellor Eldon, the Earl of Moira, Lord Lonsdale, and Lord Sidmouth. She went higher than that, as a newspaper paragraph shows:

> His Royal Highness the Prince of Wales has been graciously pleased to present Euphemia the daughter of the late well known James Boswell, Esqr. with 50l. as a tribute due to her excellent and moral conduct under the frowns of fortune.

Yale has a letter of hers to Sir Joseph Banks appealing to him to get her a pension from the Literary Fund "as a distressed Author and the daughter of one that added much to the honour of Literature". She advertised a subscription for herself in the newspapers. She solicited a pension on the Scots and presumably also on the Civil List, and did actually get from Government a pension of £50 a year. Yale has begging letters of hers to Mrs. John Landseer and to Dr. Charles Burney. (Mme d'Arblay has endorsed one of the latter, "From the dreadfully distressed, and really crazy Daughter of the famous Biographer of Dr. Johnson, Euphemia".) On 25 April 1816 Alexander wrote to James, "I know not whether the plan you have adopted with Miss B. will have any good effect, but it is at least consolatory to have it to think upon that no expedient has been left untried. She has overwhelmed me and Mrs. Cuming[5] with Letters, and two days ago I received one *open* which had been directed to *Auchinleck,* I am affraid written when drunk. She concludes by saying that she had given up spirits but that now she 'will drink the devil if she can get him'." Euphemia's problem was then in fact approaching a radical solution. Some time in that same year of 1816, probably because of physical prostration or some particularly outrageous act of self-advertisement, she was declared insane and put by her brothers in Fisher House, Islington, a private asylum for lunatics operated by Dr. Alexander Robert Sutherland. The brothers promised to pay Sutherland four guineas a week (£218. 8s. a year) for her board and maintenance as well as for medical and other attendance. Her annuity of £140 a year appears to have formed

---

[5]His wife's mother. See below, p. 37.

part of this sum, but her pension of £50 seems to have been left free for her own uses. She remained there for the next twenty years.

What would Alexander's policy have been if he had received a responsible request for access to the papers? I think he would have answered promptly and politely but that he would almost certainly have imposed a policy of censorship, limiting not only what could be published from Boswell's papers but even what could be seen.

This is not mere conjecture. Mention has already been made of Lord Woodhouselee's request of him in 1808 to be granted access to Boswell's unpublished materials for a life of Lord Kames.[6] Woodhouselee himself had published a biography of Kames in 1807, was then preparing additions for a second edition, and claimed that Forbes and Malone had granted him permission to read and quote. Since paraphrases of six brief extracts from Boswell's manuscript were added as footnotes in his second edition, it would be easy to conclude that Alexander gave him the unrestricted access he asked for. Recent publication from Woodhouselee's papers, however, shows that was far from being the case.

Alexander Fraser Tytler, judge in the Court of Session in Edinburgh with the judicial style Lord Woodhouselee, was the "young Tytler" whom Johnson in 1773 sharply rebuked for asserting, without knowledge of Gaelic, that he had heard a great part of *Fingal* recited in the original. When Boswell printed an unsoftened report of the incident in the *Journal of a Tour to the Hebrides,* Tytler sent him an angry and abusive letter which he was later persuaded to moderate without really being in the least mollified. Woodhouselee (to return to the style by which he was more commonly addressed after 1802) had known from Boswell himself that Boswell was making collections for a life of Kames, and as early as 1803 had attempted to gain access to these materials for use in his first edition. Sir William Forbes, to whom he then talked, told him there was no trace of the materials in the Boswell papers in his hands. At the end of 1806 Woodhouselee appears to have addressed a query to Malone, who assured him in a long and extremely polite letter (16 December 1806) that he was sure Boswell had never written a line of the projected life of Kames, but that he (Malone) perfectly remembered seeing the packet of materials in the papers he had sent from London to Forbes. He was planning soon, he said, to recall the papers from Forbes's son (Forbes had just died: 10 November 1806) for a more careful examination than he had ever yet given them, and would report on what he found. He could not, however, turn the papers over to Woodhouselee without the permission of Boswell's younger children. Boswell's son James, he thought, after he had inspected them, would have no hesitation in putting them into Woodhouselee's hands, but his two sisters were also concerned.

> The former of these ladies, I know, has got some strange notions in her head, of the great value of her father's papers; and supposes that if they were but properly managed,

---

they might produce countless treasures; and were I to employ any of them, though for the most reasonable and desirable purpose, might perhaps clamorously complain of the wrong I had done her.

Malone seems in the end to have left to Woodhouselee the task of appeasing Euphemia and Elizabeth: "I will carefully inspect the bundle I have alluded to, and inform your lordship of the contents; and if it shall prove such as I suppose, I should hope you would find no great difficulty in obtaining their consent to my transmitting it to you." If he wrote again, his letter has not been traced. Woodhouselee had to publish his first edition with no help from Boswell's papers.

Eighteen months later (27 June 1808, as previously stated) he wrote a rather curt letter to Alexander saying that he had learned "some time ago" from Forbes's son that the Kames collection had been found "among your Father's papers"; he does not add, "which have since been returned to Auchinleck", but we must assume that clause to make sense of what follows in his letter and of Alexander's reply. Woodhouselee says both Forbes and Malone had given their consent to his examining the papers (Malone in his letter of 16 December 1806 had certainly given no such unqualified consent), and asks for Alexander's. "Let me add only, that if I have your permission to inspect the MS. it will be an additional favour, that they come soon into my hands."

Alexander answered immediately, though by accident his letter was not posted, and his effective reply was not written till 2 August 1808. On getting Woodhouselee's request, he said, he had at once sent the Kames papers to James in London "as I conceived him peculiarly concerned in the matter, and from the manner in which my Father had directed his Papers to be disposed of I did not think myself authorised to use them". So far as he was concerned, it is clear that he would have preferred that the papers remain at rest.

> On examining the Notes concerning Lord Kames I by no means found much interesting matter and what was interesting seemed of a nature not fit for publication as touching upon private and delicate subjects.—A Letter too from his Son[7] to my Father expressing extreme uneasiness and anxiety as to what might be published, rendered such passages still more objectionable. . . . From a Letter which I had from my Brother he seems to be of much the same opinion with me.

Woodhouselee did not hear from James till 6 December 1808. James had consulted Malone (he says nothing of consulting his sisters), and was sending the papers to Woodhouselee. But not the entire lot. "One or two pages which are entirely of a personal nature I have suppressed but where any thing occurred in them which you could be desirous of seeing I have transcribed it." That is, in order not to mutilate or deface Boswell's manuscript, he has removed certain entire leaves which contain objectionable passages, but he has copied out for Woodhouselee any harmless bits occurring in the suppressed leaves. We can with great plausibility

---

[7]Kames's son, George Home Drummond. See C 1113.

equate the papers sent to Woodhouselee with a sheaf of forty-nine crumbling leaves in Boswell's hand and a single leaf of two dated extracts in his son's which turned up in the croquet-box at Malahide in 1930 and were published two years later in the fifteenth volume of Colonel Isham's *Private Papers of James Boswell*.[8] The manuscript showed only one unquestionable hiatus (it occurs in the record for 10 December 1782), but it would be careless to conclude that James suppressed matter only at that one point. Boswell had given the memoirs no overall pagination, and as his records consist mainly of dated self-contained interviews with no run-overs, James could have removed entire dated sequences of leaves without creating traces of his interference. On the evidence of the papers known in 1930 alone, he must have suppressed matter at at least three points: in the entry for 10 December 1782 (shown by the hiatus), and in the entries for 17 February 1782 and 5 December 1782 (shown by extracts in his hand so dated with no entries at all for those days in the manuscript).

We can with equal plausibility recognize the withheld leaves in a single leaf and three separate sequences of leaves, all in excellent condition, which were found in the stable-loft at Malahide in 1940.[9] The leaves which James removed, we must assume, were not restored to their proper places when the manuscript came back from Woodhouselee, and became permanently misplaced. If this assumption is correct, as I feel sure it is, James did not suppress "one or two pages": he suppressed nineteen out of a total of eighty-one, or nearly a quarter of the whole. Most of the "private and delicate" matter of course related to Kames (his love of money and his stinginess; his hardy speculations in theology, religion, sex, and morals) but some of it related to Boswell (mention is made once of his "days of dissipation", once of his having "got myself drunk or infected venereally"). The matter of greatest delicacy was a long and moving conversation between Boswell and Mrs. Drummond (Kames's wife, who resumed her maiden name as an heiress in her own right) concerning the Kameses' only daughter, Jean, who while still very young had been married to Patrick Heron of Kirroughtrie, and was divorced by him in 1772 for adultery with a young Army officer. Kames banished her to France and never after made public mention of her: from Woodhouselee's biography one would not learn that such a person ever existed. Though Kames and his wife never suspected it, this was "private and delicate" matter to Boswell too, for he himself had been Jean Heron's lover in the early days of her marriage, and his report of Mrs. Drummond's confidences reflects a personal dismay for which he advances no explanation. How much Alexander and James guessed (or knew—they could have deduced the facts, as I did, from Boswell's journal-notes and the "Ébauche de ma vie" he wrote for Rousseau) it is impossible to say, but they would obviously have considered the whole conversation matter to be suppressed.

In 1809, in *The Supplement to the Memoirs of the Life and Writings of the Honourable*

---

[8]Pages 267–302. The croquet-box is explained below, pp. 111–12.
[9]The stable-loft is explained below, pp. 161–62.

Henry Home of Kames, Woodhouselee published a small selection of passages from Boswell's censored manuscript, attributing them in an Advertisement to "some MS. collections made by the late JAMES BOSWELL, Esq. (who at one time was preparing materials for a Life of Lord Kames)". Though the passages he borrowed were quite unexceptionable to begin with, he subjected them to the disinfection of ponderous paraphrase. In 1814, when the second edition of the *Memoirs* appeared, he moved the bits from Boswell into it as six footnotes.

Alexander and James did not withhold a large portion of Boswell's manuscript from Woodhouselee because they feared he would *print* it. He was not only eminently respectable and responsible, but he was opposed in principle to the use of such matter in biography. They withheld nearly a quarter of the manuscript from him because they did not wish him to *read* it and get further grounds for contempt of Boswell's method of biography as producing "a very indiscreet farrago". If Alexander had been granted the biblical life-span, I think the policy of granting access under censorship would have been continued to 1845.

Evidence that has come to the attention of Boswell scholars only recently, however, warns us that in considering Alexander's attitudes we should not overlook the possible influence of his wife. Alexander no doubt was quite candid when he told James that he would fain find a place at Auchinleck for displaying his portrait of Johnson, but there was perhaps some reserve in his talking as though the choice was to be wholly his and that the sole obstacle to the rehanging of the picture was its "unmanageable" size. We now know that within three years after Alexander's death his wife quietly caused the picture to be sold, advancing reasons which I at least do not find altogether candid. The portrait formed one of the lots in the sale of James Boswell the younger. I had always assumed that, on finding that it was not being hung at Auchinleck, James had borrowed it for display in his own chambers, and died with it in his possession. Not at all. Lady Boswell (as she then was) sent it up to London to be included in James's sale, where it fetched the disappointing figure of £76. 13*s.* On 8 July 1825, she wrote about it to William Murray, a close friend of James's in London:

> With regard to Dr. Johnsons Picture it certainly went for its real Value. At the same time had I known it was to bring so trifling a sum I would not have sent it up, but some foolish people here talked of its bringing £1000 or *at least* £500—and I therefore thought it an excellent opportunity of realizing such a sum which it was my intention to send to the Executry fund.

We know this letter only in a retained draft. In the letter as sent, Lady Boswell seems to have condensed and altered the passage to read, "With regard to Dr. J. Picture I have no doubt it went for its real Value as it was so[10] completely faded." Did she not make the change because she feared that her first version might be

---

[10]This word may be only a deleted false start.

taken to indicate a personal dislike of the picture? And is it not probable that it did? We shall soon be informed from disinterested authority that she and all her connexions greatly disliked any allusion to Johnson, believing that Boswell degraded himself and his family by obsequiousness to him. What makes more inescapable allusion than a large portrait hung in a living-room? Was it not somewhat extraordinary that she should have taken so detached and commercial an attitude towards *this* picture? A Reynolds of Johnson, given by Reynolds himself to the author of the *Life of Johnson* in acknowledgement of the Dedication of that work, the only portrait of Johnson in Boswell's house of Auchinleck—the picture more than any other object at Auchinleck was a symbol of Boswell's deepest human commitment and of his unique achievement. Did it lose all its claims on family piety when it faded? Lady Boswell's motives, like most human motives, were of course mixed. That she wished to swell the executry was generous and deserves commendation. It still remains likely that she seized a plausible opportunity to get rid of a picture she disliked because it was a portrait of Johnson.

On this admittedly less than probative foundation, I venture to erect a considerable speculation. Alexander's bearing when Johnson or the *Life of Johnson* was mentioned *while his wife was present* may have been adopted as much to spare her feelings as his own. Euphemia Boswell more than once remarked that Alexander's marriage had isolated him from his own family and submerged him in his wife's,[11] a charge which appears to be true and which may not be without significance in the history of his father's papers. Grizel (commonly called Grace) Boswell was the fourth daughter of Thomas Cuming, a wealthy banker in Edinburgh. Mrs. Cuming's mother was a Miller, sister to Sir Thomas Miller of Barskimming and Glenlee, Lord Justice-Clerk and at the end of his life Lord President of the Court of Session. Sir William Miller, Lord Glenlee, Sir Thomas Miller's only son, was Mrs. Cuming's first cousin and brother-in-law. Grizel Cuming's marriage-contract shows Lord Glenlee to have been one of her curators. Mrs. Cuming had five daughters besides Grizel. One of them was married to Patrick Miller of Dalswinton, like Lord Glenlee a first cousin of Mrs. Cuming's; another to James Cuninghame, Alexander's first cousin. His relations after his marriage with the Cumings, the Millers, and the Cuninghames were very close.

Barskimming House, on the river Ayr, was nearer to Auchinleck House than any other gentleman's seat, but in the time of Lord Auchinleck and Boswell the relations between the two families were not cordial. Thomas Miller had been appointed Lord Advocate in 1760 when Robert Dundas resigned that post to become Lord President of the Court of Session. When in 1766 the post of Lord Justice-

---

[11]"He and Mrs. Boswel and Miss Jessy are here just now but soon set off for Polton he has a horse I hear that is to run at Leith—he seems so much taken up with his *new* female friends *I* shall soon be forgot" (To Sir William Forbes, c. 1 June 1800); "I mention this affair to you my Generous friend to give you some idea of what I have lately met with from the new connexions this family has form'd" (To the same, 13 Nov. 1800). Both letters in Fettercairn Papers.

Clerk (acting head of the High Court of Justiciary) became vacant, Miller obtained
the appointment. There was nothing in the least irregular about this, it being
accepted custom for the Lord Advocate (the highest legal officer of the Crown in
Scotland) to nominate himself for any seat that offered on the Scots bench, but the
Boswells of Auchinleck took it hard that a novice on the bench, a man of no great
antiquity of family, should be appointed over the senior judge of the High Court
of Justiciary. Lord Auchinleck, so far as is known, observed judicial decorum, but
Boswell composed a ribald song on the new Justice-Clerk's brother, while David
Boswell and Dr. John Boswell made bitter remarks about the upstart "Tam" Miller.
In 1774 Boswell had a clash with the Lord Justice-Clerk that might have had very
serious consequences. A letter of Boswell's in the *London Chronicle* signed "A
Royalist" accused Miller of partiality in the case of a client of Boswell's about to
be hanged for sheep-stealing. This brought from Miller's nineteen-year-old son, the
future Lord Glenlee, a letter giving Boswell the choice of apologizing or fighting
a duel. Matters were adjusted through the level-headedness of the Justice-Clerk's
brother, Patrick Miller of Dalswinton (father of Grace Boswell's brother-in-law),
and Boswell's reasonableness, but it is highly probable that the Miller clan thereafter
maintained an unfavourable opinion of Boswell. Grace Boswell may indeed have
found talk about Boswell and his book distressing for the reasons assigned by Scott
to her husband, and may have been particularly worried by the family problem
presented by his private papers.

Alexander was as stiff a Tory as his father, though a better party man. In 1821
he won the baronetcy which might well have come a generation earlier if it had not
been for the Biographer's flightiness, but he enjoyed his honours less than a year.
He was, like his father, given to newspaper publication of anonymous lampoons
on persons with whom he had no overt quarrel, and in 1822 had directed a really
vicious series against a political opponent, James Stuart of Dunearn, W.S., repeatedly accusing him of cowardice. In February 1822 he received word of the death
of his brother James from an illness that had not seemed sufficiently alarming to
justify warning him of it, and went at once to London to bury his brother and
make a start at settling his affairs. (James's will made him sole heir.) During his
absence from Scotland, Stuart, by none-too-scrupulous means, obtained evidence
as to who was the author of the lampoons, and sent a card which Sir Alexander
found lying for him on his return, two weeks after James's funeral. He refused all
apology or explanation, met Stuart in the field, fired his pistol in the air, and
received a mortal wound from his assailant, who had little skill in the use of firearms
and made the mistake of *not* aiming.

Sir Alexander's only son, Sir James, succeeded to Auchinleck at the age of
fifteen. Sir Alexander's will left his entire heritable and movable property to Sir
James, subject to various settlements, and, of course, to payment of his debts.
Many of the difficulties attendant on the settling of the Biographer's estate presented
themselves again, but in a much intensified form. Sir Alexander, like his father,

had been a great purchaser of land on borrowed money, and had incurred in addition the great expense of getting into Parliament. The Biographer had left debts of £13,000 which his personal estate finally extinguished. Sir Alexander's debts were estimated to be in excess of £70,000, and it appeared quite certain that neither his heritable nor his movable estate was adequate to meet the claims of the respective creditors. Sir James was advised to take the same course as Sir Alexander and to succeed only as heir of entail; and whereas it had been thought safe for Sir Alexander to be served heir to the Biographer's lands *cum beneficio inventarii* (that is, with responsibility to pay the debts only up to the value of the lands shown in a sworn inventory), the venerable Dean of Faculty who had advised Sir Alexander counselled Sir James to decline all representation of his father's estate, and especially to leave "the management disposal and application thereof [of the movable property] to some other person or persons as Executors qua nearest in kin or Creditors".

The creditors united and agreed not to take measures against the heritable estate, at least not until Sir James came of age. Interest on the heritable debts was kept up by paying over the full rents of the unentailed lands, and by an annual sacrifice of £800 by Sir Alexander's widow from her jointure. Lady Boswell also purchased the library, furniture, and other effects in the house of Auchinleck for £3,000, roughly the appraiser's valuation, which permitted a dividend of two shillings in the pound to the creditors against the movable estate. Hamilton Douglas Boswell of Garallan, one of the creditors, was on 20 February 1824 confirmed executor to manage the personal estate for the behoof of the creditors, and he dying very shortly thereafter, his wife and executrix, Jane Douglas Boswell, was confirmed in the office, 11 August 1824. On 8 August 1828 (that is, a few months after he came of age) Sir James proposed to take over the funds available for the payment of the personal debts at the valuations already approved by the personal creditors, and, in return for a complete discharge, to pay them eight shillings in the pound in addition to the two shillings already received. This scheme, or some similar scheme of composition, appears to have been effected, for on 10 January 1831 Sir James had assignations of all but £2,542 of the £30,822 of personal debt. It is not necessary for our purposes to carry further the troubled story of Sir James's dealings with his father's creditors.

To return to the puzzle of the papers of James Boswell the younger. The erratic division of those papers could be well accounted for by assuming that the only sorting they ever received was from the hand of Sir Alexander, and that when he went back to Scotland and death in March 1822, he had not finished his task. The state of his personal affairs would then explain why no further division was effected. He was sole heir to his brother's estate, but James had died in debt—apparently much deeper in debt than is indicated by the one obligation of £200 mentioned in his will. The Probate Court, after having tried in vain for two years to get Sir James or his guardians to accept letters of administration, granted them on 18 November 1824 to one William How, a creditor, and it was, I suppose, under

How's direction and management that the sale of 1825 took place. He would not have been likely to remove any saleable manuscripts from the effects as he found them, and Sir James would not have been likely to claim any, for he was under a general injunction not to intermeddle with his father's movable property "otherwise than as purchaser of any part he may wish to retain". William How died without settling the estate, and Jane Douglas Boswell finally accepted administration on 23 April 1834. A balance of £547 was paid over next year to the estate of Sir Alexander Boswell.

Sir James Boswell was laird from 1822 to 1857. He was the last of Boswell's descendants to hold the estate under the entail.

ᕃ CHAPTER III ᕄ

"TO THAT REQUEST

THE EDITOR HAS NEVER

RECEIVED ANY ANSWER"

WE HAVE SEEN THAT under Sir Alexander Boswell, Boswell's papers were open to restricted inspection by qualified applicants. At the end of 1829 a request by a most respectable applicant was completely ignored. Early in that year John Wilson Croker, an able Irish politician and man of letters residing in London, agreed with John Murray to prepare a new and extensively annotated edition of Boswell's *Life of Johnson*. He did not need to go beyond Boswell's book to learn that there ought to be "masses of manuscripts at Auchinleck", in particular, Boswell's journals, which would have been of inestimable value in filling blanks and clarifying other obscurities. He wrote to Sir James Boswell and received no answer. He then (16 January 1830) wrote asking his friend, Sir Walter Scott, to present his request:

> I wrote a month ago to *Sir James Boswell, Bart., Auchinleck, Mauchline, N.B.* asking, very civilly I hope, after his grandfather's papers; and I stated my acquaintance with his father and his uncle. I have had no answer. Now, *pray*, find out from somebody in Ayrshire whether the young Baronet is at home, or where he may be. I need not add that if you could, thro' any channell, get at him or his Mamma, and find whether the Journals are at Auchinleck you would confer a great favour on me and on the literary world.

Scott replied promptly (28 January 1830):

> I only write to say that finding Sir James Boswell was at Callender House within 20 miles I wrote to him about your letter and have as yet had no answer. He may have gone some where else otherwise I should scarce think his breeding according to Hoyle. . . . It strikes me he may be as his father certainly was rather ashamed of his fathers passion for Johnson for Boswells book though one of the most entertaining in the world is not just what one would wish a near relation to have written. But then it is but civil to say No politely.

Scott never did receive an answer either. His known letters to Croker report no further efforts on Croker's behalf, but we learn from Croker's preface that Scott later made a personal call on Sir James and missed him; Sir James returned the call but found Scott out. It has naturally been inferred from this that Scott then gave up the chase. Croker in the preface just cited reported Sir James's silence with heavy irony (after all, a Privy Councillor and Secretary to the Admiralty should have had *some* answer), but added in a footnote that he had heard from another source that the journals did not exist at Auchinleck. He expressed fear that the materials for the *Life,* whatever they may have been, had been "irretrievably dispersed". From 1831 till quite recently Sir James Boswell has stood under castigation not only for compound discourtesy but also for having initiated a policy of secretiveness at Auchinleck. Since 1925, when it became generally known that there undoubtedly was a mass of Boswell's papers at Auchinleck in 1829–30, there has been some speculation as to what would have happened if Scott had been more persistent in his inquiries. We now have evidence indicating that Scott *was* more persistent; that he carried his pursuit farther than Croker indicated, probably farther than Croker knew; and that though Sir James was undoubtedly discourteous, he was probably not responsible for the policy of blank silence as to Boswell's papers that prevailed at Auchinleck during the whole of his lairdship.

In order to obtain evidence which will enable us to explain what happened in 1829–30, we must move ahead some fourteen years. But as we pass the years 1836–37, we had better pause to complete the sad history of Euphemia Boswell.

We left her in 1816 the inmate of a private lunatic asylum in Islington, generously provided for by her brothers, who had agreed to pay four guineas a week for her sustenance and care, allowing her to keep her Government pension of £50 a year for extras.[1] Sir Alexander, as a Member of Parliament, was in London a good deal between 1816 and 1821, but I cannot picture his going to visit her. I should like to think, however, that James and T. D. Boswell did keep in close touch with her and went to see her occasionally. How long she actually benefited from her Civil List pension is not clear. Since she had been declared *non compos mentis,* her next of kin would have had to draw it for her. Lady Boswell, writing on 8 July 1825, said the money had not been drawn "since she has been so unwell", which sounds as though she had not had it since she passed into Dr. Sutherland's keeping. Perhaps that is so. It is hard for me to believe, however, that so long as Sir Alexander and James were alive (that is, until 1822) one or the other of them would not have performed that service for her. Lady Boswell says that "above two years ago" she had tried to get T. D. Boswell, as next of kin, to act in the matter, but his health had been so bad that he had done nothing about it. He died on 3 May 1826.

In September 1824, Sir James Boswell being then in his eighteenth year, his curators must have worked out a new arrangement with Dr. Sutherland. Of the sum of £218. 8s. which Euphemia's brothers had agreed to pay him annually, £140

---

[1] See above, pp. 32–33.

was the annuity with which Euphemia's father had burdened the entailed estate of Auchinleck, as he had a right to do. The other £78. 8*s.* came out of the brothers' (probably actually out of Six Alexander's) personal funds. Far from leaving personal funds to endow the supplement, James had died barely solvent and in 1824 it was long since clear that Sir Alexander's personal estate would stretch to no more than half his personal debts. Dr. Sutherland agreed thenceforward to be satisfied with Euphemia's annuity of £140 only, further agreeing, somewhat surprisingly, to let her continue to have her pension of £50 for her own purposes.

Dr. Sutherland received his £140 annually for a period of five years only, from 1824 to 1829. (Sir James came of age at the end of 1827.) Having cared for Euphemia for seven years without any payment from Auchinleck, Dr. Sutherland on 9 February 1836 discharged her as "convalescent" (!), and on 28 April 1836 brought an action against her in the Court of Session in Edinburgh. On 6 July 1836, "in absence", the Lords decreed and ordered her to pay Dr. Sutherland £1,648. 13*s.* 9*d.* "with progressive Interest thereon", plus £10. 11*s.* 10*d.* procedural fees.

The suit, of course, was aimed not at Euphemia, but at Sir James Boswell. Having got a judgement against Euphemia, Dr. Sutherland put an arrestment on her and also one on Sir James as owing her the annuity since Martinmas 1829. Sir James employed delaying tactics, and Dr. Sutherland's lawyer agreed to settle for the bare amount of the arrears in the annuity (£980 as against £1,648. 13*s.* 9*d.*). Sir James's lawyer lectured him:

> Pardon me for saying that you are placing me in a very painful situation with reference to this lady's business. Recollect that I am even yet unable to reply to Mr. Adam's[2] letter a copy of which I sent you, and now comes this official[3] from Mr. Smith to which a satisfactory answer must be made, otherwise the consequence to you may be very serious.

In this Action Euphemia is said to be living at No. 11, Grafton Street, East Tottenham Court Road, London. One hesitates to imagine the state of mind of this unlovable but pitiable woman, certainly elderly (nearly sixty-three) and eccentric, possibly insane, fending for herself in the world after being completely cut off from normal social life for almost twenty years. What on earth did she live on?

The newspapers gave the story a happy ending:

> Miss Euphemia Boswell, daughter of the biographer of Johnson, has very lately been released, through the instrumentality of a friend, who took a lively interest in her behalf, from a lunatic asylum in the Lower-road, Islington, where she had been kept in confinement for the last 19 years.

I should not be disposed to put much credence in this if its accuracy were not strongly indicated by Euphemia's will, a document that has only recently become

---

[2]Mr. Adam will be immediately explained: below, pp. 44–45.
[3]"Short for *official letter*" (OED, Official, II. 4. a).

accessible to me. The will is holograph, dated 9 November 1836, written in lodgings in Barton Street, Westminster, with a holograph codicil, 13 January 1837, written in 7, Francis Street, Bedford Square. Though in the codicil she describes herself as "feeling . . . truly afflicted in body", she was to make one more shift of residence, this time to 48, Great Portland Street, adjacent to or across the street from the house in which Boswell lived from 1791 and in which he died. She begins with directions for her funeral and burial:

> I desire to be buried in St. Pauls Cathedral as near as is possible to Dr. Johnson and I hope my honour'd friend the Revd. Sydney Smith may be able to procure me that favour for which purpose I *respectfully intreat* my Executors after named to apply to him immediately on my demise and to *urge* the point with *energy*—My funeral to be conducted in a prudent manner suitable to my means and station in life.

She goes on to bequeath "to G. Wm. Adam Esqr. Accountant General in Chancery a Gilt Silver cup of the value of one hundred Guineas for his Godlike conduct to me on all occasions and I wish the same to bear an inscription expressive of my vast gratitude and regard". She gives thirty pounds to Thomas Smith, 7, Upper Charles Street, "my worthy solicitor", and ten pounds to Robert Gregory, his clerk. She gives Mrs. Mary Suning of Cuninghame Place, St. John's Wood, widow, "one hundred pounds as a token of gratitude to her for her Philanthropy to me on my first coming to London", and fifty pounds "to her daughter Mrs. Anne Baker wife of the Revd. Mr. Baker a Clergyman somewhere in Kent". Mrs. Turnerelli, "wife of Mr. John Turnerelli of Newman Street Oxford Street sculpturer", is to receive fifty pounds "for her sole use and benefit over which sum her Husband is to have no controul". Mrs. Suning is named residuary legatee and Adam and Smith are nominated executors. The codicil revises the terms of the legacy to Mrs. Turnerelli, giving her and her husband twenty-five pounds apiece, and increases the legacy to Smith to "one hundred pounds if my means admits of it at the time of my demise which I trust it will as I hope to be able to replace the hundred I sold out ere long".

    Is it all—the burial in St. Paul's, the friendship with so prominent a person as Sydney Smith, the Accountant General in Chancery nominated as executor, legacies totalling £410—is it all mere delusions of grandeur? Not in the least. The document is quiet, coherent, and lucid, in style confirming Euphemia's assertion that she is of "sound and disposing mind". She made some mistakes in names (Turnerelli the sculptor was Peter, not John; Adam was William George, not George William), but mistakes of that kind occur in the sanest of wills. If she really meant to imply that she believed Johnson to be buried in St. Paul's, that would indeed have been what Johnson calls a morbid oblivion, but I think it is as likely that by "as near as is possible to Dr. Johnson" she meant "as near as is possible to Bacon's cenotaph of Johnson"—a larger-than-life whole-length statue of Johnson in a toga that stands at the entrance to the north choir aisle of St. Paul's.

The will was treated as quite sound. Euphemia Boswell died on 7 September 1837 and was buried on 14 September 1837 in St. Paul's Cathedral, the officiating clergyman being J. Clarke Haden, M.A., fourth Minor Canon. The undertaker was George Edward Debenham, 50, Bayham Street, Camden Town; it was he who reported the street number of the lodgings in Great Portland Street where Euphemia died. It is touching to find that in her last days she found her way back to the street and almost to the very house where she had spent the happiest years of her life.

Euphemia's madness had always consisted in asserting her right to a degree of public notice which her abilities and her means could not support. What is most surprising in this affair is that she did have funds in hand to pay for her grand funeral and perhaps to pay all the legacies besides. It was reported on 15 September 1837 "that the whole of her goods chattels and Credit are under the value of Four hundred and Fifty pounds". I take this to be a conservative way of saying that she had left an estate approaching, but not over, £450. Whether the legacies were paid in full would have depended on the amount of her funeral expenses, of which I have found no report.

Where did the funds come from? The credit, I fancy, was her claim against the estate of Auchinleck for a half-year's or a full year's annuity. Where else could the cash have come from save from her Civil List pension? William George Adam may have collected an accumulation of several years and invested it for her.

It will be noticed that Euphemia's will names not a single relative. Her provision for executors and appointment of a residuary legatee made it unnecessary to refer to her nearest of kin at all in settling her estate. She is through with the whole Family and divides her substance among those who she thinks have been good to her. When I learned from the newspapers of the "friend who took a lively interest in her behalf", I assumed that either Bruce Boswell (her nephew) or Thomas Alexander Boswell (her first cousin) had stepped forward as her benefactor and protector when Sir James Boswell (her other nephew) had failed to come to her aid. The will removes all basis for this conjecture. Her benefactor and protector was quite clearly William George Adam, no relative at all. He took a strong interest in her affairs by 1806; what he did for her in 1836 has not been determined. The Court of Chancery had jurisdiction over certain rights of lunatics.

We are left with another pretty problem about which I can only make guesses. In 1874 Dr. Charles Rogers published an extended memoir of Boswell which gave the fullest account of Euphemia that has hitherto appeared. He showed by quotation and paraphrase that he had undoubtedly at some time had in his hands a collection of Euphemia Boswell's private papers, the kind of miscellaneous collection one would have expected to find in her effects after her death. He had also read or been told about her will, for he says, "In her Will she expressed a desire that her remains should be deposited in Westminster Abbey near the grave of Dr. Johnson. She was buried elsewhere." I have been unable to decide whether this is a silent "correction" of Euphemia (every one knows that Johnson is buried in Westminster Abbey) or a mistaken report. I formerly had a theory that Rogers found Euphemia's personal papers in the hands of her niece, Mrs. Elizabeth Margaret Montgomerie Williams, through the following chain of events: Rogers acknowledged aid from "the representatives of Thomas David Boswell, the biographer's brother, and of his uncle, Dr. John Boswell". The representative of Thomas David Boswell at the time (c. 1870–74) was not a descendant of his. Thomas David's son, Thomas Alexander Boswell, having lost his only son in India at the age of eighteen, left his valuable property of Crawley Grange, Buckinghamshire, to his first cousin once removed, Col. Bruce Boswell, grandson of the Biographer, son of William Boswell and the Biographer's daughter Elizabeth. When Bruce Boswell died in 1855, the property passed to his sister, Mrs. Williams. But unless Thomas Alexander Boswell or Bruce Boswell befriended Euphemia, there is no reason to suppose that Mrs. Williams had Euphemia's papers. Our best guess, in spite of Rogers's mix-up of Westminster Abbey and St. Paul's, is to suppose that he looked up Euphemia's will and ran down Mrs. Suning, the residuary legatee, or her representative.

The earliest evidence so far recovered that in any way explains Sir James Boswell's failure to reply to Croker occurs in a letter written in 1844 by a surgeon in Edinburgh to a banker in Savannah, Georgia, neither of whom was personally interested in Boswell.

The centenary in 1832 of the founding of the Colony of Georgia naturally stimulated interest in the historical recording of the Colony's early days. The Rev. William Bacon Stevens of Athens, afterwards Episcopal Bishop of Pennsylvania, undertook a comprehensive history, but announced in a letter in the *Savannah Republican,* 1 June 1842, that he could not begin it until he had more information for the founding years 1732–35. William Mackenzie, surgeon, dissector for Dr. Alexander Monro *tertius,* Professor of Anatomy in the University of Edinburgh, whose deep interest in early Georgia history has not been explained, somehow got sight of this letter, and transcribed for Stevens's use from the file of the *Caledonian Mercury* in the Advocates' Library everything he could find concerning Georgia from 1732 to 1736. He also sent on various books and pamphlets dealing with Georgia, and engaged in extensive research on the identity and genealogy of the Highlanders who emigrated to Georgia before 1745. The Georgia Historical Society of Savannah fittingly rewarded his tireless volunteer efforts by making him an honorary member. The diploma was sent by the Corresponding Secretary of the Society, Mr. Israel K. Tefft, banker in Savannah and collector of autographs and Americana, who accompanied it with a request that concerned Boswell's private papers. His letter has not been recovered and must be reconstructed entirely from Mackenzie's reply. The following reading seems to me best to fit all the clues, but claims to be no more than inference. Tefft was trying to locate for Dr. Stevens the manuscript notes on the life of General James Edward Oglethorpe, founder of the Colony of Georgia, which Boswell in the *Life of Johnson* says he had taken down from Oglethorpe's own lips. Stevens had read and accepted Croker's discouraging report as to there being no significant deposit of Boswell's papers at Auchinleck, but wished to investigate the possibility that some at least of the papers might be in the hands of Boswell's brother's son, Thomas Alexander Boswell of Crawley Grange, of whose existence he had somehow become aware. Tefft or Stevens made direct or indirect inquiry at Auchinleck for T. A. Boswell's address, and were somehow informed by the Dowager Lady Boswell, widow of Sir Alexander Boswell, that she did not know it. Tefft asked Mackenzie to try to get the address by other means. Mackenzie's letter is so important for the present portion of this study that a good deal of it must be quoted verbatim. The date is 1 February 1844:

I have not yet obtained the address of Thos. A Boswell although I lost no time in beginning the requisite enquiries. It unfortunately happens that there is a feud in this family—who, indeed, have always been remarkable for some weak peculiarities. Mr. Miller of Dalswinton and others nearly connected with the Boswells referred me to a gentleman residing in this city who is reported to have *extraordinary* influence with them—He does not wish his name to be mentioned and considers the conversation I held with him as so far confidential. Mr. James Boswell Johnsons biographer, left two sons—the eldest Alexander was killed in 1822 by James Stuart of Dunearn in a duel. The present Sir James Boswell is his only son. Neither James the grandfather, Alexander the father, nor the present Sir James ever lived at "Crawley Grange". At Sir Alexr.'s decease he was considerably in debt, and his library and MSS were purchased by his wife the Dowager Lady Boswell. They are all at Auchinleck house, in the state in which they were found, at the death of her husband in three boxes carefully sealed up. Dowager Lady Boswell recently writes to her sister the Honble. Mrs Leslie Cumming,[4] in reply to a question from me "that she never heard Sir Alexr. B. allude to any MSS. life of General Oglethorpe, and that she does not believe that anything of the kind exists— otherwise she would have heard of it".

The second brother of Mr James Boswell was named David—he was first a merchant in Spain, and subsequently obtained a lucrative appointment in the Navy Pay Office. He used to be called "Don" David. He had one son David Thomas, who made an unsuitable marriage, went to India, acquired an immense fortune, and left one Son Thos A. Boswell, the gentleman whose present address you wish to obtain. My informant positively declares that the deceased Sir Alexander B. got *all* his fathers papers, and that none of these could by any possibility have been in the possession of "Don" David, or of his son, or grandson.

Dowager Lady Boswell and her connections dislike greatly any allusion to Dr. Johnson, considering that Mr. James the grandfather degraded himself and his family by acting the toady to the Dr. Sir Walter Scott applied to my informant to get access to Dr. Johnsons letters for Croker's edition of Boswell, but in spite of all his importunities and influence, was met with a firm refusal. It is known that many interesting papers and letters exist in the collection—and all the letters published by Boswell with the suppressed passages. If my friend survives Dowager Lady B. he will then be allowed

---

[4]Jane, eldest daughter of Thomas Cuming, widow of Gen. the Hon. John Leslie (d. 1824). She took the name Cuming as representative of that family after the death of her brothers.

to examine them all. He tells me that Boswell *intended* to write the history of many distinguished individuals,—but actually did nothing except notifying his intentions. As for instance he reported that he had written the life of Lord Kames—after B's death it was found the M.S.S. consisted of only five pages. . . . I have delayed making enquiries in England in relation to Thos A Boswell's address, because D. Lady B. is expected to visit her sister the Honble. Mrs L. Cumming in about a fortnight, when if she *really* can give me no positive information, I will at once apply elsewhere, as I cannot believe, she can be ignorant of the residence of the heir at law to the title and estates of her son Sir James.

The first question that arises is of course who Mackenzie's Informant was. However, since my answer to that question must be speculative in the present state of our knowledge, I shall defer my identification to the end of my discussion of the other problems the letter raises. The Informant must be cited again and again, and it would be intolerable on each occasion to have to tag the name with some qualifying clause like "if my identification is correct".

How accurate was the information Mackenzie obtained from his mysterious Informant? Completely accurate, I should say, in all that concerns the accessibility of the Boswell papers to qualified applicants from 1822 to 1844 and probably to 1864. There is one glaring error in Mackenzie's report, but I feel sure that it was his own and was due to confusion in his notes. His David Thomas Boswell and his Thomas Alexander Boswell are one and the same person, the second style being the correct one. Boswell's brother, as Mackenzie says, was christened David. When he went to Spain to settle as a merchant, being told that the Spaniards had a prejudice against Old Testament names, he prefixed the name Thomas to David. On his return to England he chose to retain the Thomas: Boswell usually calls him "T. D." Thomas Alexander Boswell was T. D. Boswell's only son. I do not remember reading elsewhere that he went to India and acquired an immense fortune, but it sounds reasonable. The information that he made an unsuitable marriage I at first thought wrong, believing that Mackenzie had again confused him with his father. T. D. Boswell paid court to a Miss Anne Catherine Green but showed some inclination to withdraw his suit when she developed signs of mental instability. Her family exerted pressure and T. D. Boswell married her rather reluctantly. She later seems to have been permanently put in confinement. I think now, however, that Mackenzie was reporting an important fact I had never heard of before. T. D. Boswell's marriage was unfortunate but would not have been styled unsuitable. ("Unsuitable" would have implied that the man in question married beneath him or married a woman of damaged reputation.) That Thomas Alexander Boswell as a young man committed that kind of *faux pas* I now think quite likely from a letter that became accessible to me only in 1978, when Sir Arthur Eliott of Stobs gave it to the Boswell Museum at Auchinleck. It is from Alexander Boswell, writing from London to his wife in Scotland, 6 December 1819:

My uncle is in his usual health, his unfortunate son after wandering from place to place has got to Bolougne where he feels more happy because amongst his Countrymen, but

calls it *Exile* and wishes to return home! where it must be exile indeed. Poor wretch
what a prospect he has before him.

That is exactly the strain in which Alexander would have written if his cousin
had made an unsuitable marriage. I had not supposed there was any "feud" between
the Boswells of Auchinleck and Thomas Alexander Boswell before Sir James Boswell
started proceedings to break the entail of Auchinleck, but we can now safely
conclude, I think, that there had been no communication between the parties since
1819. There is not among the Boswell papers at Yale a single letter from Thomas
Alexander Boswell or copy of a letter to him. The "Materials for Writing the Life
of Lord Kames" run to eighty folio and quarto pages, but the Informant did not
profess to have seen—much less to have handled—Boswell's papers himself. Nor,
I think, did Lady Boswell: she went on what she had heard from Sir Alexander.
(By the way, she was right in thinking that the notes on General Oglethorpe's life
were not at Auchinleck. They turned up at Fettercairn.)⁵ In matters of detail,
memory, unless checked by written records, always tends to exaggerate and to
substitute: "five pages", indeed, may be what the Informant's or Lady Boswell's
memory had made of some remark of Lord Woodhouselee's that from Boswell's
materials he had been able to extract only matter for six footnotes.

There has been of late a strong tendency to challenge the tradition that a policy
of secretiveness, "a conspiracy of silence" with regard to Boswell's papers, was
followed at Auchinleck at least from 1822 onward. The challenge has been healthy
so far as it consisted of a demand for evidence. We now have solid evidence that
from 1822 to 1844 (and probably, as I have said, to 1864) there was at Auchinleck
a policy of not letting any one whatever see Boswell's private papers. Further, I
know of no evidence that during that time any one at Auchinleck ever admitted
in writing to any one outside the family that the papers even existed at Auchinleck.

It was probably the Dowager Lady Boswell, not her son, who set and kept up
that policy. What right had she to do so? Down to the Fettercairn litigation, it
was assumed by scholars as a matter of course that Sir James inherited his grandfather's papers as he inherited the landed estate of Auchinleck. We now know that
that was certainly not the case. The papers at Auchinleck were handled as part of
Sir Alexander's personal estate, which Sir James dared not claim. When, in 1824,
Lady Boswell purchased from the creditors the effects in Auchinleck House, the
papers became her absolute property, to deal with as she saw fit. The only document
touching the matter that has so far been recovered is a minute of agreement drawn
up in 1858, the year after Sir James's death, between the Dowager Lady Boswell
and her son's widow. This document says that the effects were presented by the
Dowager Lady Boswell to Sir James, apparently soon after the purchase, and confirms
the gift by declaring that they are now the exclusive property of Sir James's widow.
It is assumed that both the Dowager Lady Boswell's purchase and her gift to Sir
James were conducted informally, without written documents, which David Buch-

---

⁵Fettercairn is explained below, pp. 126–27.

anan assures me would have been normal under Scots law. It seems clear, however, that in one respect the gift to Sir James was not unrestricted. David Buchanan says that "although Lady Boswell gave her son the contents of Auchinleck", Mackenzie's letter "suggests that she still kept the family papers under her strict control". That is, she gave Sir James only limited title to the papers. She was no doubt completely within her legal rights in sealing Boswell's papers up and in deciding that the seals should not be broken for any one.

We know that she did do that. We know on the same testimony that she greatly disliked allusions to Johnson, believing that her husband's father had degraded both himself and his family by obsequiousness to Johnson. We know that she got Johnson's portrait quietly removed from Auchinleck House, though in fairness we must grant that at least part of her motive on that occasion was disinterested. Beyond that we *know* practically nothing, and the document that tells us the most of what we do know comes wholly from outside the Boswell papers. Surely that is significant. Is it not fair to conclude that the main reason we know so little about Lady Boswell's motives is that she was so secretive, that is, that she kept so completely from putting her motives on paper? We do not *know* that Sir James ever told her of the letters from Croker and Scott. He may have carelessly ignored them and she may first have heard of them when Croker published his preface. True, but either way she was extraordinarily secretive: secretive in not telling Sir James what to write or secretive in not sending Croker belated explanation of what had happened. (Surely we should have heard of it if she had written to Croker after his book came out?) Secretiveness on this scale was hardly to be expected in a woman of breeding, a titled member of the county gentry, the widow of a public man, indeed of a Member of Parliament. She may not have known Croker very well herself, but she undoubtedly knew that he was one of the leaders of her late husband's political party and that a considerable degree of acquaintance, if not of friendship, had existed between them. Does not Mackenzie's letter imply her secretiveness outside the family in that he can get a report on the papers he wants to locate only from Lady Boswell's sister?

If Lady Boswell's secretiveness was constitutional, even morbid, one would just accept it as such, but as a matter of fact it appears to have been practically effective in furthering what I take to have been policy. She had, I suggest, a strong sense of family pride to begin with, and her pride had been stiffened by the personal responsibilities she had to assume as head of the family while her son was a minor. She deeply deplored the turn of events which had joined the name of Johnson so firmly to that of Boswell, and literally wanted to strip this association off, to restore her son to the position of head of the ancient family of Boswell of Auchinleck, with no degrading reflection from his grandfather's literary fame. She did not look beyond her son (she could have burned the papers), but during her lifetime she wanted the papers to fall into oblivion. And they would not have fallen into oblivion if she admitted publicly that they were at Auchinleck.

If Scott was told by the Informant that all Boswell's papers remained at

Auchinleck, and if Scott used importunities and influence to secure access to them for Croker, why did not Croker say so? Why did he allow himself to give the impression that there were no papers of any importance at Auchinleck? If he knew that it was Lady Boswell who was the source of the firm refusal, why did he slate Sir James? My guess is that the Informant imposed stricter limits of confidentiality on Scott than he did on Mackenzie. (Croker wanted to make extensive publication of the kind of matter Lady Boswell found most offensive; the notes on Oglethorpe were free of Johnsonian connexion and were to have only provincial publication.) Scott indeed may not have been allowed to tell Croker all he had learned. I shall venture a second guess which should probably be rated far-fetched. Croker wanted to see Boswell's *journals;* the Informant talks about *letters* of Johnson published in the *Life* and says nothing whatever about journals. Perhaps the Informant had never been told about the journals and too confidently assured Scott that they were not at Auchinleck. In that case, ironically enough, *he* would have been the "another source" of Croker's footnote. Croker's putting Sir James rather than his mother in the pillory presents no difficulties. He could not mention Lady Boswell without breaching confidence, but he had a public quarrel with Sir James. His letter had been addressed to *him;* Sir James owed Croker polite acknowledgement even if it accompanied a refusal.

Before we drop discussion of Mackenzie's letter, it is necessary to point out the serious implications for scholarship of the Informant's confident assurance that the original manuscripts of Johnson's letters to Boswell (and probably also of Boswell's to Johnson) were at Auchinleck in 1844. Of late years, scholars have begun to question whether they were seen by any one after Boswell's death, and to speculate whether they may not have been lost by having been put by Boswell himself in what he considered a place of greater security in London. The Informant's statement does not by any means prove this speculation wrong, but in my opinion it requires us to reconsider it.

Finally, who was Mackenzie's Informant? If Miller of Dalswinton and others nearly connected with the Boswells directed Mackenzie to him, he was very likely a Miller or a Miller connexion himself. The perfect candidate in most respects would be Sir William Miller, Lord Glenlee in the Court of Session and the High Court of Justiciary, first cousin to Lady Boswell's mother, Lady Boswell's own guardian and head of the Miller family. He would have been eighty-eight at the date of Mackenzie's letter, but I do not consider his age a serious objection: he sat on the bench till he was eighty-five and lived to be almost ninety-one. Obviously, if he spoke of outliving a woman nearly twenty years younger than himself, he did it with a smile which Mackenzie has not reported. But Mackenzie in one respect was not writing with complete freedom, and in that respect he may not have been perfectly frank in what he did write. He was under obligation to preserve the Informant's incognito, and any reference to extreme old age could have led to easy identification if Tefft had had another correspondent in Edinburgh. Mackenzie may have added a misleading (but not untruthful) detail at the Informant's own request

("Lady Boswell mustn't find out that I have told you all this. Throw your American off the scent by saying that I am to be allowed to read the papers if I survive her"). In spite of the difficulties, Lord Glenlee remains my candidate and I have no alternative suggestions. If Lord Glenlee does stand back of Mackenzie's report, that report is weighty evidence indeed in spite of coming at second hand.

David Buchanan thinks that if Lady Boswell had been out of the way, and especially in his later years, Sir James Boswell might have been willing to open the archives to a qualified applicant. He cites as evidence Mackenzie's letter (who but Sir James could have "allowed" the Informant to read Boswell's papers?) and another written at the end of 1856 by Hugh Bruce Campbell, a distant cousin of Sir James, to the editor of the Boswell-Temple letters, which had just appeared (more of this later). Campbell, who expressed a confident opinion that there were papers at Auchinleck that would furnish the means of tracing many of Boswell's miscellaneous letters, said that he suspected that Sir James had felt the justice of Croker's rebuke, and that it was his (Campbell's) opinion that Sir James might respond favourably if approached again. He even offered to speak personally to Sir James on the matter when he saw him the next summer. It is not known whether this offer was accepted or not. Sir James died on 4 November 1857. I personally would not base much on such evidence. Willingness to grant access to a confidential, long-time adviser and friend of the family—especially if that adviser were Sir James's venerable cousin, Lord Glenlee—tells us little or nothing about the kind of response Sir James would have made to an outsider. It would only point up the extraordinary rigour of Lady Boswell's restrictions. As for Hugh Bruce Campbell, he resided in England, and I doubt if his relations with the Auchinleck family were at all close. He clearly did not know that the Dowager Lady Boswell had kept the papers under her control at least to 1844, and if he did not know that, I do not think his opinions can be given much weight.

Sir James, for reasons soon to appear, cannot however be treated as a mere zero in the history of the Boswell papers. Very little accurate information has as yet been put in print about him. He spent two years at Oxford and is said to have had great natural abilities, but he followed no profession, sought no public office, showed no interest in literature (it does not appear that he added a single important book to the library at Auchinleck), but was content to appear before the world as an Ayrshire laird, a sportsman and a gambler. He showed temper when Miss MacLeod of MacLeod suggested that he name one of his racehorses "Boswell's Johnsoniana". David Buchanan maintains that his reaction to "this rather silly suggestion" is no real evidence as to his feelings about Johnson, but surely Mackenzie's Informant meant to include him in the general charge that Dowager Lady Boswell and her connexions greatly disliked any allusion to Dr. Johnson. Sir James wrote "Damned Scoundrell" in the margin of a transcript of the Auchinleck entail, opposite a sentence in which Lord Auchinleck says that it might be alleged that the limitations he was putting upon his heirs male were contrary to the agreements of his marriage contract; presumably Sir James's bitter resentment extended to his grandfather as well, for the deed was made jointly by Lord Auchinleck and Boswell.

Dowager Lady Boswell could hardly have been so silly as to suppose that by sealing up Boswell's private papers she could extinguish or dampen the general literary talk and writing about him and his book. She was determined, I think, that the family papers—at least in her time—should furnish no *new* materials that might increase the general talk, but her main object was to put an end to mention of the Johnson connexion in Auchinleck House.

She certainly would not have been made more communicative by Croker's edition of the *Life*. Sir James, as has been said, was paid off in the preface, and far too many of the notes were strictures, couched in a tone of extreme condescension, on Boswell's intelligence. Macaulay, whom Croker had humiliated in the House of Commons, was waiting for an opportunity to take vengeance. He reviewed the book, and flayed not only Croker but Boswell as well. There are many things in the *Life of Johnson* that could have been counted on to irritate Macaulay. Boswell was an extreme Tory and let himself go in notes intended less to assert his own political conservatism than to insult people who differed from him; he was distressingly orthodox and High Church; he printed rough remarks by Johnson on Macaulay's grandfather and great-uncle. Still, Macaulay would hardly have handled Boswell as he did if his animus against Croker had not carried over to Croker's author. His characterization of Boswell is brilliant, but its brilliance stems from a paradox stated with the simplicity and lack of qualification of an axiom: "This man wrote the greatest of biographies *because* he was a fool." He redrew the portrait on a smaller scale in his *Essay on Johnson*, originally published in 1856 in the *Encyclopaedia Britannica*. Perhaps no other essays on an English author have been so widely read; certainly no other pieces of personal disparagement of an author have been so successful. Even now, in spite of the enormous additions made to our knowledge in the last hundred years, the popular estimate of Boswell is almost pure Macaulay. If nothing had been added to the depreciations of Croker and Macaulay, Boswell's descendants through the rest of the nineteenth century might well have felt that Lady Boswell's policy of non-communication was justified, and should be continued. As it happened, the inclination to silence was probably increased by the publication of a body of Boswell's private papers not in the family's hands.

"IT IS BELIEVED
THE WHOLE WERE
IMMEDIATELY
DESTROYED."

A NUMBER OF EVENTS important for our story cluster about the year 1857. Towards the end of 1856 (the title-page is dated 1857) there appeared from the press of Richard Bentley in London a book which must have surprised and shocked the family at Auchinleck. It consisted of ninety-seven extremely intimate letters from Boswell to his lifelong friend William Johnson Temple, the first written in 1758 when Boswell was a boy of seventeen, the last in 1795 when he was on his death-bed. The story of the recovery of the manuscripts of these letters is so improbable that many people at the time pronounced the whole thing a hoax. Temple had carefully kept all Boswell's letters except a few that Boswell had begged back for various reasons. Temple's oldest daughter, Anne, married a clergyman named Powlett, a grandson of the Duke of Bolton and Lavinia Fenton, the original Polly Peachum of *The Beggar's Opera*. Mr. Powlett's tastes were more expensive than his income warranted, and he ended his life on the Continent in retreat from his creditors. He presumably took with him his father-in-law's papers, or at least a part of them. He died in 1834. Some six years later a Major Stone of the East India Company Service went into the shop of a Madame Noël in Boulogne and received his purchase wrapped in an English letter bearing the signature of James Boswell. He asked if there were any more of the same kind and was assured that there were; Madame Noël had bought them in a bundle with others from a hawker of paper and knew nothing of their history. She had already used a good many as wrappers. Major Stone secured what still remained of the correspondence, perhaps about half of it. After Major Stone's death the letters were purchased from his heir for a total of £25 (a trifle over five shillings a letter), and edited by Sir Philip Francis, barrister of the Middle Temple. The book constituted a remarkably complete and faithful *biographia epistolaris* and furnished, for any one willing to approach it with some degree of sympathy and tolerance, a characterization of Boswell strongly at variance with Macaulay's. But though Francis had expurgated the text, it still presented ample evidence of Boswell's vanity, incontinence, and intemperance. To those under Macaulay's spell it merely confirmed Macaulay's verdict of fatuity. Boswell's recordings of his incontinence and intemperance would at the present time be the principal, if not the sole, reason for a policy of family suppression or censorship. I doubt if Dowager Lady Boswell's action was primarily instigated by this aspect of Boswell's papers. Women born well within the eighteenth century, as she was, accepted rakishness and heavy drinking in gentlemen as a matter of course. What hurt Lady Boswell most, as the Informant said, was Boswell's lowering himself (as she believed) by attendance on a plebeian man of letters. But Dowager Lady Boswell's granddaughters, who were born shortly before the inception of the reign of Victoria, no doubt absorbed the moral and literary attitudes of that reign. The disclosures of the Temple letters must have been painful to the proud family at Auchinleck, and may have strengthened their determination to keep the papers from the sight of any one who might wish to publish them.

Towards the end of 1857 Sir James Boswell died, leaving the estate of Auchinleck crippled if not ruined by enormous debt. As every one who has read the *Life of Johnson* knows, Boswell and his father (both lawyers) had agonized over the drawing of an entail which would prevent any heir to the estate from borrowing money on it. Both wanted male succession, but they could not agree on the number of ancestral lines they should make eligible for the succession if their own male line failed. Lord Auchinleck was determined to go no farther back than heirs male of his own Boswell grandfather. Boswell supposed that his motive was to exclude a remote Boswell line, the representative of which at the time the entail was being debated was a dancing-master. Perhaps that was what was ultimately in Lord Auchinleck's mind, but his really pressing reason (never admitted to Boswell) was that he had already bound himself to that succession in his marriage contract. Since Lord Auchinleck had three sons, his brother John three, and his uncle John one, the succession Lord Auchinleck demanded seemed to make reasonable provision for heirs male. But Boswell, who could get very much worked up over eventualities not likely to happen, wanted heirs male back to Thomas Boswell, the founder, and for some time remained stubbornly committed to what he considered a sacred principle. Lord Auchinleck won out, but all their agonizing went for nothing. Their own male line did fail with Boswell's grandson, but the entail was broken before the males descended from Lord Auchinleck's brother—let alone his uncle—had had their chance.

As has been remarked, Lord Auchinleck had three sons. The Biographer had two sons. Sir Alexander had an only son, Sir James. Sir James had two daughters but no son. From 1826 to 1852 his heir male presumptive was his father's first cousin, Thomas Alexander Boswell of Crawley Grange. Mackenzie's Informant spoke of there being a feud—estrangement would be a better term—between the Auchinleck family and Thomas Alexander Boswell, and I have ventured to carry that estrangement as far back as 1819, when Sir Alexander was laird, and to impute it to an "unsuitable" marriage entered into by Thomas Alexander. As a matter of fact, there were two "feuds": Sir Alexander ended by being at odds with all his nearest Boswell kin except his uncle, Thomas David Boswell. I have already mentioned his disowning his sister Elizabeth ("Betsy") and having no communication with her, her husband, or her four children (Robert Cramond Boswell, d. 1821; James Paoli, d. 1820; Bruce, d. 1855; and "Monty", d. after 1871). Sir James went to court on 12 April 1849 in an attempt to break the entail. On 3 February 1852 the Court of Session declared the entail void because a material word "irredeemably" was written over an erasure. As it turned out, Thomas Alexander Boswell, who had lost his only son, predeceased Sir James, so that if the entail had stood in 1857, the estate of Auchinleck would have gone to the Rev. Robert Bruce Boswell, son of Robert Boswell's second son, Alexander. As has been narrated, Thomas Alexander Boswell, who died on 24 March 1852, gave Crawley Grange to Elizabeth Boswell's son Bruce (his brothers Robert and James had died young and unmarried) and on Bruce Boswell's death (1855) Elizabeth's daughter "Monty" (Mrs. Elizabeth Margaret Montgomerie Williams) succeeded him. Shortly before his death, Sir James Boswell made a will bequeathing his entire property of whatever description to his wife and first cousin Jessie Jane Cuninghame. This Lady Boswell held Auchinleck in her own right from 1857 to 1884. She undoubtedly owned the Boswell papers from 1858, but her mother-in-law and aunt, whom I have so often referred to above as the Dowager Lady Boswell, lived on to 1864, and it would seem highly probable that as she had certainly controlled use of the papers from 1824 to 1844, she would have continued that control to the end of her life. Sir James, as has been said, left two daughters, Julia Grace Jessie Jane, who married George Mounsey, solicitor and one-time mayor of Carlisle, and Emily Harriet, who married the Hon. Richard Wogan Talbot, eldest son of Lord Talbot de Malahide of Malahide Castle, near Dublin. Lady Boswell's settlements directed that one half of the estate of Auchinleck should go to the trustees acting under the marriage contract of her younger daughter, and that the other half should go to the same trustees if Mrs. Mounsey should die without issue, which in fact happened. The other half of the estate, including the mansion-house of Auchinleck, was to be held in trust for the liferent use of Mrs. Mounsey. The books and pictures in the house of Auchinleck were given to Mrs. Mounsey; the remainder of the movable estate was divided between the two daughters. After her husband succeeded to the title, Lady Talbot de Malahide lived at Malahide. Mrs. Mounsey opened Auchinleck for a few months each year, but made her principal residence in Carlisle. The Boswell name had left Auchinleck, and the hold of the family on the ancestral property had weakened.

In 1874, the year after Emily Boswell's marriage, the Rev. Charles Rogers, Scotsman and minister of the Church of Scotland, who had settled in England and had there brought out a long series of works on Scottish history, literature, and genealogy, published the first extended memoir of Boswell as preface to the first full-scale printing of the *Boswelliana*. (This large and important manuscript, as has been mentioned above, had escaped from the archives through having been in the library of James Boswell the younger at the time of his death. It had passed into the possession of Richard Monckton Milnes—later Lord Houghton—who in 1856 had printed a few anecdotes from it for the Philobiblon Society.) I have already drawn on this memoir to fill out Euphemia Boswell's story. I now return to it for an important statement which Rogers made as to the disposition of Boswell's papers. Rogers printed a full text of Boswell's will (minus the codicils) and gave authority to the view that Boswell's archives had perished. "The three persons nominated as literary executors," he says, "did not meet, and the entire business of the trust was administered by Sir William Forbes, Bart., who appointed as his law agent Robert Boswell, writer to the signet, cousin german of the deceased. By that gentleman's advice, Boswell's manuscripts were left to the disposal of his family; and it is believed that the whole were immediately destroyed."

Dr. Rogers was a careful writer; he made mistakes but he was not given to unsupported assertions. That his source of information was not Auchinleck is indicated by the acknowledgements in his preface: "The representatives of Thomas David Boswell, the biographer's brother, and of his uncle, Dr. John Boswell, have been most polite and obliging in their communications." Either he wrote very carelessly, or he meant to invite the reader to infer that he had applied first to Auchinleck (that is, to Lady Boswell, Sir James's widow) and that he either received no answer or received an answer that was not polite or obliging. As I have said above, I do not know whom Rogers considered to be the "representative" of Dr. John Boswell. If he meant "heir male", he was probably referring to John Alexander Corrie Boswell, grandson of Robert Boswell's second son, Alexander; this J. A. C. Boswell died in 1872. By representative of Thomas David Boswell he could only have meant Mrs. Williams, who, though not a descendant of T. D. Boswell (she was his grandniece), did inherit his property of Crawley Grange.[1] Her information, one would think, would have come from her father, William Boswell, dead since 1841, or her uncle, Alexander Boswell, W. S., who lived till 1850. William, having been a party to the arbitration over Boswell's executry, knew much at first hand, and could have learned more from his father, who was agent for the executor, Sir William Forbes. But Robert Boswell's knowledge was limited. He died on 1 April 1804, less than two weeks after Hope issued his interim decreet and a good ten months before the final decreet appeared and Forbes got his discharge. Robert Boswell could not have *known* that the papers "were left to the disposal of [the] family" (that is, handed over to Alexander), but William Boswell probably knew that they were. If he did not know from his involvement in the arbitration, he could have learned that fact from his brother, Alexander Boswell, who succeeded Robert Boswell as Forbes's agent. Robert Boswell was a good and a very pious man, a lay preacher in the strict Glassite or Sandemanian sect. He was fully aware of

[1]See above, p. 56.

Boswell's intemperance and very probably aware also of his traffic with strumpets; Forbes may have confided to him his uneasiness over "reprehensible passages" in Boswell's journals; for that matter, Robert Boswell may have dipped into the journal himself. He proposed a verse-epitaph on his cousin containing the couplet

> Bury his failings in the silent grave,
> And from unfriendly hands his memory save.

He would very probably have urged William and Elizabeth Boswell not to press for publication of any of Boswell's papers but rather to let them go quietly to Alexander. It would have been very like him to express to all concerned an opinion that the papers should be destroyed. But why would William Boswell or his brother Alexander have believed that such action was indeed immediately taken when the papers were returned to Auchinleck?

The answer may lie in a forgotten footnote of Malone's which unfortunately requires a good deal of explanation if it is to be understood.

There appeared in 1807 (only two years after Forbes's discharge) an apparently authoritative statement that a mass of papers containing at least one of Johnson's letters to Boswell had been burned in Scotland. This statement was very probably a mare's nest, but there was no reason why a reader in 1807 should not have taken it at face value. It will be remembered that in 1804 Malone had asked Forbes to try to find the originals of three of Johnson's letters to Boswell so that he could verify readings in the *Life* which he considered suspicious. In one of these letters, 3 July 1778, Johnson is credited with the expression "without asserting Stoicism". Malone believed that he had actually written "without affecting Stoicism", "asserting" being a misreading by either Boswell or the type-setter. The original not being forthcoming, Malone left the text as it was. In the fifth edition (1807), however, he added a footnote proposing the emendation "affecting", going on to say that it could not be verified, "the original letter being burned in a mass of papers in Scotland". Commander Rupert T. Gould made the ingenious suggestion that "burned" is itself a misreading, and that Malone really wrote "buried". Though the textual history of the *Life* supports "burned", the surviving letters of Malone to Forbes and to James Boswell the younger make it almost certain that Comdr Gould was right. Malone's letters to Forbes of 23 April and 2 May 1804 would certainly have alluded to the destruction of papers by fire if Forbes's untraced letters of 9 March and 25 April had contained that shocking news. And if Forbes after 25 April 1804, in some letter of which we have no record, had stated or suggested that any letter from Johnson to Boswell had perished in a bonfire, Malone would hardly have failed to allude to the report in his letter to James Boswell the younger in 1808. Pretty clearly, when he was revising for the fifth edition, he decided not to bother Forbes again but simply proposed his emendation and wrote a note saying that the original letter was "buried in a mass of papers in Scotland". In 1808, with the papers, as he supposed, all at Auchinleck and with James Boswell the younger on the spot, he tried again to get his textual puzzles searched. It is annoying that the list he sent was haphazard; particularly that it omitted all mention of the letter with which we are concerned.

It is possible that Malone's unintended record of a burning may be the ultimate source of Dr. Rogers's statement, but it is not likely that he got his information directly from Malone's brief note. That note was well hidden and was to be found only in editions of the *Life of Johnson* little read after Croker. It may well be, however, that from that note William Boswell or his brother Alexander formed a belief that the papers had been destroyed in accordance with their father's advice; that they handed their belief on to Mrs. Williams, who reported it to Rogers. It really does not much matter except to those who like to fill in, even if by pure speculation, the links which connect one bit of historical evidence with another. The important thing is that in 1874 Croker's assurance that the papers had perished received circumstantial support of a very persuasive kind.

But, after all, Dr. Rogers had said that it was *believed* that the papers had perished. So comprehensive an editor as Dr. George Birkbeck Hill should not have remained satisfied with that statement. Yet in his great edition of the *Life of Johnson,* first published in 1887, he makes, so far as I can discover, no references to any help received or requested from any descendant of Boswell. Hill's strong point never was the location and use of manuscript material; it was rather the isolation and collection, by means of a remarkable memory, of explanatory or illustrative passages from other printed books, books which he could carry with him in his valetudinary wanderings. But in 1890, in his *Footsteps of Dr. Johnson (Scotland)*—an anecdotal picture-book commentary on Johnson's *Journey to the Western Islands* and Boswell's *Journal of a Tour to the Hebrides*—he lamented that Auchinleck was not open for public inspection, discussed Sir Alexander and Sir James Boswell with hostile detail, and scolded Boswell's living descendants sharply and at length for being ashamed of their ancestor. And in an essay, "Boswell's Proof Sheets", published in the *Atlantic Monthly* in 1894, he brought out the whole story of his grievance. In 1889 (two years after the publication of his edition of the *Life*) he had "tried to penetrate into Auchinleck". It does not appear that he requested permission to search for Boswell's papers. His expressed hope was to find "many curious memorials" in the library. "Permission," he says, "was refused me." Soon after, he received a brief, badly spelled letter from Mrs. Vassall, daughter of Sir Alexander Boswell, saying that she had heard that he was about to publish "another addition of My Grandfathers book—'Boswell's Life of Johnston'," and that he professed to have got "some papers from Ayrshire". From whom did he get them? Hill assumed that his request to visit Auchinleck House (presumably addressed to Mrs. Mounsey) had not only displeased the family but had "even excited suspicion". Now that *The Treasure of Auchinleck* has been published any scholar can easily find out that Mrs. Vassall was sole heir to the estate of her mother, Lady Boswell. In view of this fact, it seems likely that Mrs. Vassall was merely (or at least primarily) expressing concern about valuable effects to which she thought she might have a claim under her mother's will. She may not have known of Hill's approach to Auchinleck at all. Hill can hardly be faulted for not being up on these testamentary intricacies, and with such facts as he had it was not unnatural for him to assume that Mrs. Vassall was speaking as a member of the Auchinleck family, and that the family harboured a suspicion that he had in some underhand way got access to papers that were, or should be, under family control. But before he *published,* he was under obligation to search out the facts, however obscure, and that is just what he did not do. He further took rather spiteful revenge by printing Mrs. Vassall's letter *literatim.* But it does not appear that he ever entertained a suspicion that the archives had survived. In the *Footsteps* he rated Boswell's executors for having destroyed the manuscripts "with a brutish ignorance worthy of perpetual execration". Rogers had not accused the executors themselves of destroying anything.

David Buchanan properly chides Hill for his shrill and careless denunciation of the executors. He considers Mrs. Vassall's letter "polite" and feels that it "gave [Hill] no cause for offence". I do not share his views as to the politeness of the letter, which is here reproduced *in toto* as Hill printed it:

44 Queen Street, Edinburgh,
June 1, 1889.

DEAR SIR,

   I am told you are about to publish another addition of My Grandfathers book— "Boswell's Life of Johnston" and that you have "some papers from Ayrshire"! May I ask you to be so good as inform me from whom you received them and oblige

Yours faithfully
M. E. VASSALL

I may tell you that I am daughter of Sir Alexander Boswell.
G. Berbick Hill Esq.

If I had received that letter from a total stranger, I should have felt it to be curt to the point of rudeness. If, after looking in books of reference, I found the writer to be an old lady of eighty-five, the daughter of a famous man, I should, I hope, have made proper allowance for old age and crustiness, but I should still have thought the writer short on manners. Mrs. Vassall was born a lady, must have moved all her life in county society, and was the widow of a general. I don't believe that was the tone and style she used when she wrote to people she respected. Hill was touchy and anxious in temperament; he suffered severely from bad reviews. But he was not a recluse and he was not socially inept. He managed quite readily to "penetrate" the mansions of the Duke of Argyll, the Earl Cawdor, the Earl of Erroll, and MacLeod of MacLeod. If he said he was "refused" at Auchinleck, it was not a matter of his having presented himself without writing ahead at a time when the family was not in residence. He may well have proposed a visit when the House was closed. But knowing the man, we can properly assume that he wrote a careful and deferential letter and that he received a curt note saying that his visit would not be convenient, without any expression of regret or invitation to make a visit at another time.

David Buchanan draws attention to the very different experience of another petitioner who visited Auchinleck at about this time, citing the fulsome acknowledgement to Mr. and Mrs. Mounsey that Jasper John Boswell included in the preface to his privately printed *History and Genealogical Tables of the Boswells,* 1906. Jasper John, who was no relation of the Boswells of Auchinleck, by his own account had visited the Mounseys at Auchinleck House "several times" and by invitation; had been given the keys to the library and muniment chest, and complained only that he had been so showered with attentions that he could not more than half look through the papers he was given access to. "Title deeds and other papers bearing on the general history of the Boswells," says Buchanan, "are one thing; the private journals and papers of James Boswell, the Biographer, are quite another. One cannot readily assume that Mrs. Mounsey would have been equally willing to show the latter to an outsider." The observation is just. I shall venture to paraphrase it with a degree of certainty which he may perhaps think reckless. The most welcome of guests at Auchinleck *would* have been a thorough-paced genealogist who was compiling a comprehensive genealogy in which the Boswells of Auchinleck would occupy a place of honour—perhaps *the* place of honour. The least welcome of guests at Auchinleck would have been the scholar who at the moment represented the Johnson connexion more fully than any other man in the world. Mrs. Mounsey lived till 1905, and Hill's book and article must have come to her attention. If he had given a misleading statement of the facts, why did not she make public reply? For the same reason that her mother had not replied to Rogers and her grandmother had not replied to Croker. Any correction would either have had to be an admission that Boswell's papers were in existence and were at Auchinleck, or would inevitably have led to that disclosure by encouraging more scholars and literary pilgrims to seek admission to Auchinleck House. And the family still deeply disliked the Johnson connexion and wanted to mute it. If people came to Auchinleck House, they wanted them to come for other reasons.

That Mrs. Mounsey did despise her great-grandfather and that she was generally a good deal of a dragon are pretty clearly established by an unsolicited family report which David Buchanan received from Miss Kathleen B. Mounsey, a grandniece of Mr. Mounsey, soon after *The Treasure of Auchinleck* was published.

> I think you may be interested in a few odd things my father told me about life at Auchinleck as he used to stay there during the lifetime of his uncle George Mounsey and Aunt Julia. He and one of his brothers, Harold Mounsey went there often as schoolboys and young men, and he told me about the utter distaste of Aunt Julia for everything concerning James Boswell. He described a portrait of James which was kept in either a large barn (or possibly attic) and visitors were invited to shoot at it—so it was practically shot to pieces! My father thought it might be a good oil painting.
>
> He also described how many chests and cabinets were stuffed with letters and papers, even bulging out of drawers.
>
> Unfortunately all invitations ceased about 1899 as these two young men ordered a coachman to drive them out on a *Sunday* to find a doctor to deal with tooth-ache—and

Aunt Julia did not forgive them, although she did leave Uncle George's signet ring to my father.

That the picture used as a target was literally a portrait of Boswell seems to me not very likely. If a portrait that could be debased to such uses had ever existed, I think we would have heard of it in the journal, and the only portraits of himself in oil that Boswell records there are the well-known ones by Willison (1765) and Reynolds (1785); both are now in public collections and both are unscathed by powder and ball. But that the Mounsey boys and other visitors to Auchinleck were encouraged to shoot at a portrait which somehow to Mrs. Mounsey represented Boswell and all his ways, I have no doubt whatever. I diffidently suggest that the target-portrait was that of John Reid, the sheep-stealer, which we know Boswell caused to be painted shortly before Reid's execution.[2] The rigour of Mrs. Mounsey's Sabbatarianism was perhaps not extreme for the time and place, but her refusal ever to invite the culprits (her husband's nephews) back was surely harsh and shows her capable of refusing Hill admission to Auchinleck.

One cannot pass by young Mounsey's recollection of "chests and cabinets . . . stuffed with letters and papers, even bulging out of drawers" without wondering whether in Mrs. Mounsey's time Boswell's private papers had been unsealed and brought down from the attic. I think at least some of them had. Jasper John Boswell later had in his possession two letters from Boswell to Margaret Montgomerie, 24 and 31 October 1769, and a considerable fragment of the diary of Boswell's brother John, 22 December 1769 to 18 June 1770, and I cannot think of any way by which he could have acquired them save by gift from Mrs. Mounsey. I fancy that he came upon them, mixed in with the cartulary papers he was copying, showed them to Mrs. Mounsey, and was presented with them as souvenirs. Lieutenant John's diary is unexceptionable—a dreary round of weather, meals, exercise, and reading—and Boswell's letters, written to his fiancée shortly before their marriage, report only exemplary behaviour, but the earlier of the two letters contains an extended encomium of Johnson which I should have expected Mrs. Mounsey to find distasteful. However, Jasper John Boswell, no literary scholar, was not likely to make any use of the documents that Mrs. Mounsey would have disapproved of.

If Hill had been admitted to Auchinleck in 1889, he would still have been too late to see all the "curious memorials" he had learned about from Boswell's will. On 2 November 1886 Alexander Dowell sold at auction in Edinburgh for Mrs. Mounsey a group of valuable articles which had belonged to the late Sir James Boswell of Auchinleck. The eighteen-piece silver-gilt dressing-set of Veronica, Lady Kincardine, about which Boswell had been so solicitous in his will, was included in this sale, the pieces being auctioned separately. Eight of the larger pieces were

---

[2] If one could assume that Douglas Mounsey's recollection had magnified matters in making the picture an *oil*, then a plausible identification would be John Jones's mezzotint, 1786, from Reynolds's oil.

most appropriately acquired by the ninth Earl of Elgin and Kincardine, heir male of Veronica's husband. The other ten pieces were dispersed. By the time Hill had printed his essay on Boswell's proof-sheets, the library also had been broken up, or broken into. Mrs. Mounsey put up "a selected portion" of it (782 lots) at Sotheby's for auction on 23, 24, and 26 June 1893. A good many books inscribed by Boswell were dispersed, as well as some of his non-personal manuscripts, such as Allan Ramsay's autograph of *The Gentle Shepherd*. The catalogue also lists one lot certainly from the archives (Lot 398: Proof-sheets of the *Life of Johnson*), but is utterly silent as to Boswell's correspondence and his journal. The legend of destruction was so far confirmed.

❧ CHAPTER V ❧

TINKER GOES TO

MALAHIDE

EMILY BOSWELL, LADY TALBOT DE MALAHIDE, died in 1898, and three years later Lord Talbot married as his second wife Mrs. Isabel Charlotte Gurney, widow of John Gurney of Sprowston Hall, Norfolk, partner in Gurney's Bank, Norwich, and one-time mayor of that city. On Emily Boswell's death, the son of her marriage to Lord Talbot, the Hon. James Boswell Talbot, became half-owner of the estate of Auchinleck. When Mrs. Mounsey died without issue, 8 July 1905, the other half of Auchinleck fell to him under his grandmother's settlements. He now received also the pictures at Auchinleck and such books as remained there after Mrs. Mounsey's sale of 1893; these had been Mrs. Mounsey's sole property and had been bequeathed to him in a will in Scots form made six months before her death. A will in English form, drawn later, directed her executor to sell all her personal estate (except for the articles specifically bequeathed) and to pay various legacies, the residue to go to the Cumberland Infirmary, a hospital in Carlisle.

Lord Talbot took over the management of the estate for his son, and for about ten years the Malahide family resided at Auchinleck for a few months each year. As soon after Mrs. Mounsey's death as could be arranged with the executor, Lord Talbot went to Auchinleck House to work out the problems posed by Mrs. Mounsey's direction that all the household effects except the books and the pictures were to be sold. He bought from the executor all the effects (mainly furniture) which his son had not inherited. Much of the furniture he kept to furnish Auchinleck House, some he sold at auction through Dowell's, in Edinburgh, 17 March 1906. Among the articles then sold were some that can be confidently identified as belonging to the Biographer. One of Lord Talbot's first acts at this time was also to examine and sort out the family papers. Thomas Drysdale, land steward at Auchinleck from about 1896 to 1920, when interviewed in 1937 said that to his own knowledge

Lord Talbot spent much time in an attic room which previously had been kept locked.

> I understood that he worked there for some time amongst old boxes containing papers and perhaps pictures etc. The joiner, who is now dead, assisted him and within a short time of Mrs. Mounsey's death, the joiner told me that there were packers brought through to pack up mostly papers, etc., and they were *I understood* all removed to Ireland. I imagine Lord Talbot took away anything of value, such as papers and pictures, etc., and I think the ebony cabinet would also have been removed. This was a large ebony cabinet which stood in the morning room and was always kept locked and sealed. We always had the idea that it contained something valuable. I am not aware of any box in any outside place or of anything of value beyond the contents of the attic room and the ebony cabinet.

We shall hear again of this joiner, who appears to have been a good deal of a gossip. It is a pity that his testimony could not have been taken down earlier and directly. Drysdale emphasized the fact that his own information was mainly second-hand, but he did have a clear personal recollection of seeing Lord Talbot coming down from the attic room "as black as a miner".

The removal from Auchinleck of the pictures, some furniture, and (our particular concern) the papers did not follow so promptly on Mrs. Mounsey's death as one might infer from Drysdale's recollection of the joiner's account. As has been said, the family continued for ten years or so to make Auchinleck its seasonal residence. All that the available evidence permits us to say is that the contents of Auchinleck House which the family wished to preserve were sent to Malahide in instalments over a period of twelve or thirteen years. Samuel Gurney, youngest son of the second Lady Talbot de Malahide, had a recollection of Boswell's journal being stored in the ebony cabinet in the morning-room at Auchinleck; he may have been right, but it could not have stayed there long, for Col. Milo Talbot, Lord Talbot's brother, who sorted out and read at least the greater part of it "during the Autumn of, I think, 1908", said he did so at Malahide. The ebony cabinet itself and the four best pictures had left Auchinleck by the end of 1914. The final clearance was said to have been effected in wartime, under circumstances that indicate late 1916 or early 1917.[1]

Drysdale's and Samuel Gurney's independent testimonies concerning the ebony cabinet call for some comment. This, like the silver-gilt dressing-table set, was an heirloom from Boswell's Dutch great-grandmother, Veronica van Aerssen van Sommelsdyck, Countess of Kincardine, to Boswell's grandmother, Lady Elizabeth Bruce. As has been remarked above, Boswell prized this cabinet so highly that in his will he attempted to keep it always in the family by devising penalties for any heir who should alienate it. It seems to have been the general impression since the recovery of Boswell's papers that Boswell himself made it the repository of his archives. That

---

[1] See below, pp. 71–72.

was not at all the case. The cabinet seems originally to have housed Lady Kincardine's dressing-table set. A few years after Boswell's death, it contained the Auchinleck collection of medals and coins, as well as various family trinkets, *objets d'art,* and curiosities. Boswell also made it the repository of selected letters that he especially prized. After it went to Ireland, it was certainly stuffed with papers from Boswell's archives: the bulk of his journal (all of it that was in bound notebooks) and a rather miscellaneous collection of letters. Samuel Gurney, as we have seen, believed that this same disposition of the papers obtained at Auchinleck, say from 1905 to 1907 or 1908. Drysdale's testimony is ambiguous, but as he was land-steward during the last ten years of Mrs. Mounsey's liferent, it might be read to mean that the journal was in the cabinet at Auchinleck when Lord Talbot took over. I very much doubt this. I think that all, or practically all, of Boswell's journal remained in the locked attic room at Auchinleck from 1824 to 1905, and that moving some of it down to the family living quarters and putting it in the ebony cabinet was a Talbot innovation.

When the journal was released from the attic and placed in a conspicuous article of furniture which every day advertised its existence to the family, the question of publication was bound to arise sooner or later. Isabel, Lady Talbot seems to have been the first to raise it. In 1907 she sought advice as to publication by letter from her brother-in-law, Henry Lee Warner, classicist, former master at Rugby, country gentleman and J.P. for Norfolk. He replied that so far as he knew the journal was at least unpublished, and suggested that she submit it, for an opinion if not for an offer, to the publishing firm of Chatto and Windus, of which his nephew, Philip Lee Warner, was a partner. This advice seems not to have been followed, but Lady Talbot continued to discuss with Lord Talbot the possibility of publication.

Why was Lord Talbot, rather than his son, making fundamental decisions regarding Boswell's private papers? The Hon. James Boswell Talbot as a child was thought to be delicate: though noticeably competent in some respects, he was backward in others. He could not learn to play cricket, but he could plan a cross-country train trip from timetables with ease and accuracy. Horse-racing was the thing he cared most about: he could cite the pedigrees of all the horses. In most other matters he turned to his father for advice and direction, gratefully surrendering to him the management of the estate. Lord Talbot, however, acted as though the Boswell family papers at Auchinleck were his own property. He apparently believed that he acquired title to them when he bought the effects in Auchinleck House.

Lord Talbot, however, had his son's best interest deeply at heart, and he knew how uneasy his first wife's family had felt about the papers. It seems to me doubtful that either he or his second wife attempted to assess the literary possibilities of the journal by reading widely in it. They probably thought merely that since Boswell had published a very successful and famous book, his unpublished manuscripts might also make a profitable publication. But in the discussions which Lord and

Lady Talbot had, she argued for it and he remained unconvinced. His feelings were deeply set against it.

He allowed himself, however, to be persuaded when his brother, Col. the Hon. Milo Talbot of the Royal Engineers, a distinguished soldier, became convinced that the journal had literary merit and should be published. Colonel Talbot spent the autumn of 1908 alone at Malahide while Lord Talbot and his family made a trip to South America; and he amused himself by sorting out, arranging, docketing, and reading the greater part of the journal. As a result of his urgings, the journal, or most of it, was submitted to the late Sir John Murray, head of the publishing house of John Murray. Sir John declined publication in a letter which for several reasons should be printed practically in full.

July 2 1911

Dear Lord Talbot de Malahide,

I have read the Journals of James Boswell which you kindly submitted to me with much care, and, as is my usual practice in the case of important works, I have also in confidence consulted a personal friend of great literary experience so that two independent opinions may be formed.

Our opinions agree in almost every detail and I am sorry to say that the prevailing impression left upon both of us is one of disappointment, I had almost said of dismay, at finding how badly Boswell's character shows itself throughout. Macaulay, as you are no doubt aware, formed but a poor opinion of Boswell: "Those weaknesses which most men keep covered up in the most secret places of the mind, not to be disclosed to the eye of friendship or of love, were precisely the weaknesses which Boswell paraded before all the world. . . . He was not ashamed to exhibit himself to the world as a common spy, a common tatler, a humble companion without the excuse of poverty, and to tell a hundred stories of his own pertness and folly, and of the insults which his pertness and folly brought upon him." But Macaulay had not seen these journals: had he done so he would have added that he was an incurable sot and libertine: conscious of his own iniquities: sometimes palliating them as "Asiatic satisfactions quite consistent with devotion and with a fervent attachment to my valuable spouse": sometimes making resolutions of amendment which were not carried into effect, but always lapsing into the slough of drunkenness and debauchery and indolence.

The occasions on which he records that he was intoxicated, and even blind drunk are innumerable, and over and over again he notes that "he ranged the streets and followed whores" or words to that effect.

Many passages have been cut out, I presume on account of their immorality, but if they were worse than many which remain they must have been bad indeed.

He calls his Father "a little wretch", his brother John "shockingly sulky" and "a man of gloomy horrid ill nature": he records "the abominable unfeeling ill nature" of Lady Auchinleck, who he says "talked with venom".

In writing thus it must not be supposed that I regard the journals as devoid of interest: far from this they contain excellent passages—chief among them being those which refer to Dr. Johnson, but these (so far as I have compared them) are reproduced word for word in the great biography. There are conversations with David Hume, Lord Thurlow and a few other notabilities, which are interesting but small in extent, but by far the larger part consists of trivialities; records of eating and drinking; bare facts and dates; and introspective reflections which rarely tend to raise one's estimate of the writer.

Macaulay wrote "There is not in all his books a single remark of his own on literature, politics, religion or society which is not either commonplace or absurd." This is unjust, but they rarely rise to the point of merit which attracts attention, or calls for permanent record.

If we eliminate the passages which have already been published: those which are unpublishable: and those which are too trivial for permanence, the residuum is I fear very small.

The books would be invaluable to anyone who was engaged in writing Bozzy's life, but if they were to be published as his authentic autobiography, the question would arise how far the editor would be justified in eliminating the true character of the man. If this were fully displayed he must inevitably fall very low in public estimation— altho' he writes of himself "I had faults but was upon the whole one of the best men that ever lived."

Boswell like Byron must ever live as the writer of some of the best English literature: his private life like Byron's is best left to oblivion. I make this comparison from some bitter experience. In my 13 volume Edition of Byron's Works I asked the editors to deal almost exclusively with his writings and to leave aside the frailties of his private life. He was dead and it was impossible to pass fair judgment on a man who could not say a word in his own defence. Byron's own grandson, Lord Lovelace, frustrated this purpose by producing a scurrilous and garbled book to vilify his own grandfather. Infinite harm has been done thereby, altho' as time goes on the tide is turning more in favour of Byron and against his detractor.

I confess however that I should be sorry to play the Lord Lovelace to Bozzy: the more so as he would be damaged not merely by inference and inuendo as Byron was but by his own explicit confessions.

And so I am reluctantly driven to the conclusion that I cannot offer to publish this book, but I thank you none the less for having consulted me. Believe me,

Yours very truly,
JOHN MURRAY

Though it must in honesty be admitted that there is no indication that Sir John would have placed a higher valuation on Boswell's journal if he had been free to make a purely literary judgement of it, it must nevertheless be noted that he did make his decision largely on non-literary grounds. In particular, it must be remembered that he made it nearly seventy years ago. Expurgation of Boswell's great autobiographical record, as he pointed out, is really not feasible, and in 1911 an unexpurgated text would not have been tolerated. Even a privately printed, strictly limited edition could not have appeared much before 1925, and trade publication before 1950 would probably have been premature. Not until authors like Maugham, Strachey, Lawrence, Joyce, Hemingway, and Faulkner had broken down the old decorums and established those we are now accustomed to could Boswell's journal be given to the world.

From Sir John's references to "books" (ninth paragraph of his letter) one might assume that he had done his reading in the manuscript journal itself, a great part of which is written in bound notebooks. A previous letter of his to Lord Talbot ("I thank you for your note and for the copies of the Boswell Diaries"), however, makes sufficiently clear that this was not the case. He may have been shown one or more of the original notebooks, but he certainly did his reading in a huge typescript made by a typing agency in London. A good part of this typescript— considerably more than half of it—survives, and most fortunately so, for it shows that the manuscripts had been extensively expurgated before they were handed to the typist to transcribe. This brings us to a very troublesome and disagreeable subject: the various kinds of disfigurement and mutilation which the manuscripts of Boswell's journal suffered before they left the custody of the family.

First, as to disfigurement. Efforts of varying degrees of determinedness have been made to render a good many relatively short passages illegible by scratching or scrawling over them with pen and ink. Among these deletions, some which were effected with quill pen-point and ink identical with Boswell's were presumably but not always certainly made by Boswell himself. Some, for which steel pen-point and modern ink were used, were pretty clearly made at the time that the typescript was prepared for Murray. Much the larger number of the inked deletions were certainly made a few years later, and will be discussed below at the proper point. In addition to the disfigurements (which are annoying to an editor but generally do not render the text illegible) the manuscripts have suffered extensive mutilation. Parts of leaves have been cut away, but not very often. The more common kind of mutilation consists of the removal of entire leaves, from one leaf (more often than not written on both sides) to nine in a row. This radical and hopeless kind of censorship seems capricious (as Sir John says, it is hard to believe that the passages that were removed were worse than many that remain), and is quite unsystematic. The censor worked through the journals written in bound notebooks to 19 April 1776, skipped to 7 May 1780, passing over some of the most scabrous matter in the whole record, worked through to 21 March 1784, and then gave up. As has been said above, the Murray transcript shows that in most cases the leaves now missing were missing when the manuscripts were given to the typist. In at least two cases the transcript contains or once contained matter not now to be found in the manuscripts, but in general the typescript reports the lacunae just as they now occur: e.g. "N.B. Original pages 65–70 missing".

Who performed this act of family piety will probably never be known with certainty. Indeed, we are perhaps not justified in speaking of "*the* censor" or *his* "act". We really have no way of assuring ourselves that earlier members of the Boswell family—Sir Alexander's widow, Sir James's widow, Mrs. Mounsey—did not engage in sporadic reading and pulling out of leaves that offended them. I used to think they probably did, but now I doubt it. I think they would have been satisfied with keeping the manuscripts locked up. We do, however, know for a certainty that Lord Talbot de Malahide sanctioned some kind of censorship. Two of the dockets he wrote on the journals read, "P. 72 to be expunged"; "July 29th and August 18 to be expunged". "Expunge" perhaps more naturally means "ink over" than "tear out", but it can have the latter meaning.[2] Perhaps for no better reason than pressure of the law of parsimony, I now incline to think that the censorship of 1908–11 was the first the manuscripts underwent after Boswell's own. Lord Talbot's notes probably show that he did not "expunge" offending passages in the manuscripts himself but left that disagreeable task to his brother. If the mutilations are capricious and sporadic, it may have been because Lord Talbot's heart was not in the job of reading and Colonel Talbot's not in the job of "expunging".

To pull out leaves that contained "personal and delicate matter" was precisely what Boswell's son James had done before lending his father's "Materials for Writing the Life of Lord Kames" to Lord Woodhouselee. The leaves that he removed, to be sure, were not stitched into a binding, and he did not destroy them but put them to one side to be restored to their places when the manuscript came back. As it happened, they never did get put back, though they survived. Perhaps Lord Talbot and Colonel Talbot (if the gaps were indeed due to them) similarly saved the removed leaves but never replaced them, and the leaves got lost by being all in one bundle. To a casual reader of the manuscripts of the journal, Boswell himself might be thought to have justified this kind of attack on the physical integrity of his manuscripts. He himself ruthlessly tore out many pages of his best-written journals to use as printer's copy for the *Life of Johnson*. Of course he preserved them carefully, but he did not put them all back where they belonged.

Murray's letter put an end to all schemes of publication during the lifetime of the fifth Lord Talbot de Malahide. When Samuel Gurney suggested that if the journal were to be published, the Medici Society, with which he was associated, might appropriately be the publisher, Lady Talbot replied that Lord Talbot was so sensitive on the subject that she disliked mentioning it to him again. "He thinks it is not fair on James or Boswell relations to see what horrors he wrote!" Throughout the Talbot regime casual Boswellian pilgrims to Auchinleck House were not unreasonably denied admission. A properly introduced scholar would probably have been received at Malahide or at Auchinleck while the family was there, and might even have been shown letters or other inoffensive documents, but would almost certainly not have been allowed unrestricted access to Boswell's journal. Lord Talbot now considered the journal a family document to be kept strictly private—not

[2]See J18 and J96.

because it degraded the family, but because it was indecent. David Buchanan reports on the testimony of the Talbot family that after the ebony cabinet went to Malahide it "was proudly pointed out to visitors, and no secret was made of the fact that it contained Boswell papers. Selected portions were sometimes read to guests after dinner." I very much doubt that random readings from the journal were allowed before the death of the fifth Lord Talbot, that is, before 1921. Samuel Gurney, with whom I corresponded extensively in 1958, though a member of the inner family, never wrote as though he had handled Boswell's journal—or for that matter had ever seen it.

Auchinleck had been encumbered with crushing debt ever since Sir James Boswell's time, and the holders of the mortgages were now pressing for payment of principal. Lady Talbot reported on 1 January 1915 that with a view to the possible renting of the house some of the more important pictures and the ebony cabinet had been moved to Malahide. Later in the year Lady Talbot said they were breaking away from Auchinleck and that the estate must go.

In March 1916 another group of important books from the Auchinleck library (111 lots this time as compared with 782 in the sale of 1893) was put up for auction by Sotheby, and a year later Alexander Dowell of Edinburgh, having previously held an auction of "superior modern and antique furniture" in Auchinleck House, completed the dispersal of the library. Except for a letter of Capel Lofft's that accompanied a presentation copy to Boswell of one of Lofft's books, Sotheby's catalogue lists no manuscripts from Boswell's personal archives. Dowell's catalogue of the sale of furniture at Auchinleck lists no books or manuscripts, but the first 160 lots, consisting of "kitchen and servant's bedroom furniture, coppers, culinary utensils, etc.", were sold with a good deal of clumping ("Box and Contents", "Tray and Contents"). Dowell's catalogue of books specifies no manuscripts of Boswell's, but since it lists no fewer than 73 totally undescribed "Miscellaneous lots" from Auchinleck, one cannot put much trust in it as a source of precise information. My friend and correspondent, the late Dr. Robert McKinlay, Congregational minister in Stonehouse, Lanarkshire, wrote me (I think in 1926) that *his* friend, Glen, bookseller in Glasgow, bought "at the Auchinleck sale some years ago" some bundles of odds and ends that contained a quantity of loose printed sheets of Boswell's anonymously published *Ode by Dr. Johnson to Mrs. Thrale on their Supposed Approaching Nuptials* (1788) and *No Abolition of Slavery* (1791). "Auchinleck sale" could mean either of Dowell's sales of 1917. If we could assume that some manuscripts of the humbler sort were dispersed at this time, it would account for the escape of a number of letters whose separation from the archives is otherwise hard to account for.

At about this time, presumably late in 1916 or early in 1917, the Talbots sent a final shipment of furniture and papers from Auchinleck to Malahide. Some of Boswell's papers that were boxed at this time seem not to have been opened on arrival but to have been stored at Malahide with the furniture. The transfer was made in wartime; Mr. Talbot was busy with Red Cross work, and Lord Talbot, who managed everything connected with the papers, was ill and never after enjoyed full health. A considerable quantity of estate papers, minor family papers, and even some scraps of Boswell's archives, remained in Auchinleck House, presumably abandoned by Lord Talbot.

In 1918 the mansion-house of Auchinleck was let for a period of five years to Robert McCrone, who appears to have dispersed some of these papers. The Auchinleck estate was broken up and sold, the sale beginning in 1920 and continuing over a period of years. Part of the farms were purchased by the tenants (families that in some cases had been there as long as the Boswells), part by the Marquess of Bute, whose Dumfries property adjoined Auchinleck. The mansion-house (subject to McCrone's tenancy), "policies" (parks surrounding the house), and some of the adjacent farms were bought by a distant Boswell cousin, Col. John Douglas Boswell of Garallan, representative of the old Boswells of Knockroon and great-grandson of the executrix of Sir Alexander Boswell's personal estate. It is perhaps not the least of the ironies of the Boswell saga that he was descended of that very branch of the Boswell family (the Craigston line) which Lord Auchinleck had wished to exclude from the entail. Lord Talbot died on 4 March 1921, leaving his entire personal estate to his son. When Boswell's great-great-grandson became the sixth Lord Talbot de Malahide, he was no longer laird of Auchinleck.

Even if Boswell's archives had remained at Auchinleck in the possession of direct descendants of his bearing the name of Boswell, the family themselves would probably have taken the initiative in opening them up to scholars before the end of the present century. The conviction that Boswell degraded the family by deference to Samuel Johnson could hardly have survived the nineteenth century; and even a family of extraordinary propriety would come to feel little reflected shame from the shortcomings of a great-great-great-grandfather. When the papers went to Ireland, when they became the possession of a man who, though proud of being a Boswell, did not bear that family name—a man who moreover was childless—the day when they could be given to the world was considerably hastened.

Nobody can give anything directly to the world; there must exist trained intermediaries. The fact is that the world got Boswell's papers about as soon as it showed itself ready to handle them. If one must fix on a single person as the initiator of modern Boswellian studies, that person would undoubtedly be Dr. Hill. Before publishing his great edition of the *Life of Johnson*, he had brought out a reprint of the *Letters between the Honourable Andrew Erskine and James Boswell, Esq.* and of Boswell's *Journal of a Tour to Corsica*—the first editing of any of the minor works which Boswell published in his own lifetime. He made the *Life of Johnson* one of the best edited and best indexed of English classics, and he defended Boswell's character and intelligence in essays of wide circulation. His notes stimulated the collecting of books and manuscripts. In his essay on Boswell's proof-sheets he pays tribute to the generosity of R. B. Adam of Buffalo, owner of "a finer collection of Johnsonian and Boswellian curiosities than exists anywhere on our side of the Atlantic". Adam (by birth a Scotsman) was a successful business man, the owner of a large department store. In his leisure hours he set himself the pleasant task of extra-illustrating with manuscripts and prints Hill's edition of the *Life of Johnson*, Hill's edition of Johnson's *Letters*, and Hill's collection titled *Johnsonian Miscellanies*, besides acquiring early editions of books by Johnson and Boswell, and all the manuscripts by either that he could come by. The collection (like the family business) was continued and was greatly expanded by his nephew and adopted son, whose family name was originally Scott. R. B. Adam, second, left school early but gave himself an excellent literary education by reading; he was a man who knew and loved books, and especially books having to do with Johnson. The great collection brought him the acquaintance and then the warm personal friendship of three men who combined to make its resources widely known: A. Edward Newton of Philadelphia, Professor Charles G. Osgood of Princeton, and Professor Chauncey B. Tinker of Yale. Newton was, like Adam, a successful and largely self-educated business man (he was a manufacturer of electrical equipment) and a collector. He was gifted with an agile and pungent style, and when he was past fifty began publishing familiar essays on books and literary men in the *Atlantic Monthly*. The essays enjoyed (and deserved) great popularity, and so did the volumes into which they were collected. One of his essays, "James Boswell—His Book", a shrewd, masculine, common-sense appreciation, probably had a wider circulation than anything written about Boswell up to that time except Macaulay's essay. Since Newton always wrote as a collector, with infectious references to the pleasures of the game, his essay on Boswell made the market for Boswellian books and manuscripts much more lively than it had formerly been.

An interest in Johnson and Boswell was being simultaneously developed at Yale and at Princeton. Osgood, while a young instructor at Yale, had introduced a course called "Dr. Johnson and His Circle", and when he left Yale for Princeton in 1905, had founded a similar course there. One of the wisest of Johnsonians, he always spoke wisely of Boswell. Tinker, a slightly younger contemporary of Osgood's at Yale, inherited "Dr. Johnson and His Circle", and under the title "The Age of Johnson" made it one of the most esteemed in the undergraduate English curriculum. He was himself a distinguished collector. His lectures and essays fired dozens of men, in Yale and outside it, with the passion for book-collecting; and his course in the graduate school produced a long succession of eighteenth-century scholars. The main scholarly project of his life was the locating and printing of Boswell's letters, a venture which he brought to completion in 1924. The edition (*Letters of James Boswell*, Clarendon Press, 2 vols.) contained 389 letters, upwards of 100 of them published for the first time. As a by-product of his research, Tinker had written for the *Atlantic Monthly* a number of biographical essays on Boswell; these he had collected and with additional essays published in 1922 as *Young Boswell*.

Young Boswell enjoyed a considerable popular success; the *Letters* was the first really large exercise in Boswellian, as distinguished from Johnsonian, scholarship. One of his pupils (Dr. Margery Bailey) published an edition of Boswell's essay-series, *The Hypochondriack,* in 1928; another (the writer of this history) undertook an extended bibliographical study, published in 1929 with the title *The Literary Career of James Boswell.*

Though Boswell has never enjoyed high popular esteem among his own countrymen, Scottish scholars and critics have done well by him. Carlyle's essay, written like Macaulay's as a review of Croker, is still the best critical appraisal of Boswell's book and the best answer to Macaulay's shallow paradox; if it fails to satisfy a reader of the present day completely, it is because it goes so far towards accepting Macaulay's estimate of Boswell's intelligence and in attributing his eminence as a biographer so much to qualities of the heart. Rogers, it will be remembered, was a Scot. Up to a few decades ago the most satisfactory life of Boswell was the unpretentious little volume by W. Keith Leask, published in the Famous Scots Series in 1897. But it is perhaps in *Six Essays on Johnson* (1910) by Sir Walter Raleigh that one first finds a characterization of Boswell that can really be considered acceptable on all counts. Raleigh was a brilliant lecturer, a quotable and memorable writer, and his paragraphs on Boswell had an immediate effect, at least on academic criticism. A little later (1913) Professor D. Nichol Smith published in the *Cambridge History of English Literature* a brief but well-informed critical survey of Boswell which needs little revision in view of our present knowledge. He also compiled for the *Cambridge History* the first systematic list of Boswell's publications and of books and articles about him. Scanty as the list now seems, it was the basis of much fruitful research. Dr. Robert McKinlay was, I think, the first to make a serious attempt to assemble a complete collection of Boswell's own publications. His knowledge of the bibliography of Boswell was extensive and his generosity in sharing it unlimited. Dr. J. T. T. Brown, lawyer and antiquary, published in the *Transactions of the Glasgow Archaeological Society* (1920) one of the solidest and most useful biographical essays on Boswell to appear up to that time: "James Boswell: An Episode of His Grand Tour". Dr. T. B. Simpson, advocate and man of letters, Sheriff of Perth and Angus, investigated Boswell's legal practice ("Boswell as an Advocate", *Juridical Review,* Sept. 1922), and for more than twenty-five years cheerfully and expertly answered questions about Edinburgh and Scots law for Boswell's American editors.

Though perhaps the chief impetus in the recovery of Boswell came from America, the honours in publication before 1950 must be awarded the great university presses of England. It would have given Boswell enormous satisfaction if he could have known that both the Clarendon Press at Oxford and the University Press at Cambridge during a certain portion of the twentieth century were to be directed by professed Johnsonians who were also warmly sympathetic to Boswellian studies. At Cambridge Sir Sydney Roberts encouraged the publication of works dealing with the Johnsonian circle, and himself edited Boswell's *Journal of a Tour to Corsica* (1923). Tinker's *Letters of James Boswell* and Pottle's *Literary Career of James Boswell*, both Yale works, appeared with the imprint of the Clarendon Press. They appeared from the Clarendon Press because the Secretary to the Delegates, Dr. R. W. Chapman, showed a lively interest in publishing them. Chapman began to have strong Johnsonian interests during the First World War. His *magnum opus*, a three-volume edition of Johnson's letters, completed in 1952, was planned as far back as 1920. Trained in classical studies, he was the first to apply rigorous textual criticism to both Johnson and Boswell (in his fine combined edition of Johnson's *Journey to the Western Islands of Scotland* and Boswell's *Journal of a Tour to the Hebrides*, 1924); he also published a number of other smaller Boswellian studies. About 1922, at his suggestion, Dr. L. F. Powell, Librarian of the Taylor Institution, was commissioned to revise Hill's edition of Boswell's *Life of Johnson*. This great project, which was triumphantly completed in 1950, soon became a major focus of Boswell research.

In surveys such as this, one tends to overlook handbooks and compendia, though they must be very influential in determining the general critical climate. Thomas Seccombe's *Age of Johnson*, first published in December 1899, contains an estimate of Boswell that is remarkable for its time. Those who feel that modern Boswellians are going too far in their praise of Boswell's powers of imagination might be surprised by John Bailey's *Dr. Johnson and His Circle* in the Home University Library (first published in 1913, revised by L. F. Powell in 1944).

Tinker once warned me not to overlook the important role played in the recovery of the Boswell papers by various booksellers, notably by James Tregaskis, who made a specialty of books and letters by Boswell. Constant intelligent search for Boswell autographs was sure, sooner or later, to uncover the archives.

Whether before 1920 Tinker had any clear notion of who succeeded to Auchinleck (that is, who was Boswell's representative) after the deaths of Lady Talbot de Malahide and Mrs. Mounsey, I do not know, but I rather doubt it. It is my impression that up to that time he held without serious question the common view that Boswell's papers had perished and that any attempt to locate a family archive would be futile. On 29 July 1920 he inserted in the *Times Literary Supplement* the customary editor's letter announcing his intention of bringing out a collected edition of Boswell's letters and asking owners of letters by Boswell to communicate with him. Two replies came at once. One (now lost with no copy reported) was anonymous; the other, written on a postcard with a Dublin address and postmark, was signed with a name that Tinker never deciphered but which nearly forty years later Robert Metzdorf made out to be that of Miss Elsie Mahaffy, daughter of the recently deceased Provost of Trinity College, Sir John Pentland Mahaffy. Both communications advised Tinker to apply to Malahide Castle, Miss Mahaffy's card giving specific details: "The last representative of Boswell and owner of Auchinleck is Honble. James Talbot Malahide Castle, Co. Dublin. He has lately imported here an escritoire of Boswell's which is full of letters, so far uncatalogued. . . . The said gentleman is not *quite* like other people you must be very simple with him." Tinker wrote to him at once and received a prompt but cryptic answer: "I am very sorry I am unable to give you any letters of James Boswell for publication. I regret I cannot meet your views in this respect." This was surely a secretive letter, and because secretive, misleading. I do not think Talbot wrote in the spirit I have imputed to his redoubtable Aunt Julia, assuming her to have refused Hill; everything I have heard of him indicates that, though a shy man who hated publicity, he was essentially friendly and naturally complaisant. I suspect that previous discussion of his reply to Tinker has not taken sufficiently into account that in 1920 he probably did not consider himself to be the owner of Boswell's papers, and that his father, who seems always to have acted as though he did own them, was ill, perhaps so ill that Talbot felt he should not disturb him with matters on which he knew him to be very sensitive. Tinker's request, to be sure, extended only to letters, and none of Boswell's letters at Malahide, so far as I can recall, presented any problems of decency, but Talbot certainly did not know that to be a fact. He probably not only accepted Sir John Murray's judgement on Boswell's journal, but also extended that judgement to the whole mass: Boswell's papers were indecent and should be kept within the family. He tried to give the answer he thought his father would have given, but he found the recital of family detail embarrassing. Instead of being explicit, he wrote ambiguously and perhaps was not unwilling to be understood as saying that there were no letters of Boswell's at Malahide. The style of his letter seemed to preclude the possibility of further inquiry by post, and even put difficulties in the way of approach through a third person. I am not saying that he was under obligation to allow Tinker to publish the Boswell letters at Malahide; I am saying that, in view of Tinker's standing (on which he could easily have taken advice), he owed Tinker a frank and explicit reply.

While Tinker pondered, he received (September 1920) from McCrone in Auchinleck House, to whom he had also addressed some queries, another of those circumstantial and apparently well-attested accounts of the burning of papers which had inhibited search so many times previously. McCrone wrote:

> There were a number of documents of one kind and another of the old laird's [that is, of Boswell's] time, and it is just quite possible that when the present proprietors came in they burnt these along with a great number of other manuscripts which were in the House. That this was done, I know from the old joiner who is still resident on the place. When James Boswell Talbot took possession he cleared out a large number of the Books and Papers which were thrown over the window into the court and he along with this same joiner made a bonfire, so little did the family think of their great predecessor.

Though later disclosures amply proved the story of a holocaust of Boswell's personal papers to be a myth, I have never doubted that McCrone's bonfire actually took place. What was burned, however, remained matter of pure speculation. Now, after more than sixty years, an eye-witness to the event has turned up with an answer. Thomas D. Drysdale, son of the land-steward of Auchinleck mentioned some pages back,[3] subscribes to the following statement which I have compiled, partly in words of my own, from various letters of his to me.

> The burning of papers which I witnessed at Auchinleck House occurred a few days before the public auction of the contents of Auchinleck House (4 and 5 April 1917). I was then a schoolboy of fourteen on holiday. The papers that were burned had been sorted out some years before by Lord Talbot, and were stored in the South Tower.[4] The burning was part of a general operation of clearing preparatory to leasing the House. Lord Talbot ordered it and the Hon. J. B. Talbot directed it, though Mr. Talbot was not present during the half-hour I was at the scene. The estate carpenter, Bob Haddow, carried the papers from the South Tower to the courtyard. The pile when ignited was about five feet in diameter on the ground and about a yard high. I did not see any manuscripts or bound books in the pile, but, as I have said, I was there only about half an hour, and do not know what may have been burned after I left. The pile appeared to me to consist of unfolded printed sheets or printer's proofs of foolscap size. Before the fire was lighted, I inspected one sheet and found that it contained a sentence which I remember as "Mr. Thrale is constantly on the lookout for a horse for his mares, a bull for his cows, and a dog for his bitches." From things I heard my parents say, I concluded that the papers were destroyed because they contained indelicate matter.

The paper that Mr. Drysdale read in was undoubtedly the first printed sheet of Boswell's ribald poem, *Ode by Dr. Samuel Johnson to Mrs. Thrale upon their Supposed Approaching Nuptials,* dated 1784 but actually published in 1788. The passage he remembered (p. 6) was an extract from a letter from Johnson to Mrs. Thrale, 29 September 1777: "Dr. Taylor desires always to have his complements sent. He is, in his usual way very busy,—getting a Bull to his cows, and a Dog to his bitches. . . . Old Shakespeare is dead and he wants to buy another horse for his mares." The substitution of "Thrale" for "Taylor" is easily accounted for, for the preceding page is all about Thrale, and Thrale and Mrs. Thrale are named on both sides of the extract. The reader will remember that Glen the bookseller picked up sheets of both the *Ode* and *No Abolition of Slavery* at one or other of the Auchinleck sales.[5] The joiner's bonfire no doubt consisted principally if not entirely of more unassembled sheets of the same—remainder stock sent back to Boswell, who had probably published both pamphlets at his own risk. Lord Talbot may have ordered their destruction as being indecent or simply as being useless lumber.

Subsequent events, as I have said, proved that Boswell's correspondence did not suffer in the bonfire of 1917. Tinker, however, did not have the benefit of later knowledge, and uneasily desisted for the time from further approaches to Malahide.

---

[3]Above, pp. 64–65.

[4]"South Tower" is the local name for the detached stone pavilion that stands at the south front corner of Auchinleck House. Mr. Drysdale tells me that it is fitted out as a storehouse, and was used for storing wines, food, etc.

[5]Above, p. 71.

He was in fact consciously or unconsciously inhibited from vigorous and persistent inquiry by not really wanting to turn up a large mass of new Boswell letters. He had only one eye, the other having been enucleated because of a tumour when he was a child. So far as I know, he had competent (that is, correctible) vision in his one eye, but he had to ration his hours of study and reading. He was emphatically research scholar as well as teacher, but the dominant passion of his life was the teaching of English literature through lectures in Yale College: in this he had no peer at Yale in his time. His lectures, delivered from very scanty notes, sitting beside a desk or table, were finished essays, capable of being printed without revision; and he delivered six such lectures a week during the college year. An unsurpassed teacher of the techniques of research, he preferred for his own publication subjects of small or moderate scope which he could handle with elegance. His *Letters of James Boswell,* as it stood in 1920, was already much the largest project he had undertaken (he was then in his forty-fourth year), and he meant it to be his *magnum opus*.

A year or so later, while he was working on the manuscripts of Boswell's letters to Temple in the Pierpont Morgan Library, where they had finally come to rest after publication, he happened upon the letter from Malone to Euphemia Boswell, quoted above.[6] This showed beyond all doubt that Boswell's literary executors had discharged their trust: that as late as 1807 Malone knew for a fact that many of the papers (including most of the journal) were at Auchinleck, and believed all of them to be there. This disposed completely of Rogers's account of early (c. 1805) wholesale destruction at Auchinleck, though it did not eliminate the possibility of the holocaust which McCrone reported as having occurred a hundred years later. Rumours that there were precious documents at Malahide continued to arrive. But Tinker went ahead and published (1924) his two volumes of Boswell's *Letters* without any further attempt to establish the real state of affairs at Malahide. He even unfortunately failed to qualify some footnotes, no doubt written years before, in which he had spoken of the destruction of Boswell's papers as historical fact, and nowhere hinted a suspicion that Croker, Rogers, and Hill might be wrong.

The Hon. James Boswell Talbot succeeded as sixth Lord Talbot de Malahide on the death of his father, 4 March 1921. He had never shown any interest in Boswell's papers, indeed had never handled them at all. Though he appears among family and friends to have made no secret of the presence of his great-great-grandfather's papers at Malahide, he had returned a misleading and secretive answer to the only inquiry we know him to have received up to this time from a recognized Boswell scholar. From the spring of 1921 to the autumn of 1924 the papers, as David Buchanan well puts it, "continued to lie undisturbed". Then matters moved very fast.

Lord Talbot on his succession displayed unexpected power of independent judgement. In September 1924, when he was turned fifty, he took the decisive step

_____

of marriage to an attractive young woman of little more than half his age. Miss Joyce Gunning Kerr came from a well-known theatrical family, and had briefly been an actress herself. Lord Talbot did not pretend to literary taste, indeed had few avocations, but she encouraged his keen interest in racing—he was a teetotaller who never laid a bet—and helped him to exploit his considerable social gifts. He gratefully resigned to her a good deal of his correspondence and much of the management of his business affairs. The reserve that her late father-in-law had shown as regards the journal was now ended. The ebony cabinet stood in a drawing-room of Malahide Castle, and visitors not only had their attention called to it, but were freely shown what it contained. The guests at Malahide were now of a more literary cast than they had been in the fifth Lord Talbot's time, and were more likely to talk about what they had seen. *Young Boswell* and *The Amenities of Book-Collecting* had appeared, Boswell was coming more and more to be regarded as a literary artist, and the market in Boswell autographs had become brisk. The new Lady Talbot soon came to realize that the Boswell archives were not only of interest to historians and literary scholars, but might also be a property of considerable commercial value. This was a matter she had to consider seriously. Lord Talbot was owner of an ancient and distinguished estate, but high taxation was depleting his income. He had in his possession manuscripts by a famous author, some of which appeared to be capable of publication with profit. If there was some way consonant with his rank and his descent from Boswell by which he could realize this income, it was incumbent on her to find that way. If Boswell had been a writer of fiction and had left manuscripts of unpublished novels, the only question to arise would have been whether they were likely to diminish his literary reputation. The problem actually posed was that the most obviously publishable portion of the collection was a private journal which was bound to affect the public's judgement of Boswell's character as well as of his skill as a writer. Lady Talbot felt that Murray's verdict should be reconsidered. She discussed the matter with her father, the well-known actor Frederick Kerr, who looked at some of the manuscripts and talked about them to friends in the Garrick Club in London. He also submitted the Murray transcript of the journal to Eveleigh Nash of the publishing house of Nash and Grayson, and in May 1925 Nash met with Lord and Lady Talbot to discuss the problem of publication. He brought along Lord Dunedin, Lord Justice General and Lord of Appeal of Scotland, to discuss matters of copyright. Nash (just when is not certain) gave as his opinion that an unexpurgated trade edition of the journal would have a large sale, and that if it were merely a question of securing maximum returns, Lord Talbot would do well to realize these publishing profits himself before selling the manuscripts. Nash and Grayson, however, would not wish to publish such an edition, and Nash doubted whether Lord Talbot would choose to appear as promoter and beneficiary of anything of that sort. On the other hand, he thought that a selective edition such as Lord Talbot would not be embarrassed to present as his own would have to be underwritten by Lord Talbot and might prove to be very expensive. His final advice to the Talbots was to sell the papers to some one who would observe their wishes as to suppression of matter which they thought unfit for publication, and who would not mind putting a considerable sum of money into any publication he might arrange. Lady Talbot was not at once convinced of the soundness of this advice and continued for some months to entertain thoughts of holding on to the papers and arranging some publication which she and her husband would have power to control.

When it had been authoritatively asserted in places like the Garrick Club that Boswell's papers were still in existence at Malahide Castle, faceless rumours soon gave way to confident reports with well-known names attached to them. On the strength of one of these reports (it came from W. S. Lewis, who had it from A. W. Evans, who had it from John Drinkwater), Tinker decided to go to Malahide himself. His Yale classmate and intimate friend, Charles M. Hathaway, Jr., American Consul General for Ireland, arranged for him to meet the Ven. Thomas Somerville Lindsay, Archdeacon of Dublin and Rector of Malahide, and Archdeacon Lindsay obtained from Lady Talbot an invitation for Tinker and Hathaway to go to tea at the Castle, 30 June 1925. The Dowager Lady Talbot was also present. Lord Talbot was cordial and charming, Lady Talbot courteous but reserved. Tinker's gift of his two volumes of Boswell's letters was received with little warmth, Lady Talbot remarking that it was her understanding that the copyright of all unpublished letters by Boswell belonged to her husband and that Tinker should not have published so many new texts without consulting him. This indicated a considerable degree of misunderstanding on her part. It is probable that when Tinker initiated his edition, he knew nothing about the Malahide connexion; certainly he did not then request permission from the family to go ahead. Nobody editing letters of authors who have been dead well over a century commonly troubles himself about copyright. Who feels any obligation to hunt for the literary representative of Johnson or of Goldsmith or of Reynolds before publishing their letters? In this matter the rule *de non apparentibus* surely obtains: let the alleged owner of copyright reveal himself. Tinker had given public notice in the *Times Literary Supplement* that he proposed to publish a collected edition of Boswell's letters, and at that time he also had written a personal letter to Lord Talbot stating his plan. He did not ask Lord Talbot's permission to publish texts he had obtained elsewhere, but he certainly *consulted* him and gave him adequate opportunity to object if he chose to. Talbot had raised no objection whatever, though he declined to assist the project. Lady Talbot seems also to have been under a misapprehension as to the revenue to be obtained from books like Tinker's *Letters of James Boswell*. A scholar publishing a book of that kind gets his return in reputation rather than in cash: he feels lucky if he can get it published without a subvention. It cost Tinker far, far more to collect and prepare his texts than he ever got in royalties or honorarium.

Tinker and Hathaway, at Lord Talbot's suggestion, were shown the ebony cabinet, and Tinker was allowed to examine some of the pieces it contained. Lady Talbot (I am not sure *which* Lady Talbot) told Tinker that there were at Malahide other papers by Boswell, including two cases from Auchinleck that had not yet been opened. From what he saw and what he was told, he concluded that most of Boswell's papers were in existence. He was not, however, encouraged to think that he might examine any of them with a view to publication. Lady Talbot said that she intended to retain control of any future publication herself, and that it might take many years to put the papers in order. Tinker understood her position and was not disposed to think himself unkindly treated, but he came away from Malahide feeling, as he himself said, that his life's work lay in ruins. The primary object of his visit, however, had been accomplished.

Popular apprehension (so far as matters of this sort can ever become popular) was encouraged by at least two printed accounts to cast Tinker in the role of discoverer of the long-lost papers of James Boswell. That he was in no proper sense discoverer has, I trust, been made clear by the preceding narrative. Tinker's visit to Malahide was belated and was prompted by no feat of detection. Yet, like no other of the personal viewings of the papers, it produced results that were direct, immediate, and conclusive. I can speak with some personal authority on the point: *pars fui*. At Tinker's request, I went over to England a little after he sailed for Ireland so as to be on hand if he found that the papers really were at Malahide, was allowed to examine them systematically, and needed help. On arrival in London I found a brief and agitated letter saying that he had been at Malahide and had "seen the valley of rubies"—a metaphor he used in other letters conveying the same news to eagerly awaiting friends. Before 30 June 1925 no recognized Boswell or Johnson scholar, collector, or dealer in the United Kingdom or the United States knew for a certainty that Boswell's papers were at Malahide. Chapman did not know, Nichol Smith did not know, Tregaskis did not know, McKinlay did not know, Adam did not know, Newton did not know. (By "know for a certainty" I mean, had handled or seen the papers himself or had been assured by some one whose competence he trusted that he had handled or seen them.) Within a month, I think, after 30 June 1925, they all knew. Roberts, alone of Boswell scholars, by his own statement did not know till a full year later. I have doubts as to the accuracy of his chronology, but shall defer stating them till we come to his own visit to Malahide, which certainly occurred in June 1926.

ISHAM GOES TO MALAHIDE

ONE OF THE FRIENDS whom Tinker reported to was Newton, and Newton passed the word on promptly to his fellow Philadelphian, Dr. A. S. W. Rosenbach. In August 1925, Rosenbach sent from London a long cable to Lord Talbot, asking to be allowed to treat for the purchase of his Boswell papers and expressing a willingness to go up to £50,000. Lord Talbot was very much upset. A widely credited story that came into circulation the following year represents him as going in person to the American Consulate in Dublin. He comes into the Consulate in a state of agitation, holding the cablegram by one corner, like a soiled handkerchief. LORD TALBOT: "Who is this person who is sending me cables?" CLERK (looking at the cablegram): "Why, that, my Lord, is the great American book-dealer, Dr. Rosenbach. He's quite good for the money." LORD TALBOT: "Will you please tell him not to correspond with me? We have never been introduced, and what is more, I don't like his name." The story was a pure fabrication, a characteristic invention by Lt.-Colonel Ralph H. Isham, still in the wings of our story, but about to step on stage in a principal role. Rosenbach was answered by post in a brief letter, 27 August 1925, signed by Lady Talbot: "We regret that such Boswell papers as are in our possession are neither for sale, nor can they be seen by anyone. Lord Talbot was very surprised and annoyed at the matter being opened by tele-gram." It should in fairness be added that the Talbots' displeasure, though mainly attributable to grossly inappropriate tactics, had other substantial grounds. The times in Ireland were unsettled and ugly, and a cablegram is not a private message. Lord Talbot feared for the safety of his family if word got abroad that he had at Malahide movable property that some one was willing to pay a quarter of a million dollars for. As a result of this alarm the majority of the papers were removed from the ebony cabinet and stored in a vault in a bank in Dublin.

In a letter dated 11 September 1925, Hathaway reported to Tinker a conference he had just had with Lord Talbot's solicitor, James Robinson. Robinson thought the Talbots were decided not to sell the Boswell collection on any terms, but he was not aware that they had reached any decision beyond that. He thought it not unlikely that Tinker might be allowed to examine the papers under a strict understanding that rights of publication were reserved. Lady Talbot was still trying to work out plans by which Lord Talbot could appropriately derive benefit from publication, either by a sale of copyright or by royalties. I assume that Tinker, through Hathaway and Robinson, expressed his willingness to accept the restrictions imposed, but nothing ever came of the scheme. Because of his classes at Yale, he could not in any case have gone to Malahide for any length of time between the end of September 1925 and the middle of June 1926, and by that time the situation had changed radically.

The resounding failure of Rosenbach's blunt tactics made it clear that the first problem any would-be purchaser would have to solve was simply that of etiquette—how to establish a relationship in which one could talk business without giving offence. Newton reconnoitred the situation but decided that he did not have the time required for a proper campaign. He suggested to his friend of recent acquaintance, Lt.-Colonel Ralph Heyward Isham (they had met by chance during an Atlantic crossing on the *Majestic*), that he have a try. Isham seized on the suggestion, and was moved to prompt action by hearing that another American dealer (probably E. Byrne Hackett) was about to sail for Ireland to try his hand. He sent a cable to an Irish friend in London, Maj. Frederick Nesbitt (later style, Maj.-Gen. Frederick Beaumont-Nesbitt) in the hope that Nesbitt might know Lord Talbot personally and would present his case; on Nesbitt's replying (27 February 1926) that he did not know Talbot, he commissioned him to find a suitable person to approach Talbot and send him to Ireland at Isham's expense. Nesbitt cabled (6 March 1926) that he had been unable to find any suitable envoy, and that he could give no further assistance as he was obliged to leave London. Isham thereupon sent a long cable to the firm of Denton, Hall, and Burgin, Gray's Inn, his solicitors in London. Nothing could illustrate Isham's character and temperament better than this cable:

LORD TALBOT DE MALAHIDE OF MALAHIDE CASTLE DUBLIN INHERITED LARGE QUANTITY MANUSCRIPTS OF JAMES BOSWELL ALL OR PART OF WHICH AM EXTREMELY ANXIOUS ACQUIRE FOR MY COLLECTION STOP CAN YOU FIND ANYONE SUITABLE APPROACH HIM TO REQUEST FIRST REFUSAL FOR ME AT HIS OWN VALUATION IF HE DECIDES TO SELL STOP ONE AMERICAN DEALER OFFENDED HIM BY CABLING DIRECT ANOTHER IS ON WAY TO SEE HIM SPEED MOST IMPORTANT IF YOU CANNOT FIND PERSON KNOWN TO TALBOT PROCEED SEE HIM YOURSELF FORTIFIED WITH ALL POSSIBLE CREDENTIALS [STOP] FROM INFORMATION JUDGE VALUE APPROXIMATELY TWENTY THOUSAND POUNDS WILL GIVE YOU ONE THOUSAND POUNDS BONUS IF YOU CAN ARRANGE MY PURCHASE OF MANUSCRIPTS OTHERWISE CHARGE ME EXPENSES AND FEES CABLE YOUR PLANS

The partnership of Denton, Hall, and Burgin at that time consisted of Edward L. Burgin and his two sons, Dr. E. Leslie Burgin and Harold Burgin. They made the sensible decision to send Harold Burgin, and to approach the Talbots through their solicitor. What happened to the American dealer I do not know, but Burgin saw Robinson promptly on his arrival in Dublin, and Robinson arranged for him to meet Lord and Lady Talbot at Malahide the very next day (11 March 1926). Lord Talbot gave an oral promise that Isham should be notified as soon as any one else of a decision to sell, but Burgin believed that he had Robinson's assurance that the Talbots would actually hold no further interviews on the subject, and that Isham in fact had the first refusal that he had hoped for. Burgin believed also that he had disposed the Talbots to sell. He had reason to be proud of his success in a delicate mission. Negotiations had been opened in a way acceptable to the Talbots. Robinson's confidence had been won and the Talbots disposed to think that Isham was the kind of man they could properly deal with. Isham could now employ his great powers of persuasion. It had already been established that money by itself would accomplish nothing. If Talbot were to be won over, he had to be made to feel that the papers were being transferred from one gentleman's library to another gentleman's library. And the gentleman had to be the kind of man he understood, with recommendations from people he knew and respected; a gentleman who would not push matters but would take time to get acquainted.

Ralph Heyward Isham, born in 1890, was an American from New Jersey, but he had enlisted in the British Army in 1915, had received a commission at Aldershot, had been promoted directly from Captain to Lieutenant-Colonel, and had ended, with the decoration of C.B.E., on the staff of General Haig and of Field Marshal Robertson. His most distinguished service had occurred in 1919, when he received official commendation for skill in pacifying disaffected troops, but of course his wartime period of command and of companionship with other British officers had given him the social training he needed to deal effectively with people like the Talbots. He had lived on in England for several years after the Armistice, and had a wide and distinguished British acquaintance—one may instance T. E. Lawrence. He retained his military title and the speech and bearing of a British officer, or perhaps one could not unjustly say that to most people he came through as a good actor impersonating a rather extreme type of British military man. By and large, his virtues and foibles can best be developed in particular episodes of the narrative that follows, but the histrionic element in his character should be stressed at the very outset because it was general and pervasive. He always acted. A brilliant raconteur, he had the disconcerting habit of infusing fiction into practically everything he said. You believed all of his utterance at your peril, but you were generally safe in assuming that the most improbable portions of his narratives were true. His staginess put many people off, but he never lacked a circle of warmly devoted friends. He was a keen sportsman (when most of his friends were undergraduates, he was shooting big game in the Malay Peninsula), very much a man's man. He was courageous to the point of rashness, and could make far-reaching decisions more quickly and firmly than any other man I have ever known. He had spent something like a year at Cornell and a similar period at Yale, had been married and divorced (he had a teen-age daughter by this first marriage), and in 1924 had married a beautiful young woman as his second wife. In 1926 he was a man of considerable, though not vast, wealth. He was also a collector. He had never been a pupil of Tinker's, but as has been mentioned above, he was at Yale in 1910–11, and the Tinkerian fascination often operated at a distance. At any rate, after the war, while he was still living in England, he started collecting books, acquiring, among others, a good many volumes that had been in the library of Lt.-Colonel F. R. C. Grant (author of the *Life of Johnson* in the Great Writers series), and going on to assemble a fine collection, especially strong in Johnsonian and Boswellian rarities. He therefore had expert knowledge of the significance and value of the separate documents in Lord Talbot's collection.

Isham cabled back at once, asking Burgin for fuller and more precise information on points that Burgin had left vague, and instructing him to write to Lord Talbot and inquire if Isham might call on him. Burgin no doubt did so, but several weeks went by before Talbot answered. Probably he and Lady Talbot were taking a spring holiday in France, and both Burgin and Isham knew that a reply could not be expected before the end of May. As that date drew near, Isham decided that he had better be on the other side of the Atlantic when Talbot's letter arrived. His decision may have been precipitated by a chance encounter he had with Newton in New York on the 27th or 28th. He then proposed that the two of them should sail next day for England in a joint attempt to purchase the papers, sharing the costs equally. Newton thought his plan "carefully matured", but after a few hours' deliberation declined to participate in a note presumably delivered by messenger. He however urged Isham to make the venture alone ("Dear Ralph, For me to go to Ireland would be as mad as for you not to. Greetings, A. E. N."). Whether Isham had already booked passage, I do not know: it would have been very like him not to have fixed so crucial a matter till after he had talked with Newton. At any rate, he sailed on the *Olympic* at 12:10 a.m. on 29 May 1926, landing at Southampton on the afternoon of 4 June. Talbot finally wrote to Burgin on 30 May, while Isham was in mid-Atlantic. The letter was extremely non-committal and sounds as though it had been composed after conference with Robinson. He said, in brief, that he and Lady Talbot expected to be at home after 10 June, and that if Isham happened to call upon them at Malahide, they would of course be very happy to receive him. At the same time, he thought it only fair to point out that he could not see the slightest possibility of its being worth Colonel Isham's trouble to make the trip.

> I do not wish to sell any of the Boswell papers, and I shall be, quite frankly, too busy to be able to show him many of them, as they have recently been moved and are now somewhat difficult to get at. We have, in the house, one or two specimen papers.

. . . I would be very pleased to show him these, but there are only one or two of them.
. . . If Colonel Isham came over, it would have to be entirely at his own wish, and
with a clear understanding that it did not alter the present position which is;—that
if any Boswell papers are to be sold, we will advise him as soon as anybody else. I
doubt if Colonel Isham will think it worth while to come under these circumstances,
but if he should, and would give us a day or two's notice, it would give us great
pleasure to meet so keen a collector, informally.

Isham landed at Southampton in the afternoon of 4 June. He would have seen
Talbot's letter in London that evening, if indeed Burgin had not already sent it to
him by marconigram aboard the *Olympic*. On 7 June he wrote the first letter he had
ever addressed to Lord Talbot, assuring him that his purpose in calling was merely
to see his manuscripts, not to try to persuade him to sell them. "I should gladly
go much farther than Dublin to see even one letter of James Boswell. Perhaps in
this I have something akin to the religious fervour that moves the pilgrims to set
out on their journeys to Mecca!" He also wrote to the younger son of the Duke of
Marlborough, Lord Ivor Spencer-Churchill, begging him to send a letter of recommendation for him to Lord Talbot. (He *may* have requested this recommendation
by cable before sailing or by marconigram from the *Olympic:* he very much wished
it to be delivered before his arrival at Malahide.) Talbot answered on 10 June,
inviting him to call on "Tuesday 14 June". In 1926 the Tuesday in question was
15 June, and 15 June was actually the day on which Isham presented himself. Lord
Ivor Spencer-Churchill had meantime sent the requested recommendation; it is
dated 11 June. Isham said afterwards that "the journey seemed interminable, the
most nerve-racking part being the hours I spent in Dublin, awaiting the time
appointed for the short motor trip to Malahide".

Isham's first visit to Malahide was no more than an afternoon call. His own
account represented him as spending the time in unreserved vocal admiration of the
few pieces shown, and in assuring Lady Talbot that the specimens on view were
worth considerably more than the tentative valuations she suggested. The most
interesting manuscript on display was a very fine letter of Goldsmith's to Boswell,
commenting on the success of *She Stoops to Conquer* and reporting Goldsmith's having
beaten Evans, the editor of a newspaper that had abused him.[1] As reported by
Isham, the conversation ran: "LADY TALBOT: 'Colonel Isham, is that letter worth
£200?' ISHAM: 'Lady Talbot, it is not worth £200; it is worth £500.' "—"I allowed
her," he said, "to sell me the Boswell papers." In this case his account seems to
have been historical except for considerable inflation of the valuations he said he
assigned. No sale was discussed at that meeting, but after it the eventual transfer
of the Boswell papers to Isham's possession was merely a matter of waiting and of
agreeing upon terms.

A week later (22 June 1926) S. C. Roberts called at Malahide and was shown

[1] See C 1378.

the same pieces that Isham had seen. Many years later he said that though he had been "deeply interested in Tinker's *Young Boswell* (1922) and in his edition of Boswell's *Letters*" and had even met Tinker at Yale in 1925, he did not hear "rumours about the Malahide treasure" till 1926 and then from Montague Rhodes James, Provost of Eton. It may be so, for the trip on which he first met Tinker at Yale occurred in the spring of 1925, that is, before Tinker went to Ireland, and they may not have got in correspondence until after June 1926. But it seems to me odd that Roberts did not hear from Chapman, or, for that matter, from Newton, whom he thought he met in London as early as 1923 or 1924, and who, according to his own account, was his guest at a dinner at Pembroke College in August 1925. His memory certainly misled him into thinking that his visit to Malahide preceded Isham's, and I do not feel at all confident of the correctness of his chronology in other respects. What matters at this point is that he was much impressed by what he was shown, and immediately wrote Talbot a letter offering him his personal services and those of the Cambridge University Press if Talbot decided to publish. This was a flattering offer, but Lady Talbot reacted to it as she had to Tinker's. She was impressed by what she had read of the journal and wanted to see it published, but she did not think that scholarly publication through a university press was particularly in her husband's interest. What would suit best, she now thought, was to sell the papers for their true value to a keen collector like Isham who would keep the collection intact, and would publish the papers himself in a style and manner that Lord Talbot would approve of.

Lady Talbot devoted the next fourteen months to a gradually revealed campaign to win Lord Talbot's consent to a sale of the entire collection to Isham. As for Isham, he thoroughly appreciated her tactics. Her first step was to encourage him and to make a breach in Talbot's instinctive aversion to selling family papers. She accomplished this by getting Talbot to allow Isham to purchase immediately a single conspicuous document, the letter of Goldsmith's already mentioned. Isham, during his call, had in fact valued this at £120 (not £500), and in a letter of 5 July said he would be glad to purchase the journal, suggesting "four or five thousand" as an opening valuation. Though she liked his frankness and his obvious expertise in pricing manuscripts, she was very far from accepting his valuations without taking other opinions and consulting catalogues herself. About this time she and Lord Talbot went to London, taking the Goldsmith letter and others from the collection with them. Eveleigh Nash, whom they consulted, strongly advised selling the letters by auction. I do not think he formally appraised those they had brought, but Lady Talbot saw auction catalogues and noted that in 1911 a letter of Goldsmith's which she considered inferior had sold for £265. She accordingly offered the Malahide letter to Isham for £400 and expressed an opinion that Talbot would probably sell most of the letters by Boswell in the collection when Nash's firm had valued them. As to the journal, she said no steps could be taken for the present. Isham promptly sent his cheque for £400 for the Goldsmith letter, and it was in his hands by the beginning of September. He always talked as though he had brought it away with him from his first visit to Malahide, and reported that he had paid £500 for it. Lady Talbot wrote, "I am so glad the letter has gone to you. It will encourage my husband to give more attention to the papers."

Lady Talbot continued to work at the letters until the end of November, when she and her husband left to spend two months at Menton. She reported to Isham that she had sorted all the letters out, and that Talbot was still undecided whether to sell all, some, or none of them; she thought an offer of £10,000 would "hurry matters". Isham was willing to go to that figure, but only if the journals and other papers were included. On her return from Menton in February 1927 she replied that Lord Talbot would not consider selling the journal, and that it would be some years before that proposal could be dealt with. She promised, however, to make a full priced list of the letters. The work went slowly: by 18 July 1927 she had listed only a quarter of the whole. She seems to have taken no further advice from professional appraisers, but to have arrived at her valuations by studying a quantity of Maggs's catalogues which Archdeacon Lindsay had lent her. She wrote now as though all the letters could be purchased, but she was finding her estimate of £10,000 for the whole too low. (She had priced about a quarter of the documents, she said, and her valuation had already exceeded £5,000.) She proposed that if Isham wished to purchase the collection, he ought to come over and spend a weekend with herself and Lord Talbot to go into the whole matter.

This was exactly what Isham had been waiting and hoping for. He was at Malahide from Friday 19 August to Sunday 21 August 1927, but it does not appear that he spent much if any time in conference with Lord Talbot. He and Lady Talbot worked long into the morning hours of three nights, handling all the papers except the journal piece by piece. Lady Talbot had listed a considerable number of letters, with descriptions of content and her own valuations. After coming to terms on this list (Isham succeeded in reducing her valuations by more than half), they agreed to a set price per page for the miscellaneous manuscripts, and valued them accordingly. The total figure was £13,585. Isham brought away with him from Malahide all the letters and miscellaneous manuscripts then known to exist. Journal, or "Diary", as Lady Talbot usually styled it, was specifically excluded, but in fact she included among her miscellaneous manuscripts a considerable number of stray bits of journal-notes written on loose leaves.

Isham's main concern from the first had been the journals, and in spite of the treasures he was obtaining, he would hardly have made this large commitment if he had not believed that Lady Talbot felt confident of being ultimately able to persuade her husband to sell the journals as well. Isham now saw her repeating for the journals the gradualist tactics that had worked so well for the letters and miscellaneous papers. There, she had broken the ice of Lord Talbot's reluctance by persuading him first to sell a single brilliant and thoroughly unexceptionable document (Goldsmith's letter about *She Stoops to Conquer*). During the August conference she obtained his permission to sell also the so-called Ashbourne Journal of 1777, the most brilliant of Boswell's Johnsonian journals after the journal of a tour to the Hebrides, which at this time was not known to exist. The grounds for exception were presumably that it recorded on Boswell's part no behaviour more exceptionable than the fondling of maids at inns, and that since he had printed most of it in the *Life of Johnson,* it could hardly be counted as a private journal. Lord Talbot however insisted that the levities of fondling be obliterated before the manuscript was turned over. Lady Talbot told Isham that no sale of the remaining journals would ever be possible unless she could assure her husband that each piece had been carefully read and censored. She promised to go through the whole series, trying from time to time to get Lord Talbot, if terms were agreed upon, to allow her to send him what she had worked through. Isham was unable to take the Ashbourne Journal with him, but it was delivered to him at Claridge's Hotel, London, on 10 September 1927, with certain passages obliterated by black paint.

Isham was not one of those collectors who hoard their treasures and consider a manuscript vitiated if it has been published. On the contrary, his passion for putting the Boswell papers into print in a publication of his own was about as keen as his passion for owning them. He contemplated extensive publication from the first, and assumed without question that Tinker would be his editor. Tinker was in London: Isham encountered him by chance in a bookshop there in late August or early September 1927 and gleefully invited him to Claridge's to see the huge suitcase full of manuscripts he had just brought from Malahide. With Isham an eager cicerone, Tinker pored over piece after piece, his brow growing steadily blacker and his gestures more agitated. He said little, and finally made a gloomy exit. Isham and his wife accompanied him to the elevator. Just as the door was closing, Tinker shook his fist and shouted in a tone of ferocious jocularity, "She was my mistress, Ralph, but you bought her with your money!"

Isham's response to this gratuitous insult was in every way admirable. Though the only fault he perhaps could charge himself with was a degree of tactlessness in vaunting his nonpareils before a rival collector, he wrote Tinker a conciliatory letter and called to express anxiety lest Tinker should be at outs with him. I do not think the question whether Tinker would serve as editor ever really got asked, but it was most definitely answered. Tinker's way of letting Isham know that he did not wish to be associated with the project was of course indefensible: Tinker, though very much a man of good will, too often allowed himself to act the prima donna. But if he had been able to deal with the situation good-humouredly, the answer would still have been the same. He was himself a collector of Boswell and could not see these treasures in another's hands without exquisite pain. He was upset to see spread before him so many texts that ought to have been in his own edition of Boswell's letters. He was temperamentally unfit to work under direction, especially under Isham's. It pained him to see the attractive image of Boswell he himself had created now threatened by masses of new evidence that could be used by new Macaulays.

He was, in fact, beginning to regret that Boswell's private papers had ever been recovered, a feeling that grew stronger after he had read the journals. But more important than all these motives was the realization that if he took on an editorial job of such magnitude, he would have to relax the standards he had set for himself as a teacher. "I preferred," he said, "my post as professor of English literature to that of Boswellian scholar and editor."

Isham's capacity for swift decisions has already been mentioned. He was in London only from some date after 21 August to 14 September 1927. After being rebuffed by Tinker, he wrote offering the post to T. E. Lawrence ("Lawrence of Arabia"), who, under the name of Aircraftman Shaw, was then in Karachi with the R.A.F. Isham's acquaintance with Lawrence had extended over a period of years and could without exaggeration be styled a true friendship. But long before he could hear from Lawrence—perhaps before Lawrence got his letter—he had made another and much more appropriate arrangement. There was no embarrassment, for Lawrence declined, as Isham no doubt expected him to.

Isham always tended to attribute his instant decisions to extraordinary coincidences and providential leadings, a habit nowhere better illustrated than in his own account of how he found his actual editor. On the day he returned to London from Malahide, he said, he took it into his head, for no apparent reason, to lunch at Simpson's in the Strand, where he had not been for five years or so. There he ran into Newton and invited him to Claridge's to dine and look at his treasure; the two friends sat far into the small hours, going over the papers piece by piece. Newton asked him what he proposed to do with them; he replied, "Obviously, publish them." When Newton asked who his editor would be and he replied that he was undecided, Newton at once named Geoffrey Scott, saying that Scott's *Portrait of Zélide* was one of the most exquisite books in the English language. The recommendation seemed to Isham instantly right: he knew the book, Scott "was the ideal man". But how would he find him? Neither he nor Newton had ever met Scott and neither had the slightest idea where he might be. Two days later Isham said he had a sudden urge to call on J. C. Wilson, manager of the bookstore of John and Edward Bumpus, in Oxford Street. When he told Wilson of his acquisition, Wilson said, "I wish you had been in here fifteen minutes earlier, Geoffrey Scott was here." Wilson got on the telephone, located Scott in a few minutes, introduced Isham to him over the wire, Isham invited Scott to Claridge's, Scott and Isham sat up all night the first night, Isham provided Scott with quarters at Claridge's. "From that time until my sailing," Isham wrote, ". . . we were scarcely separated during our waking hours. By that time we had made plans. He was to come to America to edit the papers as soon as his personal affairs could be arranged."

This is obviously fictionalized to a considerable degree. By eliminating the whole Tinkerian contretemps and telescoping time, Isham converts a frustratingly inconsequential sequence into drama. He may have run into Newton by chance on the day he returned from Malahide, but he could not then have said that he was undecided: he fully planned to offer the editorship to Tinker and expected Tinker to accept with alacrity. Newton may have mentioned Scott at a meeting on that first day but only as a second choice if Tinker declined. Isham pretty certainly did not drop work and rush off to Oxford Street merely because of a sudden vague urge: he went there because some one (why not Newton?) had told him that Wilson was the kind of man who might be personally acquainted with Scott and might know where he was to be found. Still (and this is characteristic of most of Isham's stories) *some* of the extraordinary coincidences of his account stoutly resist sceptical reduction. He probably did meet Newton quite by chance at Simpson's; he certainly arrived at Bumpus's just after Scott had left there. Wilson himself confirmed that detail.

Geoffrey Scott was at this time forty-three years old. Isham has left a brilliant description of his appearance: "He was of great height and heavy build. His head was large and fine, his face sensitive,—at times beautiful in expression. His black hair, which he wore long, was vigorous and untidy. His manner was gentle and sympathetic." Iris Origo adds sensitively perceived detail: "I think with much affection, after so many years, of his tall, ungainly figure, and of the mobile, ugly face lit by quick flashes of intelligence and laughter; the straight coarse black hair, eternally unbrushed and falling over his eyes, and the appealing, faintly bewildered look beneath his horn spectacles." Scott's father, Russell Scott, belonged to a non-conformist (Unitarian) family settled in the south of England; his mother, Jessie Thurburn, came from the north of Scotland. C. P. Scott, well known as for many years editor of the *Manchester Guardian,* was his uncle. Geoffrey Scott was educated at Rugby, St. Andrews University, and New College, Oxford; at Oxford he won the Newdigate Prize for poetry. On leaving Oxford he served for a decade or so as private librarian and secretary to Bernard Berenson at I Tatti in Florence; he also practised architecture in Florence for a few years in partnership with Cecil Pinsent. His *Architecture of Humanism,* a study centred in the architecture of the Italian Renaissance, was published on the day that the Great War broke out, 4 August 1914. In 1916 the architectural partnership was closed down, Pinsent joined the British Red Cross on the Italian Front and Scott was made Honorary Attaché to the British Embassy in Rome. In 1918 he married Lady Sybil Cutting, younger daughter of the fifth Earl of Desart, Co. Kilkenny, Ireland, widow of William Bayard Cutting, Jr., of the U.S. Diplomatic Service. (At the end of his life Cutting held the post of Deputy U.S. Secretary of Embassy at Tangiers, but bad health seems to have kept him most of the time in Florence. The Marchesa Iris Origo is Lady Sybil's daughter by this first marriage.) Scott left the Embassy on his marriage and withdrew to his wife's house, Villa Medici, Fiesole, Florence, but before long felt the need of some distraction from his writing, and accepted the new post of Press Officer at the Embassy, commuting between Rome and Florence. His liaison with Vita Sackville-West, the disclosure of which recently by Nigel Nicolson has made so much noise, began at Florence in the late autumn of 1923; his marriage ended in a divorce (1926), when Lady Sybil married Percy Lubbock. Early in 1924, while the divorce proceedings were in train, Scott returned to London and some time in that year moved into the visitors' flat of his friend Haslam's house, 8 Hanover Terrace, Regent's Park. *The Portrait of Zélide,* an imaginative vignette of Belle de Zuylen, the Dutch bluestocking who both captivated and repelled Boswell, was published in 1925. Like *The Architecture of Humanism* it was a huge critical success, but neither book was a runaway best-seller. Scott had planned to follow the *Portrait* with a short biography of Boswell, to be published in the British Men of Letters series, but on hearing of the existence of papers at Malahide, had shelved it until he could learn what disposition was to be made of them. He seems always to have been hard up, or rather, perhaps, never to have had money enough of his own completely to support himself in the style he thought suitable. His friend Haslam speaks of faking the house accounts for his benefit when they lived together in an apartment in Rome ("at the top of the Casa dei Quattro Venti over the Spanish Steps"), and was furnishing him with free quarters in London when Isham's offer came out of the blue. Isham, who was in a great hurry to leave and was only waiting for Lady Talbot to deliver the Ashbourne Journal, begged off for the time from formalizing his relations with Scott. He probably made him a generous advance to enable him to settle his affairs and pay for his passage; he certainly persuaded him to leave all the details of his remuneration as editor to be worked out at leisure after he had arrived in America.

Scott arrived before the end of October and joined Isham in the pleasant country house at Glen Head on Long Island which Isham had recently purchased. It was characteristic of Isham to have engaged his editor not merely before he had his hands on Boswell's journals—the principal matter the editor was to publish—but even before he had assurance that the journals were ever to be his. Lady Talbot had promised only to censor them, fragment by fragment, and to try to persuade her husband to sell them piecemeal. There was of course work enough to keep Scott busy for some time in sorting, transcribing, and studying the miscellaneous manuscripts Isham already owned and in planning the format of the forthcoming edition, but to plunge straight ahead on so expensive a venture with any uncertainty at all as to availability of text required enormous self-confidence. Two typists were at once engaged for the transcription, and the edition was conceived in the most splendid style. There were to be twelve stately volumes, each volume individually laid out by Bruce Rogers, foremost of American book-designers. The number of volumes was later expanded to eighteen. The type was to be genuine Baskerville in various sizes, which meant that all the italic (of which there was to be a great deal) had to be hand-set because of the swash characters. The size and shape of each volume were to be determined by the full-sized facsimiles of manuscript leaves of the text that were to be used as illustrations. The set was to be sold only by subscription: the price, $50 a volume, $900 the set. William Edwin Rudge was chosen as printer. He manufactured and distributed the work on commission; Isham remained sole owner. The title was to be *Private Papers of James Boswell from Malahide Castle in the Collection of Lt.-Colonel Ralph Heyward Isham.*

Isham began pushing Lady Talbot by letter as soon as he got back to America. On Scott's arrival, he sent a second urgent letter and then a cable, complaining that without the journals he was held up in his publication. Lady Talbot chided him for engaging himself so deeply on the strength of so tentative an agreement as she had given him, but nevertheless did buckle down to work. Lord Talbot's scruples were overcome, and the journals were sent in several lots during December 1927 and January 1928. Lady Talbot's procedure was to post a censored typed transcript to Isham and to deposit the corresponding censored manuscript at a bank in Dublin, to be forwarded to Isham on receipt of Isham's payments. Her price was £10 per page, with an agreement that if the total should run over £20,000 (it did by a considerable figure), Isham should have the excess free. Isham agreed to these terms, but asked permission to defer payment of half the price for one year. He also asked Lord Talbot to give him a document expressly declaring him owner of all the private papers of Boswell's Lord Talbot had inherited. The first request was denied, the second granted only to the extent of assuring him that if more of Boswell's journal should turn up, he should have it without further payment.

Isham had now paid or committed himself to pay Lord Talbot £35,235 for manuscripts (£400 for the Goldsmith letter, £13,585 for the miscellaneous papers and letters, £1,250 for the Ashbourne Journal, £20,000 for the rest of the journal). He had recently invested heavily in real estate—"an island off the coast of Florida, a part of an island off the coast of Georgia, an apartment at Fifth Avenue and 72nd Street, New York, and a very well established place not far from Oyster Bay", to quote Newton's admiring summary. From the time he appeared in *Who's Who* (1925, when he was still living in England) he described himself as "financier". In 1929, when my close connexion with him began, he was certainly furnishing capital for a firm named Ross Safety Switch, a partnership between himself and an inventor (Ross), formed to promote a promising electrical device. Ross Safety Switch had an office on East Forty-second Street with a full-time secretary and probably other employees. Later on Isham told me that he had acquired or hoped to acquire an automatic gear-shift for motor cars. Both devices, I gathered, were ahead of their time, and neither made any money for him. What he was financing in 1927 I do not know, but I feel sure that if Ross Safety Switch was not already in existence, he was putting money into some other similar promotion. The greater part of his income came from a trust fund of which he could not touch the principal.

It is only the outcome that finally determines whether a man's actions are to be considered intrepid or reckless. Newton, a prudent and successful business man, sincerely liked and admired Isham, but thought his publishing venture "almost impossible" of achievement.

The thinness of Isham's capital resources had shown itself before he had ever been admitted to Malahide. In June 1926 he had tried to get Newton to go halves with him in an attempt to purchase the papers; Newton reported that at some unstated time later he made the same proposal to Rosenbach. On 7 January 1927, perhaps to put himself in a better cash position for purchasing the Boswell papers, he had sold the miscellaneous portion of his fine collection of rare books at the American Art Association, New York. Though he retained the Johnson, Goldsmith, and Boswell sections of his library, this could not fail to hurt his reputation as a collector, perhaps even to raise suspicions of his solvency. To effect the purchase of the journals at the end of 1927 and beginning of 1928, he procured a short-term loan of $136,000 from James Van Alen, in three promissory notes: 3 December 1927, 4 December 1927, and 14 January 1928. He repaid $12,000 of this sum in accordance with the terms of the loan, but let $124,000 of indebtedness run. While I was working for him, I knew in the vaguest sort of way that Van Alen, whom I once met in Rudge's New York office, had lent Isham a good deal of money, but I never got acquainted with him or knew any of the details of his loans till I read *The Treasure of Auchinleck*. Van Alen, it appears, a young sportsman and member of a wealthy Newport family, came to Isham's aid out of no love for literature but simply because of his admiration for the elegance and audacity of Isham's campaign for buying the papers and his scheme for publishing them. Isham, he is reported to have remarked, "had a Rolls-Royce without an engine". He turned out to be a not-wholly-voluntary angel to the whole venture.

Isham also sold a few of the manuscripts he had obtained from Malahide. He is said on his return to New York in 1927 to have swept into Rosenbach's Madison Avenue bookstore, to have dropped on a table an armful of precious bundles, and to have assured Rosenbach that he could have the whole collection—at a price which caused even that hardened high-pricer to blench.

To one who really knew Isham the episode is startling but quite credible. In 1927 and the years following he undoubtedly more than once indicated to Rosenbach and others his willingness to treat for the sale of his entire collection. On a later occasion he deposited with Rosenbach a fantastic appraisal of his Boswell papers by the late Arthur Swann which set the total asking price at $1,736,880. Isham knew that he was gambling on a very long chance and may merely have wanted assurance of what he could count on if he were suddenly forced to sell out. It is also possible that he had thoughts of applying for a loan, with the papers as collateral. But it is almost certain that these overtures were mostly a game, the kind of acting he excelled in. All collectors like to fill their rivals with envy; all collectors savour a prospective lucrative sale of the treasures they intend never to part with. In 1927 and for many years after that, to own and to publish the Boswell papers meant more to Isham than anything else in life. Though he courted a reputation for instability and unaccountable caprice, he was actually at all times doggedly true to his central commitments. Yet he did sell Rosenbach some individual pieces from the collection: six leaves from the main draft of the manuscript of the *Life of Johnson* (at that time it was believed that only sixteen leaves had survived), a five-page "Paper Apart" from the same manuscript, and two fine letters from Boswell to his wife.[2] We should surely infer that he did not want to sell these papers or any others from the collection, but that he was forced to do so to meet pressing financial

---

[2] The total sum paid by Rosenbach for these items was $17,000.

obligations which he could not shift or postpone. That Isham had sold papers became known to dealers and collectors as soon as Rosenbach offered his purchases for sale, and the report and rumour could not fail to be damaging to Isham's publication. Did this mean that the subscribers would not get texts of all the papers promised? What confidence could subscribers have in Isham's ability to complete an edition of eighteen volumes if he was selling off papers before even one volume had been published? Actually, no one need have worried on the first score: Isham was careful to keep photocopies of all manuscripts he sold and to retain copyright. But there was nothing he could do to still the other anxiety.

CHAPTER VII

GEOFFREY SCOTT

GETS OFF TO

A BRILLIANT START

SOME PAGES BACK we left Geoffrey Scott ensconced in Isham's house at Glen Head studying the miscellaneous manuscripts and eagerly awaiting the journals. The journals have now begun to arrive and he can see the results of Lady Talbot's censorship. We had probably better go into that matter rather fully before continuing the narrative, though we unfortunately shall have to fall back on conjecture as regards some aspects of this very important problem.

Lord Talbot capitulated as to the sale of the journals, but could not be budged from his insistence that the manuscripts be properly expurgated before they left his hands. He himself had no liking or aptitude for the task, but was willing to entrust it to Lady Talbot. She had no strong feelings of her own in the matter, and cast about for some model or set of standards. By her own account, she came up with the Murray transcript. From the gaps in that transcript occasioned by the removal of leaves from the manuscript *causa pudoris,* she could have learned nothing useful unless the now missing manuscript leaves were then in existence and available to her. She always maintained that she knew nothing whatever of those missing leaves. Presumably, then, we should infer that numerous passages were typed up in the Murray transcript and then obliterated in the typescript before it was handed to Murray, but that there remained some fairly easy way of recovering these censored bits. Blotted typescript, if blank on the verso, can be easily read in mirror image from the verso if the recto is held up to a strong light, but for a reason I shall later specify, I do not think Lady Talbot knew that. It is more probable that she turned to the manuscripts and found that at least a good many of the corresponding passages there had not been obliterated or had been scored so lightly that they could be read without difficulty. Lady Talbot concluded that the matter expunged by her father-in-law and Colonel Talbot could be grouped roughly under three heads: "indelicacies" (both coarse expressions and the record of sexual licentiousness, however decent the language employed), names of persons whose descendants might be distressed by Boswell's disclosures, and extended references to the insanity of Boswell's brother, Lt. John Boswell. After the Talbots' return in November 1927, she set herself to the task of reading and blotting; when she developed eye-strain, she employed a secretary to assist her. She caused a typescript to be made for the large body of journal, journal-notes, and memoranda for which no typescript had previously existed. She first worked through the Murray transcript, marking systematically and in most cases heavily in the manuscripts the deletions already present in the transcript, with further deletions suggested by its practice. After she got the secretary, she seems to have blotted the typescripts herself and to have delegated the inking of the manuscripts. The manuscripts now show blottings in four different liquids: brown iron-gall ink of the same sort as that which the documents were written in, black paint, blue-black writing fluid, and carbon ("India") ink. The deletions in iron-gall ink are certainly in some cases and are probably in all cases Boswell's own; those in black paint and in carbon ink were pretty clearly made in 1927–28. I do not feel able on the basis of my present knowledge to say whether the others were made in 1911 or 1927. They perhaps more probably were made at both times. The blue-black ink employed was traditional at Malahide.

The precise apportionment of the blottings is not in any case a matter of much concern to any one, but assignment of the responsibility for the removal of leaves is. Lady Talbot in 1951 stated publicly that her censorship in no case went beyond blotting: that she never destroyed and never removed any portion of any manuscript physically. The Murray typescript, as I have indicated above, generally supports her disclaimer. She later in private correspondence pleaded *nolo contendere* as regards a single instance which we must now examine.

Colonel Isham, immediately after he left Malahide in the summer of 1927, reported that he had seen Lady Talbot burn in the grate the six leaves or so from Boswell's journal-notes of 12 January to 23 February 1766 in which Boswell had recorded his intrigue with Thérèse Le Vasseur, during their trip from Paris to London. According to the story as I have heard Isham tell it, he and Lady Talbot had worked late one night on the papers, and when they broke off, Lady Talbot gave him the notes with a suggestion that he read them in his room and see what they contained. When he came down the next morning, highly elated, and showed her the passage, she remarked, "We can't have that sort of thing, can we?" and thrust the offending leaves into the fire burning in a grate. He protested vigorously, but did not dare restrain her physically. From the first Isham gave a circumstantial account of what was in the missing leaves, and there is among the Boswell papers at Yale a pencilled memorandum by Geoffrey Scott recording this account as Scott heard it from Isham. The memorandum is not dated, but Isham told me that Scott wrote it in London, at the very beginning of their acquaintance, urging the importance of getting it into writing while Isham's recollection was fresh. That the memorandum was indeed early is to some extent proved by the fact that the watermark of the paper on which it is written (an ordinary 8½ by 11 inch sheet of typewriter paper) does not match that of the paper that Scott used at Glen Head in 1927 and 1928. In 1930, when the journal-notes in question were published for the first time (*Private Papers of James Boswell*, vii. 65–66), I printed a version of Scott's memorandum as revised and augmented at that date by Isham, omitting or paraphrasing as somewhat too hardy for the time some of Scott's detail, including some words which Scott reported as *ipsissima verba* of Boswell's. In 1955, when that portion of the journal-notes was reprinted in the trade edition of Boswell's journal (*Boswell on the Grand Tour: Italy, Corsica, and France,* McGraw-Hill, pp. 277–78), Professor Frank Brady and I, so far as consistency permitted, merged Scott's memorandum with the version Isham and I had made in 1930 and a third version furnished by Isham over the telephone. A reading of the accounts in succession cannot fail to raise doubts as to the complete historicity of all three. One would not be disturbed by added detail so long as it filled out a previously fixed outline, but in this case the later versions make fundamental changes in the design. They are suspicious as much in what they omit from Scott's memorandum as in what they add to it. Isham actually had a remarkably accurate and retentive memory of texts that he had really read: in the lectures on Boswell he later gave, he used to repeat whole paragraphs from letters and journal without substituting a word of his own for Boswell's. A tendency in him to *renchérir* a story could not unfairly be taken as evidence that the story was a fiction to begin with. His later accounts omitted a vigorous indecent simile which he had reported to Scott as Boswell's own. It never sounded to me much like Boswell, and it did sound to me like Isham. He may have come to the same conclusion himself.

When one's suspicion has been aroused, one begins to question details that are indeed Boswellian but which seem wrong in the given situation. Scott's memorandum and Isham's final version represent Boswell as incapable when he was first admitted to Thérèse's bed. This would have been very Boswellian if the intrigue had been in the grand style of Girolama Piccolomini (*Boswell on the Grand Tour: Italy, Corsica, and France,* McGraw-Hill, p. 130) or even approaching the genteel of "Louisa" and Miss Temple (*Boswell's London Journal*, pp. 117, 273), but it does not seem likely that Boswell would have suffered any anxiety as to his sexual adequacy with a female like Thérèse, a plebeian, not much superior to a chambermaid. I also wonder whether if Isham had really read the missing leaves, he would not have remembered and mentioned matter to which I should have expected Boswell to have given prominent mention: namely, that he and Thérèse missed the boat, with a consequent wait of four or five days for the next one, and that this involuntary sojourn at Calais was extended two or three days more by a dreadful storm that strewed the Channel coasts with wrecks.

In the situation, Lady Talbot's burning of those six leaves would have been an act of pure caprice in a woman otherwise remarkably steady. I do not know that it has previously occurred to any one who has considered this matter that those journal-notes should not at that date have been matter of treaty between her and Isham at all. Their task was to agree on a price for the letters and miscellaneous papers: the journals were specifically excluded, indeed excluded with no promise that they would be offered for sale. It is true that several loose leaves of journal-notes had strayed into the bundle of miscellaneous papers under Lady Talbot's generous classification of "oddments", but the journal-notes we are talking about were a sizable collection of nearly forty octavo leaves, most of them with writing on both sides, done up in a wrapper endorsed by Boswell, "Mem. From Paris and so forth. Some of Dr. Johnson after my return from abroad in 1766". All Lady Talbot would have needed to do in the situation Isham describes was to lay the packet to one side and say, "Those leaves are journal, and will have to wait till I have time to read and expurgate them." Instead of destroying whole leaves, she could then merely have inked out the offending passages, as she did with other journal-notes that contained indelicate matter. Isham had promised to respect her deletions, so why should she have been more drastic in this case than in others? Does it not seem more likely that Isham somehow persuaded Lord Talbot to make an exception for these notes, as he did for the Ashbourne Journal? May Lord and Lady Talbot not have allowed him to take them with him because he assured them that they *had already* been savagely expurgated? The only exceptionable passages now surviving in them are the crucial sentence with which 12 February begins, "Yesterday morning had gone to bed very early, and had done it once 13 in all" and references, in the entries for 25, 26, and 27 January, to Boswell's going to brothels in Paris, all brief, cryptic, and containing no indelicate language except the one word *bordelles*. Lady Talbot might well have let these bits stand if they had been shown to her.

Lady Talbot, as I have said, made a public statement in 1951, denying firmly and without qualification that she had ever burned or otherwise destroyed any papers of Boswell's. In private communications, however, she showed an unwillingess flatly and specifically to contradict Isham in this particular case. She said she could not remember any such happening, but she granted that she had got very tired before the three-day assessment of the manuscripts was over. She repeated emphatically, however, her certainty that during the later period when she was preparing the journals for transfer to Isham, she destroyed nothing, but limited her interferences to pen and ink. I became convinced that she did not burn the leaves as Isham said she did, and with that conviction lost faith in all Isham's accounts. If she did not burn or at least confiscate the leaves, what reason is there to suppose that Isham ever saw any such leaves at all? Should we not regretfully dismiss all the versions as "brilliant historical fiction by a highly imaginative man who knew Boswell's journal forward and backward"?

That was my verdict in *James Boswell, the Earlier Years*, and I adhere to the general judgement that Isham never had sight of the missing leaves and made up the details of all the versions by analogy with genuine incidents in Boswell's existing journal. But it was surely simplistic and careless of me to write then as though Isham knew Boswell's journal equally well at all periods of the present story. When he went to Malahide in August 1927, he did not know Boswell's private journal at all. Nobody did. In 1930 he knew a great part of Boswell's journal, but not the London Journal of 1762–63, which is of great importance for the present inquiry. In 1955 he probably did know Boswell's journal with the degree of familiarity I mean to suggest by the phrase "forward and backward". A real problem in this view is presented by Scott's memorandum. Where could Isham in August 1927 have found his analogy and warrant for depicting Boswell as embarrassingly liable to fall impotent at assignations expressly granted for the consummation of passion he had represented as uncommonly ardent? This is now a well-established quirk of his sexual constitution, but no evidence for it had been published by August 1927. Boswell recorded the evidence fully in his London Journal of 1762–63; he recorded it briefly but quite explicitly in his Italian journal-notes of 1765 (10 September). In 1927 the London Journal of 1762–63 was lying lost and forgotten in Fettercairn House; Isham could not possibly have seen it. The Italian notes were in Isham's possession by January or February of 1928, and if Scott's memorandum could be dated so late as that, the question as to where Isham found his analogy and warrant would be satisfactorily answered. But the evidence of the watermark of the paper on which the memorandum is written is against it; besides, how could Isham have explained to Scott why he had not told him sooner about so important a matter? The Italian journal-notes were of course at Malahide in August 1927, and if we could assume that Isham was given a chance to glance through them as he was to glance through the "Mems. From Paris and so forth", we should again have an answer. But in those three crowded days, would he have had time to scan over one hundred and sixty octavo pages of difficult manuscript? Perhaps he would not have needed to read it all; he might have turned up the crucial page quickly by random sampling. On the whole, in spite of the extreme improbability of this assumption, I am inclined to think that something like this was what really happened. Failing that I can only credit Isham with a truly inspired guess.

Scott not only worked but lived in Isham's home for more than a year—from November of 1927 to January of 1929. He and Isham were congenial companions: they liked each other, and they both liked to talk late into the night over new things turning up in the papers and the progress of the work. The selectivity and elegance of the first six volumes of the *Private Papers* reflect Scott's taste, but I am sure that Isham was consulted at every point, and that all the basic policies of the edition received his informed approval.

At the very outset he and Scott felt they had to make a far-reaching decision that raised an uncomfortable question of good faith. The manuscripts came to them heavily censored, with many leaves altogether missing and many passages scored out with ink. They could do nothing at all about the missing leaves except to report and bewail irreparable loss. But they found (I fancy with some surprise) that they could with little difficulty read a good many of the scored-out passages through the deleting strokes, and so could judge for themselves the nature and gravity of the alleged improprieties. It soon became evident that the censorship followed mood as much as system, the same sort of thing was struck out in one place and spared in another. It also betrayed a lack of historical and literary sophistication: passages which Boswell himself had printed in the *Life of Johnson* were bowdlerized, scandal about the Earl of Pembroke that had been common knowledge in the eighteenth century was excised. Mentions of movement of the bowels and of wayward coition were rated equally indecent. Most disconcerting of all was to find completely innocent and decent drawing-room language (e.g., "[We] brought free will on the carpet") struck out on the suspicion that it carried an indelicate meaning. The censor only too clearly had been rushed and was tired and suffering from eye-strain; she had skimmed over the tops of the words, not really read them. Scott, with Isham's approval, made up his mind to puzzle out all the deletions he could, and to follow such standards of decorum as scholars of that day would normally employ in publishing old papers of historical importance.

Some of the blottings could be freed of the deleting strokes. Paint, which had been used on some occasions, could be safely removed with turpentine. Ordinary writing fluid, extensively used in blotting the Murray transcript, could be bleached in the typescript, giving trustworthy readings or at the very least readings that helped to recover trustworthy readings from the manuscripts. (For that matter, as has been said above, blotted typescript can usually be read without difficulty from the back side without removing the deleting ink.) But for much of the journal-notes there had never been any transcript, the great bulk of the blotting had been made with carbon ink, and there appears to be no completely safe way to remove carbon ink from paper. No chemical will bleach it. Since it consists merely of carbon particles floated in a gummy vehicle, does not penetrate the fibres of the paper deeply, and undergoes no chemical change in the paper, it should be possible to remove it by using some liquid that will soften the vehicle. Draughtsmen do remove it in this way from their drawings, but this requires rubbing with balls of cotton to get the carbon particles off the surface, and old paper will not stand up to such treatment. (Draughtsman's "paper" is really a kind of a cloth.) Furthermore, since carbon black is even more absorptive of infra-red and ultra-violet rays than it is of visible light, special kinds of photography are worse than useless. The vast majority of the blotted passages were read by patient and persistent poring over them with no other aids than good light, some kind of smooth-pointed instrument to trace the shapes of letters with, and a magnifying glass. Scott, who was decidedly short-sighted, was very good at this, as was also Miss Helen Cohan, the second of Scott's secretaries.

Scott did, in fact, follow a policy of moderate expurgation, something like that adopted by H. B. Wheatley in his edition of Pepys's *Diary*. Scott's standards for excluding matter (he suppressed only a few passages) strike me as being aesthetic rather than protective. He was not bothered by the record of any kind of human behaviour so long as it was couched in decent public speech, but he disliked coarseness and bluntness.

We have now arrived at the early winter of 1928. Scott had all the manuscripts of Isham's Malahide purchases of 1926 and 1927 under his hands and could work at them in the intense way that suited him best. Isham has left a charming picture of him during this year:

> His usual method was to write or dictate during the day, which began for him at about ten o'clock. When the secretaries had gone he would write on until the last moment before dinner. If it was a family dinner the work would be discussed and he would tell us eagerly of progress and discoveries. After dinner we customarily went straight to the library, from which Boswell seldom let us emerge before morning hours.

In spite of Isham's unremitting financial worries, one would guess that 1928 was the happiest year of his life. He was constitutionally a night-hawk who seldom went to bed before four in the morning or rose before noon. To see the stately volumes of his *Private Papers* taking shape under Scott's hands, to join eagerly in discussing Scott's most recent problems with the text, to have under his roof a congenial guest whose favourite game was poker, should have been for him almost the definition of felicity. They often sat at poker as long as at Boswell proofs.

But the financial worries must not be forgotten or minimized. Isham had borrowed the entire sum needed for the purchase of the journals and had been able to pay little of the money back. Sales of manuscripts to Rosenbach had been going on at intervals since the previous autumn: two leaves of the manuscript of the *Life of Johnson*, 3 November 1927 ($3,600); one leaf of the same, 20 January 1928 ($1,800); two more leaves, 8 June 1928 ($3,600). In the last-named month the collection suffered a shocking accidental loss. Isham had sent Arthur Swann, rare-book dealer in New York, for sale if Swann made an acceptable offer, some thirty or forty letters from James Bruce to Boswell with Boswell's minute of his reply entered on each. (Bruce was overseer at Auchinleck under both Boswell's father and Boswell himself. From his early years Boswell carried on a confidential correspondence with him.) On 27 June 1928 Swann wrote that he had bad news to report. He had given the manuscripts to his secretary to transcribe; she had put them, with other important papers, in a double-deck wire basket, and had left the basket on the floor beside her desk when she went home for the day. The cleaning woman had thrown the basket, papers and all, into the waste; the night-watchman had retrieved the basket but without its contents. It was assumed that the letters were all destroyed. Scott had as yet caused no copies to be made; indeed, nobody seems to have made a record of just how many letters there were in the bundle. Isham presumably received a fair value from Swann's insurance, but the texts were lost for ever.

At the end of 1928 or early in 1929 volumes 1, 3, and 4 of the *Private Papers* (*Early Papers, Journal of a Tour through the Courts of Germany, Boswell with Rousseau and Voltaire*) were sent to the subscribers and received glowing reviews. At the end of December 1928 or beginning of January 1929 Scott moved out of Isham's home at Glen Head, Long Island, where he had then lived more than a year, and took up residence with Dr. and Mrs. James B. Murphy, 603 Park Avenue, New York City. Dr. Murphy, a distinguished scientist, was engaged in medical research at the Rockefeller Institute; Mrs. Murphy was deeply interested in contemporary writing and disposed to be useful to living authors. Neither of the Murphys had known Scott before the end of 1928. Mrs. Murphy then met him at a Christmas party given by Mrs. Reginald De Koven, a *grande dame* of the period who conducted a *salon* and aspired to know every one of note. Mrs. Murphy found Scott one of the best conversationalists she had ever met. She told him how much she had enjoyed *The Architecture of Humanism* and *The Portrait of Zélide,* and Scott—at this first meeting—confided to her that he was miserable living with Isham, whereupon she suggested that he use the guest suite on the fourth floor of her home, which was at his service if he cared to come to live and work there. The very next morning Scott turned up on her doorstep with all his luggage. Scott, however, could not keep many manuscripts at a time in his quarters in New York, and had to make frequent trips to Glen Head by train. The commuting has been blamed for the loss of eighteen manuscript letters to Boswell from Margaret Montgomerie, Boswell's wife after 25 November 1769. The manuscripts disappeared while Scott was working on them, and Isham thought he may have left them in a folder on the luggage-rack of a Long Island train. Scott hardly deserved to be called careless, but he was certainly absent-minded, and there was always rush and confusion in changing trains at Jamaica. In this case, fortunately, the letters had all been typed and the transcripts had been verified by reading them against the manuscripts, so that there was no loss of text.

Scott's long sojourn in Isham's home as a member of the family had understandably been a burden on Mrs. Isham. She said later that she never saw her husband except at meals, and that the presence of an editorial office in the house kept the telephone ringing all the time. My too-brief sketch of Scott's character makes him seem like a real-life paradigm of the man who came to dinner. Indeed he was, provided it is understood that the affluent friends who played host to him all thought they were making a good bargain when they exchanged free living quarters for his company. His protracted residence with Isham, however, was by no means a simple case of that kind of symbiosis.

I enter now upon an important aspect of Scott's relationship with Isham for which there are very few documents and I have to draw heavily on my own memory of conversations which took place fifty years ago. My most important source of information was Arthur Mallet, Scott's friend in New York, who was a just and careful man but no doubt spoke *ex parte.* I have tried to take this bias into account

in adjusting what he told me to my personal knowledge of Isham's character and
to the whole story of the Boswell papers.

Isham (in a vigorous metaphor which would have amused Scott, though Scott
would probably not have used it himself) always declared that when he first made
Scott's acquaintance, Scott was absolutely destitute. This was surely an exaggeration.
Scott had invested funds that he valued at £3,500 to £4,000, and in the autumn
of 1927 should have been receiving some royalties from *The Portrait of Zélide*, which
had appeared in 1925. But unless he drew on principal, he was by his own standards
embarrassingly hard up, and admitted as much by accepting free lodgings from his
friend Haslam. Isham's proposal that he edit the Boswell papers must have come
to him as a godsend. It would furnish him with interesting and most congenial
work quite worthy of his powers at (as he supposed) a contracted salary not only
sufficient to support him comfortably but also to enable him to save something.
Moreover, it would assure him access to the prime materials for his projected
biography of Boswell, a book from which he had every reason to expect large returns.
As I have said above, I infer that Isham got his consent to serve as editor without
any formal or even specific agreement as to what his salary would be, persuading
Scott of his bona fides by advancing money for his passage to America. From Isham's
style of living, Scott, I fancy, assumed that Isham was much richer than he actually
was, a generous, very rich man whose assurance it would be small-minded to ask
guarantees for. When Scott arrived in America, Isham, I think, continued to defer
executing the contract, meantime putting Scott up in his own home and providing
him with pocket-money by occasional hand-outs of cash. Scott settled into his
routine at Glen Head partly because Isham did not give him money enough to live
in such style anywhere else. The situation in many ways suited him perfectly. He
disliked the United States and had no wish to travel or to meet many people there.
To be able to concentrate furiously on congenial work, finish the job, and go back
home, was just what he would have chosen to do. Living in Isham's home was
convenient and very comfortable. He was not lonesome, or as Nigel Nicolson
concluded, "loveless", having with his usual flair soon formed an amorous intimacy
with a gifted woman who shared many of his tastes and was happy to invite him
to spend his week-ends with her. But of course he wanted more than present
amenity. He wanted to live comfortably while he edited Isham's Boswell papers,
but he wanted also to leave Isham's employ with a sum of money large enough to
support him comfortably while he wrote his own life of Boswell. If the cash was
forthcoming when he needed it, he was quite willing that it should accumulate in
Isham's hands. But when (again this is inference) he finally got anxious and pressed
Isham, Isham declined to give him a contract for anything like as much money as
he had counted on, perhaps declined to give him any contract at all. Isham had all
his life been a tough business man who regarded a business contract as something
one did not hesitate to break if one thought it would be more advantageous to settle
a suit than to honour the terms of the contract. In dealing with individuals who

performed some kind of non-menial professional service for him, he had many of the characteristics of a feudal baron: he enjoyed bestowing largess and did it rather generously, but he chafed at being bound by contract to pay a fixed salary for such services. I fancy he reminded Scott of the low state of his finances when he offered him the editorship: told him he would get fame from the *Private Papers* and both fame and fortune from his life of Boswell, which would be mainly based on Isham's papers. Why should he expect more than to be kept free while he did the editing? Isham would have said that kind of thing quite sincerely. He was through and through a speculator, an adventurer, who scorned security and braved enormous risks, and he would not have thought it unreasonable to demand that Scott take risks too. I got the impression that Scott never allowed the controversy to develop into overt hostility: he was a seasoned poker player like Isham. But in the spring of 1929, when the reviews of volumes 1, 3, and 4 of *Private Papers* were still fresh, he signed a contract for his biography of Boswell with Harcourt, Brace, and Co., and Harcourt, Brace, and Co. entered into treaty with the Curtis Publishing Co. for the serial rights of the biography at an asking price of $30,000, though not a word of it had yet been written. With this contract Scott could have secured so much of an advance from Harcourt, Brace as would have made him independent of Isham. He then calmly issued an ultimatum: if Isham did not give him a satisfactory contract, he would resign as editor of *Private Papers* and go back to England. Isham capitulated and on 20 May 1929 the contract was signed. Scott was to receive from that date a total remuneration of $75,000 plus half the royalties of his life of Boswell; if he was called on also to edit any public or trade edition of the papers, he would receive an additional sum, that sum to be covered by another contract. Isham was to receive the other half of the royalties of the life of Boswell. If Scott should die before publishing the biography, his estate was to be paid $25,000. (My guess is that Scott stipulated a salary of $16,000 a year for five years from the time he began work, and reckoned $5,000 as the value of what he had already received in lodging, sustenance, and cash. At that rate Isham's support so far would have averaged something like $275 a month or $3,300 a year.)

I have heard Isham say with considerable bitterness that "Scott held me up", but it did not appear to me that whatever hard feelings he retained were more than occasional and momentary. When Scott soon after sailed for England, Isham sent two detective stories to the boat for him to read, and Scott sent back cordial and intimate letters of news and humorous chat. I feel sure that Isham held Scott in affectionate remembrance. After all, the contract that Scott exerted pressure to obtain was as favourable to Isham as it was to himself. If Scott had lived, he would in effect have earned at least half of his own salary, leaving Isham not more than $8,000 a year to pay out of his own funds.

Contract signed and the editorial work on volumes 2, 5, and 6 completed, Scott sailed to England for a two-months' holiday, the first he had taken since he began working for Isham. Even so, he mixed business with relaxation by excursions to Auchinleck and Crawley Grange. He came back on the *Adriatic,* accompanied by his friend and former partner, Cecil Pinsent. He landed on 4 August, in good health and spirits, so far as any one has reported, and on 7 August had lunch (probably a business lunch) with Rudge at the Biltmore. After lunch he complained of a chill. He must have grown worse very rapidly, for on the following day he was entered in the Rockefeller Hospital, his illness diagnosed as bronchial pneumonia. He died there on the morning of the 14th. A commemorative article by Isham appeared in the *Saturday Review of Literature* on the same page as a review by me of volume 6 of *Private Papers.* Pinsent carried his ashes back to England, where they were deposited in the cloisters of New College, Oxford. The memorial plaque reads simply "Geoffrey Scott, 1884–1929, Architect and Humanist".

The total period of Scott's connexion with the Boswell papers was less than two years, but no name in the history of Boswell studies will ever shine more brightly than his. Though he was not a scholar by profession and always depreciated his accomplishments in research, he set and achieved high standards of accuracy for his text. He was particularly skilful in recovering deleted passages. On the critical side, he stands without peer. His introductions are the most brilliant of all writings on Boswell, and his study, *The Making of the "Life of Johnson"* (volume 6 of *Private Papers*), handles in a revolutionary and definitive manner the fundamental problems of Boswell's powers of recollection and the relations which his journal-notes and journal bear to the great biography. Scott's deductions in this quarter are the more brilliant because his evidence in one crucial area—the manuscript of the *Life of Johnson,* of which only sixteen leaves were then known to exist— was very scanty and not wholly representative. His premature death deprived the world of one of the great literary biographies of all time.

The author of this history was immediately selected by Isham to pick up where Scott had left off. I was at the time just thirty-two years old, son of a Maine farmer, A.B. of Colby College and Ph.D. of Yale; had served as enlisted man with the rating of surgical assistant in an evacuation hospital, A.E.F. (France and Germany), 1918–19, and at the time was teaching English at Yale with the rank of assistant professor. I had that spring published at the Clarendon Press *The Literary Career of James Boswell,* a bio-bibliographical study of all Boswell's publications, a radical reworking of my doctoral dissertation which had won the John Addison Porter prize at Yale in 1925. My favourite field of literary study was the English romantics, but I had taken an eighteenth-century topic in order to have Tinker as my supervisor. A history by me of my army unit was about to be serialized in *Outlook,* and was published that autumn as *Stretchers* (Yale University Press).

Though I never met Scott, we had been in correspondence for several months before his death. As far back as September 1926 (that is, at a time when Isham possessed none of the Malahide papers except the Goldsmith letter), I had got in touch with Isham on Tinker's introduction, and had consulted him on various bibliographical problems which his fine collection of Boswell's works held promise of resolving. Isham was generous and communicative, as always in such matters, and when Scott arrived at Glen Head, Scott joined in the correspondence. I sent them all my proofs, receiving many useful additions and corrections. Scott's manuscript minutes of the journals were extremely useful to me in collecting the scattered evidence the journal provides as to Boswell's authorship of various anonyms. Scott did not report this matter to me systematically, I think, but he collected it, and Isham showed it to me during a visit I made to Glen Head when Scott was unfortunately absent. After Scott's death, an unposted letter to me was found in the pocket of a suit he had been wearing at the time he fell ill. It was written to tell me that during his vacation in Britain he had read my *Literary Career of James Boswell* which he had formerly only consulted piecemeal in proofs, and was gratifyingly complimentary: "I cannot refrain from writing to express my profound admiration—amazement, rather—at the total achievement, which sets an altogether new standard in a field of scholarship already exacting enough. No one is better able, perhaps, than I to appreciate one particular aspect of the miracle—namely, your faculty of forestalling evidence." I have already mentioned Isham's tendency to attribute his important decisions to providential leadings. In a printed Announcement informing his subscribers of his choice of an editor to succeed Scott, he said that in his "perplexity and distraction, this letter seemed to be nothing less than a message of guidance".

As soon as word got about that Isham was in treaty with me, my friend W. S. Lewis passed on to me a message he had received from friends in New York: that before committing myself I should consult Scott's friend Arthur Mallet. I came down from Maine on the State of Maine Express (Yale's summer vacation had some weeks yet to run), arriving in New York at something like seven o'clock in the morning. To my great surprise and gratification, Rudge met me at the train and took me to breakfast at the Biltmore. His transparent friendliness and honesty were wonderfully encouraging. I managed to see Mallet and (then or later) Scott's lawyer (Melville Cane) and his publisher (Alfred Harcourt), and was given a full and I think not unfair account of Scott's difficulties in securing a firm agreement as to the remuneration he was to receive. To me a firm contract and a regular monthly salary were absolutely necessary. A young self-made man at the beginning of a professional career, I had no inherited wealth and very little in the way of savings. My wife, a professional librarian, had a position in the Yale Law Library, but would lose it if we moved to Long Island. I would have expenses of moving, and a good deal to pay for travel, for it was too late to negotiate a full leave of absence from Yale for 1929–30, so that for that year I would have to spend half of each week in New Haven. I engaged Cane to negotiate and draw a contract for me, and I think it may have been he who suggested that Rudge pay my salary, of course charging it to Isham. Rudge was quite willing to assume this responsibility. Isham showed some of the irritation at being bound that I had been warned to expect, but his counter-proposals during the negotiations were reasonable and the terms of salary which he offered seemed to me generous. He made no objection at all to having Rudge made my paymaster—in fact, he seemed to like it.

I agreed to edit the twelve remaining volumes of *Private Papers* and some kind of trade edition, not yet defined (more of this later). My total remuneration was to be $18,000, all of which should be considered earned by 1 October 1931. During Yale's academic year 1929–30 I was to divide my time between teaching at Yale and Isham's Boswell editions; after that I was to give full time to Isham. From 1 October 1929 to 1 October 1930, Isham was to pay me $5,000 (Yale paid me $2,500); from 1 October 1930 to 1 October 1931 Isham was to pay me $8,000 (Yale paid me nothing). The remaining $5,000 was to be considered earned and claimable on 1 October 1931. Until October 1933 I was to be allowed exclusive use of the papers for writing a short trade biography of Boswell for Harcourt, Brace, and Co.; after that I was to have non-exclusive right to prepare a scholarly annotated edition of Boswell's journal and a multiple-volume biography.

My wife and I took an apartment in Glen Cove, Long Island, about two miles from Isham's home, and my wife's godmother gave us our first automobile, a Model A Ford. I secured a room for myself in a boarding-house in New Haven. I taught at Yale on Mondays, Tuesdays, and Wednesdays, going by train to Glen Cove Wednesday evenings. I worked on the papers in Isham's home at Glen Head on Thursdays, Fridays, and Saturdays, returning to New Haven on Sunday evenings. It was a crowded, exciting, and very happy period in my life.

THE CROQUET-BOX

WHEN I TOOK OVER THE EDITORSHIP, the papers were uncatalogued, not even filed in order, and some of the most difficult portions of the journal-notes had not yet been transcribed. I had had no opportunity to make an informed estimate of the amount of material remaining to be published. And the work of publication began to expand from the very outset. As soon as I got into the manuscripts, I found myself questioning the austerity of Scott's editorial policy. He had printed one page of the Italian memoranda-notes for dates (13–14 May 1765) for which no journal had ever been written, and in volume 6 (*The Making of the "Life of Johnson"*), where his purpose was to show the development of the conversations in the *Life* from notes to fully expanded speech, he had printed a sizeable specimen of the journal-notes for 1773 and quite brief ones for days in 1768, 1775, 1776, 1781, and 1784. Otherwise he had excluded Boswell's abundant memoranda and journal-notes from *Private Papers*. This of course suited the elegance which gave his work such distinction, but in my practice it seemed over-fastidious. Some parts of the memoranda and journal-notes, for all their being abbreviated, elliptical, and obscure, were still more personally revealing than some parts of the fully written journal. It seemed to me that we had been entrusted with a great multifarious human document which was misrepresented by anything less than full publication. I also felt unhappy about Scott's policy of occasional (sometimes silent) suppression of gross passages, and wished to print the documents henceforth with no expurgation at all. What can or cannot be printed at any given time is much more a matter of taste than of morals, and taste in this matter is determined by the reigning mode in contemporary literature. Though in 1929 popular taste had by no means become so liberal as it is now, *Ulysses* and *Lady Chatterley's Lover* had both appeared, and the direction things were going to take was clear enough. Sir John Murray was right in thinking that there are only two defensible choices to make with regard to Boswell's journal: not to print it at all or to print it as he wrote it. Bowdlerization vitiates its artistic integrity, as one can easily prove to one's self by reading the savagely mutilated London Journal of 1768 after the unmutilated London Journal of 1762–63. It also vitiates the integrity and usefulness of the journal and journal-notes as historical and autobiographical documents. Some of the blotted passages, when puzzled out, prove merely to contain gross *words*, not a record of gross behaviour by anyone; some show Boswell *resisting* temptation. Others, which do record gross behaviour on his part, often contain innocent and important information intertwined with their indelicacies.

On both points Isham told me that for some time he had felt just as I did, and he gave me his permission both to enlarge the text by including the journal-notes from the point where I took over, and to print everything I (with all the help I could get) could read in the inked-over passages.

In agreeing to a considerable enlargement of the text of *Private Papers* Isham again demonstrated his intrepidity. Scott's six volumes had brought him no profit. (I shall return to this point later.) His contract with Scott required him to pay Scott's estate $25,000 in case of an eventuality which had occurred. Scott had died intestate and his elder sister Dorothy became administratrix. I do not know just when she presented her claim, but it makes little difference: Isham knew from the day of Scott's death that it would be forthcoming. He characteristically resisted it, maintaining that the contract was invalid but probably hoping for no more than delay and a composition. He kept the claim hanging for nearly two years but finally settled for little less than the stipulated sum. At the end of 1929 his debt to Van Alen, including interest, amounted to $122,836. Van Alen, presumably to prevent the frittering away of the collection piece by piece, in effect became joint owner of the manuscripts. Isham was allowed full control over publication, and if the collection was sold, all expenses, including costs of editing and publishing, were to be paid before Van Alen received any part of his investment. From the date of this most generous arrangement (1 January 1930) Isham made no more sales of manuscripts from the collection as it then stood.

At just the time I went to work on the papers, Lady Talbot, who had learned that Scott had recovered and printed matter which she had struck out, sent Isham a letter charging him with breach of faith. It was an extremely difficult letter to answer: Isham consulted me and took his time in drafting a reply. He had certainly at various times encouraged Lady Talbot to believe that he would respect her censorship. On 5 July 1926 he had written to her saying that he sympathized with her desire to suppress certain passages in the journals and that if Lord Talbot would sell him the papers, he would sign a formal agreement not to print anything which did not meet her approval, under penalty of having to return all the papers and forfeit the purchase money if he broke his word. But as his offer to purchase the journal (and it was only the journal that was censored) was at that time firmly declined, it would appear that this promise lapsed, and could have been put in force later only if he offered it again or implied it in some other promise or act. The tone of his correspondence did imply it. Lady Talbot's letters, written while she was censoring the journals, take for granted that he will not only accept her censorship but will also cooperate with her in making it more systematic. And Isham, though deprecating extensive blotting and any mutilation whatever of the manuscripts, in at least one letter of that period did express approval in principle of a policy of censorship: "I do not, of course, have in mind such things as from sheer grossness should very properly be struck out. In this I am of one mind with you." The formal bill of sale made no mention whatever of censorship and contained no penalty clause, and the determined character of Lady Talbot's deletions surely indicated less than perfect trust in Isham's professions. Yet to argue that he stood completely free of commitment in the matter would be sophistical. Assurances he did give, both direct and by implication, which though probably not legally enforceable, certainly constituted a bond in good faith.

When Isham did write, he wisely made no attempt to disown or to explain away his assurances, but simply attributed Scott's action to his and Scott's having found on a fair trial that the deletions were unworkable. I have given his reasons above in a passage which in fact summarizes the letter we are now discussing.[1] As David Buchanan says, Isham's action, so far as the Talbots were concerned, was indefensible, but he had the choice of either breaking his (at least implied) word or sanctioning a publication that he and Scott knew responsible critics would denounce as fundamentally vitiated. "For Isham there was only one possible decision."

> As we were dealing with MSS. of great age and of the utmost historic and literary importance, both Mr. Scott and I felt very strongly that our duty was not one that would admit of a *general* suppression of such words and passages as we found deleted. We believed that such a frequent recurrence of omissions as would be entailed by following this course, could only deceive the reader into unfortunate surmises regarding Boswell and his circle, for of course it is incumbent upon an editor to indicate by suitable printer's marks wherever any word in the MSS. has been omitted in type. We therefore, after consulting many of the foremost scholars of England and this country—and on their urgent advice—adopted the procedure of either printing or not printing the censored portions, wherever we could decipher them, according to the standards usually followed in a scholarly publication of historic MSS.

Lady Talbot in due time made dignified remonstrance. She and Lord Talbot were naturally displeased, but they did not propose to let the offence cause a breach. On the contrary, the main object of her writing when she did write was to report a piece of news that would have been most damaging to Isham's interest if they had ignored him and announced it elsewhere. An overlooked box which had once held

---

[1] Page 101.

the four balls and clips of a croquet set, stored at Malahide years before in a cupboard that was not thought to contain any papers, had just turned out when opened to be three-fourths full of a confused mass of papers from Boswell's archives. They were wrapped in newspapers of the year 1907 and were generally in very bad condition, having rotted after long exposure to damp. Lady Talbot thought her father-in-law had probably put them there to dry out, the cupboard being near a fireplace. On first view the papers seemed to Lady Talbot of secondary value, and she thought Lord Talbot would sell them for a nominal sum; but the valuation would have to wait on sorting. Isham replied at once that of course he was interested, but that he was short of funds and that he might not be able to raise the sum the Talbots might require. Experience by this time would have warned him to assume that a mass of Boswell manuscripts of the size reported would contain some items of great value. In any case, because of *Private Papers* he could not afford to have it known that a considerable quantity of "new" Boswell papers had been discovered and had not passed into his collection. It was probably at this time that he began saying that he was a man who had caught a bear by the tail—he could not let go. On 16 June 1930, he sold at auction at Sotheby's in London a magnificent collection (eight-five lots) of rare books, mainly by or relating to Goldsmith. He may have ordered this sale on getting Lady Talbot's letter, so as to provide funds against her forthcoming appraisal, but it is perhaps more likely that the sale had already been arranged, and was occasioned by the shortness of funds he reported to Lady Talbot. David Buchanan tells me that he thinks the sale was probably forced by the need to raise funds to settle with Scott's estate.

After the sale was arranged but before it was actually held, he got a measure of relief from another quarter. Since the *Private Papers* were limited to 570 sets and were sold only by subscription at a total price of $900, few readers other than collectors and scholars have ever seen that work. Isham from the first had planned a trade edition of some sort, partly to give Boswell's journal wider circulation, but also partly to recover some of the money he had sunk in the manuscripts. On first acquiring the papers in 1927, he had joined in inconclusive negotiations concerning such an edition with Doubleday, Page, and Co. Nelson Doubleday had procured for him from the New York *Herald Tribune* an attractive offer for world-wide newspaper serialization ($10,000 plus fifty per cent of syndicate profits), but Isham had to decline this because it stipulated that all book publication should be held up until fifty-two weekly newspaper extracts had appeared. Isham also discussed with Doubleday, Page the publishing of a trade edition in three volumes after the completion of *Private Papers*, but this also failed to materialize. When I first came on the scene in the autumn of 1929, he was engaged in equally inconclusive negotiations with Simon and Schuster, who talked only of a single volume of brilliant extracts from the journal, with a small amount of annotation. It was the latter concept that governed everybody's thinking at the time my contract was drawn. But when on 1 May 1930 Isham finally did succeed in negotiating a contract, it was with the Viking Press; and the Viking Press stipulated that the trade edition should consist of all of Boswell's fully written journals, connected by editorial links, annotated, and furnished with an index. It was agreed by Isham that I should deliver complete finished copy for this trade edition by the spring of 1934.

I was not present at the discussions that ended in this contract and in fact knew nothing of its terms until after the document had been signed. I then told Isham that though the editorial work on the trade edition had now been made many times more onerous than I had been given to understand when I signed my contract with him, I was quite willing to do it with no increase in my contracted remuneration, but that I could not do it in anything like the time specified. I was under obligation to return to full-time teaching at Yale in the autumn of 1931, and thereafter could expect little time for my own publication except in the summer months. Isham assured me that nobody expected the impossible, and that no doubt reasonable adjustments would be made.

On the strength of its contract, the Viking Press made Isham an advance of $7,500, as did also William Heinemann, Ltd., which had acquired the British rights to the trade edition. Isham's sale, as has already been mentioned, occurred on 16–19 June 1930, and brought him in about $11,500 more.

Lady Talbot progressively revealed the contents of the croquet-box in letters dated 26 May, 14 June, and 27 July. Most of the items turned out indeed to be minor—a dozen stretches of journal-notes, a handful of letters by Boswell (mostly drafts and copies), a larger handful of letters to him—but the tattered mass of papers also contained three large manuscripts, two of them of the very first importance: Boswell's "Materials for Writing the Life of Lord Kames", 110 more leaves from the printer's copy of the *Life of Johnson*, and the journal of the Hebridean tour with Johnson in 1773. The last-named was in some respects a double prize, for it had also served as printer's copy, and preserved between the lines, on versos, and on interleavings, the revision by which Boswell and Edmond Malone had converted it into the book published in 1785. Lord Talbot sent Isham without charge all the stretches of journal-notes as part of his purchase of 1928, but ruled that the Hebridean manuscript was printer's copy, not journal, and asked £500 for it. Isham in a transatlantic telephone call tried to get Lady Talbot to include it among the items sent without charge, failed to persuade her, and acquiesced. If any price at all was to be put on the manuscript, £500 was a very low one (I should myself rate it the most important single recovery from Boswell's papers), and in any case Isham was not in a strong position to argue that a promise should be kept. Because Isham reported himself low in funds, Lady Talbot at first said that Lord Talbot would sell the leaves of the manuscript of the *Life of Johnson* at auction. When Isham begged to be allowed to treat for all the newly discovered papers, she set a price of £3,000 on that manuscript. When Isham said he thought it a hardship to have paid £450 for 16 leaves of the manuscript on the representation that that was all of it that had survived, she offered to buy his leaves back at the purchase

price, combine them with the 110 newly discovered leaves, and sell the whole at
auction. Finally, she priced at £500 all the remaining papers, bringing the total
for the contents of the croquet-box up to £4,000. Isham's acceptance would bring
to slightly less than £40,000 the total sum he had paid to Lord Talbot for his great-
great-grandfather's papers.

In the summer of 1930, volumes 7, 8, and 9 of *Private Papers* (the first volumes
appearing under my editorship) were sent to the subscribers. My volumes contained
on the average much more text than Scott's, but I was told by Rudge's foreman,
Melvin H. Loos, that they cost less to produce. Scott was as gifted in book design
as he was in critical prose, but he tended to earn his happy touches experimentally
by lavish reworking of matter already expensively set in type. Loos told me that
one of his volumes (I should have guessed volume 4 but I seem to remember volume
5) cost more to produce than the $50 the subscribers paid for it. I left design to
Rogers and imposed restraint on my itch to make radical changes after my copy
was once in type. There should have been profit for Isham from these volumes,
profit enough to give him substantial relief. Actually, as he insisted to Lady Talbot,
his financial situation and prospects were very bleak.

Private Papers had undoubtedly been planned with intention of profit. My guess
is that Isham hoped to recover by his publication the full sum (roughly $175,000)
that he had paid for the papers up to the time the set was launched. If 500 sets
had been subscribed by 1930 and if all 500 subscribers had promptly paid their
subscriptions for the half of the set so far issued, Isham could have paid all the costs
of production and distribution to date with a handsome surplus to apply to the cost
of the manuscripts. Unfortunately, the whole crucial business of getting a full
complement of dependable subscribers had been handled casually and unprofes-
sionally. Isham was extremely generous in making presents of the books, but the
total number of sets printed (570) made allowance for gifts and review-sets. More
dangerous was his practice of taking subscriptions himself at social parties from
friends who were not too clear as to what they were committing themselves to.
What was sinking the venture was that Isham was committed to produce 570 copies
of each volume while he was getting paid for not much over 200. On 12 September
1930 Rudge reported to him that the costs for the first nine volumes (all of Scott's
and three of mine) were $154,907.26 while the money received from subscribers
amounted only to $103,555.08.

Still, if the euphoria of 1927 could have continued for five or six years more,
Isham's audacious venture might still have paid off. *Private Papers of James Boswell*
may be taken as a perfect symbol of the ascendant self-confidence of the glittering
twenties. I suppose only readers of or approaching to my own age would feel the
irony implicit in my remark if I said that I signed my contract with Isham on 29
October 1929. On that day ("Black Tuesday") occurred the appalling crash in the
stock market that inaugurated the Great Depression. No one now living who was
not in 1930 an adult seriously enmeshed in the American economy can have any

sense of the shock, the incredulous hopelessness of those days. Of course on 29 October and for some time after we were confident that the Depression would soon be reversed. The fact was that from that day forward very few more people were going to subscribe to an eighteen-volume set of books costing $50 a volume, and many people who had subscribed were going to default. Rudge was going to be ruined. *Private Papers of James Boswell* could still be a surpassingly beautiful set of books, it could still be an admired interim work of scholarship and of criticism, but it was not going to bring Isham the large return in cash he needed to clear himself of debt.

He finally got by private agreement from Harold Guinzburg of the Viking Press the full sum of money he needed to purchase the entire lot of croquet-box papers. Guinzburg advanced $20,000 specifically for that purpose. The 110 pages of the manuscript of the *Life* were to be ostensibly Isham's property; they were to remain in Isham's collection and be used in *Private Papers* as Isham saw fit, but they were actually to belong to Guinzburg. Isham could include them, at a price of $50,000, in any sale of his entire collection of Boswell papers made to a public institution in two years' time. After two years, Guinzburg could sell them, but Isham had the right of purchase before any one else. If the leaves were sold, Guinzburg was to get back his $20,000, plus interest and expenses, plus half of whatever they fetched over $20,000. Guinzburg's rights to a trade edition of *Private Papers* were enlarged to allow him to publish a trade and a limited edition of the journal of the Hebridean tour from the manuscript.

Isham agreed to Lady Talbot's terms and sent the money. The croquet-box papers were delivered in August, September, and November 1930. Isham sent a printed circular letter to his subscribers announcing his acquisition of the new papers and his intention of including all of them of date later than the ninth volume (1774). "This has meant a virtual doubling of the size of the volumes as originally planned. Even so, it now appears that there will not be space in volume xviii to include the index. For this reason we announce an additional volume No. xix, which will go to subscribers without cost." The information as to the doubled thickness of the volumes was quite correct; the reason assigned showed perhaps too much of a wish to stimulate interest by emphasizing up-to-the-minute recoveries and to spare Scott an implied stricture. The croquet-box papers actually added little to the bulk of volumes x–xviii—perhaps a hundred pages distributed over nine volumes. The real reason for the greater thickness of the volumes was that I was printing all the journal-notes, as explained above. The promise of a full-volume index would have been magnificent in any circumstances.

Two more discouraging chapters remain to be added to this gloomy chronicle of Isham's finances in the second year of our association. At the end of 1930 he moved out of his house at Glen Head and took a suite in the Hotel Pierre, New York City; he sold the fine Long Island estate early in 1931. He told Newton that he paid $175,000 for the property, but he no doubt had a large mortgage on it.

Even this did not relieve him, for in February 1931 he got another advance of $20,000 from Van Alen, who offered to increase his already large investment in the Boswell papers by putting that sum into the new papers, exclusive of the leaves of the manuscript of the *Life of Johnson*. David Buchanan writes to me that he saw correspondence both in Isham's files and in those of Van Alen's lawyer indicating that this loan was "under continual consideration and review at least during the whole of the latter half of 1930". It looks as though Isham's original wish and endeavour was to get the money from Van Alen, but that Van Alen did not this time move so quickly as the circumstances required; that in order to send the money when Lady Talbot announced that it was due, Isham was forced to turn to Guinzburg and get it on terms which must have been very repugnant to him; that Van Alen belatedly acquiesced, and that Isham took his money for another purpose—perhaps to make up a payment towards the more than $50,000 that he owed to Rudge. It was no doubt generous of Van Alen to lend Isham any more money.

From the 18th of December 1930 to the 7th of February 1931 the entire collection was exhibited at the Grolier Club in New York. This was a very great honour for a collector, and Isham was determined to handle it magnificently. He asked me if I would be willing to prepare copy for a full descriptive catalogue of the collection, to be printed and presented gratis to all the members of the Club. The proposal to prepare such a book was attractive both to me and to my wife: it was in the line of her training and interest, and would be of the greatest use to me in editing the remainder of the papers. Indeed, by rights some such catalogue should have been compiled (though not necessarily printed) before any systematic publishing of the papers was undertaken. I told him that my wife and I would be glad to prepare such a catalogue without any addition to the remuneration received by my contract. I pointed out to him, however, that the task would take a good part of my best working year and could not fail to delay the publication of *Private Papers*. He understood this, but decided that we should nevertheless undertake the catalogue. We spent something over three months compiling it and seeing it through the press. Rudge was the printer. Paperback copies entitled *Catalogue of an Exhibition of the Private Papers of James Boswell from Malahide Castle Held at the Grolier Club, New York, December 18th 1930 to February 7th 1931* were distributed to the members and an edition of 415 bound copies entitled *The Private Papers of James Boswell From Malahide Castle in the Collection of Lt.-Colonel Ralph Heyward Isham . . .* by Frederick A. Pottle and Marion S. Pottle, 1931, was published by the Oxford University Press, American Branch. I prepared the copy for Part I (Journals by Boswell) and Part III (Manuscripts by Boswell); Mrs. Pottle was responsible for Part II (Letters by Boswell) and Part IV (Letters to Boswell). The published version was prefaced by a brief history of the Boswell papers in which, by quoting from letters by Forbes and Malone, I was able to show that the literary executors performed their trust and that Rogers's circumstantial account of a general destruction of the papers was certainly untrue. That a great many papers were missing was only too obvious, but

I was uneasily prepared to attribute the losses to the confusion in which Boswell left them, subsequent house-cleaning (including perhaps some burning), careless handling, imperfect protection, and family censorship. That further large finds might be made I did not hint or suspect.

When Isham moved out of his Glen Head house, my wife and I left Glen Cove and took an apartment at 400 East Fiftieth Street, New York City, making the move in Christmas week of 1930. Through the kind intervention of Harry K. Lydenberg, Assistant Librarian of the New York Public Library, I was given work-space in the Library, and the Boswell papers were moved there when the exhibition at the Grolier Club was over. Helen Cohan was given working quarters in Rudge's New York office nearby. I worked daily on *Private Papers* in the New York Public from January to August and part of September 1931. We remember our more than eight months in New York as the time when we went to a play every week. In that year I brought out volumes 10, 11, and 12 of *Private Papers*. A survey of the remaining copy after volume 12 was made up convinced me that if we continued the format of volumes 8–12, the last six volumes would be unpleasantly thick. Bruce Rogers gave us a taller, broader page with less white (the date-lines of the journal run-in instead of centred) which I found especially pleasing and which enabled us to get a good deal more copy into a column without increasing the number of pages.

Within a year or less of that morning in 1929 when Rudge met me at the train in the Grand Central Station, he made application for a large life-insurance policy. The physical examination he was required to take raised a question about his health which he characteristically made a matter of jest. I remember his relating a very vivid dream he had had in which he found all his pockets stuffed with two-dollar bills. He professed to regard this as an augury of greatly increased personal prosperity, but it soon became evident that his illness was not merely serious but terminal. He died on 12 June 1931 in his fifty-fifth year, before the insurance had become binding. His death was a sad loss to his friends and a serious blow to the success of *Private Papers*. He had been, with Isham, Rogers, and Scott, one of the planners of the edition, and he had a deep personal concern in making it beautiful. Rudge was by no means a mere entrepreneur who made a profitable business out of an art and skill he had not himself mastered. As a business man, I fancy he was like Isham sanguine and adventurous, and his firm might have proved to be dan-gerously over-extended even without the Depression. It was not, however, for his own sake that he wanted to gain large returns. His own preferred style of living was modest, even frugal. He wanted unlimited means of producing beautiful books. It was as a practical printer that he shone: he had worked his own presses in his father's printing-house from the age of ten or eleven, and had had a long and solid training in the craft. His printing-house in Mount Vernon was the most attractive workshop I have ever seen: beside the presses, it contained a library of books on the art of printing and a fine collection of famous exemplars. "Expense, profit, all the limits of the ordinary printer," as was well said in a contemporary commemorative article, "[were] brushed aside by the largeness of imagination which touched everything he did." As a man, he was utterly unassuming, transparently good all the way through. I have never known a man I respected more.

It is probable, as I have said, that the firm would have gone under even if Rudge had lived and had kept his health. The business was kept going for five years more, at first under its own officers remaining after Rudge's death, then in a reorganization with Mitchell Kennerley as president. The skilled personnel drifted away. Melvin Loos became head of the Columbia University Press. Printing was kept pretty much up to standard (I think the quality of the facsimiles in *Private Papers* declined), but the management of Isham's edition was neglected. Old subscribers were not encouraged and new ones were not sought out. A really large number of volumes (over four hundred) through the incredible carelessness of a workman in the bindery were sent to the dump as surplus stock. This of course meant that a shocking number of sets became permanently unsaleable. In May 1936 the firm was shut down.

"TIMES 9 MARCH ANNOUNCES DISCOVERY SCOTLAND MANY MISSING BOSWELL PAPERS"

My return to New Haven put me out of daily touch with the manuscripts (which remained in the New York Public Library), a very awkward situation for an editor. Dr. Lyndenberg, for the Library, came to my assistance with a generous proposal: if Isham would allow the Library to make at its own expense and to retain negative photostats of the entire collection as it then stood, the Library would furnish me with positive duplicates at its regular rates. The Chairman of the Department of English at Yale, Professor Samuel B. Hemingway, assigned me up to $1,000 out of the Departmental research fund, which covered the entire expense and enabled me to do most of my editing after that at Yale. As I had expected, my time for independent research was limited during term-time, especially during the academic year 1932–33, when I served as interim Chairman of the Department, but for many years I worked on through the summer in New Haven, allowing myself only the vacation of two weeks I had taken in the summers of 1930 and 1931. I brought out volumes 13, 14, 15, and 16 by the end of 1932, volume 17 in the autumn of 1933, and volume 18 early in 1934. After 1 October 1931 I received no further salary from Isham, but he continued to pay Helen Cohan's salary ($50 a week), and she went on working, mainly on *Private Papers,* in Rudge's office in New York, I think through 1934.

By Isham's decision, I spent all my research time on *Private Papers* and its *Index* until that project was completed, but I took such steps as I could, short of personal participation, to collect materials for the publications that were to follow: Viking's trade edition of the journal, my two biographies, and my research edition of the journal. For five years, beginning with the academic year 1931–32, I offered at Yale a small graduate course called "The Boswell Papers". As the chief exercise of the course, each student prepared an edition—introduction, text, research annotation, and index—of an assigned portion of Boswell's journal, beginning with the earliest fragments. Charles H. Bennett, a member of the first class (his assignment was the London Memoranda of 1762–63), also chose as his dissertation for the doctorate (1933) an edition of the correspondence between the Hon. Andrew Erskine and Boswell which Boswell himself had published in 1763. Bennett had already had experience of teaching and had found that he did not much care for it, and when in 1933 Professor Edgar S. Furniss, Dean of the Graduate School at Yale, assigned me a grant of $1,500 (later $1,800) a year, I was enabled to engage Bennett as full-time research assistant for seven years. Before he left the Boswell Office in 1943 to join the editorial staff of Dr. Wilmarth S. Lewis's Yale Edition of the letters of Horace Walpole, he had prepared new or revised text of all the journal then in Isham's possession, and had collected research annotation for all the portions of the journal not covered by the students' exercises. These collections still remain the most massive body of Boswellian annotation extant; they underlie most of the annotation of Yale's trade edition, later to be mentioned, and will not be fully exploited until Yale's research edition of the journal appears. Mention should also be made of other Yale doctoral dissertations which have been of incalculable help to the editors of the Yale Editions: Robert Warnock, "Boswell in Italy" (1933); Joseph Foladare, *James Boswell and Corsica* (1936, University Microfilms); Inge Probstein, "Boswell's London Journal of 1778" (1951); and Frank Brady, *Boswell's Political Career* (1952, Yale Studies in English, 1965).

In the spring of 1932 Isham felt himself so hard pressed for funds that he asked me to explore seriously the possibility of Yale's purchasing his entire collection. I was able to return only a discouraging answer, and a few days later had to follow discouragement with shock. Sotheby, I found, was putting up for sale at auction on 1 June as "The Property of a Lady" a group of nineteen very miscellaneous lots of manuscripts by or relating to Boswell. The lot contained three fine letters from Boswell to his son Alexander, some letters and verses by Alexander himself, a letter from Rousseau to Boswell, and a letter of condolence from Sir Walter Scott to Alexander's widow; autograph scraps of the kind of material that Boswell collected for his Boswelliana; a Boswell notebook; and autograph verses by Johnson. None of the pieces had ever appeared in a previous sale, which made it almost certain that the lot had just been released from a family archive. I knew of no family archive that contained private papers of Boswell except Malahide, and too hastily concluded that Lord Talbot had found these manuscripts and put them up for auction without informing Isham of their existence. Isham sent a cabled protest, but Lord Talbot assured him that he knew nothing whatever about the papers. Efforts to find out from Sotheby who the "Lady" was failed. (Chapman told me he knew, but was not at liberty to pass on the information.) Isham did not bid at the sale himself, but was able to acquire from a dealer, Alvin J. Scheuer, who did bid, the letters from Margaret Montgomerie and Rousseau and one of the letters to Alexander. (Scheuer charged Isham only a ten per cent commission, and in addition allowed him to print the other two letters to Alexander.) Scheuer also learned who the "Lady" was and told Isham, but I think I did not know till I read Buchanan's book. She was Mrs. Lawrence Eliott, born Emily Wood, granddaughter of Sir William Francis Eliott of Stobs, seventh Baronet, and Janet Theresa Boswell, elder daughter of Sir Alexander Boswell and Grace Cuming. Emily Wood's husband, Lawrence Edward Eliott (d. 1902), major in the Indian Army, was her second cousin, both he and she being descended from Sir William Eliott, the sixth Baronet.

It is certain that Mrs. Eliott's handful of Boswell papers escaped at some time from the Auchinleck archives, and if the papers escaped as a group, it is certain that they left the main deposit no earlier than 1822.[1] Their being in 1932 in the possession of a member of the Wood branch of the family of Eliott of Stobs suggests that they should perhaps be grouped with another highly important stray from the Auchinleck collections: I mean the portrait of Boswell painted at Rome in 1765 by George Willison. Mrs. Lawrence Eliott's father was Capt. James John Wood, late of the 45th Regt., her mother was Jessie Blanche Adelaide (she was called "Blanche" in the family), daughter of Theresa Boswell and Sir William Francis Eliott. Mrs. Wood died in 1898. In 1912 Captain Wood presented the portrait with no history to the National Portrait Gallery of Scotland.

It also seems certain that Mrs. Eliott's Boswell papers were a haphazard gathering from the Auchinleck archives, not a completely deliberate selection. Boswell's letters to Alexander, Margaret Montgomerie's letter to Boswell, Alexander's verses, Sir Walter Scott's letter of condolence—Lady Boswell might well have selected these to give to Theresa as mementoes of her father and grandfather. But she would never deliberately have included letters by Francis Gentleman, Sir Alexander Dick, and Rousseau in such a selection. If the group was put together by Lady Boswell, it was as a miscellaneous handful of strays that had turned up after Boswell's papers were sealed, a handful that she might have taken, among current papers of her own, to Ochiltree House or Stobs. Beyond that everything is guess-work. I suggest that Lady Boswell gave Theresa the portrait of her grandfather, and that it went to Stobs. Theresa, after only ten years of marriage, died in 1836 in giving birth to her ninth child. Her husband retreated to England, leaving Lady Boswell in Ochiltree House to bring up her numerous brood, among whom was Blanche, later Mrs. Wood. Young William, the heir, angered his father by marrying without parental consent. Sir William thought his son irresponsible, and put the estates of Wells and Haddow under a trust, the trustees including two of his own brothers, his brother-in-law General Vassall—and Blanche. Blanche outlived all the others and ended as sole trustee. She occupied Stobs and engaged with her brother in a long litigation over the rents of Wells. I suggest that at some time she removed to her own house in Edinburgh the Willison portrait and Lady Boswell's separated packet of Boswelliana, which she had picked up at Ochiltree or Stobs.

---

[1]Scott's letter of condolence was written in that year.

This speculation has recently received some unexpected confirmation. At about the time I was putting it down on paper, Sir Arthur Eliott of Stobs gave to the new Boswell Museum at Auchinleck a thick sheaf of Boswell-related documents. I have only just (January 1979) been able to study these through the kindness of Gordon P. Hoyle, Honorary Curator of the Auchinleck Boswell Society, who has sent photocopies to the Boswell Office at Yale. The papers have not yet all been transcribed and catalogued, but it is clear that they came from Auchinleck and that they contain bits from the Biographer and a good deal from Sir Alexander Boswell. A considerable number in a difficult angular hand, mainly in verse, I take to be private papers of Lady Boswell, Alexander's widow. The scarcity in the collection of autographs of the Biographer (there are only three scraps in his hand, all brief) is hardly compensated for by eleven new letters in French, written to him by his Dutch cousin, F. C. van Aerssen van Sommelsdyck, but is to a large extent balanced by another letter in French, unsigned, which turns out to be the hitherto missing letter from Belle de Zuylen ("Zélide"), 27 March 1768, acknowledging the gift of *An Account of Corsica:* "Vous m'inspirez une si grande admiration pour Paoli que si j'etois fort riche je n'hesiterois pas á le demander en mariage. Je me trouverois seulement un peu embarrassée s'il exigeoit que je crusse á ses songes prophetiques. Il est encore plus difficile d'être un prophete pour sa femme qu'un Heros pour son valet de chambre." The documents by Sir Alexander include the first letter he ever wrote to his father (all in straggling capitals) and an important one he wrote to his wife, 6 December 1819; there are also several specimens of his verse in various modes, and altogether much politics. Lady Boswell's papers, if they are indeed hers, show that she both copied verse and attempted verses of her own. Sir Arthur Eliott's wife wrote about this collection to Hoyle, 13 May 1978, "We suspect that all these letters may have come to us through Mrs. Emmy Eliott née Wood, grand-daughter of Theresa." It indeed seems likely. Mrs. "Emmy" Eliott was Mrs. Lawrence Eliott: she was Boswell's great-great-granddaughter, as Sir Arthur is Boswell's great-great-great-great-grandson. The papers he gave to the Boswell Museum look very much like the residue of a general Boswell collection from which the more brilliant items have been sold.

The portrait of Boswell is a single indivisible object: now that we have it back in good condition, it really does not matter very much where it was located at any given moment in the nineteenth century. Uncatalogued or only partially specified manuscripts are a quite different matter. With them, our joy at the recovery of indubitable strays must always be mixed with the fear that what has reappeared is less than what disappeared, that more remains to seek than we like to think.

The year 1933 was perhaps the most difficult that Isham had to face. His lovely young wife of eight years divorced him. It was always my impression that he was genuinely and deeply fond of her, as he certainly was of his two boys. David Buchanan is inclined to date his domestic troubles back at least to the end of 1930, when he sold his charming estate at Glen Head and moved into the Hotel Pierre.

Buchanan attributes the break-up to Isham's "preoccupation with the Boswell papers and the depletion of his private fortune in acquiring them". He is probably right, though my own guess would be that preoccupation with Boswell and insecure finances only exacerbated a strain caused by Isham's incurably undomestic nature. It is hard to go on living with a man who habitually gets up at noon and goes to bed at four in the morning, especially if he continues to make domestic engagements which he fails to keep. In the year 1930 Isham's income from his family trust stood at $36,350; in 1932 it had shrunk to $29,400; in 1933 it was $17,050; in 1934 $7,396. On 4 May 1933 he sold what remained of his private library at the American Art Association, Anderson Galleries, and the result was a shambles. (Newton in fact dubbed it "the Isham slaughter".) A copy of Boswell's extremely rare bankruptcy pamphlet sold for $12, and most of the other prices were in proportion. Isham turned for income to a radio programme on "The Romance of Literature" and lectures on the Boswell papers. His lectures on Boswell received high praise and gave him intense personal satisfaction, but probably left him no more than bare sustenance when expenses of travel were paid. In February 1935 he sold to Rosenbach for $35,000 the 110 leaves of the manuscript of the *Life of Johnson* which had been recovered from the croquet-box. As will be remembered, he was only the ostensible owner of this manuscript. Guinzburg was the true owner, having advanced the $20,000 needed to buy the croquet-box papers, with an understanding that after two years Guinzburg could sell the leaves and take from the proceeds his $20,000 plus interest at six per cent, plus half of what the leaves fetched over $20,000. Guinzburg accordingly took about $33,000 of the $35,000, leaving Isham with $2,000 and the rest of the manuscripts from the croquet-box. This was no bad deal in itself, but Isham must have felt keenly his failure to retain so major a manuscript as the leaves of the manuscript of the *Life of Johnson*. Rosenbach afterwards sold the leaves to Arthur A. Houghton, Jr.

During the autumn of 1934, an unfortunate necessity of rethinking the terms of my contract irritated Isham and left a permanent sore spot in his feelings towards me. My contract assumed that in two years' time from September 1929 I would complete *Private Papers*, and would also plan and execute a popular edition of Boswell's journal. The scope of this popular edition was not defined in my contract because at the time the contract was drawn Isham had not yet found a publisher for the work. However, he and I both assumed that it would be a volume, or at most two volumes, of extracts with rather light annotation. Isham indeed gave me to understand that I could work on the two editions concurrently. My remuneration for these services was to be a total of $18,000: $5,000 during 1929–30, $8,000 during 1930–31, and the remaining $5,000 on 1 October 1931. For reasons already given (Isham's decision to enlarge the scope of *Private Papers* and his request that I drop *Private Papers* for close to four months to prepare his *Catalogue*), *Private Papers* was not finished by 1 October 1931, and the popular edition was then not even begun. Viking Press did not sign a contract with Isham till 1 May 1930 (by which time seven months of my first year had passed), and as I later discovered, I could never have worked concurrently on the two editions, for Isham had agreed in his contract with Rudge not to publish any part of a popular edition until six months after the last volume of *Private Papers* was ready to go to the subscribers.

As I have already explained, Rudge was my paymaster, but of course paid my stipend from subscription-money collected by him for Isham. I received from Rudge, as stipulated, $5,000 in 1929–30 and $8,000 in 1930–31. In the autumn of 1934 the affairs of William Edwin Rudge, Inc. were being wound up. When Isham came to settle his account, he found that Rudge's treasurer was holding out $5,000 of his subscription-money to meet a possible claim by me. Rudge's lawyers had assured the then president, Mitchell Kennerley, that I could have claimed that sum at any time after 30 September 1931. Isham asked me to sign a formal release so that he could get the money, which was likely to be lost to both of us unless it was promptly claimed.

I greatly regret now that I did not instantly sign the release with generous expressions of good will. But I was troubled and perplexed. I was not prepared to forgo the $5,000, actually a nominal remuneration for the quantity of editorial labour I should have to perform to produce Viking's popular edition, but I could not look forward with equanimity to having Isham in my debt for a period of years. I felt quite sure that if he became directly responsible for paying me any fixed sum of money under the terms of a contracted agreement, I would run into the same kind of difficulties with him that Scott had encountered. The arrangement of getting my pay from Isham through Rudge had worked perfectly. My relations with Isham down to this time had been pleasant, even affectionate, and I wanted to keep them so. I hesitated, and engaged Cane again. He interviewed the people at Rudge's and reported that they were friendly to me and not particularly so to Isham. I do not remember what he counselled, but I fancy the main points were embodied in a letter I sent Isham on 10 October 1934. In that letter I asked for a formal revision of my contract which would enable me to draw from Rudge's collections after 1 September 1934 and from Viking's and Heinemann's first royalties on the popular printing, a possible total sum of $10,000. This would have been an increase of $5,000 over my original contract. But after thinking the matter over more carefully, I decided not to push at the time for these sums or any other. I resolved not to take advantage of a situation that my contract had not contemplated, and I further decided from that time forward to forget about precise contractual details and to try to handle all my problems with Isham by ordinary principles of friendliness and decency. The money at Rudge's was really Isham's, and he needed it badly. I gave the release and Isham got the money. He promised (over the telephone and later in a signed letter) to put it in a trust account for me, he to receive only interest on the sum, but he didn't, and I didn't expect that he would.

The whole episode was strung out over no more than eight months of sporadic bargaining, but the delay did our relations a good deal of harm. Isham afterwards remembered, not that I finally granted all he asked, but that I had for a time opposed him, had "held him up".

Isham had agreed to have copy for the Viking-Heinemann popular edition ready by 1934, but he instructed me, after finishing volume 18 of *Private Papers,* to devote my energies to the *Index* to *Private Papers,* a work not contemplated in our contract of 1929 and probably not in his mind when he made his contract with Guinzburg in 1930. Accordingly, that order was followed, in spite of the strong desire of Guinzburg and especially Frere, to get on with the popular edition of the journal. Slips for the *Index* were prepared by Mrs. Pottle (working gratis), Helen Cohan, and Bennett (working on my Yale research grant). Some 50,000 turned out to be necessary. When the slips were all in hand, Bennett started the huge task of entering identifications of all the persons and places named in them. (*Private Papers* had been essentially a text without annotation.) Down to 1769, Bennett could draw on the student collections; beyond that, he was pretty much on his own. By the summer of 1934 the slips were ready for compilation. That summer I devised style-rules and typed up copy from the first entry to BOSWELL, EUPHEMIA (thirty-four pages of the printed book). From that point Isham authorized me to engage Joseph Foladare, one of my graduate students, for six months at the monthly rate of $125. Foladare went on to the article MISCHI (pp. 34–244 of the printed book), omitting the articles BOSWELL, JAMES and JOHNSON, SAMUEL but going beyond to prepare the article PAOLI (pp. 265–67 of the printed book). John P. Kirby, another graduate student, working on the same terms as Foladare, then completed the alphabet (pp. 245–357 of the printed book). In the summer of 1935, I added the very long articles BOSWELL, JAMES and JOHNSON, SAMUEL and a key to Johnson's conversations, and revised the entire copy. Chapman, Powell, and Frank Miller of Annan, a Scots antiquary and scholar who had given me much help, read the proofs.

Guinzburg and Frere of Heinemann were meanwhile becoming very impatient for copy for their popular edition of the journal. They requested a meeting with me and Isham, I think early in 1935. My entire commitment to Isham was discussed, and I asked to be allowed to write the biography as my next assignment. Isham said nothing to indicate that he did not regard my claim to use the papers for a biography good, but Guinzburg and Frere naturally opposed my plan, not being the publishers of that book. They proposed instead that I next turn to the popular edition of the journal, and that Isham engage Bennett at a salary of $1,500 to assist me for one year on that project. They also proposed to begin with the Hebridean journal of 1773, and to publish that work by itself, though the other volumes were to be brought out as a set. Since the Hebridean journal had not been in Isham's collection when I made my contract with him, they proposed that he pay me $1,000 for editing it. Viking and Heinemann offered to advance the $2,500 for Bennett and me, charging the sum against Isham's royalties. Agreement was reached on those terms and considerably later embodied in a new contract.

Bennett transcribed, restored, and annotated the long, defective manuscript of the Hebridean tour. I tested (but did not completely collate) his text, and revised his notes with some additions of my own. Kirby collected the materials for the index (which gave fuller identifications than the work had ever before received); I think he was paid from a WPA grant to Yale University. The $1,000 I received on completion of the copy was the last remuneration I received from Isham. It brought the sum he paid me to the modest total of $14,000.

The first months of 1936 passed in delusive calm. The *Index* to *Private Papers* was in press on terms favourable to Isham. He was to pay Oxford Press for manufacturing the book and mailing it to subscribers, but Oxford was to buy from him 250 sets of sheets which it published with its own imprint. The copy for the Hebrides volume was also being readied for the press. The heavy expense of producing *Private Papers* was now ended, and some sums were still coming in from subscriptions. The trade *Hebrides* portended profit, with more money-making volumes (the trade journal and my popular biography) to follow. But on 10 March out of the blue I received a cryptic cable (night letter) from Chapman:

TIMES 9 MARCH ANNOUNCES DISCOVERY SCOTLAND MANY MISSING BOSWELL PAPERS
STOP AM SENDING YOU COPIES WITH LETTER

I was completely mystified, and posted the cablegram to Isham with a hasty scribble on it saying I had no notion what had been found but suspected that it was a cache of letters. (Several of Boswell's longer correspondences have never been recovered: for instance those with the tenth Earl of Eglinton and with Lord Mountstuart, later fourth Earl and first Marquess of Bute.) When Chapman's letter arrived ten days later, the discovery proved to be of something quite different from a single correspondence and vastly more important. Professor Claude Colleer Abbott, then of Aberdeen University, had late in 1930 found at Fettercairn House, Aberdeenshire, a mass of miscellaneous private papers of Boswell's amounting in bulk to roughly half that of the papers Isham had acquired from Malahide. These papers of Boswell's were found mixed with papers of Sir William Forbes, and clearly were a portion of the Boswell manuscripts which Forbes was holding as literary executor at the time of his death. By some oversight they had never been returned to Alexander Boswell, and had been completely lost sight of.

The ebony cabinet, the croquet-box, and Madame Noël's counter symbolize three of the kinds of oblivion that may overtake a man's papers. They may be lost to scholars but not to the family; they may be lost to both scholars and family though physically in the family's hands; they may be lost to everybody. We have now to consider a fourth and more unusual variety.

It seems odd in retrospect that some one was not moved sooner to make effective search for the private papers of Sir William Forbes. He had been the confidential friend and executor of Boswell, had written the official biography of James Beattie, and had known many of the members of The Club. As a man of consequence, the holder of an old title, and an author, he must have had an interesting correspondence. Yet his papers dropped completely out of sight for reasons very similar to those which finally eclipsed Boswell's: they descended through a female representative and came to rest in a house that Forbes himself never lived in. His heir married Williamina Belsches Wishart Stuart, the heiress of Fettercairn in Aberdeenshire (she, by the way, was the young lady who broke the youthful heart of Walter Scott), and since Fettercairn was a large and comfortable house and the old castle of Pitsligo, Sir William's country property, was antiquated and ruinous, Fettercairn became the seat of the family. Forbes's heir (also Sir William) had a son, Sir John Stuart Forbes; there the male line ended and the Forbes baronetcy passed to a nephew. Sir John Stuart Forbes's only child married the twentieth Lord Clinton; their son, the twenty-first Lord Clinton, was consequently heir of line and representative of Sir William Forbes. He had extensive properties in Devon, where he made his principal residence, occupying Fettercairn only about two months of each year.

In 1929 or earlier the late Alistair Tayler, author, with his sister Henrietta, of many antiquarian studies, chiefly on Jacobite topics, was at Fettercairn in connexion with some Jacobite papers in Lord Clinton's possession. One group of these they published some time in 1930 (Preface dated 1 February) as *Jacobite Letters to Lord Pitsligo . . . preserved at Fettercairn House.* Lord Pitsligo (generally so called; his actual style was Lord Forbes of Pitsligo), an active and unreconstructed Jacobite, was great-uncle of Sir William Forbes, who purchased a good part of the Pitsligo lands and had the Pitsligo papers by gift. I do not know whether Tayler approached Lord Clinton or vice versa, but as the Preface says that the editing of the letters has been undertaken at Lord Clinton's desire, the latter alternative is perhaps the most likely. What other papers Tayler glimpsed or was told about will probably never be known, but he somehow learned that there was at Fettercairn a quantity of papers by or about James Beattie.

Professor Claude Colleer Abbott, then Lecturer in English Language and Literature at the University of Aberdeen, had in 1928 begun to read through the collection of Beattie papers which had come into the possession of the University and were then being catalogued. These papers had already formed the basis of Margaret Forbes's *Beattie and his Friends* (1904), and Abbott naturally wished to determine the relation which they bore to the materials used by Sir William Forbes in his official *Life.* As Abbott continued to work on Beattie, he found himself continually wishing to know more about Forbes. It seemed strange that a man so prominent in his own time and the friend and correspondent of so many famous men should not have had a biography; stranger still that his correspondence should not have come to light. For example, though Forbes must have received many letters from Boswell, not a single letter from Boswell to Forbes had appeared in Tinker's collection (1924). It looked, in short, as though Sir William Forbes's papers were somewhere in hiding, possibly all in one place. But Abbott was unable to trace them.

Dr. W. Douglas Simpson, the Librarian of the University of Aberdeen, was
then Secretary of the Third Spalding Club, and in that capacity was in close contact
with Tayler, who, with his sister, was editing two of the Club's publications.
Tayler, hearing from Simpson of Abbott's interest in Beattie, told Simpson that
there were Beattie papers at Fettercairn. Through Simpson, Abbott asked Lord
Clinton to send these papers to the University Library for his use. In due course
Lord Clinton, through his factor, caused a box of papers to be sent to Aberdeen.
In the box, besides miscellaneous papers connected with Beattie, was a large part
of the manuscript of Forbes's *Life of Beattie,* with the originals of Beattie's letters
used in it, as it had been sent to the printer. Abbott's previous concern about Forbes
made this for him an explosive discovery. Though Beattie material of the first rank,
the printer's manuscript of the *Life of Beattie* was even more significantly a *Forbes*
document, and where it had been, the rest of Forbes's papers might be. Abbott,
through Simpson, applied to Lord Clinton for permission to make a search of the
papers at Fettercairn. The request could not be granted for several months, the
house being closed, but what Abbott learned in the mean time about Clinton's
ancestry and the Forbes connexion with Fettercairn made him confident that discoveries were to be made there. Sir William Forbes was now the main quarry.

Abbott went to Fettercairn on 6 October 1930 for a three-day visit and found
a selection of papers in boxes and loose piles laid out for him. He had barely begun
to look into the boxes when he found that his surmise was correct. Mixed in a
confusion of papers of the various owners of Fettercairn—Baron Sir John Stuart, Sir
William Forbes (1773–1828), Sir John Stuart Forbes—were papers of Sir William
Forbes the biographer of Beattie and friend of Boswell. Among them were letters
to Sir William from Boswell's children and drafts of Sir William's letters to various
Boswells. More than that, the stacked piles of papers revealed, along with more
manuscript of the *Life of Beattie*, a stout package containing Boswell's journal from
15 November 1762 to 4 August 1763, the now famous *London Journal*. This was
clearly matter separated from *Boswell's* papers, and Abbott, who knew that many
documents known to be part of Boswell's archives had not turned up in Isham's
purchase, began to think that any or all of the missing papers might be at Fettercairn.
He saw that the whole house—a rambling seventeenth-century structure with two
nineteenth-century additions—would have to be searched systematically. There was
a large cupboard full of confused papers at the foot of the attic stair; there were two
large wooden chests standing one upon another in a covered courtyard; there was
a long double attic containing lumber and some more boxes. None of these receptacles gave any appearance of having been looked into for years; some of the boxes
indeed were secured with locks for which the keys had been lost. On his second
day at Fettercairn he found the main deposit of Sir William Forbes's correspondence,
including his letters from Boswell, in one of the courtyard chests.

The rest of the story of Abbott's searches, conducted in the five subsequent
visits, should be read in his own absorbing account. Suffice it here to say that his
persistent and skilful probing and sifting ended by turning up another large journal

of Boswell's (the greater part of the London Journal of 1778), upwards of three hundred drafts or copies of letters by Boswell, over a thousand letters received by Boswell, and over one hundred letters from Johnson to various correspondents. In bulk these papers, as has been said, amounted to about a third of Boswell's archives as then known. Isham's purchase had contained most of the journal, but the Fettercairn cache was much richer in letters.

How these manuscripts got merged with Forbes's papers is anybody's guess, but the mixing was probably not due to any carelessness on the part of Forbes himself. As has been stated above, he did not get his discharge as executor of Boswell's estate until December 1805, and at that time reaffirmed his obligation as literary trustee. Presumably he continued to hold the papers for James Boswell the younger to read, in accordance with his agreement with Malone, but James had not asked for them when Forbes—perhaps suddenly and unexpectedly—died on 10 November 1806. It was perhaps Sir William's death and a query from *his* executor as to what was to be done with the Boswell papers in his possession that finally set James reading. Sir William's habits of packaging and docketing, as shown by the Fettercairn papers, would make it most unlikely that he had not kept Boswell's papers segregated from his own and clearly labelled, but without him to direct the job, the assembling and boxing may have been bungled. Or James may have asked that a package containing as much of the journal as could easily be assembled should be sent to him (Malone's "a large parcel of them" sounds like less than the whole), and after reading that may have asked Alexander to call for the rest of the papers and take them to Auchinleck—which Alexander neglected to do. People always tend to put off the task of dealing with recent family papers. James and Alexander both died suddenly and in middle age, James at forty-three and Alexander at forty-seven. When Sir William's papers were moved to Fettercairn, what remained of Boswell's went along with them. This probably happened many years after Forbes's death. Abbott found one lot of the Boswell papers at Fettercairn wrapped in newspapers of the year 1874.

By 18 January 1931, Abbott had completed his search and had made a rough catalogue of his findings. Clinton, who was in residence at least during Abbott's first and last visits and had seen him at work, was delighted with his discoveries and strongly disposed to aid him in his plans for extensive publication. When Abbott left at the end of his first visit, Clinton allowed him to take back with him to Aberdeen the fine journal of 1762–63, Boswell's letters to Forbes, and other selected letters, so that he might copy them at once and begin the work of editing them. Some time not long after the last visit, Clinton caused the whole mass of Abbott's Boswell discoveries to be deposited in the library of the University of Aberdeen. Abbott caused a typed transcript of the London Journal of 1762–63 to be made, and a volunteer assistant, Miss A. M. Davidson, set herself happily to the long task of making a manuscript copy in copperplate hand of each of the remaining documents save the London Journal of 1778.

§ C H A P T E R X §

"OPERATION HUSH"

EARLY IN 1931 Clinton, at Abbott's suggestion, and under conditions of secrecy, opened negotiations for publication with Humphrey Milford, (later knighted), Publisher for the University of Oxford. Milford brought in Chapman, Secretary to the Delegates of the Clarendon Press, under the same conditions of secrecy, and in early April 1931 Clinton, Abbott, Milford, and Chapman met to discuss the proposal. Clinton's plan was that Abbott should copy and catalogue the papers, that Oxford should publish them in twenty volumes; and that Clinton, at some unspecified time, should sell them, presumably as a lot, to a British library. Clinton (I do not know whether or not he had yet taken legal advice) believed that Forbes acquired both ownership and copyright by virtue of being the executor of Boswell's estate, and that Forbes's right had descended to himself as Forbes's representative. I do not know how long secrecy was to be observed, but I assume at least till the documents had all been copied.

The Clarendon Press was given responsibility for the venture, and Chapman, who savoured allusion to his fairly recent wartime experience as an artillery-officer in Macedonia, dubbed this one "Operation Hush". Like Milford he at first assumed that Clinton's claim was good. He thought that Abbott's estimate of twenty volumes of trade publication was unrealistic, and himself saw not more than two or three volumes, but as late as the end of July he had beaten Abbott down only to fifteen volumes.

By this time Milford and Chapman were beginning to have misgivings as to Clinton's claims. Sir Frank MacKinnon, Judge of the King's Bench, when consulted informally, had been inclined to think Clinton's claim sound, though he warned that Lord Talbot might contest it. He pointed out, however, that the question of ownership would be decided by Scots law, and suggested getting an opinion from Sir Wilfred Normand, K.C., Solicitor-General for Scotland. Normand's preliminary opinion, after studying Boswell's will, was that Clinton's claim was "very groggy", but he promised a formal opinion later. Chapman drafted a Case for him. The Case reviewed the background of fact so far as it was then known from my Preface to the *Isham Catalogue*. Counsel was asked to advise Milford both as to ownership of the papers and copyright in them. Did Forbes, who was sole executor of the estate but not last survivor of the literary executors, have any right to retain the papers? If he had, did Clinton now have that right by prescription?[1] On the other hand, ought the papers to have been turned over to Alexander Boswell, Boswell's heir? If so, who was now the rightful owner? As for copyright, did Clinton own it by virtue of possession? If not, did copyright belong to Boswell's legal personal representative? Who was that representative? Could he suppress publication by Clinton and claim damages? If Clinton surrendered the originals, would publication from copies be included in the surrender if the owner of the manuscripts and owner of the copyright turned out to be the same?

At Normand's request, another Scots advocate, Archibald Campbell Black, K.C., later knighted, was associated with him. On 6 November 1931, Normand wrote that he and Black found the uncertainties of Boswell's will too difficult for counsel to decide, and that they were agreed that a Judicial Factor should be appointed and the whole problem taken for judicial decision to the Court of Session in Scotland: "Lord C. himself cannot give you a fair passage." Chapman now thought that Milford should refuse to commit himself to publication: "It is pretty clear that C. ought to throw himself on the mercy of the Court, who may give someone a good title to publish. If C. kicks (as A. may incite him to do) I guess you and I will have cold feet."

On 23 November 1931 Normand and Black returned their formal opinion. ". . . Lord Clinton has not an exclusive title to the MSS. and other papers now in his possession in virtue of which he can deal with them as his own property. . . . He is, in our opinion, under a distinct duty to regard himself as a trustee of the papers under obligation to make them forthcoming to the persons, of whom he may be one, who have legal rights to, or in, them. . . . The proper course for him to adopt is to apply to the Court of Session in Scotland for the appointment of a Judicial Factor. . . . It will be the duty of the Judicial Factor, who is an officer of the Court, to take the necessary steps to ascertain who are the persons interested and what are their respective rights." (The legal fees for this opinion were paid by the Press.) This was only a bit more than a year after Abbott made his first discovery at Fettercairn. Yet in spite of this clear and unqualified advice (advice, indeed, which emphatically stated obligation and implied urgency), Clinton did not petition for the appointment of a Judicial Factor until 5 March 1936—four years and three months later. During that time I had brought out volumes 10–18 of *Private Papers* and Powell had published the first four volumes of his revision of Hill's edition of the *Life of Johnson*, both of us in complete unawareness of the documents which

---

[1]See Below, p. 154.

Abbott was working on, documents enormously relevant to the works on which we were engaged.

Indeed, Chapman continued to read my proofs and Powell's, had been constantly reporting to us on our proofs, and had been urging Powell on to publication in his role of head of the Clarendon Press. Not until 1934, when our volumes had all been published or committed to the press beyond recall, did he begin to express some degree of uncertainty and uneasiness as to the effect of his policy on other scholars. This was caused, I fancy, by my opening negotiations with him for the printing and publishing of Isham's *Index*. In the spring of 1934 he wrote to Milford that if the Clarendon Press published the Fettercairn journals, the Press ought afterwards to make those journals accessible to me for my (that is, Isham's) trade edition. "If Cl. cared to pay" for a general publication of the Fettercairn Boswell papers, Abbott should not be sole editor, "but the editing clearly ought to be pooled." If "pooling" were adopted, he saw that it might entail sacrifice on his own part. From the beginning of "Operation Hush" he had of course hoped to have first use in his collected edition of Johnson's letters of the more than one hundred miscellaneous holograph manuscripts of letters by Johnson in the Fettercairn haul. But now, "if necessary, I must make up my mind to losing J.s letters". He and Milford, for some unstated reason (perhaps a new opinion from Clinton's lawyers), seem now to have begun to fear that Elizabeth Boswell's descendants (rather than Lord Talbot) might cut Clinton out: "Perhaps the Beneficiaries will swoop down like harpies and release us from the troubles of a decision."

Abbott in 1932 was appointed Professor of English Language and Literature at the University of Durham, and I suppose thereafter did a good deal of his cataloguing there from copies. By September 1934 he was within sight of the end of his work, and seems to have felt that Milford and Chapman were dragging their feet. He said he was planning to send a specimen of his copy and hoped that soon "this absurd holding back will come to an end and the book be rushed on". What Chapman replied, I do not know, but when Abbott in the following January tried again to get the printing started, he reminded him that Normand and Black had said that legal process should begin as soon as the Catalogue was ready for the printer, and that Clinton's solicitors would have to assume the responsibility of ordering the go-ahead. They presumably were consulted, and Abbott turned in his complete copy on 22 April 1935. For the sluggish progress of affairs that followed, Clinton or his lawyers were responsible. Clinton, Abbott, Milford, and Chapman did not meet till 24 July 1935, when it appeared that Clinton had only got to the stage of agreeing to see the solicitors about the appointment of a Judicial Factor. The solicitors thought that the Judicial Factor would need the Catalogue to enlighten him in his inquiries. On 12 September 1935 Clinton gave authority for Oxford to set the Catalogue in type, but not to print it. On 12 December Chapman sent a set of proofs to Milford. "Concurrently (it makes me feel like a conspirator)," he wrote, "we are printing Pottle's Index. . . . It may be a question at what point the

Pottle-Isham interest should be informed. I should not like them to hear of it first from a newspaper or an outsider." The petition for the appointment of a Judicial Factor was lodged with the Court of Session on 5 March 1936, Ernest M. Wedderburn, Edinburgh solicitor, Deputy Keeper of H. M. Signet, later knighted, being nominated for the post. Abbott's letter appeared in the *Times* and the *Scotsman* for 9 March, and Chapman cabled me that night.

One of the most astonishing silences of "Operation Hush" was that which Chapman observed towards his own board, the Delegates of the Clarendon Press. Although the Catalogue had been set in type at the Press's expense, he did not say a word about it to the Delegates until a day or two before the public notice appeared. He appears also to have left Kenneth Sisam, his Assistant Secretary, completely in the dark. Chapman and Milford kept "Operation Hush" strictly to themselves for five years.

For this extraordinary delay Clinton was undoubtedly the person ultimately responsible. I have no doubt that he was wrong: that he should have broken silence as soon as he was told by experts that he had in his keeping a valuable property that probably did not belong to him. Why did he delay for more than four years after Normand and Black returned their opinion?

My own answer is favourable to his character, though it can fairly be objected that I did not know his character well enough to venture an opinion. I was in correspondence with him from 1949 but did not meet him till 1953, and was then in his company only the better part of a day. In 1953 he was a very old man (ninety), and he lived four years more. He and Lady Clinton (who was the same age as he) received Mrs. Pottle and me with a kindness that captivated both of us. He was, in a sense that Boswell was fond of using, a very old peer, his title dating from 1299. In the English peerage only three or four baronies dispute precedence with his. In the days when the Peerages listed acres and rents, his father, the twentieth Lord Clinton, was credited with 34,776 acres and an annual rental of £32,613. He himself inherited 70,000 additional acres from a relation. He represented no fewer than four families (his name was Charles John Robert Hepburn-Stuart-Forbes-Trefusis), and he was a godson of Queen Victoria. From talking with him I got very much the impression of a man who would take the prescript *noblesse oblige* seriously.

I have no doubt that he did take it seriously. I can well believe, however, that he was constitutionally opposed to haste, was innocently stubborn, and that he read the prescript not just *noblesse oblige* but *noblesse oblige—avec sage lenteur*. The depth and complexity of his roots made it hard for him to entertain the possibility that papers that had been at Fettercairn, mixed intimately with Stuart and Forbes papers from farther back than he could remember, could really belong to people who did not know that they had lost them. Though the recommendation of Normand and Black constituted virtually a first and a second opinion, he seems to have thought that another should be taken. He felt that the evidence in his favour at Fettercairn had not yet been read and studied. Even if it should finally seem wise to seek the appointment of a Judicial Factor before any of the papers were *published*, he did not feel that there was an overriding need for haste. He thought Abbott's Catalogue should first be published "to see what happened".

If we grant that it was Clinton's obligation "to transfer the responsibility for the papers to a Judicial Factor as soon as possible, so that other interested parties might not suffer from being kept in ignorance", we must make sure that we are limiting the word "interested" to its strict legal sense: "having a colourable claim to ownership of the papers at law". In the everyday sense of the word, nobody could be more "interested" in Abbott's discoveries than Isham was. He was interested as a collector. But Clinton was under no obligation to inform Isham qua collector, Isham without an assignment from a Boswell heir. Collecting is an avocation, often an admirable avocation, but its claim on public respect is that of a game in which the collector neither asks nor expects favours. Qua collector, Isham would certainly have thought it permissible to hide information from a rival or actually to mislead him. He would have delayed public notice of papers he was in treaty for or had acquired just as long as he thought secretiveness was to his advantage. He resorted even to out-and-out misrepresentation, as when he told me in the autumn of 1927 that it had turned out that Boswell kept only occasional journals, like the Ashbourne Journal, which he had just acquired. (He was at the moment negotiating with Lord Talbot for the purchase of the other journals.) Isham, the public-spirited sharer of his treasures, Isham the patron of scholars, had a claim on general good will, but it was a claim to be weighed with others. Powell and I were deeply "interested" in Abbott's discoveries (more of this later), but Clinton was not under obligation to prefer our claims to Abbott's.

In 1936, when I heard the news, I had no doubt at all that the papers belonged to Talbot, and I said that Clinton, with no action at law, should have turned them over to Talbot as soon as Abbott had gathered them together. Now that I know the tortuous route by which, according to the finding of the Court, such right as Talbot had to his great-great-grandfather's papers descended to him, I am less critical of Clinton's delay. Private papers descend through the law of succession, not through the blood relationships of heir male and heir of line. How much did Talbot and the other legally interested parties really suffer by the prolongation for a little over four years of a state of ignorance that had already lasted for one hundred and twenty-five? Talbot thought his claim so risky of expense that he assigned it gratis. The person whom Clinton wished to preserve from suffering was Abbott. Abbott was close at hand and had won Clinton's loyal support; the rest of us were shadowy figures in comparison. Clinton was convinced (correctly, as it turned out) that the papers and the copies of the papers would be sequestered the moment a Judicial Factor was appointed, and that unless Abbott's Catalogue was then ready in type, he might be unable to complete it, and might be excluded from all exploitation of his brilliant discovery.

Did Abbott take an unreasonable time? His progress seems slow, but it has to be remembered that the work he had laid out for himself included more than merely preparing copy for a printed catalogue and reading the proofs. He was causing copies to be made of 1,606 manuscripts, and was himself checking or causing the transcriber to check all the transcripts by reading them back against the originals before he made minutes of the contents. If he took an unreasonable amount of time, it was because he was held back by the remarkably old-fashioned method of copying he was employing. Miss Davidson offered free assistance, and she presumably could not type. Her hand-written copies would have been adequate for the preparation of a catalogue, and would have been some insurance against the destruction by accident or the dispersal of the originals. But surely anything less than complete photography plus typed transcripts with a carbon duplicate was very antiquated for the 1930's. Abbott afterwards estimated that he spent a total of four thousand hours himself on the job. Assuming that his total work-span was fifty forty-hour weeks each year, this would amount to about two-fifths of his working time from November 1930 to March 1936. I should guess that Mrs. Pottle and I together spent perhaps twelve hundred hours on the *Isham Catalogue,* but during that time we undertook no making of transcripts. If transcripts did not already exist, we worked up our copy from the originals.

Abbott appears to have had no plan or strategy of his own except to get on with his Catalogue and then, when he was given the word, to embark on a massive project of publication. Of necessity he left the decision as to secrecy to Clinton and the decision as to publication to Milford and Chapman. Secrecy, as a matter of fact, worked troublesomely to his disadvantage when in 1932 he became a candidate for the chair at Durham: he had a good card in his hand that he could not play. He was restive and critical towards Milford and Chapman (punctilious and even courtly when met face to face, he allowed himself to write rude letters), but completely and touchingly loyal to Clinton. "When it eventually became plain," he afterwards wrote, "that Lord Clinton's ownership might be difficult to establish, I begged him to consider only what might be best for himself and offered to put the papers in order and leave them to sleep at Fettercairn. But he was clear that the ownership should be settled." Abbott seems to have worked quietly away at his Catalogue till September 1934, when he informed Chapman that he would soon be sending him a specimen, his object apparently being to get a firm commitment to publication and a production schedule. He hoped, he said, that before long "this absurd holding back will come to an end and the book be rushed on". David Buchanan interprets this as meaning that "for at least eighteen months before his letter appeared in the *Times*" Abbott wanted the veil of secrecy lifted, "even though he must have realized that to do so could result in his being deprived of all further work on the papers". This, I think, is mistaken. Abbott was not castigating a policy of secrecy, he was scolding Chapman for declining to be pushed into type-setting before the whole copy was in hand and Clinton's lawyers had taken definite steps to secure the appointment of a Judicial Factor. Buchanan infers that Abbott had developed a bad conscience after he had had an opportunity to study the set of *Private Papers* that the Library of the University of Aberdeen had purchased for his use: "he realized how serious his own discovery would be for Isham". I saw a good deal of Abbott, first and last, and I never heard him express any compunction for the policy of secrecy so far as Isham was concerned. To me, as a member of his own guild, Abbott was disposed to be friendly so long as my interest did not conflict with his own, but for Isham he at all times showed deep and unreasoning animosity. "As for Isham," he once said to Chapman, "I consider him to be no better than a pirate."

Chapman's role in the Fettercairn imbroglio was extremely complicated and difficult to assess. Unlike Clinton, Abbott, and Milford, he was a personal friend of both Isham and me. He first got in touch with Isham in 1923 in his capacity of editor of the collected letters of Johnson, asking to be permitted to inspect Isham's collection. After that, they corresponded freely and on the most cordial terms. He had been Isham's guest at Glen Head in 1927 and, like me, had been shown all the papers Isham had just brought back from Malahide. He begged (the term is not too strong) the gift of a set of *Private Papers,* saying that he could not afford to purchase one; when he received the books, he professed himself "humbly and profoundly grateful", promising to do his utmost "to promote the great enterprise". He reviewed the work in the *Times Literary Supplement;* he read and reported on all the proofs after I took over. I do not remember whether he was instrumental in getting Isham's *Catalogue* published by the American Branch of the Oxford University Press, but that publication should in any case have tended to strengthen the ties between himself and Isham. In the midst of "Operation Hush", he became publisher of the *Index* to *Private Papers.*

Chapman accepted my first important book (*The Literary Career of James Boswell*) for publication, returning a brief but most helpful series of suggestions for revision: learned, masculine, thoughtful, but large-minded and generous. He pointed to ignorances and crudities in such a way as not to wound a young scholar eager to excel. An established and most respectable scholar himself, he treated me as an equal. My other readers sometimes accompanied correction and dissent with a tone of superiority and sarcasm. Chapman also returned spare but decisive comments on the proofs of that book and of *Private Papers.* Our correspondence usually concerned the books we were working on, but his side was witty and entertaining. Though he never claimed credit for it, I have always assumed that he recommended me for the honorary degree which Glasgow University conferred on me in 1936, the first such honour I received.

As editor of the collected letters of Johnson, Chapman had a considerable personal stake in the Fettercairn manuscripts himself. "My prime ambition," he wrote in his Preface, "has been to furnish an accurate text", and indeed he received the keenest delight from setting up a correct text of previously unpublished letters, from correction of previously published texts by accurate collating of them against

Johnson's difficult hand, and finally, from conjectural emendation of texts which he could not compare with the originals. The Fettercairn papers contained 119 letters from Johnson to twenty-one different correspondents (Brocklesby, Langton, Lucy Porter, Reynolds, Windham, etc.)—letters that Boswell had solicited from their owners for use in writing the *Life of Johnson* and had failed to return. Some of these letters Boswell had abridged, some he had paraphrased, some he had not used in any way. After the Adam Collection, Fettercairn contained the largest group of Johnson letters to be found anywhere in one place. Chapman had hopes that Clinton would sometime and somehow grant him as much access to these manuscripts as would be necessary for a careful collation. For this reason, among others, Chapman may have hesitated to annoy Clinton by prodding him to secure the appointment of a Judicial Factor.

As Secretary to the Delegates, Chapman had a clear duty to foster the legitimate business of the Oxford University Press. At the beginning, when it seemed to Milford and Chapman that Clinton's claim was probably sound, a good deal of possibly profitable publication was proposed. When I later told Chapman that I thought he should have told Milford, Clinton, and Abbott that his personal and professional commitments to Isham, Powell, and myself made it inappropriate for him to discuss secret agreements affecting the publication of Boswell documents not known to us, he said, "What good would that have done? They would have gone directly to Eyre Spottiswoode. Oxford might have lost good business, and Isham, Powell, and you would not have been a whit better off. Because of course my declining to enter into Clinton's and Abbott's scheme would not have left me free to reveal their secret. It was better for me to stay in touch with Clinton and Abbott, and to use such influence as I had to get the documents copied and to keep the collection from being broken up." I was inclined to think that a claim of loyalty between friends was absolute, but if balancing was allowed, I could not gainsay his utilitarian argument.

The fact was, of course, that he was in an unsought conflict of loyalties, and by that I mean more than loyalty to friends versus loyalty to his employer. His strongest motive for acting as he did was undoubtedly loyalty to his country. It hurt him deeply as a Briton when important British papers were purchased away from the United Kingdom. Though he had not complained publicly, he had deeply deplored Isham's acquisition of the Malahide papers. He felt that in his conflict of loyalties, he had to opt for the course of action that held some promise of keeping the papers in Britain. "If you had been an independent scholar," he said to me, "we might indeed have insisted as part of our agreement that you be let into the secret. But you were in Isham's employ, and we could not assume that you would feel that you could keep such a secret from him; and he is a mighty hunter before the Lord. The moment he heard of this great cache, he would have been down on us with power and might to bear off the spoil. Would you have considered it a favour to have been let into this secret but enjoined not to tell Isham? You know, I assume, that you and Isham were not the only concerned parties who were kept in ignorance. There is one Powell, our own man, who was told as little as you were."

He spoke expressly of his great concern that nothing should prevent the complete copying and cataloguing of the Fettercairn papers. POTTLE: "You could have photographed the whole lot in two weeks or less." CHAPMAN: "We don't do things as you do."

I think these were his more important motives, but two other traits of his character probably had some effect in his action. He loved ciphers, mysteries, secrets for their own sake. His personal letters were rendered hard to read in any case by a difficult hand, but he made them harder by abbreviation of words, and the use of elliptical constructions. How much this quirk contributed to "Operation Hush" I do not know, but I am sure that it was more than the name.

Finally, Chapman had another quirk, almost an obsession, that had developed in years of trying to get authors not to rewrite their books at the stage of proofs. I never knew any one who carried a prejudice against proof revision to such lengths. He literally held that type once set should be upset by nothing except the correction of literal misprints attributable to the printer. When you send your copy to the printer, he maintained, you abide by it, even though you acquire important new knowledge while the book is in the press. You do have one recourse: you may print your revisions as addenda at the end of the article or book. His own *Letters of Johnson* is the prime example. Several of his friends read the proofs, and of course we were sometimes able to suggest improvements in the annotation. He let his notes stand as he wrote them (by the way, he did not send us anything to read till his book was in *page*-proofs), but printed detailed addenda in appendices. For example: JOHNSON (26 May 1775): "I have taken the place for Monday. I could not get one for any day sooner. My cloaths came home last night but I could not depend upon them, and therefore could not go to day, and for the two next days the coach is full." CHAPMAN (ii. 34, n. 1): "Until he had tried them on and approved the alterations?" ADDENDUM (ii. 528): "Dr. Pottle corrects me. J means that he could have 'taken the place' for Friday if he could have been sure his clothes would come as in fact they did." A really puzzling and perhaps disquieting case is presented by his own essay "Boswell's Archives", which appears in *Essays and Studies by Members of the English Association* for 1931 (pub. 1932: xvii. 33–43). The essay makes no mention whatever of the Fettercairn discovery, though Chapman knew about it from early April of 1931. "It is astonishing," says David Buchanan, "that a scholar such as he should have *chosen* to publish a learned essay on a subject about which he had vital information which he was temporarily unable to use." This may be right. I should rather guess that he wrote and submitted the essay early in 1931, just after he had seen the *Isham Catalogue*. By early April he had learned of the Fettercairn hoard, which of course made his essay obsolete. He was unable because of his promise of secrecy to incorporate his new knowledge, but one would have expected him at least to try to withdraw the essay. Perhaps he did, but the essay was already in type, or he made a weak case and was overruled. Perhaps he thought that a request to withdraw would cause dangerous speculation. At any rate, the essay went through without the slightest hint of Fettercairn. Though conscious that his essay was grossly incomplete, he owned it with equanimity, sending me a copy inscribed "FAP fr RWC".

When his letter arrived in 1936, I replied that I was not satisfied with his explanation, but that I was willing to postpone judgement till we could talk together. Mrs. Pottle and I went over to Scotland in June 1936, my immediate goal being Glasgow, where, as I have said, I was to receive an honorary degree. After that we visited the major sites of the Johnson-Boswell tour from Inverness to Oban. I picked up some important corrections and additions for both text and notes of the Viking Press edition of the *Journal of a Tour to the Hebrides,* then in proof, and for the first time met Frank Miller and Flora MacLeod of MacLeod, who entertained us at Dunvegan. I also spent a day and a night with Chapman in his home at Oxford. He talked to me in a manly fashion with complete frankness. I have already presented most of what he said, but one important area of our discussion remains to be related. He maintained with conviction that his silence had caused me and Isham much less trouble and embarrassment than a full disclosure would have: that from a practical point of view, Isham and I were better off *not* to know of the Fettercairn discovery until *Private Papers* was completed and the books sent to the subscribers. I had laid out the matter carefully for the twelve volumes I was to do, he said, and had more than enough material to fill them. It was better for us to go ahead on that plan and finish the work, keeping as closely as possible to our schedule as originally planned, than to halt publication and attempt to reorganize in the interest of a problematical greater completeness.

This sounded like his well-known prejudice against radical revision of any book after printing has started, but on thinking things over, I came to agree with him. I had planned, from the point where I took over, to make *Private Papers* essentially a complete publication of Boswell's journals in their various forms, beginning with 22 November 1765. To this each volume would add selected letters, but I never committed myself to anything like full presentation of letters. There were 118 fragments of journal in Isham's Malahide purchase, but only three at Fettercairn: the brilliant London Journal of 1762–63; the London Journal of 1778 (a mixture of fully written entries and rough notes); and the journal of the Northern Circuit, 1788, pretty much rough notes, much of them in macaronic Italian used as a cipher. 1762–63 was much too early for my scheme (that journal should have been in Scott's first volume). If we had had it, we might have printed it in a trade edition, like the Viking Press *Hebrides,* though it was risky stuff for trade publication at that date. I could have made good use of the other two journals, but I was in fact finding I had rather too much material as it was. (With volume 13 I had to ask Rogers to redesign the format so as to admit more text.) If I had had access to the Fettercairn papers, I could undoubtedly have given the subscribers a more brilliant selection of letters, but letters were never the main feature of that edition.

When David Buchanan speaks of the great advantage it would have been to

Isham to have known of Abbott's discovery in 1930 or early in 1931, I cannot think he realizes how disastrous a suspension of publication of *Private Papers* in the midst of the Depression would have been. The rumour that Isham's collection was not complete of course made it harder to sell sets of *Private Papers* after 1936, but a complete cessation of publication from 1931 to 1934 would have been much more dangerous. Isham's financial situation was desperate as it was, and to have faltered in publication would in my opinion have meant that publication could never have been resumed. Judging from the court action that actually started on 5 March 1936 (there is nothing else to base a judgement on), Isham would not have been able to push his case to a judgement of the Court and to settle the ensuing claims within less than three years. That would have meant finding a new printer, for as it was W. E. Rudge, Inc. barely lasted out *Private Papers*.

Some have thought that Chapman's treatment of Powell was especially cruel as being merely a face-saving gesture. Without telling Powell why—so runs the argument—he could have directed him to lay his work aside till further notice. This would have saved Powell chagrin and would have been no real breach of Chapman's pledge of secrecy. I myself have never seen any merit in this argument. Powell's revision of Hill was a work commissioned by Chapman and paid for as such. It was Chapman's right (indeed, responsibility) to order all matters concerning the schedule of its publication. The work was an expensive one, tying up a good deal of capital. Chapman's near-obsession about extensive revision of type already set no doubt counted for something in his decision to go ahead with publication, but it seems to me that his decision was a reasonable one for any publisher to have made. I never saw any reason why Powell should have felt chagrin over deficiencies of text and annotation which were not in any way his fault. I did find Chapman's even-handedness morally admirable, and I (and I think Isham) would have felt that the proposed special treatment of Powell was a subterfuge if not a mean evasion.

Isham, like me, was no doubt hurt by Chapman's ordering of his loyalties, but I do not remember that he allowed his sense of hurt to interrupt or impair his friendship. When in the course of time an action at law and purchase placed the Johnson letters at Fettercairn in his hands, he immediately gave Chapman free access to them: in short, gave him everything he had hoped to obtain from Clinton.

ᘒ CHAPTER XI ᘓ

THE FETTERCAIRN CAUSE

ON 20 MARCH I FORWARDED to Isham the letter containing cuttings from the *Times*, 9 and 10 March, which Chapman had promised. I may already have read the cuttings to him over the telephone, or he may have had access directly to the *Times* in New York before he received word from me. At any rate, he decided on the strength of the scanty information furnished by the *Times* that he would make the papers his in spite of the desperate state of his finances; and he was moved to precipitate action when he saw in the communication in the *Times* for 10 March what appeared to be official notice that claims, to be admitted, must be lodged by the 23rd: "Lord Wark has ordered intimation and advertisement of the petition [Clinton's petition for the appointment of a Judicial Factor] allowing all parties having or claiming interest 14 days within which if so advised to lodge answer." He sailed at noon on 21 March for Plymouth, having cabled to Lord Talbot, apparently with no previous communication, "Sailing today steamer Paris account report published London Times regarding Lord Clinton manuscripts. Believe these yours and think essential we meet London 29th work out plans avoiding possible legal complication. London address Garrick Club."

This was instructing Talbot on very short notice to make a special trip to London and to attend a conference on a Sunday. Since Isham could not be sure that the Talbots were not still displeased with him for ignoring Lady Talbot's censorship, one might have expected him to adopt a much more ingratiating tone. The extreme need for haste, as Isham understood the situation, explains his bluntness partially but I think not completely. He wanted to get into the action himself, and since he believed that Talbot had by far the best claim, the course indicated for him was to relate himself beneficially to Talbot's claim. He knew Talbot well enough to know that he would have to be pushed if he were to stand forward. By speaking

of "possible legal complicaiton" he was hinting that he had a *right* to the Talbots'
cooperation, perhaps a right that was legally enforceable. When he purchased
Boswell's papers, the Talbots had assured him that he was purchasing *all* of them.
Talbot's deed of sale could perhaps be construed to mean that he already possessed
title to all papers of Boswell's belonging to Talbot, whether Talbot had known of
their existence or not.

Isham was in London on 28 March, but Lord Talbot neither put in an appearance nor explained his absence. This must have been a keen disappointment.
On 31 March or 1 April, however, Isham received a letter from Talbot's solicitor
in Dublin, Robinson, saying that the Talbots were in Italy and would not be back
before the end of May. Isham telephoned to Robinson in a tone more conciliatory
than that of his cable, saying he only wanted to help Lord Talbot in any way he
could to recover the Fettercairn papers, and would be glad to put his expert knowledge at Talbot's disposal. If Talbot got the papers and wished to sell them, he
would be interested in making an offer. Isham no doubt also consulted his London
solicitors, who would have been able to get him assurance that the Court of Session
would allow ample time for the lodging of claims. Then, seeing that he could
accomplish nothing further in Britain while the Talbots were abroad, he came back
home. He immediately, however (17 April), wrote a strong letter to Robinson,
arguing that in fairness to himself Talbot should press his claim:

> It was always my understanding that I was purchasing the entire collection, as left by
> Boswell in so far as it survived. Indeed, had this not been so, it is questionable whether
> I should have purchased them at all, and it is certain that the price I agreed upon was
> largely influenced by this consideration; for publication rights, which were part of my
> purchase, gained their main value from the completeness of the collection.

He quoted Talbot's deed of sale of 21 August 1927, which seemed to transfer
to him "the collection of papers, Manuscripts and letters, by or belonging to James
Boswell, inherited by me as his great-great-grandson", and went on to summarize
the great expense he had been under: "The cost of editorial and secretarial work
alone, entirely paid for by me, has been, to date, over $70,000, no part of which
has been recovered by the sale of the private edition."

Talbot, as it turned out, had already been notified of Abbott's letter in the
Times by his accountant in Edinburgh and by his cousin, Sir Gilbert Eliott of Stobs
and Wells, who had put in a claim himself and proposed that he and Talbot should
claim jointly. Talbot instructed his solicitors to notify the Judicial Factor that he
intended to claim, and notice was given accordingly on 30 March, Wedderburn's
appointment having been confirmed on 27 March.

I was in Edinburgh in July, and T. B. Simpson, advocate, already a friend
of some years' standing, arranged for me to meet Wedderburn. Wedderburn told
me he could not decide between the claims and that he would have to raise an action
in the Court of Session. The Court would insist on public advertisement, plenty

of time would be allowed for interested parties to hear of the action, and several more claims might appear. The Court had given permission for Abbott's Catalogue to be printed and published. Wedderburn estimated that the case would not open for six months or more and would not be decided in less than a year. Legal expenses of the Judicial Factor and all accepted claimants would be paid out of the fund *in medio,* that is, would be charged against the manuscripts and paid by the winning claimant. At Aberdeen I met Dr. Douglas Simpson, Librarian of the University. He was very courteous to me and Mrs. Pottle, but naturally could not show me or even discuss the Fettercairn papers, which were locked up in his strong-room. I also met Abbott in London, when he invited me to luncheon at Simpson's in the Strand. He talked with me frankly and honestly, but did not subscribe at all to my view that Clinton should have turned the papers over to Talbot as soon as their nature became clear. (I know now that my opinion was bad law, but it still seems to me to have been good morality.) My meeting with Chapman at Oxford I have already discussed. I learned from both Abbott and Chapman that a claim was expected from Elizabeth Boswell's descendants, a line which I had been inclined to think extinct.

The Talbots returned from Italy in early summer. Lord Talbot, as has been mentioned, had on 30 March intimated through his solicitors that he intended to lodge a claim, which he finally did on 17 September 1936. He however did not like the publicity at all, and it took a good deal of persuading to keep him from withdrawing. Lady Talbot had lost her copy of the 1927 deed of sale, and was considerably alarmed by Isham's hints that he might seek legal reparation. She corresponded earnestly with Robinson and no doubt had consultations with him. She studied Boswell's will and came to the conclusion that Boswell intended to transmit his papers in such a way as to benefit the "younger children". Of the "younger children" only Elizabeth had married, and Lady Talbot, on making in-quiries, found that three great-grandchildren of hers (a brother and two sisters) were still living. She decided that these three (Charles E. Cumberlege Ware, Mrs. Edith Marriott, and Mrs. Elizabeth Hailey) were morally entitled to the papers, but she seems to have been given to understand that they would not be able to produce legal evidence of it. (Earlier than most of us—perhaps from talking with Robinson—she had come to see that family papers do not descend automatically by blood-lines, but are transmitted by the law of succession from generation to generation.) Unless they could produce wills going back to Elizabeth, she thought, her husband ought to continue as "chief claimant". If he won, he could then do what he thought fair to Elizabeth's descendants—I suppose sell the property and divide between the three what was left over after all the bills were paid. She persuaded Sir Gilbert Eliott to withdraw his claim so as to make this programme simpler. But she was still uneasy over Isham's representations and felt that he ought to be consulted before any active steps were taken. On 12 October she wrote to him proposing that he come from the U.S.A. to Dublin. Isham of course had been impatiently awaiting just such a

summons. He came to Dublin promptly, talked with Robinson, and then met the
Talbots and Robinson on 29 October. He was not at all persuaded by Lady Talbot's
advocacy of the moral claims of the three great-grandchildren of Elizabeth Boswell.
True, Boswell had appointed trustees to publish more or less from his papers for
the benefit of his younger children, and it might be argued that Elizabeth Boswell's
descendants had some claim to publication rights in the papers. He and Robinson
did not think so. But Boswell said nothing in his will about giving the papers
themselves to the younger children. He had not said anything in his will as to who
should have them, but his journal showed clearly that he expected them to pass
into Alexander's keeping and from him to the succeeding heirs of entail. Isham also
took a firm position as to the rights conferred on himself by the deed of 1927,
insisting that it gave him grounds for claiming that it amounted to an assignment
to himself of Talbot's right in any papers found later that Talbot did not know of.
Robinson doubted that the document conferred any such right, and of course he
was quite correct. Taken in isolation the words "I have this day sold and delivered
to Lt. Col. Ralph Isham the collection of papers, Manuscripts and letters, by or
belonging to James Boswell, inherited by me as his great-great-grandson and otherwise" do seem to have that meaning, but when read in context they clearly mean
only that portion of Boswell's papers ("Manuscripts and letters") actually delivered
into Isham's hands on 21 August 1927. At the time that paper was signed, Isham
was not even in treaty for the purchase of the journals, which he had seen in Talbot's
hands. When he did acquire the journals, he tried to get from Talbot a document
saying that Talbot was transferring title to the entire journal, whether or not known
to him or in his hands, but Talbot had refused to sign such a statement. Lady
Talbot had not merely lost the deed of 1927 but had also forgotten the tenor of
her correspondence of nine years before, and she did not want to risk litigation with
Isham. "It is worth a good sum of money to have Colonel Isham as a friend instead
of an enemy." She was also clearly persuaded by Isham's representation that in
fairness to him Lord Talbot should make it possible for him to sue for the new
papers. "James . . . was moved to do this by a feeling that Colonel Isham's collection
would be practically ruined in value if it were not the complete collection of the
Biographer's letters and works which we thought it was when we sold it to him."
Talbot agreed to withdraw his claim; he assigned his rights to Isham gratis and
Isham agreed to keep him free of all expense. This left Isham free to prosecute the
claim with no reference to Talbot, which suited Talbot exactly. Lady Talbot however
still thought that Cumberlege Ware was morally entitled to something (why she
preferred him to his sisters, I do not know), and Isham offered to make him a
gratuitous payment of £500 if he would make no claim. Cumberlege Ware chose
to take time to consider the offer and so lost the money, for later study of the wills
showed that if his mother, Mrs. Elizabeth Anne Cumberlege, had any right to
claim the papers, that right had passed exclusively to his sister, Mrs. Elizabeth
Hailey.

Isham was in a hurry to get back home in order to give a well-paying series of lectures at Northwestern University, and had accordingly secured passage on the *Normandie* for 4 November. But Lord and Lady Talbot were due soon to leave for Italy until spring, and he was determined not to leave till Talbot's claim had been withdrawn, his own assignation prepared, and his own claim formally intimated. He got Robinson to instruct Scott Moncrieff and Trail, Talbot's solicitors in Edinburgh, to withdraw Talbot's claim and to prepare the assignation in his own favour. Then he went to London to consult his own solicitor, Humphrey Thackrah of Denton Hall and Burgin. Thackrah told him that since the action would be tried by Scots law, he would have to have a Scots solicitor, and engaged for him Eric P. Buchanan of the Edinburgh firm of Steedman Ramage and Co. The Judicial Factor told Thackrah, who had made tactful inquiries in Isham's behalf, that the action would begin after Christmas at soonest, and that Isham could safely go home till then. Isham thought best, however, to cancel his lectures and stay on in Britain till the assignation had been formalized, Lord Talbot's expenses paid, and his own claim formally intimated (30 November). He dashed home for Christmas, but was back early in January 1937.

In the month of November 1936, by a remarkable coincidence, two important Boswell books appeared from different presses. The Viking Press (William Heinemann, Ltd. in Britain) published the trade edition of Boswell's *Journal of a Tour to the Hebrides with Samuel Johnson, LL.D., Now First Published from the Original Manuscript*, edited by Frederick A. Pottle and Charles H. Bennett, and the Clarendon Press published *A Catalogue of Papers Relating to Boswell, Johnson & Sir William Forbes Found at Fettercairn House a Residence of the Rt. Hon. Lord Clinton* 1930–1931, by Claude Colleer Abbott.

Nobody knew what to expect from the new *Hebrides*. If Boswell himself had not published a heavily edited version of it in 1785, I am sure that our edition would have had a very large sale. But although a good third of the text was quite fresh and new, the book was not able to rise above the imputation of being a reprint of a classic. On those terms it did extremely well. It was the choice of the Literary Guild for November 1936, and Viking's edition had a general sale of about ten thousand copies. It was not so successful in Britain, one printing of five thousand copies proving to be rather more than enough. Still, it must have come close to earning for Isham the advances made to him in 1930 ($15,000) and 1936 ($2,500). Abbott's *Catalogue* was hardly a book for the general reader (five hundred copies were printed), but received some general attention because of the absorbing Introduction in which Abbott related the tale of his successive discoveries.

On his arrival in America Isham immediately conferred with Guinzburg. The Fettercairn find with its important recovery of Boswell's London Journal of 1762–63 completely upset Viking's scheme for a complete trade edition of all Boswell's fully written journal. (The Hebrides journal, as published by Boswell himself, had deliberately been conceived as outside the reckoning, but no excuse could be made, now the journal of 1762–63 had been recovered, for beginning the trade edition without it.) Isham agreed to do all he could to obtain the new papers, promising, if he got them, to give Viking the rights of publication in the United States and in Canada at the rates formerly agreed upon. Guinzburg gave him a further advance against royalties of $5,000, and no doubt treated with Heinemann for the British rights.

So far as I know, Alistair Tayler had up to this time made no public statement of having discovered Boswell papers at Fettercairn. But on 12 February 1937, in an address given in London at the annual general meeting of the Clan Chattan Association, he is reported to have asserted, though in a guarded fashion and without any elaboration, that he had been the first to see and recognize the nature of the papers which Abbott had catalogued: "At another house, when searching for and finding Jacobite material, I was delighted to discover a collection of letters from James Boswell, which has proved a somewhat important literary discovery." He died later in that same year (8 November 1937).

Tayler's remark was published very obscurely, but it seems necessary to quote it in order to challenge it. He knew that Lord Clinton was Sir William Forbes's representative, and he knew that the Jacobite papers he was editing had once belonged to Sir William. His report of Beattie papers at Fettercairn is most naturally explained by granting that he had turned over some papers there besides the ones he had come to fetch. He may have glimpsed something by or relating to Boswell. But until evidence is presented that before 9 March 1936 he gave some one a reasonably specific account of Boswell papers seen at Fettercairn, his claim to a discovery will have to be disallowed. Certainly he did not follow up any clue that may have confronted him. He did not have the energy, the knowledge, or the interest in Boswell which a genuine discovery of the Boswell cache would have required. He and his sister were specialists in Scottish genealogy and history (especially Jacobite history); they were committed for at least two more laborious studies after the Pitsligo volume; they were getting on in years. It is clear that any search he may have conducted at Fettercairn must have been of the most limited sort. If he recognized the manuscript of Forbes's *Life of Beattie* for what it was, he did not say so. He failed to locate a number of Pitsligo documents (found later by Abbott) that were his special interest. He saw no "collection of letters from James Boswell". The only collection of letters from Boswell at Fettercairn was the packet of forty letters to Forbes, and this Abbott found in the courtyard among papers that had clearly not been handled for years. He may well have seen the papers that Abbott found laid out for him on his arrival at Fettercairn: the very important London Journal of 1762–63 and a packet labelled by Sir William Forbes, "Letters from Mr. Boswell of Auchinleck and from his brother Mr. James", but he did not report the first, and if he had opened the second, he would have found that "Mr. Boswell" was Alexander, not the Biographer. The great haul of letters *to* Boswell, found by Abbott in the last corner of the attic, he certainly never saw. He put aside as important no papers other than the ones connected with his and his sister's publications. He appears not to have told Lord or Lady Clinton that he had found any other papers of interest. He passed on no information as to Boswell papers. His remark in the Clan Chattan address shows that even after the publication of the Fettercairn *Catalogue* he had only the vaguest notion of what actually had been found. He *could* have discovered the Boswell papers at Fettercairn, but his actual role consisted of no more than furnishing an essential clue to the man who did discover them.

The Fettercairn cause was before the Court of Session in Edinburgh from the end of March 1937 to the middle of July 1938. It was what in Scots law is called "an action of multiplepoinding". (The verb *to poind,* pronounced "pīnd", corresponds to the English noun *pound,* and means "to shut in, to impound".) A piece of property called "the fund *in medio*" (in this case the Fettercairn papers) is claimed by several parties called "defenders". The person holding the property (in this case the Judicial Factor) raises the action against the defenders. The first step is to advertise the cause in newspapers of wide circulation, announcing the date by which claims must be lodged. Ample time is given; indeed, as we shall see, a party with a colourable claim can get admitted long after the deadline.

In Scotland, causes like that of the Fettercairn papers are not tried by juries but by a judge sitting by himself. If the litigation is of the magnitude of the Fettercairn cause, the judge is from the bench of the supreme court for civil actions (the Court of Session) and, though not a peer, is styled "Lord". Scots courts make far more use of written and printed papers in the early stages of a civil cause than American courts do. The "claims" that are lodged are long *ex parte* pleadings of fact and law. In Scotland (as in England, though the terminology there differs somewhat) there are two kinds of lawyers: *solicitors,* who manage causes and collect the evidence, and *advocates,* who prepare the pleadings and, at the proper time, plead viva voce in court. Isham's principal solicitor, as we have seen, was E. P. Buchanan of the firm of Steedman Ramage and Co.; his counsel (advocates), whom Buchanan had engaged, were J. R. Wardlaw Burnet, K. C., and W. P. Milligan, later raised to the bench as Lord Milligan. When all the claims are assumed to be lodged, the cause does not proceed at once to a hearing, but the pleadings are printed and each claimant, through his counsel, is allowed to study those of his opponents and to change his pleading so as to answer their arguments. After due time for "adjusting the record", as this stage is called, the record is "closed" and a date is set for a hearing in presence. The judge, after study of the points of fact and law and hearing counsel, makes his decision.

On 5 January 1937 Wedderburn formally raised the action of multiplepoinding against Clinton, Isham, and Sir Gilbert Eliott, the only parties who by that time had indicated an intention of lodging claims. Isham returned from his Christmas dash to America in time to attend a conference in London with E. P. Buchanan and Thackrah the next day. E. P. Buchanan was confident that because of the requirement of advertising, it would not be necessary to lodge elaborated claims before May. A great deal of work had to be done in the meantime. Talbot's solicitors, Scott Moncrieff and Trail, must have gone to work on the Boswell legal documents in their hands, if they did not make search in the public registry, immediately on Abbott's announcement of his find. By June 1936 they had traced the wills of all the members of the Boswell line through whom Talbot claimed: that is, Boswell himself, Sir Alexander Boswell, Sir James Boswell, Lady Boswell (Sir James's widow), Lady Talbot (Lord Talbot's mother), and Mrs. Mounsey. By paying Talbot's legal costs, Isham acquired all this invaluable collection of evidence already transcribed. He deeply enjoyed working up a legal case, and had a distinct aptitude for that kind of work. He vowed that he would do everything in his power to build up a strong claim, promising to be in Edinburgh with E. P. Buchanan and his counsel, and joined in close scanning of the materials collected by Scott Moncrieff and Trail. Areas that obviously needed much more investigation were the arbitration proceedings between Alexander and Boswell's other children and how the property of the younger children transmitted on their deaths. The voluminous correspondence between the Boswell children and Sir William Forbes needed to be borrowed from Clinton and studied. Isham, soon finding that Lady Talbot could give him no help while she was in Italy, decided to stay in Britain till her return. When the Talbots passed through London in early March on their way home, he begged permission to visit Malahide and make a thorough search himself for papers bearing on his case. Lady Talbot believed he would find nothing, but agreed.

Isham went to Malahide in the middle of March 1937 and spent two days (probably the 14th and 15th) searching every room of the Castle systematically. In the strong-room he came upon a metal dispatch-box filled with papers from Boswell's archives that Lady Talbot had somehow overlooked. Besides bits of journal and some letters, the box contained a diary of Johnson's, Boswell's Book of Company at Auchinleck after he became laird, his Register of Letters, 1782–90, and Johnson's D.C.L. diploma from Oxford. The Talbots gave Isham all these papers. Lady Talbot also showed but did not give him a legal document which Scott Moncrieff and Trail had found among their office-papers: the deed, made in 1795, by which Boswell provided £500 of additional fortune for his daughter Veronica because she had shown "infantine attention" to Johnson in 1773. He also unearthed a mass of later correspondence and sale catalogues from Mrs. Mounsey's time that furnished evidence for his suit. In a close connexion, he caught the *Queen Mary* on 17 March and sailed home to deliver the postponed lectures at Northwestern University.

Knowing that the story of the discovery was bound in no long time to get into print, E. P. Buchanan and Thackrah tried to head off exaggerated reports by a brief and soberly worded announcement which they sent on 18 March to the leading Scottish newspapers and to London press agencies. On landing, Isham declined to make any comment, but he held a press conference after various conjectural reports had appeared. He stated that he had had the papers as a gift from Lord Talbot, and on other matters was reasonably accurate, but the London newspapers printed wildly irresponsible stories, converting the strong-room into a gloomy dungeon, the tin dispatch-box into a huge iron casket, and reporting that Isham had paid Talbot as much as £100,000 for the newly recovered papers. Talbot was naturally very much upset and published a letter in the *Times* (5 April) deploring the "exaggerated stories about my great-great-grandfather's papers". Besides affronting his shyness the report put him in an awkward position with the tax authorities.

That Isham was innocent of planting or encouraging any such Gothic nonsense may well be granted, but that is not to say that he did not embroider the tale in a more down-to-earth fashion. He begged Lord and Lady Talbot to let him say that he found the dispatch-box in the kitchen, "because that would make 'such a good story' ". He gave me a minutely detailed oral account (which I never doubted till I learned the truth from David Buchanan) of how *he* found the Grant to Veronica:

> We were standing in the entrance hall of the Castle, and I said to Lady Talbot, "You have no notion where papers may be hidden in a house like this. Look at that hat-rack" (pointing to a thing with stag-horns to hang hats on, and rails for walking-sticks, and in the middle a seat, with a lid). "Now there's a place where a paper of Boswell's might very well be." I lifted up the lid, and there was the Grant, right on top of a heap of papers. Lady Talbot gave it to me with the other papers, but I said, "No, no, Lady Talbot. It should stay here because it's a legal document and belongs with all the other Auchinleck deeds."

While Isham was in America, E. P. Buchanan remained hard at work on the evidence. Two discouraging pieces turned up. Sir Gilbert Eliott's solicitors sent him a deed in which Sir James Boswell renounced succession to his father's personal estate. Isham's case had somehow to carry the papers from Sir Alexander to his granddaughters Lady Talbot and Mrs. Mounsey, and his lawyers were naturally assuming that Sir James was one of the links. Also it turned out that Mrs. Mounsey had left the residue of her estate to the Cumberland Infirmary, a hospital in Carlisle. It could be argued with considerable cogency that Mrs. Mounsey's half-share of the papers came under this residuary clause, and hence that the Infirmary had grounds for a claim. Buchanan went on searching in Scott Moncrieff and Trail's papers and in the Register House, not solving the problems, but at last locating the very important decree in the Arbitration between Sir Alexander and his brother and sisters, which had been incorrectly indexed, and building up a full picture of the confusion in which Sir Alexander's personal affairs had been left at the time of his unexpected death.

The day set for lodging claims was 4 May 1937, but no one was ready then and the time was extended to 19 June. E. P. Buchanan badly wanted Isham back, and he appeared in Edinburgh on 16 June to help complete his claim, which was duly lodged by the 19th. Only two claims were lodged: Lord Clinton's and a joint claim by four Eliott heirs, grandsons or granddaughters of Sir Alexander's daughter Theresa, Lady Eliott: Charles W. Eliott, Mrs. Louisa Scott, Mrs. Emily Eliott (same as Mrs. Lawrence Eliott), and Thomas E. Forrest. Sir Gilbert Eliott withdrew, as did two other parties who had intimated an intention of lodging claims: the Dowager Lady Forbes and Dr. Henry St. George Boswell, a descendant of Robert Boswell and Boswell's heir male.

E. P. Buchanan warned Isham that other claims might turn up and be admitted in spite of the announced deadline. He also advised him to inform the Cumberland Infirmary of its interest, for the Court would do it sooner or later if he did not, and might scold him if he had kept silent. Isham spent a day in the office of Clinton's solicitors reading the mass of letters between Boswell's children and Sir William Forbes, and found several that helped his case. By early July he was back in New York.

I suppose that when Abbott's letter appeared in the *Times* on 9 March 1936 I was the only person anywhere who knew very much about the history of the Boswell papers from Boswell's own days to Isham's purchase in 1927. The Preface to Isham's *Catalogue* (1931) had given a fuller and far more trustworthy account of the dealings of the literary trustees than had previously appeared. After Isham entered the Fettercairn cause, I wrote many long letters to him answering historical questions put by him or his counsel or volunteering conclusions to which I had come. David Buchanan is kind enough to say that I gave valuable help to Isham's case, and points to the fact that Lord Stevenson named me in his judgement, accepting my "views on a number of points . . . without challenge or proof".

I now report an episode concerning which I never knew much of anything. On 12 June 1937, that is, four days before Isham appeared in Edinburgh to put the final touches on his claim, he married in the Paddington Registry Office, London, Christine (Sinclair), widow (second wife) of the first Viscount Churchill. I never met the lady and never heard talk about her from any one except Isham. Her first husband had died in 1934 in his seventieth year, but she, I fancy, was still in her thirties. (Isham was now almost forty-seven.) She had two small children, a daughter of six and a son (heir presumptive to the title) nearly three. Isham sent me a cable at the time asking my "blessing" and saying she was "a very old friend", from which I assume that they had known each other at least as far back as 1925. One hopes that the marriage gave both parties some satisfaction, but it must have failed in a few months, for it was terminated by a Reno divorce on 1 November 1938, the charge cruelty. A year later she married Sir Lancelot Oliphant. There is a story which I cannot vouch for that trouble started at the very outset when she indicated an intention to continue to call herself Viscountess Churchill.

On 19 June 1937 the limit set for the lodging of claims expired, the Court directed a record of the claims to be printed, and gave the parties till 13 October to adjust their pleadings. The interval, which was made necessary by the summer vacation of the Court, seemed long, but E. P. Buchanan was grateful for the extra time. It is very easy in going through his collection of neatly typed and usefully arranged transcripts of wills and deeds to forget the patient expert labour that went into locating and typing the individual pieces. He continued to burrow in the confusion of papers connected with Alexander's affairs, and turned up the potentially very important fact that Lady Boswell (Alexander's widow) had purchased the furniture and library of Auchinleck from her husband's creditors. He ran down the will of Lady Boswell and found that she had left her property to her younger daughter, Mrs. Vassall. He enabled Thackrah to find (in London) the will of James Boswell the younger. He learned something about Sir James's efforts to settle with his father's creditors.[1] He read straight through all eighteen volumes of *Private Papers* and others of Boswell's writings, and went systematically through the various Scottish registers: the Books of Council and Session, the Sheriff Court Books in Ayr, the Ayr Commissary Court records. A consultation, from which Isham was absent (he was in America), was held on 21 September. Isham yielded at last to the strong urging of his counsel that the Cumberland Infirmary be notified of its interest. Since the Infirmary's case would be identical with (lawyers say "ride astride") his own down to Mrs. Mounsey's settlements, he lent the Infirmary's solicitors any of his papers they wished to see. His counsel's motive for urging this action was to get the record closed sooner: the Infirmary was bound to be told sooner or later, and its entry while the record was fluid would save time in the long run. Actually, from one cause or another, there were seemingly endless delays. Nobody was ready on 13 October: each claimant wishing to see what changes the others had made before filing his own. Whenever it looked as though the record might be closed, a new claimant appeared. The date was extended to 10 November, to 8 December, to 5 January 1938, to 2 February, to 2 March, to 23 March, to 4 May, to 11 May. Until nearly the end of this series of manoeuvres, it did not seem necessary for Isham to be in Edinburgh. He was kept very fully informed, mainly through Thackrah, of what was going on, and commented on the various claims and pleadings. He stayed in the United States till early November, when Thackrah reported him arrived from America and planning to spend the winter in Europe. Early in January he was in France. He seems to have remained in France or England (probably London) till some time in April, when he showed up in Edinburgh, presumably summoned by his lawyers to help with the final arguments. He was deeply anxious for the record to be closed, but he heard of nothing but postponement and new claimants. Since all the legal costs of all the losing claimants would in the end be charged against the fund *in medio,* he saw every new claimant and every postponement as additions to a steadily mounting bill—a bill which he feared he could pay only by selling some or all of the manuscripts.

The entry of the Cumberland Infirmary (which was not effected till 8 December) sent Buchanan out into further researches on Mrs. Mounsey. He interviewed representatives of the Edinburgh firm who had factored Auchinleck in her time. (It was through this connexion that he learned of Thomas Drysdale.) He consulted Dow-

---

[1] See below, pp. 38–40.

ell's auctioneers in Edinburgh, who had sold much of Mrs. Mounsey's furniture and effects and the lesser books from the library. The time allowed for the Infirmary to adjust its claim (2 February) had not expired when he learned that another new claimant was on the horizon. The four Eliott heirs were withdrawing in favour of the trustees of Mrs. Vassall. Mrs. Vassall was sister to Theresa, Lady Eliott, but the claimants were a quite different lot. The Eliotts would have had to prove somehow that Theresa, Sir Alexander's elder daughter, had acquired the right to Sir Alexander's personal estate when her brother, Sir James, declined succession. Mrs. Vassall could have advanced that same claim, failing Theresa.

Mrs. Vassall's trustees were admitted and given to 2 March to adjust their claim, but before the time was up, another claimant knocked on the door. Mrs. Hailey, great-granddaughter of Boswell's daughter Elizabeth, whom we have heard of before, at last decided to enter the cause. Her entry forced Isham's lawyers to work out the whole tangle of the claim of the younger children, which they had so far been able to dodge, both the Eliotts and Mrs. Vassall's trustees assuming, like Isham, that the papers passed from Boswell to Alexander. Lord Stevenson allowed her lawyers two weeks and then six weeks more (to 4 May) to prepare her claim. Isham appeared in Edinburgh at this point (13 April 1938) and worked almost daily with his lawyers. When 4 May arrived, Mrs. Hailey's lawyers tried for another extension, but were refused more than a week. The record was closed on 11 May. The Clerk of Courts could see no time in the calendar for the hearing of a cause requiring so much of the Court's time, and wished to put the hearing off until after the vacation (that is, to October), but Isham pushed so hard for a hearing before the Court rose that the date of 12 July was set. Since it would cost Isham more (supposing him successful and paying the costs of all the parties) to defeat his opponents in court than to buy them out beforehand, he next attempted to settle with the other claimants. Lord Clinton and Mrs. Hailey declined, and the Cumberland Infirmary wanted an independent expert valuation (for which there was not time) before entertaining any proposal. Mrs. Vassall's trustees agreed to settle for £200 plus costs, and their claim was assigned to Isham the day after the hearing commenced. In order not to complicate his own argument, he decided not to argue her cause at all. He worked night after night on Talbot's claim; David Buchanan says that "to a large extent, he dictated the presentation of his case in court".

I remember vividly an impromptu dash of three hundred miles which I myself made to get information for him that July, probably only a day or two before the hearing. I was in Maine for my brief vacation, staying at camp on a lake at some distance from a telephone. Word was got to me that Isham had called me from Edinburgh by transatlantic telephone at the nearest telephone office, Oxford village, and would call back that evening. What he wanted, it turned out, was the text of a passage in Boswell's journal in which Boswell spoke of his hope that when Alexander some day read the journal at Auchinleck, he would be grateful to him for his thoughtful care of him as a child. The point of course was that this reflection implied an assumption on Boswell's part that his papers would descend to his eldest son and representative. I remembered that there was such a passage, but had no notion where in the journal it was to be found, and had no set of *Private Papers* at hand to consult. Isham said the matter was urgent. When I hung up the receiver, baffled, my mother-in-law, who was at the switchboard (the central was in the house of my wife's parents), reminded me that the Bar Harbor Express from Bar Harbor to Washington would be going through Danville Junction (some fifteen miles away) in forty-five minutes. My brother-in-law volunteered to drive me, and I borrowed his hat and went just as I was, with no overnight case, caught the train (they held it for a minute or two), got to New Haven at dawn next morning, worked all day in the Boswell Office, sent a long cable to Isham, and caught the night train back to Portland about 10:00 p.m. I cite this story partly for the pleasure it gives me to recall those days, partly to support David Buchanan's conclusion that my services to Isham were performed in a spirit of friendship and were not restricted to the agreements of a contract.

The hearing, with Lord Stevenson presiding, began on Tuesday 12 July 1938. In order to save time by restricting the debate to legal issues, all claimants agreed to admit certain facts and to accept certain documents as authentic. Lord Clinton's junior counsel spoke all of Tuesday and most of Wednesday morning. Milligan replied for Isham, using Wednesday afternoon, all day Thursday, and most of Friday. Junior counsel for the other two claimants managed to say what they had to say in what remained of Friday. This used up all the time that had been allotted to the hearing, and extra sittings had to be scheduled for Monday 18 July (the Court of Session does not ordinarily sit on Mondays) and Friday 22 July. Senior counsel for the four parties finished summing up by lunch-time on Friday. Lord Stevenson took the cause under consideration for a period that nobody could confidently predict. He actually took a little over three weeks. On 14 August 1938 he issued his judgement, awarding the Fettercairn papers in even shares to Isham and the Cumberland Infirmary. Isham heard of it at Dunvegan Castle, where he was visiting Mrs. Flora MacLeod.

§ C H A P T E R   X I I §

THE STABLE-LOFT

As PRELIMINARY TO a discussion of Lord Stevenson's judgement, a succinct review of the four claims may be useful.

Lord Clinton claimed first by prescription: that is, that since his forbears had had uninterrupted use and possession of the papers for considerably more than a century, his title to them could not be challenged at law. Alternatively, he claimed that Boswell's will had bequeathed the papers to the literary executors, and that since he had inherited Forbes's rights, he was entitled to one third of the fund *in medio*.

Isham claimed that the papers fell to Alexander Boswell by specific bequest under the Biographer's will ("all manuscripts of whatever kind, lying in the house of Auchinleck"). Alternatively, that if they fell to the younger children as part of the movable estate, they then became Alexander's property through the Assignation of the younger children to him of 21 and 31 December 1805. Or (another alternative) that if the papers ever did pass by deed or otherwise to the younger children or their descendants or other parties, said children, descendants, or other parties abandoned all claim to them in favour of the heir of entail in possession, and later to the proprietor for the time being. Or (finally) if the papers passed on Boswell's death to the younger children as part of his movable estate and were not conveyed to Alexander by the Assignation of 21 and 31 December 1805, they then passed in whole or at least in part "to the said Sir Alexander Boswell or to his son Sir James Boswell in virtue of the testamentary writings or as intestate estate of said younger children". That is, supposing the papers to have passed to the four younger children, Alexander would still have inherited three-eighths of the property by will from James and by intestate succession from Veronica; and if Euphemia too had died intestate, Alexander's family would have divided her five-sixteenths with Elizabeth's family. (As a matter of fact Euphemia did leave a will, as we have seen,[1] which would have conveyed her share to her residuary legatee, Mrs. Suning, but by some accident Isham's lawyers failed to find it.) From Alexander, Isham's argument ran, by virtue of the respective wills, deeds, and settlements, the papers passed to Sir James Boswell and to his widow, Lady Boswell. Or alternatively, if they did not pass directly from Sir Alexander to Sir James, they became the property of Sir Alexander's widow when she purchased the library of Auchinleck House and that she then gave or abandoned them to Sir James. By the bequest of Lady Boswell (Sir James's widow) to Mrs. Mounsey of the "books and pictures in the Mansion House of Auchinleck", they then passed to Mrs. Mounsey, and by a similar clause in Mrs. Mounsey's will, to Lord Talbot, whose assignee Isham was. Alternatively, Isham claimed that on Lady Boswell's death one half of the papers passed as part of her movable estate to Mrs. Mounsey and half to Lady Talbot de Malahide, and that Lady Talbot's half descended to her son by the terms of her marriage contract.

Mrs. Vassall's trustees advanced the same main argument as Isham in getting the papers to Alexander, and also backed it up with his first alternative. They then claimed that Sir Alexander bequeathed his entire movable and heritable estate to his son James and the heirs male of his body, "whom failing to Janet Theresa Boswell and Margaret Amelia Boswell his daughters". The Settlement provided further that "if his sons or their heirs male shall repudiate this deed or decline to make up titles under it, then his [Sir Alexander's] younger children shall succeed to the subjects". Sir James, they said, did formally renounce representation of his father in a deed dated 22 October 1831. Theresa and Margaret Amelia consequently succeeded to the movable estate including the documents making up the fund *in medio*. The trustees accordingly claimed one half of the fund.

The Cumberland Infirmary, accepting Isham's case with its final alternative claim, asserted its right to one half of the fund as residuary legatee of Mrs. Mounsey.

Mrs. Elizabeth Mary Hailey (*née* Cumberlege), great-granddaughter of Boswell's daughter Elizabeth, claimed five thirty-seconds of the fund on the ground that the Biographer's will gave the papers to the younger children, both in the disposition of the movable estate and in its clause creating literary trustees, and that she was heir to half of Elizabeth's five-sixteenths (Elizabeth's original fourth plus a fourth of the share of Veronica, who died intestate).

Lord Stevenson did not rule at all on the claim of Mrs. Vassall's trustees, because, though the case appeared in the Closed Record, it was in fact not pleaded in court. Isham had acquired it on an assignation, but he did not get the assignation till 13 July 1938 (the day after the hearing commenced).

Lord Stevenson dismissed the claims of Lord Clinton and Mrs. Hailey summarily. Forbes, Malone, and Temple, he said, "got no beneficial gift" under the clause appointing them literary trustees, but rather "had imposed upon them a

[1]See above, pp. 43-45.

duty". Forbes having received the papers for a trust purpose, the plea of prescription was not applicable. Also, "I certainly do not think the clause can be read as a gift of the papers to the younger children." The younger children were entitled to the proceeds of publication, if publication had been decided on, but not to the papers themselves. Though they knew that a mass of papers, supposed to be the entire deposit, had been returned to Auchinleck after Sir William Forbes's death, there is no evidence that they put forth any claim to ownership.

Lord Stevenson's judgement found for Isham's main argument and the argument of the Cumberland Infirmary down to the point where the two diverged; from that point he found for the Infirmary. He ruled that by the clause "all Manuscripts of whatever kind lying in the house of Auchinleck" Boswell gave his personal papers to Alexander. The mislaid papers, then, were the property of Alexander. He had a right to demand them from Forbes, and under his will this right passed to his son, Sir James. By the terms of Sir James's will, it passed to Sir James's widow. She, it will be remembered, divided her estate evenly between her daughters Mrs. Mounsey and Lady Talbot, but she gave the "books and pictures in the Mansion House of Auchinleck" solely to Mrs. Mounsey. Lord Stevenson considered it doubtful whether "manuscripts" would pass under a gift of "books", and in any case the manuscripts in question were not in Auchinleck House at the time Lady Boswell made her will nor at the time of her death. "The right to demand the manuscripts therefore passed equally to her two daughters as part of the residue of her estate." Lady Talbot's share of the right passed under her marriage contract to her son (that is, to Isham), but Mrs. Mounsey's share passed by the residuary clause of her will to the Cumberland Infirmary. Lord Stevenson therefore awarded the fund *in medio* in equal shares to Isham and the Cumberland Infirmary, continuing the cause to ascertain which of the documents in Abbott's *Catalogue* were from Boswell's archives and which (e.g. the originals of Boswell's letters to Forbes) were from Forbes's. Isham's senior counsel advised against appeal, and Isham acquiesced. Since none of the other parties appealed either, Lord Stevenson's judgement became final.

I have no doubt that Boswell wished all his personal papers to be gathered at Auchinleck as the property of Alexander, and I am glad that Lord Stevenson found the clause in the will "as also all Manuscripts of whatever kind lying in the House of Auchinleck" "habile" (his own word) to effect that disposition. As I have said above,[2] however, I doubt that Boswell in that clause meant to refer to his own papers. The Auchinleck library contained many literary and historical manuscripts of considerable antiquity (for example, the so-called Asloan Manuscript now in the National Library of Scotland), and I have little doubt that Boswell meant "all the book manuscripts in my father's collection, regardless of the language they are written in". I think too that the mention of "Classicks and other books" followed by a specific bequest to the heirs of entail of only "greek and latin Books" was not

---

[2]See above pp. 19–20.

accidental. Boswell wished Alexander to have the whole library, but he was worried by the small provision he had made for the other children, and he was willing that Alexander should pay something to get the "other books". The construction of his sentence shows that he was deliberately allowing the "other books" to fall into the executry, which he was leaving equally among the younger children, not expecting that they would really keep all or any of them, but that they would release them to Alexander on payment of a negotiated sum of money. The provision for his "Manuscripts of my own composition and all my letters from various persons" is not structured in that way at all. It occurs in a later portion of the will which contains no reference to the executry, embedded in a series of legacies. It makes specific provision for handling possible profits arising from publication of the papers—and that is all. Boswell seems to have felt that no more was necessary. "He just assumed," as David Buchanan writes to me, "[his papers] would remain at Auchinleck where they properly belonged." Whether they in fact landed in the executry is for lawyers to decide. I should myself get them to Alexander by Isham's first or second alternative.

Any historian of the Boswell papers who probes at all deeply will find the problem of the transmission of the Fettercairn hoard from Sir Alexander Boswell to Sir James Boswell the toughest in the entire sequence. Lord Stevenson is no help at all on this point: he simply accepts the arguments of Isham and of the Cumberland Infirmary that the papers passed to Sir James by Sir Alexander's will. This was no doubt because the matter was not debated in court, Isham's case and that of the Cumberland Infirmary being the same on this point. If Mrs. Vassall's case had been argued, Lord Stevenson would have had to be more specific as to how Sir James acquired his right, but in the circumstances he seems to have concluded that ownership of the papers got from Sir Alexander to Sir James in one way or another, and that he need not settle the details.

Sir Alexander left his entire free estate to Sir James, but he died hopelessly in debt, and Sir James declined his succession, later even executing a formal deed of renunciation. Boswell had attempted to keep Lord Auchinleck's library for ever at Auchinleck by bequeathing it to the heirs succeeding under the entail, and Sir Alexander confirmed this attempt by bequeathing it to Sir James, to be his whether he otherwise accepted Sir Alexander's succession or not. Isham argued that this bequest included the Fettercairn papers, because Sir Alexander meant Sir James to have all the papers, and would have included them if he had known about them. Alternatively, Isham argued that Sir Alexander's daughters declined the succession, and that if none of Sir Alexander's children (James, Janet Theresa, Margaret Amelia) inherited the papers, they must have gone to Sir James's children, since Sir Alexander's bequest was to "James Boswell, my son and the heirs of his body".

David Buchanan thinks the most compelling argument (which Isham did not use because his lawyers did not understand a certain episode in Sir James's dealing with his father's creditors) would have been to claim nothing under the will, which

Sir James really and completely repudiated, but to locate his claim in his status as creditor to his father's estate. He bought out and secured formal assignations of the claims of almost all, if not all, of the creditors. "I am confident," David Buchanan says, "that either he satisfied *all* the creditors before he died, or that his executors could easily have done so after his death" (Sir James had insured his life for £35,000). The Fettercairn papers were his as sole remaining creditor to Sir Alexander's estate.

Lord Stevenson's ranking of the Cumberland Infirmary to half the Fettercairn fund was moral nonsense. Mrs. Mounsey would have been shocked and infuriated by it. Isham maintained that by "books in the Mansion House of Auchinleck" Mrs. Mounsey meant "the library at Auchinleck". Boswell, he argued, had regarded the library as a family heirloom which ought to pass to each successor to Auchinleck House. The "library" was an entity to which all the books *and all the family papers* belonged, wherever they happened to be situated at any given time. The Boswell papers at Fettercairn got there by accident, and they were constructively part of the library of Auchinleck; Mrs. Mounsey, if she had known of them, would certainly have wished them to remain in the family. Isham's senior counsel, Wardlaw Burnet, believed this to be not only just reasoning but sound law, and cited judicial precedents for bringing "manuscripts" in under the heading of "books". If the legality of sometimes making the term "books" include manuscripts had been the sole point at issue, he would probably have advised Isham to appeal. But Lord Stevenson had only found that part of the argument "doubtful"; his unqualified reason for rejecting the claim was that "the manuscripts which are claimed in this case were not in Auchinleck at the date of the Settlement of James's Widow or at the date of her death". "It is very difficult," as David Buchanan says, "to argue that a testator meant constructively to include in a bequest items of the very existence of which she was unaware." Wardlaw Burnet therefore advised against an appeal, David Buchanan thinks rightly.

Lord Stevenson gave no judgement on the case of Mrs. Vassall's trustees because Isham had purchased it and chose not to present it. However, if David Buchanan's analysis of Sir James's tactics is accepted, it would appear to be possible to dispose of Mrs. Vassall's claim summarily. By declining to enter upon the succession, Sir Alexander's daughters forfeited any right they may have had under his will in consequence of Sir James's renunciation. But if they had entered upon the succession, the will would have conferred no benefits. Sir Alexander was hopelessly insolvent. *All* his personal estate was the property of his creditors and was not nearly enough to satisfy their claims. The only way an heir could have made anything out of the situation would have been to do what Sir James did: buy up the unsecured debts for less than their face value. (Sir James secured assignments of nearly all the unsecured debts by paying ten shillings in the pound.) Whatever assets of Sir Alexander's personal estate could be located in the end were Sir James's property as sole creditor.

Exactly ten years elapsed before the cause was finally wound up. The course that would undoubtedly have been best for Isham to follow would have been to move promptly and decisively; to push the Court to separate the papers that were to be returned to Clinton and to decide how the expenses of the action were to be borne. That accomplished or put in train, he should have bought out the Cumberland Infirmary and have paid whatever expenses were assessed. He delayed, not from choice but from sheer lack of funds. It was almost certain that the Court would hold him and the Infirmary responsible for the total expenses and certain that the Infirmary would expect to be relieved of its share of the bill, and the whole came to a sum that he simply did not have. Furthermore, once the Court held its hearing on expenses, he would have had to pay the bill within a very short time or the Judicial Factor might auction the papers.

Isham remained in Britain for some months but risked nothing that would have changed the situation. When he sailed for home at the end of November, it was with an agreement from E. P. Buchanan and the solicitors for Lord Clinton that so far as they could, they would delay court action till it was convenient for him to return. In America Isham again explored the possibility of selling all the papers to a university. Harvard expressed interest and Yale strong interest, but Bernhard Knollenberg, Librarian at Yale, said he could not approach a donor with any hope of success till Isham had title to the Fettercairn papers.

None of the other parties pushed for a hearing till after the beginning of the new year. On 1 February 1939 E. P. Buchanan cabled Isham that he could not get any further postponement, and that a hearing was set for 9 February. Isham replied by cable, in terms that indicated that he did not intend to be present. Represent to the Court, he said, the injustice of Boswell's heirs' being put to great expense "to obtain what had always been theirs by right". Instead of recovering his costs, Clinton ought to be assessed the entire expenses because of the negligence of his ancestor Forbes. A cable from E. P. Buchanan which crossed this caused him to change his mind. On 31 January Clinton's solicitor had intimated to Buchanan that Lord Clinton, in addition to expenses, would be claiming £225 which he had given Abbott to reimburse him for what he had paid to one of his two copyists. Isham thought this latter claim proper. But Abbott himself now intimated an intention of making a claim of £1,080 against Isham and the Cumberland Infirmary for out-of-pocket expenses and four thousand hours of personal work on his *Catalogue*. Isham was violently opposed to this, and came instantly to Edinburgh to oppose it. He refused to make any settlement, and declined to allow the matter to be referred for decision to the Court or the Judicial Factor. Abbott threatened to sue the Judicial Factor as well as Isham and the Cumberland Infirmary. Counsel had given opinion to the Judicial Factor that Abbott had no grounds of action against him, and that though he might perhaps make a case against Isham and the Cumberland Infirmary, the chance of his succeeding seemed small. E. P. Buchanan agreed with this opinion, but warned Isham that in the end it might be cheaper to settle for a reasonable sum than to defend a suit or let the claim dangle. The threat of a suit in fact produced immediate paralysis in the proceedings. The Judicial Factor wanted to be indemnified against possible action, and the Cumberland Infirmary returned no answer when asked to state its position. The hearing was postponed from 9 February to 17 February to 22 March. On that date, Lord Stevenson was ill and the hearing was again postponed. He was still unable to attend the Court at the beginning of the Summer Session and it did not look as though he would resume his duties before the autumn. E. P. Buchanan thought it better to wait instead of taking the matter to a judge who was not familiar with the case. Isham meantime made a serious effort to come to terms with the Infirmary. He had attempted by telephone conversations with the Secretary in the previous September to bypass the lawyers and go himself to Carlisle to talk directly with the governing body of the institution. The answer then had been that all matters must be left in the hands of the solicitors. He now tried again by a long and eloquent letter (9 March 1939) to the Chairman, and was again told in effect to send his solicitors to talk with the Infirmary's solicitors. Isham through E. P. Buchanan offered £800 plus all expenses. The counter-proposal of the Infirmary's lawyers was £10,000 minus half the total expenses of all parties. Buchanan had to reply that those terms were so much above Isham's as to offer no basis for discussion. Isham went home in May. When Buchanan cabled on 12 October that Lord Stevenson was again available, the war had broken out and Isham was in no mood to press matters. His aim was somehow to acquire title to the whole Fettercairn hoard and to move the papers to America. He could not raise the necessary funds, and if he had been able to would hardly have cared to risk them on the Atlantic in wartime. He replied in non-committal fashion on 24 October, sent one brief cable in 1940 and two more in 1941, and then was silent on Fettercairn business for four years.

I may use the lull in Isham's activities to recapitulate my own so far as this history is concerned. The *Index* to *Private Papers* was published in July 1937. Before that time I had turned to preparation of the copy for Isham's multi-volume trade edition of Boswell's journal, to be published as a unit by the Viking Press. As I have said, this was to contain all of Boswell's fully written journal, with annotation for the general reader. Except for the time I took out in 1940 and 1941 to prepare the Messinger Lectures which I gave at Cornell in the spring of 1941 (published later that year by the Cornell University Press as *The Idiom of Poetry*,) all my research time for eight years went into Viking's unlucky trade edition. In the second term of 1938–39 (my first sabbatical leave), I sought a change of scene by moving my family to Cambridge and working for six months in the Harvard College Library. We rented a large furnished house on Channing Street, the Library assigned me and Charles Bennett (who went along with me) the Charles Eliot Norton study in the stacks of the Library to work in, and every one was extraordinarily kind to me and Mrs. Pottle. I think perhaps I never enjoyed my research on the papers so much at any other time.

Isham's original and principal solicitors in the whole Fettercairn business had been Denton Hall and Burgin of London, and now that the action before the Court of Session in Edinburgh had been carried through to a decision, the London firm began again to take general direction. Humphrey Thackrah had been called up for military service, and Dr. E. Leslie Burgin had taken charge of Isham's affairs. Both Burgin and E. P. Buchanan repeatedly tried by cable and letter to get instructions, but Isham ignored most of these approaches. He no doubt feared that any sign of activity on his part would cause the unappealable setting of a date when he would have to produce money to pay all the expenses. It seems extraordinary that none of the other claimants had pushed vigorously for a hearing, for, as David Buchanan says, "all the solicitors involved in the case were still lying out their fees".

In March 1940 Isham again approached Yale about selling the entire collection. Before he could sell, he needed to borrow. He thought he could buy out the Cumberland Infirmary and pay all the costs for £5,000, but Knollenberg naturally needed a definite figure. Isham cabled E. P. Buchanan (1 May 1940) to try again to get a figure from the Cumberland Infirmary. The solicitors, who were now considerably less toplofty, said that their clients would consider nothing less than £1,000, but declined to commit themselves to anything more specific (15 July 1940). It was a pity that Isham could not follow this up, for it was a great come-down from the Infirmary's former position and less than he later had to pay. But he simply could not raise any money at all in the usual way. The income from his trust fund had been reduced, and he owed Van Alen $142,836, not counting interest.

On 10 January 1941, Isham received from Burgin a cable that exactly paralleled the one I had had from Chapman in 1936. It was alarming but totally incomprehensible till explained by a following letter: "Long and curious letter received Joyce Talbot reporting existence many further originals. . . . " Burgin as a matter of fact had had the letter for three months: Isham's remissness in correspondence did not encourage alacrity on the other end, and in any case Burgin wanted to discuss the letter with Thackrah, who had a leave coming up. It seems curious that Lady Talbot did not write directly to Isham, but after the croquet-box in 1930 and Isham's own search in 1937, the news she had to report was so staggering that she probably felt up to imparting it only through an intermediary. Her letter, of which Burgin forwarded a copy five days later, could not have arrived before the 20th, but Isham had meantime cabled to Burgin and received a cable in reply.

In December 1939, she reported, the Malahide Parish Council had requested space at the Castle for storing grain reserves for the village, and the loft of a stable was promised for the purpose. The stable selected was used for cart-horses and had formerly been a cow-shed: it was not in the stable-yard but stood farther off, and was more of a farm-building than a domestic structure. The loft was reached by an exposed outside wooden stair.[3] The steps of the stair were rotted and had to be

---

[3]For a good photograph of the exterior, see TA, p. 242.

replaced before loads of any weight could be carried down or up. It was October
1940 before the loft was cleared. The space above-stairs was found to be jammed
with furniture, pictures, and empty boxes: towards the back, furniture that had
been sent over from Auchinleck; in front a further mass that had been crammed
in when Lady Talbot rearranged the Castle in 1925. Several men worked two days
carrying out the lumber. On the second day, word was brought to Lady Talbot that
two boxes of papers had been found at the very back of the loft. One of the boxes
contained papers of the Biographer, the other papers of earlier and later Boswells.
Some of the papers were wrapped in newspapers of the year 1917, and both boxes
had been labelled for shipping by the Dowager Lady Talbot, Lord Talbot's step-
mother. From the appearance of the papers, Lady Talbot concluded not only that
her father-in-law had never handled them, but also that he did not know of their
existence. The Dowager Lady Talbot, she thought (she had died in 1932), had
found them in some out-of-the-way place at Auchinleck when the furniture was
being removed and had labelled them for shipment; but she had forgotten to tell
her husband about them, and at Malahide they had been put in the back of the loft
by some officious (the word was her own) unpacker and lost from that time. It
would have been impossible, Lady Talbot said, to get at them without some such
clearing as had just occurred. She had not been able to make anything like a full
listing of the documents, but mentioned six letters from Garrick, correspondence
with John Johnston of Grange, part of the Temple correspondence, letters from
Boswell to his children, some fragments of journal—and the remainder of the
manuscript of the *Life of Johnson.* She announced Lord Talbot's intention to give
Isham the journal fragments (this, as has been said, had been a consistent policy
since 1927), and suggested that Isham and Lord Talbot should pool their respective
portions of the *Life* manuscript and sell the whole for the benefit of air-raid victims
in Ayrshire. "Beyond this we have no plans and as I mentioned—no time to go
into the matter at present."

By "appearance of the papers" Lady Talbot presumably meant that the majority
of the letters in the new find gave every indication of having been undisturbed since
Boswell's time. It was his practice in filing to fold letters into packets just as they
had gone through the post, and the majority of the letters from the stable-loft were
found in that condition. Certainly, nobody since Boswell had *read* many of the
newly discovered documents, but I find it hard to believe that either Colonel Talbot
or the fifth Lord Talbot had not handled them to some extent. Their interest, after
all, had been in the unpublished journal, especially journal in bound notebooks,
and apart from fragments edited to serve as copy for the *Life of Johnson,* little journal
was found in this lot of papers. In a search for journal it would not have been
necessary to open out folded letters. The letters that were given a place of honour
in the ebony cabinet were probably always a choice collection.

Isham, whose grip was already tiring, was deeply shocked to discover that the
bear he had by the tail was twice as big and twice as lively as he had supposed. He

was convinced this time that either Lady Talbot had been culpably careless or had known about the existence of the "new" papers all along and had been holding them out deliberately. He instantly cabled Burgin to take steps to claim them as his own under the agreement of 1927, as confirmed by the assurances of 1930 and 1937 that there were no more papers in the Castle, and by the free delivery to him of the papers he himself had found in 1937. He offered to join the Talbots in a joint contribution of not more than a thousand guineas to the Ayrshire air-raid victims.

Burgin had not waited for instructions, but had already put Talbot under notice, formally reserving any rights Isham might have in the papers. This was a bad tactical error, for it was in Isham's interest to keep on friendly terms with Lady Talbot, whatever his suspicions might be. She was not one to be scared. Talbot's solicitors sharply repudiated Burgin's claim for Isham and referred to Isham's lack of good faith in ignoring Lady Talbot's censorings. Burgin referred Isham's cable to E. P. Buchanan, with instructions to take the necessary steps, but Buchanan urged caution. He doubted that Isham's claim was founded in law, and pointed out that in any case any legal action resorted to would have to be taken in the courts of Eire. On this, Burgin went to Edinburgh for a consultation with E. P. Buchanan and Wardlaw Burnet, and the three decided that unless Isham could show better evidence, he had no enforceable claim to the new papers. They so notified him, but he remained silent for more than a year.

While Burgin, E. P. Buchanan, and Wardlaw Burnet were together, they also discussed Fettercairn business. Isham had recently (7 January 1941) cabled asking Buchanan if he could now get a firm figure from the Cumberland Infirmary. The Infirmary's solicitors made definite their former tentative figure of £1,000 plus legal costs of about £400. Burgin, E. P. Buchanan, and Wardlaw Burnet decided that it was no time to reopen negotiations, because the news of the recent discovery might leak out, and the Infirmary might claim half the new papers. As David Buchanan says, "this was an extraordinary and an unfortunate decision". As recently as 1938, E. P. Buchanan and Wardlaw Burnet had been quite clear that the Infirmary could prove no claim to any papers that were in Auchinleck House at the time of Mrs. Mounsey's death. If Mrs. Mounsey's gift of books did not convey all the papers to the sixth Lord Talbot, the purchase by the fifth Lord Talbot of all the effects in Auchinleck House from Mrs. Mounsey's executor did. It is remarkable too that Isham, if he was consulted, should have forgotten so important a link in his argument. If Isham could have closed promptly on the Infirmary's then terms, he would have saved more than £1,000. But it may not have made any difference. If Isham had been able to find £1,400, he might not have dared to close with the Infirmary, because that settlement would have precipitated demands for the remainder of the expenses, a total sum he could not manage.

Though nobody seems to have been aware of it at the time, Tinker had preserved evidence that Isham could have made very embarrassing to the Talbots. Tinker had reported to Adam in 1925, only a little more than four months after his visit to Malahide, that "Lady Talbot" had told him that there were at Malahide "two cases of papers from Auchinleck that had never been opened since their arrival in Ireland". There can hardly be any doubt that he had reported correctly what he was told, or that the two cases were the ones found in the stable-loft in 1940. When David Buchanan, many years later, called Tinker's statement of 1925 to Lady Talbot's attention, she replied that she had no memory whatever of having heard of the cases before 1940, and could only suppose that in 1925 she was prompted by the butler or some other member of the household-staff who knew of the arrival of the cases at Malahide. By 1927 she "had completely forgotten about the two unopened cases if she ever knew of their existence". I have suggested above[4] a much more likely informant than the butler: namely, the Dowager Lady Talbot, who had packed and labelled the cases, and on Tinker's testimony was present when he made his call. It would seem somewhat remarkable if the Dowager Lady Talbot, who lived nearly seven years more, should have mentioned those cases in Lady Talbot's presence just that once, but it could have happened. Through repeated experience of Lady Talbot's forgetfulness (we are by no means at the end of the list of occurrences) I have come to the conclusion that it was quite genuine. It sprang, I suggest, from an excessive ingrained cautiousness, a deep native disinclination ever to make a clean sweep, that caused her unconsciously always to drop a remnant of things out of memory to be "discovered" later. I think she knew of the remnants at the time, but gradually persuaded herself that she was mistaken, or that the remnants were negligible, or would be too hard to get at, and finally ended by genuinely forgetting them. Above all, in assessing Lady Talbot's many remnants, it must be remembered that her interest in old papers, though lively on occasion, was not sufficient to sustain her through a long bout of systematic examination.

Isham made no direct approach to Lady Talbot for more than a year. In March 1942 he finally wrote her a long letter complaining of ill usage. He pointed out how important it had been to him from the first to be able to assert that he was in possession of *all* Boswell's archives as they had come down to his great-great-grandson and representative, and detailed the many assurances the Talbots had given him that every possible hiding-place had been searched. He implied that he ought to have the papers at a no more than nominal figure. Lady Talbot sharply repelled the charge of ill usage and turned over further negotiations to A. B. Spingarn, a lawyer in New York. She told Spingarn that in spite of Isham's complaints, she was still sympathetic with him and still hoped that the papers could somehow all be united in his collection. Isham soon wrote in a much more friendly tone, and Lady Talbot sent a long and generous reply: "We both sympathise with your anxiety over the situation, and Lord Talbot will take no step regarding the papers without first acquainting you. . . . I would . . . like you to believe that no-one has been as much to blame as you were first inclined to think. We must

---

[4]Pages 80–81.

all face the matter with goodwill, and at the end of the war see what suggestion can be made." She still, however, left all negotiations as to price in Spingarn's hands.

From June of 1942 to March of 1945—almost three years—Isham seems completely to have shelved the tantalizing quandaries of both Fettercairn and Malahide. He lived in diminished splendour in the Hotel Gladstone, New York, degenerating in health, saddened by the untimely death in 1941 of his daughter Samantha, lonely except for visits of his schoolboy sons, morose and unhappy about the progress of the war and his inability to get into it himself. By early 1943 he came seriously to the conclusion he had so long debated as a possibility: that his uniting Boswell's archives could only be a step towards immediately selling the entire lot. Having announced this decision to his co-investor Van Alen (the "manuscripts just must be sold in the immediate future"), he arranged with Van Alen the percentage of Van Alen's investment Van Alen was to get back in case of a sale—a matter in which Van Alen showed himself remarkably generous: "I understand fully the hardships you have undergone to attempt to preserve these valuable sources of scholarship and I will be gratified in this day of war and uncertainty if anything can be salvaged for us from this venture."

As the end of the war approached, Isham reopened negotiations with E. P. Buchanan, explaining all his difficulties and dilemmas. He had brought suit against the trustees of his family trust, and the issue of the litigation was still undecided. He assured Buchanan that when it was decided, he planned to have matters out with Abbott and to obtain the Fettercairn papers. He asked Buchanan to inquire whether the Cumberland Infirmary still stood by its figure of £1,000. He said he would negotiate with the Talbots for the stable-loft papers as soon as the war was over.

Wardlaw Burnet had died during Isham's long silence, and Isham was shocked to learn now that E. P. Buchanan was so seriously ill that there was no likelihood of his returning to business for some months. Before Isham got around to consulting Burgin, Burgin died too. Thackrah was still in the Army.

At this time occurred an episode in the history of scholarship greatly to the credit of all concerned. In September 1945 Chapman asked permission from both Isham and the Cumberland Infirmary to consult whatever manuscripts in the Fettercairn hoard were relevant to his scheme, then far advanced, of preparing a complete edition of Johnson's letters. As has been remarked above, there were at Fettercairn over a hundred letters by Johnson, some of them partially or totally unpublished, which Boswell had collected from many correspondents while he was writing the *Life of Johnson*. In spite of Chapman's secretive behaviour in "Operation Hush", Isham was disposed to grant the request to the fullest extent, allowing him unrestricted use of the manuscripts, as well as of Boswell's two letter books, also in the Fettercairn deposit. I shall desert chronology and complete the episode at this point. The Infirmary having concurred, Chapman went to Edinburgh in May

1946 and was given unrestricted access to all the papers, which were at that time in seven boxes stored in the vault of the head office of the British Linen Bank. In November of 1946, Chapman feeling the need of further study of some of the letters, the Judicial Factor handed some thirty of them to the Librarian of the Signet Library, to be transmitted to the Bodleian for Chapman's use. It is very pleasant to record this placid observance of scholarly courtesy breaking in upon an unfinished litigation. Abbott, however, was offended when he heard of it, feeling, I suppose, that his permission should also have been obtained.

I turn back now to the autumn of 1945. All Isham's advisers having dropped away, he on 19 October 1945 wrote directly both to Lady Talbot and to the Cumberland Infirmary. From this point on he was engaged simultaneously in negotiations for acquiring both lots of papers.

Before we end with the year 1945 it will probably be well to add a few words about my own activities. After completing the *Index* to *Private Papers* in 1937, I had continued to work away at the popular edition of the journal, and at the end of the summer vacation of 1944–45, I was approaching the end of that task. I had petitioned Yale for a full sabbatical release from teaching during 1945–46, and had applied successfully for a Guggenheim fellowship. The first task of my leave was to complete the copy for the popular edition of the journal. Accordingly, on 24 November 1945 I notified Guinzburg and Isham that the copy was as complete as I could make it without access to the Fettercairn papers. I then turned to the writing of the extended biography of Boswell.

I learned more than a year later that Isham was annoyed at me because I had not consulted him before applying for a Guggenheim fellowship to write a life of Boswell. It had not occurred to me that I needed to consult him. It was obviously my duty to finish all the work I had contracted to do on his Boswell publication before I started on any of my own, and that I had scrupulously performed. But I should have realized that it was a matter he was bound to be very sensitive on. It must have been very galling to him, delayed and frustrated in his own projects, to see his long-time partner in adversity apparently breaking free. I should have made an effort to see him often, but in fact stopped seeing him at all. He was frequently in communication with me during the year (always by telephone), asking my advice and reporting on what was being done. When in the spring of 1946 (as will later be explained) he acquired a small batch of new papers, he called me in high excitement and read some of them to me over the telephone. Though he did not ask me to come down, I should have gone at once to help him gloat over them. But, as I have sufficiently indicated, I found his nocturnal regimen physically unendurable; I was on leave (the first year-long leave for personal work I had ever had) and was working with intense concentration to get as much written as I could before I went back to teaching, and though of course I was deeply interested in the new bits of journal he had acquired, I could tell from his description that none of them concerned the portion of the biography I was engaged on. Since he assured me without prompting that he was going to send me photocopies, I concluded that he did not resent my failure to visit him. Then I heard nothing of him for some time, and was so absorbed in my own work that I did not realize that his telephone calls had ceased. It turned out later that he had been seriously ill and in the hospital, and I knew nothing about it till he was up again and about to leave New York for the summer. In short, his later charge that I neglected him was not without foundation.

When Isham in October 1945 reminded Lady Talbot of her promise to send a list of the stable-loft papers, she replied that because of illness, bad eyesight, and war work, she had made little progress in listing the documents, and suggested that I come over to Ireland to go through them and make the detailed identifications and literary evaluations that Isham wanted. She repeated the invitation to me. The commitment of my fellowship would have made an extended change of work awkward for me, and in any case Isham did not think an expert report that Lady Talbot would see would be to his advantage. Except for the large fragment of the manuscript of the *Life of Johnson,* concerning which she was informed from earlier Malahide sales, she seemed decidedly to be undervaluing the papers. He countered with a proposal (not accepted) that the papers be deposited at Yale, where I could work on them more effectively and at much less expense.

In February 1946 he met with Spingarn in New York and proposed a division of the new papers. The portion of the manuscript of the *Life of Johnson* was bound to be out of his reach at Lady Talbot's previous prices (£450 for 16 leaves in 1927, £3,000 for 110 leaves in 1930), not to mention his own prices to Rosenbach, which she presumably did not know about. He accordingly asked to be allowed to treat only for the other papers, leaving the fragment of the manuscript of the *Life of Johnson* to later negotiation. He offered £2,000 as a "token payment", repeating the hardship caused him by the successive Malahide discoveries. Lady Talbot accepted the offer, and sent gratis (March 1946) the few bits of journal. Isham seems to have suffered a belated access of caution, for he now demanded some indication of what he was spending £2,000 for. Lady Talbot told him the *bulk* of his purchase: the papers would fill a steamer trunk one foot by a foot and a half by three feet, and she had divided them into just twenty-six bundles, a bundle for every letter of the alphabet ("Bundle A, 57 misc. letters to J. Boswell . . . Bundle E, Odd Poems by J. Boswell and some misc. . . . Bundle H, Misc. literature by J. Boswell . . ."). There she stuck, declining to give any less-general description. He acquiesced, but beat her down to £1,750. We are now in the summer of 1946. As David Buchanan drily remarks, "The . . . list of bundles . . . as the basis of a major literary purchase, must surely be unique for its lack of informative detail."

§ CHAPTER XIII §

THE ADVENT OF

DONALD HYDE

RELATIVELY SMALL AS the sum needed was, Isham did not have it. In April 1946 he had sold to Guinzburg for $8,600 all the remaining stock of *Private Papers* (25 complete sets, nearly 250 volumes in various states from broken sets), but the money merely repaid a loan of the year before. The sum needed to acquire both the new Malahide and the Fettercairn papers was to come from his lawyer and friend, Donald F. Hyde, whom he had known since 1942.

In 1946, Hyde was thirty-seven years old, a Phi Beta Kappa graduate of Ohio State University with a law degree from the Harvard Law School. Since 1939 he had been married to Mary Morley Crapo, three years his junior, who was to take the degree of Doctor of Philosophy in English from Columbia University in 1947. Both Hydes had means.

Hyde had practised law in Michigan before coming to New York in 1940 to join the firm of Greene and Greene. After discharge from the Navy as Lt.-Commander, he in 1947 rejoined the New York firm, now named McKenzie, Hyde, Murphy, and Law. Mrs. Hyde, as has already been indicated, was professionally trained in English scholarship, and both Hydes were keen book-collectors, nursing an ambition to make their collection one of the most distinguished in the country. (In 1948 they attained this end by purchasing the entire great Johnsonian and Boswellian collection of R. B. Adam.) Both became warm and attentive friends of Isham at a time when he was feeling lonely and neglected. Hyde became very much his champion, and generously put his mind to the problem of Isham's painful position and to ways of extricating him from his most pressing difficulties. Though, as has been said, Isham needed relatively little cash to acquire both the new papers from Malahide and the Fettercairn papers, and so to accomplish his life's goal of uniting Boswell's archives, there appeared to be just no way for him to keep that magnificent collection together once he had it in his hands. Hyde came firmly to the conclusion which Isham had already waveringly adopted: that Isham must unite the collection and then immediately sell it as a whole, preferably to a university, for a sum large enough to enable him to settle his debts and have a competence left. Hyde offered, if Isham would put himself unreservedly in his hands, to carry him through to that conclusion. The plan he offered had a frank element of personal concern. He would furnish Isham with as much of an interest-free loan as would enable Isham to get the new Malahide papers into his hands. If Isham still found himself unable to raise the sum necessary to settle all the claims in which the Fettercairn papers were entangled, Hyde would advance what he needed on condition that Isham then sell him a relatively small number of selected items which the Hydes wanted for their own collection. Meantime, since the attractiveness of Isham's papers to an institutional purchaser would probably be directly proportional to the amount of unpublished matter they contained, publication, even from the papers Isham had held since 1927, was completely to cease, and everything possible was to be done to stress the freshness of the materials from the stable-loft and from Fettercairn.

It is impossible to state too emphatically that this was a complete about-face from the policy that Isham had consistently followed hitherto. Down to 1946, the idea of keeping papers unpublished to protect their sale value had been totally foreign to his thought. He loved to publish: in fact, I am not sure that he did not get more pleasure from having brought out *Private Papers* than from owning the papers that those volumes put into print. He wanted me to publish the journal more fully than Scott had done; he wanted to publish a trade edition. That unlucky trade edition was *his* venture, not mine. He granted permission to publish in the freest way not only to proved scholars, but even to graduate students who still had reputations to make. He wanted a published catalogue, he wanted a published index to *Private Papers*. Scott and I were hired to *publish*. We were his editors and advised him as editors. The new policy was not in any way intimated to me, and I could not fail sooner or later to collide with it.

After committing Isham to the first half of his plan, Hyde worked with extraordinary energy and persistence to bring it into effect. His first loan (it was interest-free) was of $5,000, roughly the sum needed to conclude with Lady Talbot. Lady Talbot, with unusual specificity, had described one bundle ("Small Bundle O") as consisting of " 'A letter to the People of Scotland' by J. Boswell". This looked as though it might be the printer's copy for one or the other of the political pamphlets that Boswell published in 1783 and 1785. Isham showed his gratitude by offering to sell Hyde this manuscript at half an appraised valuation.

Since Lady Talbot was insistent that there should be no press releases not approved by her, Isham saw to it that the steamer-trunk containing the manuscripts was not handled by any agent with a knowledge of the antiquarian trade. He was also warned not to let the papers enter the United Kingdom, since once there, they might be held because of new British regulations as to customs and control of exchange. Accordingly, Lady Talbot having obtained a customs-clearance, the steamer-trunk full of papers was put on the *American Forwarder* at Dublin, and arrived at Boston on 14 September 1946. Isham was on hand to receive it, hoping to show, or at least to report on, the papers at a first American Birthday Party for Dr. Johnson, 18 September 1946, which the Hydes were holding at their country house, Four Oaks Farm, Somerville, New Jersey. The port of Boston, however, was having a strike of dock-workers, and Isham impatiently paced the docks for three days without being able to get his cargo delivered. Having waited as long as he dared, he dashed by train to the Birthday Party at Four Oaks Farm, gave an interim report, and hurried back to Boston. He got delivery of his treasure around midnight on Saturday 21 September and transported it to New York in a railroad drawing-room. On the way, he opened the trunk and explored its contents with a young woman named Boswell who happened to be aboard.

I should suppose that Isham got more intense delight out of this exploration of Boswell's papers than from any other, because these papers came to him with less identification than any other group he had ever handled. There were in the trunk, to begin with, 85 pages of Boswell's journal, quite additional to the bits Lady Talbot had sent free. The new fragments were leaves of fully-written journal that Boswell had used as printer's copy for the *Life of Johnson,* most of them filling gaps in journals that Isham already owned. There were hundreds of letters to Boswell, including many from well-known correspondents: Baretti, Barnard, Beauclerk, Burke, Dr. Burney, George Dance, Henry Dundas, Garrick, Lord Hailes, Warren Hastings, Langton, Malone, Reynolds, Temple (160 letters, the same number as at Fettercairn), Mrs. Thrale, Wilkes. There were 139 letters from Boswell to his Edinburgh chum John Johnston of Grange, plus (an unexpected bonus) 24 fine long letters from Boswell to Temple, letters that Boswell had begged back from Temple to use in a projected book of travels. There was a letter from Boswell to Voltaire. There was the greater part of the "Ébauche de ma vie" that Boswell wrote for Rousseau (a unique and invaluable source for the biography of Boswell's early years), a leaf of Boswell's conversation with Rousseau, and two letters from Rousseau to Thérèse Le Vasseur. There was a letter from Fanny Burney to Johnson, a fine group of Johnson's autographs including manuscripts of *London* and *The Vanity of Human Wishes,* and a hitherto unknown memoir of Goldsmith by Reynolds. And besides, as David Buchanan says, "there was a mass of memoranda, jottings, newspaper clippings, invitations, and other documents of all kinds". In the last-named group was a slip of paper on which Boswell had written two verses from *The Vanity of Human Wishes,* in which he had persuaded Johnson to change a word in order to avoid a repetition. Boswell, who mentions this in the *Life of Johnson,* says that he had given the slip to the Bodleian Library, but he failed to do so. When David Nichol Smith, Professor of English Literature Emeritus of Oxford, called by invitation to see the new papers, Isham gave him the slip to take back to Bodley as a gift.

I was unfortunately prevented by duties in New Haven (the opening lecture of a large new undergraduate class in Romantic Poets) from attending the gala event at Four Oaks Farm on 18 September 1946. Isham called me on the telephone to urge me to attend; he told me afterwards (again over the telephone) that I did right in meeting my class, but I think probably he interpreted my absence as a snub to friends he wished attention paid to. At the dinner, he made unfriendly remarks about me to friends of mine who were present, saying in effect that I needn't suppose that I should have the new papers to edit. I had asked him for nothing from the new papers except photostats of the new fragments of journal, which I needed to edit and insert in the proper places in the copy for Viking's popular edition of the journal, it having been agreed in repeated conferences that that edition was to contain all the fully written journal. I had worked on this copy for eight years, with regular reports as to my progress, and had never been given a hint that there was any change of plan as to its publication. Indeed, I had supposed Isham was as impatient to get it into print as ever. He appeared now to be representing it as *mine*, a venture that I was pushing against his interest and wishes.

I resolved to keep strictly away from the new papers until he gave me a firm invitation to come to see them in New York. His telephone conversations during this period were affectionate: in fact (though our common acquaintance will find it hard to believe), Isham never then or later uttered one unkind word to my face. On one week-end during this period, he was my overnight guest in New Haven, and wrote expressing pleasure at the way he was entertained. Finally early in October he invited me down to see the papers and to stay overnight, and I went.

While I was there, I pretty much looked at things he showed me, with no attempt at systematic survey. I did ask to see certain documents that might be of use for the biography, but I made no notes and asked to take nothing away. He showed me a pile of papers which he said was leaves from the journal, and I gave it as my opinion that I should take these back to New Haven to incorporate in the popular edition. He was non-committal, and did not show them to me. Just as I was going away the next morning, he shoved into my hands some folders containing the Boswell-Temple letters, saying, "Why don't you take these back to New Haven with you?"

As soon as I could (the correspondence was voluminous and was in complete disorder) I sorted out the letters, listed them, and caused transcripts of the Boswell letters to be made. I wrote, telling him what I was doing, and proposed a date for bringing the manuscripts back. In this letter I told him flatly that on this trip I wanted to get all the new portions of fully written journal so that I could edit them for the Viking copy. I reminded him that he hoped before long to have the big 1762–63 London Journal from Fettercairn, and told him that I wanted to get the fragments done before the Fettercairn journal was dumped in my lap, so that there would be no unnecessary delay. I had seen among the new papers a number of transcripts of letters by Johnson to Boswell that Boswell had used as copy for the *Life of Johnson,* and I also said I hoped he would let me borrow these so that I could get them photocopied for Chapman. Or, since the documents (all copies) were of little intrinsic value, I suggested that he might perhaps send them direct to Chapman by post.

Isham made no reply to this letter; in fact, from that time on he did not communicate with me directly in writing at all. But a few days after I wrote, my friends James T. Babb (Yale's Librarian) and Frederick W. Hilles (Professor of English at Yale) met Hyde, and Hyde asked them to let me know that Isham was upset by my letter and did not wish to answer it. Hyde said that Isham considered my requests officious. I was not sufficiently sensitive to his difficulties as a collector: I assumed that he existed merely to acquire manuscripts at great difficulty and cost for me to carry off and print. Hyde had my letter; Hilles read it and attempted to convince him that it furnished no basis for such accusations. Hyde said that, well, anyway, Isham thought it did, and didn't want to answer it. It was clear that Hyde was now directing Isham's actions, and also that Hyde was very imperfectly informed as to the nature of the long-standing agreements between Isham and me. Hilles suggested that I write to Hyde.

I wrote Hyde a careful letter (22 November 1946), stating what I have said above: that I had tried to be very scrupulous about making personal requests, that the manuscripts I requested were needed as copy for the popular edition of the journal, a work which Isham had hired me to edit and had never countermanded. That the request I had made for Chapman was exactly of the same tenor as one I had made before, one thoroughly in line with Isham's announced policy and gladly granted. I was careful to make no complaint and to write as though the whole matter was a misunderstanding which a word of explanation would clear up. I did not think the situation was actually so simple. I was being given the outlines of Hyde's current strategy, but not with complete frankness. Isham had decided to sell; he had been persuaded that publication of the popular edition would detract from the price he might obtain for the papers, but instead of saying so frankly and directly, he (or Hyde) was pretending to misunderstand me. I had not yet met Hyde, but I expected a friendly and understanding reply. Babb and Hilles and I, up to this point, supposed that Hyde's attitude towards me would be disinterested and helpful.

His reply (26 November 1946) disturbed me, because though friendly in tone, it showed a determination to call in question the validity of the whole contractual agreement between Isham and me. Up to that time I had not suspected that it was proposed to go so far. I was warned off the new papers, which was fair; Isham now proposed to suppress the popular edition, which was his right; but I had supposed that he acknowledged the popular edition to be his own venture, and that he owed me a fee for editing it. I also had not suspected for a moment that he meant to challenge my right to make free use in my biography of any of the Malahide papers that were in his possession when our contract was drawn in 1929.

Early in April 1947, I happened to be in New York on other business, and called Hyde's office on the telephone in the hope of getting a clarifying conversation with him. His secretary reported that he was just going into a conference. I perhaps too suspiciously took this to mean that he wished to avoid frank discussion with me viva voce. But soon after, Isham invited me down to see the papers, saying that I would also have an opportunity to meet Hyde, and I went. This was at the end of April 1947. The meeting was actually a foursome, for Mrs. Hyde was also present. Hyde came late. He pitched directly into the business at hand, with bare exchange of civilities, and went away in fifteen or twenty minutes. I think we did not sit down.

His attitude towards me, though not overtly hostile, was that of a lawyer confining himself strictly to the interests of his client. He said that though there were many issues involved, the primary one in his mind was Isham's financial position; that he hoped other interests could be worked out satisfactorily, but that he had to concentrate on the problem of the advantageous sale of the manuscripts. That as a consequence, no one would be allowed to quote from the papers or even use them as a source for facts. That he could not learn that the Viking Press had any wish at the then time to proceed with the publication of the popular edition. (That accorded with my own impression. After Guinzburg got some return from the Hebrides volume, he became progressively less interested in the popular edition.) I repeated what I have said above as to my relation to that edition, agreed that it was Isham's venture and that he stood under no obligation to proceed to publication, but asked what it was proposed to do about my fee if Isham suppressed the work. Hyde asked what my fee was; I replied that under the contract there was still $5,000 due me. Isham confirmed this. I said that if the papers were sold to a university and I were allowed to retain the copy I had made for the Viking edition, I should be quite willing to take my chance of making arrangements for a publication by which I would recover my fee. Hyde seemed to deprecate this. He said that in his opinion it might be better for Isham to clear up at once any financial obligation to me, but expressed a wish to see the contract. It then came out that Isham had lost his copy. I promised to send Hyde one and Hyde agreed to report when he had studied it. During this interchange Isham was extremely friendly, denied nothing I said and made no complaints, and after Hyde had gone, assured me that if we both would trust Hyde, everything would come out right for both of us.

I then sent Hyde a copy of the contract, with a letter correcting some things I had said from memory about the date on which the $5,000 became due to me. I referred to the negotiations which Isham and I had had in 1934–35 over the $5,000 withheld by W. E. Rudge, Inc. I explained why the work had taken so much longer than had been contemplated when the contract was drawn: that by mutual agreement, oral and expressed in letters, we had expanded the limited edition far beyond Scott's plan; that we had expected the popular edition to be a small affair and that it had turned out to be six or seven large volumes with annotation. That it had become clear that it was humanly impossible for me to complete both projects in two years. That we both understood this, and that Isham had made no protest or complaint when I returned to Yale at the end of the second year; that on the contrary he had agreed both orally and in writing to extend the time-limits. That in addition to what I had contracted to do, Isham had asked me to prepare a printed catalogue of the manuscripts, and later to supervise and personally prepare a good part of the *Index* to *Private Papers.* That I did not receive and did not ask for any remuneration for these additional labours, but that I did regard them as valid reasons for an extension of time.

I now drop our negotiations at this interesting juncture, and return to the Fettercairn ring of Isham's circus, which I have not been reporting on since 19 October 1945, the events in the stable-loft ring being quite enough for any reader to follow. Actually for nearly a year after that date, the two shows ran concurrently.

On 19 October 1945,[1] Isham, deprived of his advisers, had written directly to the trustees of the Cumberland Infirmary, asking if their offer to sell for £1,000 plus expenses their half-interest in the Fettercairn papers still held. He pointed out reasons for moderation on the Infirmary's part. The expenses the Infirmary would have to share, he said, would run to £3,000, a figure that would be increased if Abbott brought suit and won. The trustees of the Infirmary took three months to get expert advice, and then replied that they felt they must ask £2,250 free of all costs. At that point (4 January 1946) E. P. Buchanan reported himself back at work, and Isham gratefully turned the negotiation over to him. Thackrah, who was now out of the service and also returned to work, warned in May that if the hospitals in the United Kingdom were nationalized, as a current Bill proposed, dealings with the Infirmary would be dealings with Government, not with a comparatively flexible board of trustees. Dealings of another sort with Government were unavoidable and did cause great delay. As Isham had found out when the stable-loft papers were shipped from Eire, the British Government had placed restrictions on the export of rare manuscripts, and he would need an export licence from the Board of Trade to get the Fettercairn papers out of Britain. Negotiations with the Board of Trade were somewhat facilitated by the fact that the late Dr. E. Leslie Burgin had once been Minister of Supply, but even so there were difficulties, and they seemed to be insuperable. Isham obviously did not want to buy the papers if he was going to be refused permission to take them to America; the Board of Trade could see no way to issue a licence to Isham to export papers he did not yet own. After six months of persistent pushing of the case (including an item-by-item run-through of Abbott's *Catalogue*), Thackrah got the conditional assurance that Isham needed. We are now at 9 October 1946. (Three weeks before that date the stable-loft papers had arrived at Boston and that ring of the circus had closed down.) On 10 October Abbott's solicitors again called attention to his claim. E. P. Buchanan advised caution, but Isham had had enough. He concluded that Abbott never would risk

---

[1]See above, p. 166.

the costs of an action, and told E. P. Buchanan to try to get the Infirmary to reduce its figure to £2,000, but to close at once. The Infirmary declined to make any reduction. E. P. Buchanan asked Isham for £2,700 (£2,250 plus £450 for the Infirmary's costs) and Isham promised to remit the sum after the new year. He had none of the money and did not know where he was going to get it.

Hyde at this point gave as his opinion that the only way out was to sell some of the stable-loft papers. Isham was strongly opposed to this action and went from bank to bank for a loan. After many refusals, he obtained a three-months' loan of $12,000 from the Continental Bank and Trust Co. in New York, putting up some selected papers as security. The Infirmary closed with Buchanan's offer on 23 January 1947, but declined to accept any responsibility for delivery of the papers or for their condition. This meant in effect that Isham had to bear the whole responsibility for checking the papers in the Judicial Factor's hands against Abbott's *Catalogue* and for separating out for return to Lord Clinton the not inconsiderable number of papers in the Judicial Factor's hands (e.g. Boswell's letters to Forbes) that had never formed part of Boswell's archives. Isham at E. P. Buchanan's suggestion asked Dr. Malcolm (mentioned above as Librarian of the Signet Library) to make this time-consuming review and allocation. His report, which was delayed by the difficulty he had in locating five apparently missing items, was not submitted till 21 March. More delay occurred when E. P. Buchanan learned that the board of trustees that had governed the Infirmary in 1938 had been superseded in 1945 by a new corporate body, which meant a check of title by Denton Hall and Burgin. Thackrah was no longer on hand to help: in February he had entered a Carthusian monastery. But on 2 May 1947 settlement with the Infirmary was finally completed, and all that stood between Isham and full ownership of the Fettercairn papers was payment of the remaining costs and the Court's decree.

E. P. Buchanan therefore wished to push on at once to costs of the unsuccessful parties, Lord Clinton and Mrs. Hailey. He strongly recommended that Isham pay these. It was, he said, almost invariable practice in actions of multiplepoinding to allow all claimants with a colourable case to charge their costs against the fund *in medio,* and he thought Isham would only incur needless expense if he opposed these claims in court. Abbott's claim remained a threat. Because court action was necessarily public and might precipitate an attachment of the papers, Buchanan wished to avoid such action as long as possible and then to make it brief. His recommended strategy was to settle quietly by private treaty all the matters left undecided in Lord Stevenson's interlocutor. That having been done, the case could very simply be disposed of by lodging a Joint Minute stating that costs were not owing to or by any parties except by Isham to the Judicial Factor, and that that sum had been approved in advance. The decree pronounced and the last costs paid, Isham could secure immediate delivery of the papers and remove them from Edinburgh. Buchanan thought he would need another £2,500 to wind matters up, and reported that he could do nothing until he had the money.

Isham could not raise the money and matters stagnated for nine months. But while the Fettercairn business languished, Hyde pushed through the action which he described to others (never, I admit, to me) as "getting tough with Pottle" or "washing Pottle out".

It will be remembered that Isham had lost his copy of our contract, and that I had furnished Hyde with one (2 May 1947). Hyde replied on 21 May, first stating his conviction that Isham and I must "maintain the friendly relationship of many years standing", and then proceeding to find me in the wrong as to every claim against Isham my contract appeared to support. By his reading of the contract (he said), it was never intended to be "a profitable undertaking"; what was contemplated was merely to compensate me for salary I lost at Yale by reducing or discontinuing my teaching. "I am sure that, today, not only would Ralph not need to pay for the editing of the Papers, but several would compete to pay him for such an opportunity. It is now recognized that access to them practically assures 'fame and fortune'." He found me solely to blame for the non-observance of the time-limits of the contract, and made an immensely flattering estimate of what I could have accomplished if I had had a mind to: "Had the work [on *Private Papers*] been completed on schedule, the popular edition would have been marketed before the discovery of the Fettercairn Papers with the recovery of at least a part of the investment that Ralph had made." He described my release of the fund at Rudge's as merely a giving up of a claim against a bankrupt firm, and reported that he could find no written agreement of Isham's to place the $5,000 in a special account; "and Ralph tells me there was no oral understanding to that effect".[2] My right to use the Boswell papers for writing a popular biography had expired fourteen years ago. I do not think, however, that at this stage it had been decided to refuse me the $5,000, for he went on, "Ralph expects to fulfill whatever obligations he may have under the agreement with you. The Rudge settlement does not in any way alter your rights as far as he is concerned."

I replied on 24 May 1947, attempting to assure him of my complete willingness to accommodate Isham in all the points which seemed to be raised, so far as I understood them. I asserted no rights, I said, in any of the new papers, and had deliberately refrained from visiting Isham and looking at them because I was writing a biography of Boswell and could not learn new facts without making use of them. I told him that I should make no immediate demand for the $5,000 due me under the contract. Because I understood him to say that Isham planned, when convenient, to pay me the $5,000, I did not repeat the offer I had made to him orally to free Isham from ever paying me the sum if he sold the papers to a university, but I assumed that he would remember it. At the same time I said it would be a great favour to me to be allowed to read the new papers for facts, to be used without quotation or acknowledgement. My letter, on repeated readings, seems to me to imply a complete willingness to consider further concessions.

---

[2]See above, p. 124.

Some time towards the end of June 1947 (I think probably on Saturday 21 June), I met Isham by Herman Liebert's arrangement at Liebert's house in New Haven. He seemed to find the meeting momentarily awkward, but was as friendly as ever. Before I took my leave, he said that Hyde was sending me a letter. "Don't you worry," he added. "Don't you worry. Everything will be all right with you." Hyde's letter, which was dated 23 June, was forwarded to me in Maine, shortly after we had arrived there for the summer. I opened it on our pleasant porch and received a severe shock.

DEAR PROFESSOR POTTLE,

I conclude from your letter of May 24th that you take the position that all of the provisions of the contract between you and Ralph are still in force and effect and are enforceable by you. Hence, I have studied the contract in more detail, and I have had several conferences with Ralph in order to determine the actions the parties have taken in the execution of the provisions of the contract.

I wish to emphasize that there is no change in attitude on either Ralph's or my part since the receipt of your letter, but you have made it necessary to answer the points that you have raised, and state Ralph's position with particularity.

1. You failed to carry out the terms of paragraph Four of the contract. Inasmuch as that paragraph is of the essence of the contract and its performance is a condition precedent to the payment of money to you, it is denied that a balance of $5,000 is owed to you.

2. Under the terms of paragraph Six of the contract all rights that you may have had to Ralph's material expired on October 1, 1933. Therefore, none of his Papers, whether acquired before or after 1946, may be used by you at this time by direct quotation, reference, or otherwise in any publication undertaken by you. . . .

I am sure Ralph completely understands why you have not made frequent visits, for he too realizes that you cannot, as you say, "look at the new papers without learning things, and cannot learn them without using them." I think you should refrain from seeing any more of the new papers, and you can rest assured it will not be considered unfriendly by Ralph.

If this letter is not a happy one for you to receive I hope you will appreciate its necessity for the safeguarding and preservation of Ralph's rights and interest in the Papers, the acquisition of which has cost him so much in terms both of investment and endeavor.

> With best personal regards,
> Very truly yours,
> DONALD F. HYDE

I waited several days to think things over, and then sent a letter of quiet protest to Isham. The following extracts will sufficiently illustrate its tone.

When I went to New York to meet you and Mr. Hyde, I assumed that you and I, in his presence, were to begin a frank and patient discussion of our relations, a discussion in which he would serve as a friendly mediator. You encouraged me at that meeting to consider him in that light. But what has actually happened is that you have not opened your mind to me at all, whereas he has from the first acted solely and simply as your lawyer, intent on gaining every advantage for you and quite unconcerned as to my interests. . . .

I have attempted in my letters to Mr. Hyde to be frank and conciliatory, but the result has merely been to increase the sharpness and severity of his replies. . . .

You must not suppose that I am, or ever have been, stubbornly insistent on the letter of a contract made many years ago in circumstances very different from those which now obtain. I have for a long time realized the need of a patient and friendly survey of the whole situation, looking to a possible redefinition of the terms of our agreement. In an atmosphere of *mutual* concession you will find me ready enough to accept revised terms. . . .

The letter was never answered.

We return now to May 1947 and the stalled Fettercairn negotiations. Months went by: spring and summer. Heyward Isham, Isham's older son, briefly in Edinburgh, got a glimpse of the papers in the Signet Library. Autumn: the Hydes also saw and handled them. Winter: by February 1948 Isham was no nearer the cash he needed, and was being pressed by the Continental Bank for repayment of his supposed three-months' loan of the year before. Then, on 4 February 1948, Hyde proposed a solution: he would pay Isham $12,500 (later increased to $14,000) for the 119 Johnson letters in the Fettercairn hoard and the Johnson diary Isham had found at Malahide in 1937. Isham apparently had been gravitating, however unwillingly, towards a sale. In November 1947 he had secured from R. J. Barry of C. A. Stonehill, Inc., a valuation of the Johnson letters. Barry thought them worth about $10,000, but of course the fact of deferred delivery put difficulties in the way of a sale. Isham accepted Hyde's offer and on 9 March cabled to E. P. Buchanan, "After infinite difficulty have arranged to cable you within fortnight requisite funds complete transaction." The money sent, he became impatient for delivery.

In fact, though E. P. Buchanan knew just how he was going to proceed, a good deal of time-consuming negotiation remained to be conducted. In David Buchanan's concise summary, "The amount of the Judicial Factor's and the other parties' expenses had to be negotiated and agreed upon; a joint minute had to be prepared and approved by all the solicitors concerned; an indemnity in favour of the Judicial Factor had to be adjusted and signed; and a court hearing had to be arranged so that the final decree could be pronounced."

At the very end the negotiations ran on an overlooked snag. The Judicial Factor intimated through his solicitors that before he could obtain his discharge, he would have to satisfy the Court that no death-duties were owing on the fund *in medio*. E. P. Buchanan had forgotten this, Isham (if he ever knew it) had forgotten it, but once encountered, there was no way round it. From the time that the Fettercairn papers dropped out of sight down to 1905, when Mrs. Mounsey died, the right to claim all or half of them had passed through five estates (Sir Alexander Boswell's, Sir James Boswell's, Lady Boswell's, Lady Talbot de Malahide's, and Mrs. Mounsey's), and no value had been assigned to this right in any of the inventories. One could not argue very plausibly that the right was valueless, at least of late years, for the Cumberland Infirmary had just been paid £2,250 for a half share of the property. The Estate Duty Office at first thought the duties might amount to £600, but was prepared in the circumstances to settle all claims for £400, of which it suggested that the Cumberland Infirmary might be assigned the larger share. E. P. Buchanan, however (writing on 25 June), pointed out to Isham that the Infirmary had been guaranteed expenses and was most unlikely to assent to such a proposal, and that obviously time would be saved if Isham paid the whole.

For Isham this very nearly proved the last straw. He drafted a violent cable in 136 words arguing that *he*, by his investment of time and money, had created the current value of Boswell manuscripts; that the earlier heirs would have assigned no value to Boswell's papers in an inventory, and that the later heirs, when Boswell manuscripts did have value, had no knowledge or enjoyment of the papers at Fettercairn. He would pay £125 nuisance value, he said, and if this was not acceptable, he would get his congressman to start an investigation in Congress. There is, however, no trace of this cablegram in the remarkably complete and accurate files of Steedman Ramage and Co. Apparently he suppressed it and worked off his pent-up emotion by calling E. P. Buchanan by transatlantic telephone, running him down at 1:30 a.m. in a remote farmhouse in Dumfriesshire, where he was for the moment staying with clients. E. P. Buchanan was vexed and perhaps not so effective as usual in calming him down, for Isham cabled tersely and angrily on 29 June:

CANNOT SUFFER FURTHER RED TAPE AND NONSENSE KINDLY RETURN MONIES CABLE
LET JUDICIAL FACTOR SELL MANUSCRIPTS AUCTION ARRANGE UNLIMITED BID FOR
ME JOHNSON LETTERS

On the same day he got off another cable, one that to me is utterly mysterious:

GOVERNMENT ADVISER REQUESTS CANCELLATION EARLIER CABLEGRAM OTHERWISE
HIS ACTIVITY AND INTEREST POSSIBLE KINDLY CONFIRM CANCELLATION BY CABLE

Surely the cable of 29 June, though angry in tone, could have raised no Government hackles? If the message in the long draft had actually been sent, one could imagine (though it seems very cloak-and-dagger) that some over-vigilant Government inspector might have ordered Isham not to charge the Crown with injustice, even by implication. But, as I have said, the long draft is not merely not preserved in Steedman Ramage and Co.'s files; there is no record there that it was ever received. E. P. Buchanan, however, seems to have understood what Isham meant and to have taken the action Isham wanted him to take.

The two following cables are cited to the honour of both men and of the Scottish legal profession. Buchanan sent the first on 1 July (night letter), Isham the second on the next day but one:

NOTE EARLIER CABLE CANCELLED LONG MEETING TODAY WITH HEAD OFFICIAL
WHO EVENTUALLY OFFERED WITHOUT PREJUDICE ACCEPT TWOHUNDRED AND
SEVENTY FIVE POUNDS COMPLETE SETTLEMENT ALL CLAIMS WHICH I CONSIDER
VERY FAVOURABLE STOP STRONGLY RECOMMEND YOU AUTHORISE ME PAY
IMMEDIATELY SAID AMOUNT TOWARDS WHICH AS GENUINE FRIENDLY GESTURE
WILLING ON FINAL ACCOUNTING WITH YOU DEDUCT ONEHUNDRED POUNDS FROM
OUR LEGAL COSTS BEYOND ABATEMENT I ALREADY CONTEMPLATED PLEASE CABLE
BUCHANAN

ANSWERING AUTHORIZE YOU PAY IMMEDIATELY TWOHUNDRED SEVENTYFIVE
POUNDS AS RECOMMENDED STOP WISH CONSIDER FURTHER BEFORE ACCEPTING
YOUR OFFER DEDUCTION WHICH I GREATLY APPRECIATE STOP CABLE
ACKNOWLEDGEMENT RECEIPT OF THIS REGARDS
ISHAM

Buchanan paid the death-duties on 5 July. The Hydes were in London, Heyward Isham was in Paris, and all three were booked to sail from Southampton on the *Queen Mary* on Friday 23 July. It was planned to get the papers on board. Time was short, but E. P. Buchanan managed it. Between the 5th and the 15th the Judicial Factor's indemnity was adjusted, the bills of all the solicitors were paid, application was made for an export licence, and the papers were packed in five large boxes under Malcolm's direction. In the charming terminology of Scots law the case had "fallen asleep" because no motion for its continuance had been made by the Judicial Factor since 1945. A "Minute of Awakening" was lodged by the parties, and the final interlocutor was pronounced on 16 July 1948 by the Hon. J. G. McIntyre, Lord Sorn, confirming the arrangements already agreed upon. 16 July was a Friday. Buchanan sent the papers to London by train, and went down himself to deliver them to the Hydes on Monday the 19th. Denton Hall and Burgin procured the export licence on the 21st. On the 23rd, Heyward Isham met the Hydes to drive to Southampton in a Rolls-Royce with the five boxes of papers strapped on top. A flat tire failed to prevent a timely arrival. The *Queen Mary* sailed at 1:00 p.m., the Fettercairn papers ensconced in a private cabin by themselves. Isham telephoned one night to inquire about the health of the "quintuplets". But when the *Queen Mary* docked on 28 July, he was in a hospital bed himself, struck down suddenly with mononucleosis. His friends Halsted VanderPoel and Herman Liebert had to take his place on the pier.

The Judicial Factor had required an indemnity from Isham against any claim that might be made by the parties or by Abbott, but none was forthcoming. He received his discharge on 1 January 1949, and the Fettercairn cause was over.

CHAPTER XIV

YALE BUYS THE BOSWELL

PAPERS

IN THE SUMMER OF 1948, then, Isham's unremitting campaign to unite Boswell's archives was crowned with a high degree of success. If the plan of 1930 had then been followed, the next step would have been to renegotiate the long-delayed trade edition of Boswell's journal. Supposing the Viking Press and William Heinemann, Ltd. to have remained in charge, supposing them to have had the judgement not to sink the London Journal of 1762–63 in a set of books but to publish it immediately by itself, Isham's publishing schemes would have been rewarded with a brilliant best-seller, and he would at last have had the satisfaction of making a good deal of money out of his manuscripts. Knowing him from the 1920's, I cannot keep my fancy from playing with that possibility, from picturing him as spurning prudence for a glorious gamble. But it is all fancy. The Viking Press in 1948 felt no disposition to risk but wanted to balance accounts, and Isham was no longer the man I had known in the 1920's. He was approaching sixty and was slipping into chronic bad health. Publication could furnish no final solution to his problem. His trust income had dwindled, his free capital was all invested in the papers; and even if the London Journal had recovered his free capital, no conceivable further publication could have extinguished his huge obligation to Van Alen. Hyde in fact had won him firmly over to a policy of selling before he had title to the stable-loft papers, let alone those from Fettercairn. The papers were to be sold, were to be sold as a unit, were preferably to be sold to a university. Further publication was to be absolutely prohibited, and every effort was to be made to emphasize the quantity of brilliant unpublished matter in the new papers from the stable-loft and from Fettercairn. Isham's previous publicity (of which there had been no dearth) had been fragmented and directed merely towards self-gratification; his publicity henceforth was to be hoarded and managed to promote a sale.

First of all, Isham had to get back on his feet again, which took some weeks. A new adviser, Herman W. Liebert, then research assistant in the Yale University Library, a seasoned newspaper man, had to plan and organize the new strategy. It was not till 23 October 1948 that the first of two skilfully managed exhibitions of the papers was staged. Isham sent the following invitation to a relatively small group of collectors, scholars, librarians, and representatives of publishing houses:

> The Boswell Papers discovered at Fettercairn House in 1931 and for twelve years in the custody of the Court of Session are now released and have reached these shores.
>
> The cases in which the MSS. are contained will be opened at eight-thirty on Saturday evening, twenty-third October, 1948, at One Hundred Sixteen East Fifty-third Street, New York City. . . .

Two weeks later (Friday 5 November) a second exhibition, again featuring the boxes in which the papers had arrived from England, opened at the Grolier Club, New York. Over the week-end a long press release composed by Liebert with Isham's help was sent out. On Monday 8 November, all the leading newspapers printed a feature story on the new papers. The *New York Times* carried a photograph of Isham on the first page, devoted a full inside page to the story, and added a long descriptive and evaluative article by Liebert.

Unsolicited funds for purchase of the papers were immediately forthcoming. Paul Mellon (Yale '29) advised the University that his Old Dominion Foundation was prepared to contribute $300,000 towards a purchase for Yale. The McGraw-Hill Book Co. (Edward C. Aswell, vice-president of the company, had attended the showing on 23 October) announced its willingness to pay any institutional purchaser $150,000 for rights to all kinds of commercial publication of the papers.

Negotiations preparatory to a sale extended over several months. Before Isham could give a clear title, various encumbrances had to be cleared away. He had to repay his loan of $8,500 to the Chemical Bank and Trust Co., which was holding some of the manuscripts as security. He had to obtain a series of releases from agreements involving the manuscripts: from Brandt and Brandt, literary agents, whom he had engaged as far back as 1930 to procure trade publication of his papers, and who had brought him and Guinzburg together; from the Viking Press and from Guinzburg personally; from William Heinemann, Ltd.; from Van Alen; and from me. Last of all, he had to discharge certain real but largely uncontracted obligations to Hyde.

Brandt and Brandt obligingly signed off for $875, the bare sum of their commission, without interest; William Heinemann also granted a release for the mere difference between royalties advanced and royalties actually earned ($5,189.41). Van Alen, with truly extraordinary generosity, accepted $100,000 as complete discharge of an investment of $142,836 plus many years' interest. (Buchanan computes the interest alone as $163,000 uncompounded. Van Alen, in short, ended by making a cash contribution of something like $200,000 to Isham's venture.)

Guinzburg was harder to deal with. He and Isham differed as to the exact nature of his rights. Did he, for example, have any rights in the stable-loft papers? Did he have rights in more than half of the Fettercairn hoard? He offered to release all his rights provided he be given first offer of commercial publication by an institutional purchaser. Yale, with McGraw-Hill's large offer already promised, would of course have opposed this. Hyde warned Guinzburg that he might prevent the sale altogether. A sharp but inconclusive correspondence followed, and Babb was sent to Guinzburg to mediate. Guinzburg finally agreed to withdraw completely for a payment of $25,000 and continuing right to publish the Viking Press *Portable Johnson and Boswell,* which contained extracts from Boswell's journal. Isham submitted, but thought Babb had been too gentle.

Babb was also delegated to get from me an agreement to sign an unconditional release, as intimated in Hyde's letter of 23 June 1947. Until Babb opened the matter with me, I had not supposed that Hyde and Isham really meant to carry matters to a conclusion without providing me any opportunity for frank and patient discussion. I told Babb that of course I would do anything in my power to facilitate or expedite the sale of the manuscripts to Yale, but that I felt great distress at being treated so unfeelingly. There was still time to retreat from cold legalism. In the spring of 1949, Hyde stood to gain nothing for his client by being severe with me. It must not be forgotten that he had declared my contract broken and my rights terminated in June 1947, better than sixteen months before any prospective purchaser of the papers put in an appearance. In June 1947 he had reason to be concerned both with Isham's obligation under the contract to pay me $5,000 and with my contracted right to use the original Isham papers as materials for a biography of Boswell. He may indeed at the time have considered the latter claim a more serious obstacle to a sale than the former. It may then have seemed essential to him to be able to assure any prospective purchaser that Isham had declared my contract broken and was prepared to repel any attempt of mine to enforce any part of it. But from early November 1948, when Mellon made his offer to Yale, my right to use material in the papers ceased to be an encumbrance, became rather an incentive to the purchase. In the spring of 1949 the only encumbrance my contract presented was the obligation it laid on Isham to pay me $5,000, and I had told Hyde at our first meeting that if the papers were sold to a university, I should release Isham from that obligation.

David Buchanan says, "Pottle must have felt hurt that the question of his contract was not dealt with on a more friendly basis." I was indeed badly hurt and I behaved very unwisely. Hyde's letter was a blow to my pride, my self-respect, my sense of justice, but in practical consequences finally did me no harm at all. The moment the papers became Yale's, I had free access to all of them for life, whereas my contract with Isham gave me access only to those he owned in the autumn of 1929. I lost $5,000 due me from Isham, but got authority from Yale to claim an equivalent sum from royalties earned by Yale's trade edition of Boswell's journal. Instead of shutting myself up in bitterness and shunning Isham and Hyde, I should have made extraordinary efforts to meet both of them frequently and familiarly, willing a friendly aspect until I got back genuinely friendly feelings towards them again.

The ultimate responsibility for all the pronouncements that made me so unhappy of course lay with Isham. David Buchanan explains Isham's conduct as caused by exhaustion: he "was weary after years of stress and pressure". Undoubtedly by 1947 Isham had failed considerably in health, but I doubt that this caused him to adopt a hitherto uncharacteristic mode of behaviour. His repudiation of my contract strikes me as unpleasantly parallel to his refusing to give Geoffrey Scott one twenty years before. Hyde's dictum that as editor of Isham's publications I should have expected only to be kept free of expense pretty certainly reflected Isham's views, as did also the concurrent dictum that an editor of the Boswell papers got fame and fortune from the connexion and hence deserved no stipend. Isham would never willingly have paid me the $5,000 due me under my contract, he would have spoken violently of me to other people, but he would never have sent me that devastating letter of 23 June 1947, and he would always have been affectionate when we met. I could have managed that situation with no more than temporary disquietude. I did in fact finally arrange to pay him a friendly call in New York: I do not remember the date but think it would have been in 1951 or 1952. I arrived in late afternoon and stayed perhaps two hours. His gracious and solicitous fourth wife, Sarah Lummus McAdoo, whom he had married in the spring of 1949, withdrew to leave us alone. He was much subdued and unusually gentle. Both of us, I think, had expected to air the matters in dispute between us, but neither actually made any reference to past griefs. We rather talked quietly of matters pleasant to both of us, mainly, I fancy, reminiscential of *Private Papers* or dealing with the Yale Boswell Editions. I came away by no means forgetful of our differences but able to recall those differences without rancour.

With Hyde I managed less commendably. He made overtures of conciliation to me twice, but when we met, each of us was defensive and the magnanimous word failed to be spoken on either side. I am now deeply sorry that I was not more generous.

"Last of all," I have said, "[Isham] had to discharge certain real but largely uncontracted obligations to Hyde." Hyde's legal fees were nominal and his services to Isham so considerable that Isham allowed his gratitude to overcome his strong repugnance to parting with any of his papers. David Buchanan's useful list shows that the Hyde Collection ultimately acquired 161 items, the first purchased in December 1945, the others following thereafter in a steady flow. The papers sold deal mainly with Johnson or Mrs. Piozzi, but included two major Boswell manuscripts: his Book of Company at Auchinleck and a collection (printer's copy and proof sheets) of miscellaneous documents relating to Boswell's *Letter to the People of*

Scotland, 1785. The Hyde collection was already strong in Boswelliana, and these additions made it second only to Isham's.

On 28 June 1949 Isham signed an agreement to sell his collection to Yale for $450,000, reserving only a few pieces which he wished to retain as mementoes or to make gifts of to persons who had been especially helpful to him. The closing took place in New Haven at ten o'clock in the morning on 22 July 1949. Isham put on a characteristic performance. On 21 July he was to go by train to New Haven with the Hydes and Robert F. Metzdorf, at that time a member of the staff of the Harvard University Library. The supporting cast got early to their reserved seats on the train and waited anxiously for Isham, who failed to appear at the rendezvous. The train left, apparently without the lead. Hyde, to make absolutely sure, toured the coaches and found Isham in the very last one, telling a stranger about the Boswell papers. In New Haven the party was entertained overnight by the Lieberts. The closing was to be at 10:00 a.m. sharp, with photographers and representatives of the press on hand. Isham again caused great anxiety by not making himself visible till 9:45 a.m. (car waiting, motor running), when he appeared immaculately garbed and remarked on the brilliance of the sunrise. When the signing was over, he collapsed and spent three more weeks abed, with a nurse in attendance.

It will be remembered that when Isham purchased the stable-loft papers in 1946, Lord Talbot had retained one very important manuscript because Isham could not then raise money enough to bid for the entire find.[1] This was what from Lady Talbot's description appeared (and later proved) to be practically all the leaves of the manuscript of the *Life of Johnson* hitherto unaccounted for. Yale was naturally eager to fill in so important a gap in its holdings, and authorized Isham to purchase the manuscript for Yale at the lowest possible price, not to exceed £10,000. The sixth Lord Talbot de Malahide had died on 22 August 1948, at just about the time the Fettercairn papers arrived in the United States, and the title and estate had been inherited by his first cousin, Milo Talbot of the British Foreign Service, son of the Colonel Talbot who had persuaded the fifth Lord Talbot to submit Boswell's journal to a publisher. The sixth Lord Talbot, however, had given all the Boswell papers to his wife, and she had meantime moved out of Malahide Castle, taking, as was supposed, all the papers with her. Isham, continuing to act through Spingarn, offered her £8,000 for the manuscript. This was a low price (especially in view of the recent devaluation of the pound), but Lady Talbot accepted it on condition that the manuscript should go to Yale and that nobody should make a profit or commission on the sale. The Hydes were in mid-Atlantic on a European tour when Isham telephoned them, begging them to go to Ireland and make sure that the manuscript Lady Talbot was selling really was what she reported it to be. They went on to Paris, but dropped a letter at Southampton, and came back to London four days later. On arrival, they found a letter from Lady Talbot urgently inviting

---

[1] See above, p. 167.

them to Mount Shannon, the country home in the west of Ireland in which she was
staying. She greatly wished to see them because she had a problem. It was a problem
by now grown familiar.

> I have here a suit case full of the final residue of Boswell papers, the present Lord
> Talbot having combed the papers at the Castle very thoroughly. I think Colonel Isham
> has seen these few oddments but I would prefer you to judge of whether or not they
> go to him. I do not think they are important, except for one printed first proof of the
> *Tour* . . . which I would be willing to sell. Any mss. in Boswell's hand (except *the*
> mss. of the *Life* of course) I would consider as Colonel Isham's.

The "oddments" in fact proved to be an extraordinarily rich sample of the
stable-loft papers. Besides the remainder of the manuscript of the *Life* (over 900
pages) and a nearly complete set of first proofs of the *Journal of a Tour to the Hebrides,*
the papers contained practically all the copy by which Boswell supplemented his
manuscript journal in sending the *Tour* to the printer, important letters sent and
received during the period of 1762–63 and the two following years on the Continent,
the missing portion of the "Ébauche" that Boswell wrote for Rousseau, and much,
much more.

Lady Talbot, as will be remembered, had already accepted Isham's offer of
£8,000 for the manuscript of the *Life*. She now asked £2,500 more for the proofs
of the *Tour,* on condition that he sell them to Yale at the same price, and gave him
the rest of the papers as part of the purchase of 1946. Isham paid her $29,400
(£10,500) for the manuscript of the *Life* and the proofs, and sold those items and
the "oddments" (25 July 1950) to Yale for $51,650, the money to pay this sum
being provided by the Old Dominion Foundation and the McGraw-Hill Book Co.
in the same proportions as formerly. This brought to $501,650 the sum he received
from Yale for his collection. As a token of appreciation for his handling of the
purchase of the manuscript of the *Life,* Yale permitted him to retain another leaf
of that manuscript in addition to the one he had been allowed to keep in July 1949.

Stories widely circulated at the time made the "new" papers out to be a recent
discovery. A press release from Yale (18 September 1950) stated merely that the
seventh Lord Talbot had found them when he himself conducted a thorough search
of the Castle on his succession. Hyde, in a talk he gave at the Grolier Club on that
same date, presented a more dramatic version. In this account, the seventh Lord
Talbot and his week-end guests at a house party at Malahide turned them up while
sorting the family papers for amusement. All versions of the story appear to have
originated with Hyde and all are inaccurate. He apparently took as serious some
jocular remark made by the seventh Lord Talbot and in consequence misinterpreted
what Lady Talbot said about the seventh Lord Talbot's "having combed the papers
at the Castle very thoroughly". The "new" papers were simply left-overs from the
stable-loft find of 1940. Lady Talbot had found the task of sorting them fatiguing
as well as hard on her eyes, and the inventory she sent to Isham was as incomplete
as it was uninformative. In sorting the papers from the two large cases of the stable-

loft, she no doubt put various handfuls into smaller piles and receptacles, and ended by overlooking some of them. When she left Malahide, she probably left some box or bundles behind, and Lord Talbot did find the residue and send it after her. The whole episode is probably the best example we can recover of her tendency always to "forget" something, never to make a clean sweep.

Isham acquired the new papers in June 1950 and at once placed in my hands all the documents which looked as though they might have a bearing on the London Journal of 1762–63, with permission to use them in any way I thought desirable.

Isham lived five years more (he died in New York on 13 June 1955, shortly before his sixty-fifth birthday) but he no longer played more than a casual role in this history.

The candid historian, taking a long-range view of Isham's dealings with the Boswell papers, will rate his foibles as of small permanent importance in the story. His temperament was histrionic, and his love of being noticed (a trait which he shared with Boswell) distressed the fastidious and caused them to undervalue the papers with which his name was so emphatically connected. His practice of selling items from the collection, though it was done partly in order to provide funds for purchasing others, bred suspicion of his *bona fides* as a collector. The *Private Papers*, ostensibly a gesture of princely magnificence, had also some of the aspects of a grandiose business venture. But he accomplished what was essentially desirable for Boswell's papers: he brought them together and then turned them over to a great institutional library where they could be expertly handled and made available to scholars and the general public. In a period of a little over twenty years, working deliberately, adroitly, and with great courage, he reassembled Boswell's archives in the face of a complication of difficulties which no ordinary collector would or could have surmounted. He hoped from the first that his papers would go to Yale, and the transfer, when it came, was part of one developing action which he initiated. The publicity which some deplored was an essential feature of that action: both tenders of funds undoubtedly came as the result of a front-page story in the *New York Times*. Isham, I think, had read all the documents in his collection and knew many of them by heart. He sold few items before 1945, and bitterly regretted having parted with any at any time. He had excellent literary taste, wrote well, had a high regard for scholarship, and should be emphatically commended for his wish to share his treasures. The *Private Papers*, for all the limitations of circulation imposed by expensive format, have been a most useful publication. He encouraged me to expand the scope of that work, knowing that it would cost him a good deal of money, and he underwrote an elaborate *Index* which was no part of his contract with his subscribers. He gave sets of the *Private Papers* to many scholars. He was very generous in showing the papers and in allowing scholars to draw on them: I may instance my own *Literary Career of James Boswell*, L. F. Powell's revision of Hill, and R. W. Chapman's *Letters of Samuel Johnson*. He deserves the unstinted gratitude of posterity.

YALE'S ACQUISITION OF PAPERS SINCE 1950

THOUGH ISHAM CONTINUED for some time to send on to Yale over-looked Boswell strays that had turned up in his apartment, the transfer to Yale of his Boswell collection was virtually complete by July 1950. A great many pieces have been added since by purchase and by gift, but a complete listing of them would be tedious to any but specialists. However, since my narrative has been principally designed to show Isham's gradual reassembling of Boswell's scattered archives, I have thought that the reader will wish also to hear of such recoveries from his archives as have been made since 1950. There have been several, and the quantity of papers involved is considerable. I have also assumed that the reader will have a similar interest in recoveries from other family archives. And finally I have thought that any acquisition of as many as fifteen pieces at one time was worthy of mention, though the papers involved may appear to have had no common history of descent.

The first considerable supplement to the Isham collection came on 5 September 1952 by gift from Mr. and Mrs. Donald F. Hyde. It consisted of fifteen documents, mostly letters, purchased as Lot 214 of Hodgson and Co.'s sale, London, 19 June 1952, of the Johnsonian collection of A. H. Hallam Murray, originally formed by J. T. Smith, Keeper of Prints in the British Museum. The gift contained letters of T. D. Boswell, Sir Alexander Boswell, James Boswell the younger, and Euphemia Boswell, besides genealogical and biographical notes on the Biographer by Mark Noble (1754–1827). The lot sold for £12. Clearly none of these papers came from Boswell's archives, but were picked up piecemeal from various sources in the usual collecting way by Smith and perhaps by Hallam Murray.

The next three supplements (they came to Yale in 1953–54) seem all to have been ultimately purchased from the same person, a woman whose husband was a

Boswell descendant but not a descendant of the Biographer. A great part of the papers, however, definitely came from the Auchinleck archives. How this could happen is best explained by successive examination of the contents of each purchase.

In June 1953, S. C. Roberts wrote to me from Cambridge to inform me that he had in his hands a packet of sixty letters from Boswell to Robert Boswell, W.S., his cousin and legal agent. At the suggestion of a friend of Roberts's, they had been sent to him for his advice by a Mrs. Edith Roxburgh of Locks Heath, near Southampton. Roberts did not know her at all, but it was represented to him, probably by the friend, that her husband's mother had been a Boswell, and that she was "quite an old lady". She was in fact the widow of Alexander Bruce Roxburgh, F.R.C.S., well-known ophthalmic surgeon in the London Hospital, who had died at the age of ninety-two so recently as 17 March. Alexander Bruce Roxburgh was the son of William Roxburgh and Ann Eliza Boswell; Ann Eliza Boswell was the fourth daughter of Alexander Boswell, W.S., second son of Robert Boswell, W.S., and successor to him in his legal business. Alexander Bruce Roxburgh being grandson of Alexander Boswell, W.S., and great-grandson of Robert Boswell, it should cause no surprise to find him in possession of papers descending from either or both of them.

Roberts inferred that Mrs. Roxburgh wished to sell. Negotiations followed, and in January 1954 the papers were purchased for Yale by the Boswell Papers Editing Fund at a cost of £300. Roberts reported the incident in a brief article published in the *Times Literary Supplement,* and was allowed to keep one letter of his own choice in recognition of his friendly mediation. Not counting this letter, Mrs. Roxburgh's packet contained fifty-four complete and seven fragmentary letters from Boswell to Robert Boswell, of dates ranging from 1777 to 1793, six letters from Boswell's wife to Robert Boswell, and nine miscellaneous letters, partly to the Biographer, partly to Robert Boswell, with some by the Biographer to other correspondents. The fragmentary letters had all been trimmed to narrow slips preserving Boswell's complimentary closings and signatures, with a bit of text, plus, of course, whatever happened to be written on the other sides of the slips. These fragments had clearly all been prepared to sell or give to be mounted in copies of the *Life of Johnson.* (I in fact had in the Boswell Office in 1953 a one-volume Croker edition of the *Life,* 1860, given me by Tinker, which contained a strikingly similar strip trimmed from a letter of Boswell's. It proved on close examination to be indeed a fragment of a letter to Robert Boswell. An accompanying trimmed letter signed "W. Bulloch," which I had forgotten, says that Bulloch got the scrap "from Wm Roxburgh the ophthalmic surgeon." My slip, in short, had been in the collection Mrs. Roxburgh was selling, but had been separated from that collection many years before.) The letters in Mrs. Roxburgh's hands, supplemented by letters of Robert Boswell to Boswell already in the collection at Yale, now constitute one of Boswell's larger preserved correspondences, a correspondence not the less valuable in the whole corpus because it is mainly devoted to business.

This group of manuscripts obviously did not come from Boswell's archives. It came from Robert Boswell's, though the line of descent of Mrs. Roxburgh's husband might make one suspect that he had it *via* Alexander Boswell, W.S.

On 9 October 1953 Yale acquired by gift from H.W. Liebert a group of what Boswell would have called "writes": fourteen legal documents (instruments of seizin, contracts of excambion, minute of sale of a superiority, precepts of clare constat, etc.) all dealing with farms or larger units of the estate of Auchinleck from 1693 to 1791. That they came from Mrs. Roxburgh's papers appeared pretty clear, for they were accompanied by four fragmentary letters from Boswell to Robert Boswell, mutilated exactly like the ones I have just described. Liebert no longer remembers the gift, but assumes that the papers were a lot he paid C. A. Stonehill, Inc. for on 28 May 1954. R. J. Barry, head of C. A. Stonehill, has forgotten the transaction too, and has no record of it.

Except for the letters, this group of documents did not belong among Robert Boswell's papers; the "writes" belonged in the Auchinleck charter-chest. It is easy enough to see, however, how they could have got into Robert Boswell's hands. They were put there by Boswell for business purposes, and were never returned to Auchinleck. But the fifteenth paper in the group reminds us again that we cannot solve all our problems by the simple expedient of assuming that Mrs. Roxburgh had acquired at least some of the office papers of Robert Boswell. The fifteenth piece is a probate of the will of James Boswell the younger, and bears the date 19 March 1822, seventeen years after Robert Boswell's death. We must rather assume that Mrs. Roxburgh became possessed of at least a portion of the office papers of Alexander Boswell, W.S., who in turn had become possessed of at least a portion of Robert Boswell's.

The last of these three supplements, acquired by Yale in April 1954, consisted of a mass of charters and "writes" (more than sixty items) starting off with a charter by the Commendator of Melrose Abbey, 20 February 1555, of the lands of Over Meiklewood, later part of the Auchinleck estate, and ending, 5 June 1841, with the commission as lieutenant in the Army of William Henry Boswell, fourth son of Alexander Boswell, W.S. Further reference to Alexander Boswell, W.S., occurs in a document of 1825, Probate of the Will of Nicholas Carnegie, Esq., who was the husband of Alexander Boswell's sister Margaret Catherine. Yale acquired the lot from C. A. Stonehill, Inc., but Barry does not remember the details. Yale drew the money to buy them from the Boswell Papers Editing Fund, but I find no record of the price. Hilles, of our Editorial Committee, a seasoned book-collector, thought such papers of little utility for our publishing venture. Liebert and I (the other members) moved whenever we could to recover all parts of the Auchinleck archives, feeling that the papers as a whole had value for social, political, and economic history hardly less remarkable than their acknowledged values for literary studies.

The next supplement, which came to Yale in August 1955, gave me personally more pleasure than any of the others. In the summer of 1953 Mrs. Pottle and I were in England and Scotland, our first visit there since 1936. The Earl of Crawford, with whom I had been in correspondence since 1939, was an original member of our Advisory Committee. When he learned that I was in Britain, he wrote to me twice inviting me to visit him and Lady Crawford at his seat of Balcarres, Fife, saying that he had something to show me at the house of a neighbour which would be of interest to me. I went on Friday 24 July and was met by him at the Elie railway station. After luncheon he took me to Balcaskie House, some three miles away. The owner, Sir Ralph Hugo Anstruther of Balcaskie, major in the Coldstream Guards, was absent on military service, but his mother, Mrs. Anstruther, was a most cordial hostess. Hardly within the door, Lord Crawford went to a chest standing (as my memory has it) near the main entrance, opened it, showing it to be full of papers, extracted a packet, and handed it to me with a triumphant flourish. I saw at once that the papers I held in my hands were the originals of Boswell's side of the correspondence which he had published in 1763 as *Letters between the Honourable Andrew Erskine and James Boswell, Esq.* (He apparently sacrificed Erskine's originals to make copy for the printer, but used retained copies of his own for that purpose.) I had not for a moment suspected what Lord Crawford wished to show me at Balcaskie, but when I saw the letters I had no difficulty in conjecturing how they got there. Andrew Erskine was a younger son of the Earl of Kellie; Kellie Castle, the ancestral seat of the earls of Kellie, lay less than a mile away. (Lord Crawford had taken me there, too.) Erskine had two brothers and three sisters. The family was poor. Of the Erskine brothers none ever married; of the Erskine sisters two married but only one had children. Lady Janet Erskine, youngest of the sisters, married Sir Robert Anstruther, third Baronet of Balcaskie, in 1763. Andrew's keepsakes, such as they were, came to rest at Balcaskie.

Sir Ralph (whom I never met) generously allowed photocopies to be made for Yale, but at first was indisposed to sell the manuscripts, especially if a sale meant their leaving Scotland. After a considerable interchange of letters involving Yale, Lord Crawford, Mrs. Anstruther, and Sir Ralph, however, Sir Ralph finally consented to part with the letters, and they were purchased for Yale by the Boswell Papers Editing Fund at a price of £600. The letters were carried to Edinburgh, where another member of our Advisory Committee, William Beattie, Librarian of the National Library of Scotland, kindly attended to packing and posting them. As I have said, they arrived at Yale in August 1955.

Boswell's letters to Robert Boswell came to Yale in 1954 through the mediation of S. C. Roberts, who from 1922 to 1948 had been Secretary of the Cambridge University Press; two years later Yale acquired through similar mediation by Geoffrey Cumberlege, Publisher to the University of Oxford, a small but useful group of letters received and in part written by members of the family of Boswell's daughter Elizabeth ("Betsy"). Cumberlege informed Professor Richard L. Purdy of Yale by letter in May 1956 that a relation of his, a Miss Elma Hailey, had some Boswell-related letters and a seal-ring with Boswell connexions which she was willing to sell. He included a list of the letters: three from Sir Alexander Boswell to William Boswell, written before William had incurred Alexander's displeasure by marrying Betsy, and four from T. D. Boswell, two of them to Betsy and two to her husband. The seal-ring, to judge by an impression, appeared to be the very "seal of investiture" that T. D. Boswell had used on 27 October 1767 in signing the "Family Oath" which Boswell had devised for him when he left Scotland to make his fortune in Spain. The daughter of Elizabeth and William Boswell, Elizabeth Margaret Montgomerie Boswell ("Monty"), married John Williams; their daughter, Elizabeth Anne Williams, married the Rev. Charles Cumberlege; their daughter, Elizabeth Cumberlege, married a Mr. Hailey and was a party to the Fettercairn suit; their daughter, Elma Hailey, was consequently Boswell's great-great-great-granddaughter. Purdy handed the information and the list on to the Editorial Committee, which expressed interest and asked him to ask Cumberlege for more details. Miss Hailey, Cumberlege said, thought that the seven letters listed might be worth $60, but meantime two more had turned up: both by William Boswell to "Monty". He thought Miss Hailey would want about $100 for the ring. Since Metzdorf was planning to be in Britain in the autumn, Cumberlege suggested that Metzdorf come and see him then. The plan was followed: Metzdorf saw Cumberlege on 9 October 1956 (I think he also saw Miss Hailey) and secured the letters for Yale and the ring for himself. Yale paid Miss Hailey $80 for the nine letters; I seem to remember Metzdorf saying that he purchased the ring for $50. The documents were received in the Yale Library on 12 December 1956.

It will be remembered that Boswell's great-great-grandson, the sixth Lord Talbot de Malahide, died on 22 August 1948, about a month after Isham received the first consignment of papers from the stable-loft at Malahide. He was succeeded in his title and estate by his first cousin, Milo Talbot, son of the Colonel Talbot who in 1911 had been principally responsible for getting a typescript of a large portion of Boswell's journal sent to Sir John Murray. The seventh Lord Talbot, of the British Foreign Service, a bachelor of thirty-five who owned a plantation in Tasmania, at first could occupy Malahide Castle only during periods of leave, but took up residence there in 1956. Lady Talbot on the death of her husband moved out of the Castle, supposedly taking with her all the papers she thought to be her own, and was living at Mount Shannon in the west of Ireland when the Hydes visited her in June 1950. On 3 October 1951 she married Brig. John Smith McCombe, and lived thereafter at Abbeylea, Ballybrack, near Dublin. For nine years she employed the style Mrs. John Smith McCombe, but on Brigadier McCombe's death, 19 October 1959, resumed the style of her first marriage. I think I have had no occasion to mention her between June 1950 and 1 January 1960, but in any case I have styled her "Lady Talbot" throughout to avoid confusion.

Milo, Lord Talbot was unexpectedly in New Haven in the spring of 1958, coming not on Boswell business but to visit a young friend of his, Charles R. McVicker, Jr., Instructor in the Department of Political Science at Yale. I was able to meet him then and to be assured by him personally that we were mistaken in our report that the "new new" papers which Yale acquired in 1950 were discovered at Malahide in a general search made at a house party after his succession. He told me also that there was still at Malahide a mass of Boswell family papers from before and after the Biographer's time. Though of great interest to me, this was not a surprise, because Lady Talbot's letters to Isham at the time of the stable-loft discovery had mentioned a case filled with papers of earlier and later date. On 9 November 1959 Metzdorf, at my request, made inquiry of Lord Talbot concerning these papers, apparently offering to sort and inventory them if he would lend them to us. He replied that he was not sure that the papers in question were his to lend, but in a later letter reported that Lady Talbot had "agreed that all Boswell and other MSS. etc. which are still here or may yet be found here, are my property". He went on to say that on 10 June he had found in one of the trunks in the strong room a bundle of papers in the Biographer's hand, most of which were so badly rotted that he did not dare to handle them. He assumed that they were "another lot of stragglers from pre–1948 finds". He had put with them six other papers which he had found scattered among the contents of the tin boxes in the strong room, and was giving the whole "tomorrow" (25 July) to McVicker, then a guest at Malahide, to carry to New York. Metzdorf picked up the parcel there on 4 August 1960. Mrs. Pottle was not available for cataloguing, she and I having been spending the spring and most of the summer in a tour of Italy and Corsica. We came back through New Haven, however, at this juncture, on the way to a few weeks in Maine, and conferred with Metzdorf, Liebert, and Frank Brady (co-editor of *Boswell on the Grand Tour: Italy, Corsica, and France* and *Boswell in Search of a Wife*), agreeing on the importance and interest of the material. Metzdorf made as much of a report to Lord Talbot as he could without handling the rotted papers, and recommended that all the leaves that were at all friable should be immediately turned over for repair and mounting to Miss Virginia Lawrence, who in 1930 had vetted the material in the croquet-box for Isham.

It was clear to us even from such cursory inspection as could be made that the most valuable portion of the bundle was not the miscellaneous manuscripts in it that Talbot had found scattered through various tin boxes and had placed on top of the pile, but rather the confused and heart-breakingly shredded mass of journals, journal-notes, and memoranda, wrapped in the *Morning Post* for 12 February 1907, that made up the greater portion. The wrapping was probably put on when the papers were packed at Auchinleck to send to Malahide. They appeared to be, and no doubt were, a residue of the croquet-box of 1930, deliberately held back by Lady Talbot at that time either because she thought them so badly damaged as to be valueless or perhaps merely because they presented such problems in packaging.

When Miss Lawrence had finished assembling and mounting and Mrs. Pottle had done a careful job of inventorying, it appeared that some of the fragments came from sequences of diary not formerly represented at Yale, while more filled gaps in journals we already had. The recovery was especially rich for the autumn of the year 1769 but included recoveries in 1773 and 1779. The recovery of some fifty leaves and many unnumbered scraps of matter of this sort, though tantalizing, was highly gratifying.

The remaining manuscripts were a mixed lot and in general not particularly exciting: a journal of Lt. John Boswell's, 1764–65, a water-colour sketch of a flower, painted by Boswell's daughter Veronica as a child, some missing leaves of miscellaneous manuscripts of Boswell we already had.

The Editorial Committee was in some doubt as to whether Lord Talbot realized that the best part of his bundle was of the sort that the sixth Lord Talbot, beginning in 1930, had given Isham without further payment as part of his purchase of the journal in 1927 and 1928, and if he did realize it, whether he proposed to observe that precedent in dealing with Yale. It was decided not to assume that he intended a gift, but to ask him what price he set on the papers. In reply he asked the Committee to give him some idea of their value. We engaged Barry to appraise the papers, and he gave the figure $2,000 to $2,500. Metzdorf wrote a careful and tactful letter to Talbot in Tasmania offering him $2,250, but pointing out that we had paid $287.70 to get the manuscripts repaired, that the cataloguing had taken a good deal of Mrs. Pottle's time, and that "much of the material . . . completes items which were transferred to Isham in 1930 and which might have been expected to have changed hands at that time". Talbot replied that he was preparing to head for home, and would postpone discussion till he and Metzdorf should meet at Malahide. Metzdorf was leaving his post as Secretary to the Editorial Committee on 15 July to become Assistant Vice-President of the Parke-Bernet Galleries in New York, and as a final service to us had offered to invest part of his last vacation in personal visits to Malahide, Abbeylea, and Auchinleck. We had had trustworthy reports that there were more papers at Malahide and Auchinleck, and were uneasy at the possibility of a further "residue" at Abbeylea.

Metzdorf was at Malahide by 20 May 1961, and reported that Talbot had decided that because the manuscripts concerning which we had been in treaty had remained at Malahide after 1930 "by carelessness, inadvertence, or negligence", they ought to go to Yale without further payment. He asked only that the little sketch by Veronica should be returned to him. He was considering negotiations with the government of Eire to secure some relief in taxes if Malahide Castle should be opened to the public, and wished, if that could be arranged, to have a small display-case of selected documents that had been found at Malahide. We agreed, but I find with some embarrassment that the sketch is still in New Haven. I should like to think that this did not happen "by carelessness, inadvertence, or negligence", but that in some letter that has strayed from the Talbot file Lord Talbot asked us to hold the sketch till he had reached the hoped-for tax agreement, and that we never received further instructions.

With the welcome news of Lord Talbot's generosity, Metzdorf also sent us a hasty list of items he had glimpsed among the very numerous earlier and later papers Talbot had told us were in his possession. But Metzdorf advised us against making any offer at that stage. Talbot, he said, felt that he lacked the time, the knowledge, and the interest to sort out and appraise the papers himself. He wanted to box them all up helter-skelter as they stood, and to send them to Yale for proper identification and valuation. Nothing could have suited us better.

From Malahide on 21 May 1961 Metzdorf dashed over to Abbeylea. I do not find that we had anything more than past experience to make us suspect that Lady Talbot might have more Boswelliana in her hands than the few mementoes (for example, Mrs. Boswell's purse and wedding ring) which we knew she had retained in 1950. But we were hopeful, and our hope was realized. Metzdorf found Lady Talbot strongly desirous to raise money for an urgent benevolent purpose and eager to take his advice even on material she had formerly dismissed from consideration as valueless. We had known since 1957 that Auchinleck House was in a sad way. It had been used during the war as a billet for soldiers, and had become infected with dry-rot. Very extensive repairs—a new roof and rebuilt chimneys to begin with—were called for. The Ministry of Works was prepared to advance the major part of the funding, but required from J. P. D. Boswell, the owner, a larger share than he could manage. Lady Talbot wanted to make a substantial contribution herself. The material she showed Metzdorf came out of an old oaken chest-on-chest which had come from Auchinleck to Malahide, probably already stuffed with papers; from Malahide it had travelled to Mount Shannon and from there to Abbeylea. The lower part had never been cleared out because the door was stuck tight. At Mount Shannon the door was coaxed open. I allow Lady Talbot to continue:

> It was full of Papers of the 18th century, legal papers and newspapers, and it did not occur to us it would ever have any value to scholars, but was merely a mass of family MSS., interesting only to the family and to some extent to anyone interested in the 18th century. After a quick look we tried to shut back the outer door, and had so much trouble doing so that once it had clicked back (and then would not open again) we forgot all about it. . . . It was moved last year by workmen, and the front suddenly fell off, and I left it off in case anyone would be interested in the contents. Very fortunately I thought of it when Mr. Metzdorf came to Abbeylea.

We meet here for the last time the pattern of "forgetting" we have seen so many times before, and should by this time have little difficulty in accepting Lady Talbot's explanation of it. Her education in assessing the market value of Boswell family papers had been gained almost entirely through actual bargainings in sales to Isham, but there had now been five of these transactions, and she had taken brilliant advantage of each successive opportunity to increase her knowledge. What she had learned principally in her last sale was that some unbound printed matter may be of considerable value. Her depreciatory reference to "legal papers and newspapers" shows that down nearly to 1950 she had pretty much taken for granted that it was Boswell's *manuscripts* (letters and journals) that collectors and scholars were eager to obtain. What turned up conspicuously in 1950 besides the manuscript of the *Life of Johnson* were the nearly complete proofs of the *Journal of a Tour to the Hebrides*. Having long ignored these, thinking them to be merely unbound sheets of the first edition, she finally recognized them for what they were and put an informed price on them (£2,500). When (I assume sometime between 1948 and 1950) she wrestled the old chest open long enough for a hasty glance at the contents, she got a general impression of printed papers, and with that identification dismissed the mass from further consideration. It was not remarkable that in a context of appraisal for sale she should have forgotten matter which she—too hastily, to be sure—had judged to be unsaleable. When in 1960 the front of the old chest fell off, she saw the contents with a changed eye. Lord Talbot having told her that Metzdorf was about to become a professional in the rare-book business, she gratefully seized the opportunity to consult him as to values.

It would be wrong to give the impression that the papers in the old chest actually contained no manuscripts. There were in fact in the lot over a hundred letters of earlier and later years, twenty by Boswell. His letters, as one would have expected, were mainly drafts and copies, but contained among them the original of a long, hitherto unknown letter to Temple, 6–8 July 1784, which is my personal favourite in that entire correspondence. But surely the distinguishing feature of this recovery was its large number of printed broadsides and separates ("off-prints"). This was a kind of publication in which Boswell was remarkably active, using it for songs, satirical squibs, signed letters to newspapers, unsigned paragraphs to newspapers, and the like. I count nine of these pieces in Mrs. Pottle's "Summary of 'Abbeylea' Material", one of the nine a "lot" of eight items. Isham had been on the look-out for pieces of this sort from the very first, but Boswell's own papers had so far yielded only one, and Isham had not recognized that for what it was. I find also in the "Summary" two annotated lots of Boswell's *Hypochondriack* essays, removed from the *London Magazine,* with a parcel of notes for additions to be made to them when the series should be collected; sixteen of Boswell's *Rampager* (occasional essays published in the *Public Advertiser,* a series for which we have no complete listing); *Proposals* by Boswell for a new edition of Charlotte Lennox's *Shakespeare Illustrated,* and, finally, a quantity of annotated newspaper cuttings, the majority of them written by Boswell himself. The Abbeylea recovery of 1961 was *the* recovery of Boswell's broadsides and newspaper paragraphs.

Metzdorf (who took instantly to Lady Talbot) found her prepared to drive a firm bargain (the firmer because the money was to be used for a charitable purpose), and confident that the papers were valuable. He was called upon to make some nice professional decisions. She asked him if she would not gain by selling certain of her things at auction. He urged her strongly not to auction any of the manuscripts, but agreed that where she had more than one copy (as was the case for several of the printed pieces), it would be defensible as well as more lucrative to auction the duplicates. When Lady Talbot expressed a wish that the Hydes be allowed to purchase several desirable items only one of which was specifically Johnsonian, he thought it not wise to oppose her.

I had asked Metzdorf while he was at Abbeylea to try to get copies of some letters of Isham to her of which Isham appeared to have kept no copies, as well as of a few legal documents of the late seventeen and early eighteen hundreds of which no copies appeared in the Isham legal transcripts. She gave him free access to her Isham file, but had at Abbeylea only a selection of the legal documents. The rest, which had been in the hands of Scott Moncrieff and Trail, Edinburgh solicitors who had handled Boswell legal affairs for more than a century, she had recently transferred to Messrs. David Shaw and Co. of Ayr. Because of her gratitude to Metzdorf, I fancy ("Mr. Metzdorf . . . got through more work in $9^{1}/_{2}$ hours than I could have believed possible"), she tried this time to assure Yale that she was making a clean sweep by sending instructions to William McHarg of David Shaw and Co. to deposit the papers—some seven or eight boxes of them—at Auchinleck, where Metzdorf was to be allowed to search them and to select any he thought Yale might be interested in.

These papers did not arrive at Auchinleck till after Metzdorf had been there and gone, but he scheduled a brief return visit at the end of his tour. On his first visit to Auchinleck he found plenty of others to occupy his attention. We had known since 1959 that the then Boswells of Auchinleck had in their hands a considerable body of Boswell papers which they had found in Auchinleck House when they took over after McCrone's tenancy. These papers had been left behind when the fifth Lord Talbot moved the archives to Malahide. Lord Talbot had presumably abandoned them, but it did not matter, for Lady Talbot waived any claim she might have to them. The first report was of scattered letters, perhaps a hundred of them, by and to Andrew Gibb, Sir Alexander Boswell, and James Boswell the younger. In the autumn of 1960 Charles Ryskamp, one of Yale's Boswell editors, visited Auchinleck and brought back word that the Boswells had found a whole trunk-full of estate papers. Metzdorf, who was already planning his trip of 1961, asked and obtained permission to visit Auchinleck and see them. He went directly there from Malahide on 22 May 1961, ran through the papers, and gave an appraisal. I venture to divulge his formula:

> Boswell signatures . . . lumped at $10 each, endorsements . . . at $25 . . . letters by Gibb, Bruce, B. Campbell, Sandie and TDB . . . at $5, estate papers at $2 each, and the notebooks, account books, and similar items . . . grouped at $285. Add to this a figure for the en bloc value.

This very miscellaneous collection of letters and legal documents concerning the management of the estate of Auchinleck ran to several hundred pieces which bore dates from about 1720 to about 1835. The bulk of the material is indicated by the fact that Metzdorf's very modest piece-rates produced a total which caused J. P. D. Boswell to set a price of $4,750 on the whole. The Boswells' lawyer, the Hon.

D. A. Balfour, reported this offer to the Yale Editorial Committee, it was accepted, and a cheque for that amount was sent for Metzdorf to deliver personally. We indicated a hope that he could bring back not only the papers at Auchinleck, which were now our property, but also those at Abbeylea, subject to return if Yale could not meet Lady Talbot's figure. Metzdorf saw Lady Talbot in Edinburgh and obtained her consent; he met the Hydes in London, delivered to them the papers which Lady Talbot had selected to sell to them, and borrowed enough money from Hyde to meet the extra costs of his re-routed flight home. He bought two suitcases: a small one for his own unneeded clothes, to be taken home for him by his travelling companion Robert H. Taylor, the Princeton book-collector, and a large one to pack all three lots of papers in:

> A new factor enters the picture: it is an earnest of Lady T's interest to send us everything she has that she's instructed her Ayr solicitors . . . to pass over to the Boswells the boxes of papers in their keeping. I'll go through them at Auchinleck—if it means staying up all night!
>
> I've phoned the Boswells and shall deliver the check on June 22. I'm to fly [from London] to Renfrew and they will pick me up there—stay at Auchinleck that night and pack the papers; June 23rd—fly from Renfrew to Dublin.
>
> Lady T's chauffeur will pick me up and drive me to Abbeylea—there I'll pack her papers and probe for everything that may be in the house. On June 24th I'll fly from Dublin to Shannon and on to New York. . . . Do you think some one can meet me at Idlewild? I'll have one suitcase (heavy) of papers and one of clothing, plus my attaché case, an umbrella, etc. Gad!

From the number of documents that Metzdorf picked out of McHarg's seven or eight boxes, it looks as though he might well have stayed up most of the night he spent at Auchinleck. He found only one new document in Boswell's hand (a list of wines at Auchinleck), but he selected several large bundles of family legal papers (some hundreds of separate items) similar in nature to the "writes" that came down from Robert Boswell to Mrs. Roxburgh.[1] Papers dealing with Sir James Boswell's efforts to break the entail of Auchinleck bulk largest, but the papers in this lot that have so far interested me most are those that enable us to reconstruct the unhappy story of Euphemia Boswell's later years.[2]

Metzdorf arrived at Idlewild on the evening of Saturday 24 June, was *not* met at customs, and struggled through to New Haven with his heavy suitcases the next day.

Lady Talbot set a price of £10,000 on her two lots of papers, which we at Yale still distinguish as "Abbeylea" and "McHarg". The Editorial Committee estimated that it would require a total of $34,750 to meet her terms, recoup the sum already paid for the papers from J. P. D. Boswell ("Auchinleck I"), and to photograph all

---

[1]See above, pp. 189–90.
[2]See above, pp. 42–46.

three lots. Metzdorf suggested that we again approach the Old Dominion Foundation and the McGraw-Hill Book Co., asking them to award us this sum in the same ratio (two to one) as in the purchases of 1949 and 1950. The Old Dominion Fund accordingly made us an outright grant of $23,000; McGraw-Hill made us an advance of $10,900 against royalties.

On 4 October 1961 the Parke-Bernet Galleries in New York sold a number of the small printed pieces which Lady Talbot had retained. Five of the pieces of which she had sold duplicates to Yale realized a total of $3,175.

Lord Talbot had meanwhile caused his papers to be packed in five suitcases and a carton for transport to America. In the autumn of 1961 Herbert T. F. Cahoon, Curator of Autograph Manuscripts at the Pierpont Morgan Library, New York, brought over three of the suitcases, which seem to have remained at the Pierpont Morgan Library till the following summer.

In the summer of 1962, Metzdorf went abroad and again devoted some of his vacation to a Boswell quest. The Ian Boswells of Crawley Grange, Bucks, and the Philip Boswells of Peebles in Scotland (Dr. Philip Boswell was heir male of Boswell of Auchinleck) were able to show him no considerable deposits of Boswell family papers, but at Auchinleck, which he reached on 8 June, he was rewarded with the kind of news that in earlier years had been almost predictable. There were more papers, quite a lot of them. Miss Margaret Boswell, aunt of J. P. D. Boswell (Mrs. Pottle and I had met her at Auchinleck House in 1936), had died in February at the age of ninety-seven, and when her house of Sandgate, Ayr, was cleared, four deed-boxes full of Boswell papers were found. One lot of them was papers of the Douglas Boswells of Knockroon and Garallan (her family and J. P. D. Boswell's), but the larger part were family papers of the Boswells of Auchinleck which had been moved for safety to Sandgate when Auchinleck House was requisitioned during the war.

In reporting this recovery to Yale, Metzdorf properly distinguished the Douglas Boswell portion from the rest, describing it as being particularly rich in papers dealing with the notorious Douglas, Heron bank failure, which ruined so many Ayrshire land-holders. (John Boswell of Knockroon lost Knockroon because of involvement in Douglas, Heron; his son, Hamilton Boswell, married Jane Douglas, heiress of Garallan.) J. P. D. Boswell wanted £100 for this lot. For convenience of description Metzdorf divided the Auchinleck papers into two chronological groups. The first (about 130 pieces), ranging in date from 1781 (well within Boswell's lifetime) to 1833 (eleven years after Sir Alexander's death), consisted mainly of estate business letters and the accounts of improvement on the entailed Auchinleck properties that had to be reported annually to Government for tax credit. In the lot were several of Sir Alexander's poems and some letters referring to his death and funeral. J. P. D. Boswell set a figure of £400 on these. Metzdorf sent an inventory of this lot. For the second lot of Auchinleck papers he sent no inventory, and I can characterize the papers forming it only by a brief and to me not wholly intelligible summary sent in a letter: "a suitcase full of material (letters and documents) dealing with the Auchinleck Estate after the death of Sir Alexander up to the death of John Douglas Boswell of Garallan, who was one of the factors for the court. It contains the complete financial history of Auchinleck after Sandie left it in such a muddle." John Douglas Boswell (d. 1863) was the son of Hamilton and Jane Douglas Boswell, who served in succession as executors of Sir Alexander Boswell's personal estate. For this lot J. P. D. Boswell asked £200. Metzdorf bowed out of the Auchinleck picture at this point. He flew home from Dublin on 15 June, bringing with him the remainder of Lord Talbot's parcels. He probably left them at the Pierpont Morgan Library with the instalment Cahoon had brought back in the previous autumn. Some time during the summer of 1962 some one transported the five suitcases and a carton to the Yale Library.

Yale declined to purchase the Garallan papers, and offered £300 for Metzdorf's two Auchinleck lots. J. P.D. Boswell finding this unacceptable, Yale on reconsideration offered £400 for Metzdorf's Lot 1 and £100 for his Lot 2. The Boswells accepted the offer of £400 for Lot 1 and sent it over to us promptly by Nellie P. Hankins, one of our editors, and her husband, Professor John Erskine Hankins, who had been some weeks in Ayrshire and had established friendly relations with the Boswells. The cheque for £400 was ordered on 3 October 1962. Mrs. Boswell, writing for her husband, said they felt that Lot 2 was worth more than £100, but expressed willingness to send that lot over to Yale to be studied and appraised if we could arrange with some one we knew to call at Auchinleck and pick it up. It was a great pity that this proposal was made after the Hankinses had been and gone. We approved the arrangement, but for six years were not able to find a proper conveyer.

Mrs. Pottle, when her other tasks permitted, set herself to the long labour of inventorying the papers Lord Talbot had sent. By 28 January 1964 she had sorted these out and listed them in six sections corresponding to the five suitcases and the carton in which they had arrived. Within each section she arranged the papers chronologically under the successive lairds of Auchinleck. Lord Talbot requested us to make an offer, and we made one which he thought far too little. In the same letter in which he said so he mentioned another "find" which should perhaps be chronicled as *not* the last in a series which must long since have lost its power to surprise the reader.

> Incidentally, I have come across about a dozen more Boswell items when going through my family papers. I have given these to Warren Howell [rare-book dealer], who came to lunch on Monday [14 September 1964], and asked him to forward them to you when he gets home. You may prefer to defer your reply to this letter until Mrs. Pottle has had a chance to look at them.

These papers (there were actually seventeen pieces, one a letter by Sir Richard Steele) duly arrived in a parcel "forwarded" from San Francisco, that being Warren Howell's home and place of business.

Liebert then wrote proposing to swell the offer by dividing the purchase between himself and Yale. He would buy for his own collection (destined to come later to Yale) three items of unusual interest for exhibit (Johnson's LL.D. diploma from Dublin, a burgess-ticket from Lichfield to Michael Johnson, a playbill for a performance Boswell and Johnson attended in Lichfield, the occasion being mentioned in the *Life of Johnson*), and Yale would buy the remainder. The total was considerably above the original offer, and Talbot found it acceptable. He said, however, that instead of receiving it in cash, he would prefer to have Yale locate and pay the sum towards the purchase of a complete set of *Curtis's Botanical Magazine,* a periodical with many plates that had begun publication so far back as 1787 and was still running. (He has been characterized as "a passionate plantsman".) Yale agreed and, since the pound was in trouble, fixed the amount in dollars. In 1967 Talbot declared himself satisfied with a set of *Curtis's* offered for sale by Wheldon and Wesley, dealers in London. Yale's offer amounted to about sixty per cent of the purchase price. He paid the remaining forty per cent, and was very much pleased.

It is impossible to characterize meaningfully in a few words a collection so extensive and various as "Talbot Papers 1–6". There are probably in it some documents of as early date as the thirteenth century (more work needs to be done to distinguish copies from originals before one can be sure); there are certainly many of the fifteenth, sixteenth, seventeenth, and eighteenth centuries. (For that matter, there are many of the nineteenth.) Most of the papers are "writes", as one would expect, but there are a great many personal letters of the various lairds and their wives. There is a surprising quantity of Bruce (Kincardine) material, and many interesting documents relating to Boswell's maternal grandfather, Col. John Erskine, and the furnishings of his house in the Colonels' Close, Culross. Undoubtedly after the demands on the papers of James Boswell, journalist and biographer, have been met, the collection will continue indefinitely to be useful as matter for British social history.

It will be remembered that in 1962 we had promised the Boswells of Auchinleck that when a proper emissary appeared, we would send him to Auchinleck to pick up and bring to Yale the group of nineteenth-century Boswell papers for which, without seeing them, we did not feel justified in paying more than £100. Mrs. Pottle and I made a very pleasant luncheon-visit with the Boswells on 25 May 1964 at their cottage of Barnsdale on the Auchinleck estate, the interior of Auchinleck House having been stripped down for eradication of dry-rot. I cannot remember why I did not offer to take the manuscripts, but it may well have been because I did not wish to subject them to the risk of transport in a motor car through the rest of our tour, and could not arrange for a return trip to Auchinleck at its end. J. P. D. Boswell died in May 1966. Two years later (1 May 1968) I wrote to Mrs. Boswell that one of our editors, Richard C. Cole, Professor of English at Davidson College, had expressed a wish to see Auchinleck House, reminded her of our inconclusive dealings of 1962, and asked her if she would allow him to bring the papers to America. He was at Auchinleck at the end of July, and found Mrs. Boswell most hospitable but unable to recall the papers we had corresponded about six years earlier. She had recently been in an automobile accident and was unable to make a search herself, but she allowed him to go through the three boxes of papers which she knew she had. It was his impression that these were all the Garallan papers which we had declined. Perhaps the two lots had got merged. Though the unlocated papers would have contained few if any autographs of James Boswell, I feel uneasy about having allowed matters to rest in so inconclusive a state.

Yale's latest considerable accession of Boswelliana from Auchinleck has fittingly enough been of what Boswell once described as "my honoured Father's Volumes bound in turkey and gilt—the *Palladia* of our Family". Since David Buchanan was solely responsible for this acquisition, it is but fitting that I end this Epilogue with his own words:

> I also took with me to America [in the summer of 1971] an offering for Yale. Shortly before leaving Lady Talbot's house [Abbeylea], I noticed in her sitting room a small bookcase containing mostly modern volumes; but what caught my eye were twelve quarto volumes splendidly bound in red morocco. I pulled one out and found it was a chartulary volume with a fine eighteenth-century binding, containing various Auchinleck charters and deeds copied by hand in impeccable copperplate. The other eleven volumes were the same. Lady Talbot agreed that these volumes should be offered to Yale, along with some old title deeds and an Auchinleck estate cash-book for 1790–91 which I found in the bottom drawer of the filing cabinet. Yale accepted, and the purchase has now been concluded.[5]

---

[5]Lady Talbot also sold to Mary Hyde at the same time a number of papers and mementoes that David Buchanan found still in her possession. I do not remember that she played any further part in the history of the Boswell papers. She died on 1 July 1980 as this book was going through the press.

HISTORY OF

THE PUBLICATION OF

THE BOSWELL PAPERS,

1949–79

YALE'S PURCHASE OF THE BOSWELL PAPERS from Isham involved a commitment to McGraw-Hill to publish. President Seymour immediately made the project a grant of $50,000 from Sterling funds. Yale's Memorandum of Agreement with McGraw-Hill, 22 July 1949, named an Editorial Committee of the Private Papers of James Boswell as already nominated and approved: Frederick A. Pottle (Chairman), Edward C. Aswell (representing McGraw-Hill), Frederick W. Hilles, and Herman W. Liebert. At its very first meeting, 23 August 1949, the Committee addressed itself to plans for publication. It will be remembered that so far back as 1929 I had planned to edit both a popular and a scholarly edition of Boswell's journal, and that complete copy for text for those editions and voluminous collections for annotation, to the extent of Isham's holdings in 1937, had been lying in store in the Boswell Office since 1945. My old plan was now confirmed and enlarged. The Yale Editions of the Private Papers of James Boswell, it was decided at this and subsequent early meetings of the Committee, should consist of a research edition for scholars and a trade or reading edition of a part of the same material for the general public. The research edition was later defined as comprising at least three coordinated series: first, the entire corpus of Boswell's journal in all its varieties (fully written journal, journal-notes, memoranda); secondly, Boswell's entire recovered correspondence, all known letters by and to him whether at Yale or elsewhere; and, thirdly, a full critical text of the manuscript of the *Life of Johnson* in an arrangement which would show the method and progress of its composition. It was estimated that the entire research edition would run to at least thirty volumes. Within a policy of standard conventions, letters and fully written journal would preserve the spelling, capitalization, paragraphing, and pointing of the manuscripts. Annotation was envisaged as excursive and historical in character, aiming to relate the documents to the various areas of historical scholarship which they seem capable of illuminating. The research series was planned as a cooperative venture in scholarship, numerous scholars working simultaneously under the Committee on different portions of the text.

Except for a parcel of biographical and critical papers by Sir Joshua Reynolds, which had turned up unexpectedly in Boswell's, we saw the reading edition as consisting only of so much of Boswell's personal life-record as seemed likely to interest the general reader. Whether we had as yet agreed to relax the standards I had set for the Viking Press edition and to admit some of the condensed and abbreviated journal-notes, I do not remember. The problem did not arise till we came to our second trade volume, and will be discussed when I reach that point in the story. It was agreed that in the reading edition spelling, capitalization, paragraphing, and pointing should be standardized and modernized. The annotation should aim to facilitate and enhance the reading of Boswell's journal as a species of autobiographical literature.

If there had been no pressure for the immediate publication of a volume promising wide circulation, and if the editors could have been assured of preternatural longevity, the tidiest and most efficient course would probably have been to complete the entire research edition of the journal before doing anything else. The journal, in all its degrees of fulness, is the centre of reference for Boswell's papers, and by printing it entire with copious systematic annotation of an historical cast, we could have reduced much of the annotation of the other volumes in the research series to mere cross-reference, besides avoiding some repetition of labour in working up annotation for the trade edition. But there was understandably and properly strong pressure for sales. McGraw-Hill agreed to publish the research edition without subsidy, but naturally wished to get some immediate return on the huge sum it had advanced against royalties. It was decided at the first meeting of the Committee that the first publication in the Yale Editions of the Private Papers of James Boswell should be the first volume of the trade or reading edition. The Viking Press had always planned to publish its trade edition of the journal all at one time in a set which would have run to seven or eight volumes; McGraw-Hill opted for separate, independent volumes, each to be published as soon as it could be prepared for the press. Viking had stipulated that its trade edition should contain all of Boswell's fully written journal, and I had assumed in preparing the copy that the fragments were to be arranged in strict chronological sequence. If we had followed this plan, our first trade volume would have begun with "Journal of My Jaunt, Harvest 1762", the opening section of an elaborate self-conscious record which Boswell began on 14 September 1762 and continued without break for more than two years. Aswell, after reading the "Jaunt", argued strongly that in order to secure greater unity of theme and a more dramatic opening for our first volume— besides getting a slimmer book—we should pass over all the journal before 15 November 1762 and should choose as our entire matter the brilliant and totally unpublished London Journal of 15 November 1762 to 4 August 1763, which

Boswell himself had given its own identity by a new heading and a brief "Introduction".

I offered to withdraw as editor of this volume in favour of Abbott, if the Committee thought best, but Aswell was strongly opposed, and Hilles and Liebert supported his view. We set publication for the end of 1950.

Publication within little more than a year presented a very tight schedule, for since the manuscript did not come into Isham's hands until shortly before the transfer of the papers to Yale, we had hardly any office collections on it to help an editor. Except for a typed transcript of the text made by one of Abbott's assistants and Bennett's research annotation to the concurrent London memoranda (J 3), which had been a part of Isham's original purchase of 1927, I had to start pretty much from scratch. My undergraduate bursary assistant, Robert Burlin (Yale '50), did a great deal of the typing for me. I was much helped in gathering annotation by two Yale graduate students, Florence G. Marsh and Rufus Reiberg. Reiberg was also chiefly responsible for the index.

The "residue" from Malahide, which Isham received in June 1950, contained several documents highly relevant to the editing of the London Journal. He sent them to Yale immediately on receiving them, and though the copy had gone to the printer, it proved possible to print or draw evidence from the most important by extending a footnote here and there and adding an appendix.

I had prepared for the volume a longish Introduction, presenting various kinds of information—historical, biographical, critical—which I thought the general reader might find helpful. It opened with a brief history of the Boswell papers (the first form of the present account), which Aswell thought too systematic and dry to occupy so crucial a position in a volume for which great sales were hoped. I had no confidence that I could write the sort of thing he wanted, and remarked that it was a job for Christopher Morley. Aswell picked up the suggestion, Morley accepted the commission with enthusiasm, and a highly readable but in various respects inaccurate twenty-one page Preface by him was prefixed to a thirty-seven page Introduction by me. The book ended by being somewhat over-introduced, as Aswell later admitted. Morley's Preface was extracted as leading article of the *Saturday Review of Literature* for 7 October 1950. Selections from Boswell's own text appeared in *Harper's Magazine* for November, and in the *Sunday Times* shortly before the publication of the book in England. *Omnibook Magazine* published a surprisingly cautious abridgement.

Boswell's London Journal was published in New York on 6 November 1950 and a little later in England, and was a very successful publication. In the United States, the Book of the Month Club contracted to distribute it as a "dividend" book (free book for members) some time in the first six months of 1951, guaranteeing to take for that purpose not fewer than 200,000 copies. The British Book Society made it an alternative choice for its members for December 1950, which meant a distribution in the United Kingdom from that source of at least 10,000 copies. McGraw-Hill's first printing for general sales was 20,000 copies, and paper was ordered for an immediate second printing. In order that publication in Britain might not fall too far behind that in the United States, William Heinemann imported plates furnished by McGraw-Hill. A. S. Frere, Chairman and Managing Director, disliked the arrangement as implying that Heinemann was subordinate in the venture, and complained of difficulties and imperfections in the British printing because the American plates did not quite fit the British machines. He asserted independence by substituting for Morley's Preface (which he did not like) a Publisher's Note prepared in Heinemann's office; it was less lively than Morley's, but not more accurate. Heinemann also signalized the venture by bringing out in 1951 a *de luxe* extra-illustrated edition of 1,050 copies, printed at Heinemann's own press. On my suggestion this *de luxe* printing included two pieces which by Aswell's decision had not appeared in the trade volume: my History of the Boswell Papers and a text of "Journal of My Jaunt, Harvest 1762", annotated in the style of the trade *London Journal*. Some reviewers chided us, we came to think justly, for giving the readers of the luxury edition more text than was in the trade book, and we decided thereafter to restrict to illustrations the matter added to *de luxe* printings. *Boswell's London Journal* was reprinted for the Reprint Society in England, and appeared in the New American Library's Signet Books (New York, 1956; I revised text and annotation for this reprint), in the Harborough Publishing Co.'s Ace Books (London, 1958), and in Penguin Books (Harmondsworth, Middlesex, 1966). It was translated into Danish (1951), Finnish (1952), French (1952, Preface by André Maurois), German (1953), Italian (1954), and Swedish (1951). I have no information as to the number of copies of the reprints and translations sold, but by the beginning of 1953 McGraw-Hill had sold 347,000 copies (this figure includes those distributed by the Book of the Month Club) and William Heinemann had sold 111,000 (including sales of the British Book Society and the *de luxe* edition). I remember Aswell's remarking that McGraw-Hill had got back on its first book all the money it had advanced for the purchase of the papers.

Because of the difficulty we encountered in making up a qualified staff at the stipends we were able to pay, we did not get to the systematic transcription of the documents till September 1950, when we engaged Mrs. Patricia Wells as executive assistant and managing editor. A graduate of Bryn Mawr, she had previously held a position in the editorial department of John C. Winston and Co. Mrs. Lucyanna Fitzgerald, a graduate of the University of Arizona who had worked in the production department of Simon and Schuster, joined her as stenographer and typist. Various other full or part-time typists were engaged from time to time in the long task of typing in quadruplicate nearly all the documents from the Boswell collection which Mrs. Pottle had catalogued. Mrs. Wells managed the office and directed the typists in the making and filing of the transcripts. She also managed to get our various research files well started before she left at the end of the academic year to accompany her husband to a teaching position in Puerto Rico. She adapted the index of *Boswell's*

London Journal to the *de luxe* edition, repaging it and adding entries for "Journal of My Jaunt, Harvest 1762". It will perhaps be better if I desert chronology and trace the succession of our office managers all in one place.

The Boswell Office was without a managing editor through the academic year 1951–52. In August 1952 the Editorial Committee and Yale University jointly engaged Dr. Robert F. Metzdorf, formerly of the staff of the Houghton Library, Harvard University, to become Secretary to the Editorial Committee of the Boswell Papers and Curator of Manuscripts in the University Library. Two thirds of his time was allocated to the Boswell Office. He had an enviable faculty of being able to compose long, detailed letters rapidly and accurately on the machine in a first draft, and he cheerfully relieved me and Hilles of much time-consuming but necessary correspondence. He expertly enlarged all of our files locating or listing Boswell manuscripts not at Yale and of books once owned by Boswell. He directed a staff of three typists and three undergraduate bursary assistants, the latter furnished to us free of charge under Yale's bursary programme. In the summer of 1961, as this account has already related at some length, he performed a uniquely valuable service by going personally to Malahide, Abbeylea, and Auchinleck, and arranging for the transfer to Yale of an extraordinary quantity of important Boswelliana. He served us very usefully for nine years, leaving at the end of the academic year 1960–61 (as has already been mentioned) to take up an important position with the Parke-Bernet Galleries in New York.

Mrs. Iola S. Haverstick succeeded Metzdorf as managing editor and Secretary to the Editorial Committee: she was appointed on 2 October 1961 and resigned her appointment on 13 April 1962. Though the period was short, it was very active, and her name properly appears on two volumes of the trade or reading series published in 1962 and 1963.

Benjamin F. Houston, formerly of the Yale University Press, became Secretary in the spring or summer of 1962 and held the appointment till 31 January 1969, when he took a position at the Princeton University Press. The period was also one of considerable activity, his name appearing on the first two volumes of the research edition of the correspondence (published in 1966 and 1969) and one volume of the reading edition (published 1970).

Mrs. Helen Cooper served as Secretary to the Committee from 11 February 1969 to 30 June 1970, that is, to the end of the academic year 1969–70. Thereafter the post was vacant till 1 January 1975, when Dr. Irma S. Lustig assumed it under the NEH grant which became effective at that date. She had herself prepared the application for this grant, working as unpaid volunteer.

At the time Yale acquired the Boswell papers I had informed the Treasurer of Yale that I expected no stipend from the Boswell Papers Editing Fund for work done on the papers after they came to Yale, but that I did propose to collect from royalties (so far as royalties permitted) the $5,000 for work on Viking's suppressed trade edition which I had released Isham from paying me. The royalties on *Boswell's London Journal*, even at so low a rate as three per cent, were considerable ($8,003.40 for 1950 and $6,673.68 for 1951), and I withdrew $2,000 from that source as part of my fee for past labours, extending over many years. I shall anticipate, so as not to seem to recur unnecessarily to this topic. When the second trade volume of the journal was published, I withdrew $500 from royalties, as I did also when the third volume of the journal appeared. After that I withdrew no more, and in effect made the Boswell Papers Editing Fund a gift of $2,000. That much I thought I could afford; the full $5,000 seemed to me beyond my means.

Hilles went on half-time teaching at Yale in the academic year 1950–51, and during that time not only did much of the editing of our third trade volume, but also organized the research edition of Boswell's correspondence, of which he was general editor. As we had expected, graduate students at Yale had begun to select portions of the papers as matter for doctoral dissertations. Inge Probstein (Ph.D. 1951) edited Boswell's largely unpublished London Journal of 1778. Marshall Waingrow (Ph.D. 1951) edited five of the correspondences by which Boswell collected materials for the *Life of Johnson*. Frank Brady (Ph.D. 1952) made a study of Boswell's politics (published in 1965 as *Boswell's Political Career*), which entailed close study of Boswell's correspondence with Henry Dundas. Charles McC. Weis (Ph.D. 1952) edited Boswell's correspondence with Sir David Dalrymple. To move ahead a bit, Arthur W. Dixon chose for his doctoral dissertation (1953) an edition of Boswell's correspondence with his sons, with the prospect of enlarging it later for research volumes including all Boswell's family correspondence. Charles N. Fifer (Ph.D. 1954) edited Boswell's correspondence with six members of The Club, with a similar invitation to expand the book into a research volume containing all Boswell's correspondence with members of The Club other than Burke, Garrick, Johnson, and Malone. Mary E. Dukeshire made a dissertation (1955) of selected correspondences of the years 1770–73. Scholars applied for permission to edit particular correspondences in the Yale research edition: I shall list them without regard for chronology. Ralph S. Walker, then Lecturer in English Literature at the University of Aberdeen, was selected to edit Boswell's correspondence with John Johnston of Grange, one of the larger groups of Boswell's letters addressed to a single individual. As the best amends we could make to Abbott for his disappointment in not being chosen to edit *Boswell's London Journal*, we offered him the editorship of the Boswell-Temple group, the largest of Boswell's correspondences and by far the richest in biographical detail. James M. Osborn, a non-teaching scholar affiliated with Yale, author of much important research on Edmond Malone, was assigned the Boswell-Malone group. Percy Laithwaite of Lichfield agreed to edit Boswell's correspondence with Anna Seward. (He died before making any headway in the work.) Alexander F. Falconer, then Senior Lecturer in English at the University of St. Andrews, asked permission to edit a group of letters tentatively titled "Boswell and the Scots Literati". David M. Little, Professor of English at Harvard, and George M. Kahrl, Professor of English at Elmira College, editors of the Garrick *Letters,* assumed responsibility for Boswell's correspondence with Garrick. Thomas W. Copeland, then Associate Professor of English at the University of Chicago, editor of the multi-volume Burke *Correspondence,* was given the Boswell-Burke letters.

As has been said above, the Editorial Committee had decided that the research edition of the journal and its related notes and memoranda should be presented in one chronological sequence, but the requests for assignments of blocks of letters both by graduate students and by established scholars soon showed that if the research correspondence was truly to be a cooperative undertaking, a different arrangement would be required. Three kinds of volumes, all chronologically arranged, appeared to be called for: first, *subject* volumes like Waingrow's, collecting letters to and from various correspondents relating to a topic or theme; secondly, *single-correspondence* groupings like Walker's, collecting the entire correspondence of Boswell with an individual correspondent (some of these would be too short to make a volume, and would be grouped with other similar collections in volumes of multiple editorship), and, thirdly, *miscellaneous chronological* volumes collecting all the remaining letters. The volumes of this last class would be provided with lists that would enable readers to read the entire corpus of correspondence chronologically if they wished to. One of these miscellaneous chronological volumes was undertaken by Richard C. Cole, who chose Boswell's correspondence in 1769 as the subject of a Yale doctoral dissertation. After he took his degree in 1955, the Editorial Committee invited him to expand his study to include also the miscellaneous letters for 1766–69 and to make it the third or third and fourth volumes of its kind in the Yale research edition of the correspondence.

If we had followed Viking's decision to restrict the trade edition of Boswell's life-record to fully written journal, we should have had to reduce to a mere editorial link more than nine months of what, in spite of irreparable loss, still remains one of the most heavily documented periods of Boswell's entire life. While he was in Holland, August 1763 to June 1764, he wrote hastily every morning a combined review of the events of the previous day and a list of hints or resolves for the day ahead. From these notes *cum memorandis* he constructed at intervals a fully written literary journal, continuing and in the style of the London Journal of 1762–63. As an exercise in learning French he also wrote daily one-page exercises in that language on topics that interested him at the moment. He wrote ten lines of heroic verse every day on the first subjects that came into his head. Like all travellers abroad, he wrote long news-letters to friends and confidants at home. He fell in love with a remarkable Dutch bluestocking, Belle de Zuylen, and before he left Utrecht had begun to receive long inimitable letters from her. Except for thirty-two quarto pages at the end (perhaps a dozen pages if printed continuously in the format of *Boswell's London Journal*) the Dutch journal was lost in Boswell's own lifetime, but the other documents survive. I resolved to construct a substitute for the journal by abridging and stitching together at will memoranda, letters, verses, and translations of French exercises. In literary organization and expression, of course, the resulting book fell far below *Boswell's London Journal,* but as acute and revealing autobiographical introspection I thought it perhaps superior.

Boswell in Holland, 1763–1764, which appeared on 28 April 1952, was the first volume in the reading series for which I had full use of the cooperatively gathered collections I had twenty years earlier founded the Boswell Office to provide. It would be tedious to detail the research underlying each successive volume of the series, but perhaps I may be permitted to illustrate our general method by giving a rather full account of the stored information which I was able to draw on in setting up a text for the Holland book and annotating it. Scott had printed the surviving fragment of Boswell's journal in Holland (24 May to 17 June 1764, the beginning of J 6), had also printed and translated all but two of the letters that passed between Boswell and Belle de Zuylen, and had provided the letters with a charming Introduction. A Yale graduate student, Joseph Foladare, in my course on the Boswell papers, had reviewed Scott's text of the Holland journal and had collected annotation for it. Another Yale graduate student, Hale Sturges, in the same course, had transcribed and annotated the long and difficult manuscript of the memoranda in Holland (J 4). Charles Bennett had reviewed both these exercises and had added greatly to the annotation of the memoranda. I had at hand a spirited translation of the French themes (M 87) made for Isham by Professor Elizabeth W. Manwaring on the Atlantic crossing in 1927 when Isham was bringing back his first miscellaneous lot of papers from Malahide. Of course too I sought and got much help from specialists as I needed it. Professor Henri Peyre, beside reading my proofs, allowed me to consult him freely on problems of translation. (Many of the documents that make up the book were written in French.) The Dutch member of our Advisory Committee, Dr. Paul S. Breuning, Deputy Librarian of the University of Utrecht, read the entire book carefully in typescript and gave me invaluable assistance with the spelling and annotation of place and personal names. Marshall Waingrow collated text against the documents, collected annotation, and was mainly responsible for the index.

Extracts from *Boswell in Holland* were published serially in the *Daily Mail* and selections appeared in the *Atlantic Monthly.* There was an abridgement of it in Danish. It sold very well, though nothing like as well as the *London Journal.* By the beginning of 1953 McGraw-Hill had sold 20,000 copies of its edition. Heinemann this time printed its own edition at its own press, also bringing out a *de luxe* extra-illustrated impression from the same setting of type. Sales of these two British printings amounted to 31,500 copies for the same period. Because I put so much of myself into *Boswell in Holland,* it has always been a favourite of mine, and at the time of its publication I had little doubt that the response of the public had vindicated my experimentation. It appears pretty clear to me now, however, that the large sale was mainly due to expectations raised by *Boswell's London Journal,* and that to the majority of non-specialist readers the book came as a disappointment.

Reviews generally were favourable, but the *Times Literary Supplement* declared the matter of the volume of no great importance, either literary or historical. As biographer of Boswell, I am no doubt too ready to see literary merit in any of his autobiographical records that provides me with acutely and subtly observed characterizing detail. But I continue to think the book undervalued, and expect that its reputation will rise when Boswell's journal ceases to be a literary newcomer and becomes a classic. In any case, the experiment had a permanent effect on editorial policy in the later volumes. *Boswell's London Journal*, a book-length narrative with no break in it, left an editor unprepared to solve the problems of fragmentation which are characteristic of most of the rest of the journal. *Boswell in Holland* demonstrated various methods of weaving that could be used to effect in later volumes.

During the academic year 1952–53 I again went on full sabbatical leave, and was again awarded a Guggenheim fellowship. I first put the copy of *Boswell on the Grand Tour: Germany and Switzerland, 1764* in shape for the printer, and then worked on the Boswell biography.

On 17 November 1952 Hilles brought out the third volume in the trade edition, *Portraits by Sir Joshua Reynolds*, the only volume in the series not devoted to Boswell's journal. How the new Reynolds materials in that book (character sketches of Garrick and Goldsmith, with other brilliant bits) came into Boswell's hands is not known, but he is much to be commended for preserving them. All the materials in the book are quite charming, and Hilles put them together gracefully. The *Saturday Review of Literature* bought the right to pre-publication of the Garrick and Goldsmith sketches. But some reviewers, though they had only praise for the material and Hilles's editorial handling of it, questioned the wisdom of bringing out the work as a trade book. The total sales (3,359 copies in the United States, 2,417 in Britain) seemed to support their verdict. Isham thought the Committee spoiled the book's chances for wide sale by giving it an ambiguous and unexciting title ("Portraits" was my suggestion), but I think rather that we have here a prime illustration of a contention of mine that almost alone among eighteenth-century authors Boswell can compete with writers of our own day on their own terms. It is not necessarily either to their credit or to his, but Boswell in style and content writes like a modern, like one of us. Reynolds's sketches seem quite admirable to scholars and literati, but to the general reader they appear "historical", "literary", the sort of thing one reads in school.

The dissertations of Probstein and Waingrow were completed and accepted in 1951, Brady's and Weis's in 1952. Waingrow was authorized to convert his dissertation into a volume of the research edition by expanding it to include all Boswell's correspondence dealing with the collection of materials for the *Life of Johnson*. As has been said, Arthur W. Dixon chose for his dissertation (1953) an edition of Boswell's correspondence with his sons, with the prospect of later editing all Boswell's family correspondence for the research edition.

Towards the end of 1953 we published the fourth trade volume (third of Boswell's journal): *Boswell on the Grand Tour: Germany and Switzerland, 1764*. I remember the book now as having been comparatively easy to prepare for the printer. I was very well served by Scott's text, translations, and introductions in *Private Papers,* by the collections of my students, reviewed and augmented by Bennett, and also had a good deal of help from experts in matters French and German. Mrs. Annemarie Holborn, German by birth, a Berlin Ph.D. in classics, prepared the first typed draft of the book and was constantly on hand for advice and research, as were my colleagues and friends in the Yale Department of German, Curt von Faber du Faur and Konstantin Reichardt. W. David Patton, formerly of the Department of French at Yale, gave me invaluable assistance in everything concerning Rousseau and Voltaire. It was with this volume that I began to benefit from the dedicated researches of Robert Warnock, Professor of English at the University of Connecticut. A remarkable linguist with near-native fluency in French, German, Italian, and Spanish, he had written his doctoral dissertation at Yale many years before (1933) on the journal and journal-notes of Boswell's Italian tour. It had long been his custom to travel in Europe every summer to improve his languages. I proposed to him that he edit all Boswell's foreign journal and correspondence for our research edition. He accepted enthusiastically, and spent several summers annotating Boswell from foreign archives. He was in Italy during the summer of 1950. From March to August of 1952 he performed a similar service in West Germany and Holland. From his preliminary reports, sent in letters, I was able to extract some very useful notes, besides fixing the spelling of many family names and supplying Christian names. He also directed us to some of our best illustrations.

Boswell on the Grand Tour: Germany and Switzerland was published on 19 October 1953. A considerable portion of the conversations with Rousseau appeared in the *Saturday Review of Literature* for 3 October, and selections from various parts of the volume, with pen-and-ink sketches by Ronald Searle, were printed serially in *Punch* (26 August, 2, 9, 16, 23 September). *Der Monat* (Berlin, August and September 1954) published two extracts, "Boswell in Berlin und Potsdam" and "Besuch bei Rousseau". Many of the reviewers expressed irritation at Boswell or even dislike of him (he is indeed in this volume and the succeeding at his least attractive), but the great majority declared the volume to be interesting as literature and important as an historical document. The *Times Literary Supplement* again dissented. I wrote a private note to members of the Advisory Committee predicting that the *Times Literary Supplement* would ultimately "reverse its position . . . that is, in reviews of future volumes will refer back to these in terms very different from those the reviewer is now using". Which has certainly proved true, at least of *Boswell on the Grand Tour: Germany and Switzerland*. Sales kept up very well. By the beginning of 1954 McGraw-Hill and Heinemann had printed 40,000 copies and had sold over 28,000. There was a German translation and a French translation (prefaced by an essay by André Maurois).

I had now brought out three large trade volumes in four years, a feat I could hardly have accomplished without having had full sabbatical leave during the academic year 1952–53. I could not expect to have such relief again till 1959–60, and my progress on *James Boswell, The Earlier Years* was disappointing. The Editorial Committee agreed with me that the trade volumes ought henceforth to be done in collaboration. Frank Brady, then Instructor in English at Yale, was my immediate choice for the next volume. He had been a student of mine in the Yale Graduate School and had taken his doctorate at Yale with a dissertation on Boswell which I had supervised. I admired his powers, especially his capacity for turning out accurate finished work of high quality in a seemingly impossibly short space of time. The method I followed with him became a model for my later collaborations. Using all the stores of the Boswell Office, including my abortive edition for the Viking Press, he first constructed a finished proposed volume: a complete text edited for the printer, tied together by editorial links, and fully annotated. I then reviewed his typescript minutely, making suggestions for additions to the text and changes in the links and annotation. He then went through the book again with my suggestions before him, making such changes as seemed to him desirable. Finally, he wrote a critical Introduction, on which I again gave him some suggestions for revision, and we joined in writing a textual note and a statement of editorial method.

Boswell on the Grand Tour: Italy, Corsica, and France, 1765–1766 resembles *Boswell in Holland* in being constructed largely from memoranda, notes, and letters. Except for sparse occasional scraps, Boswell wrote no journal from February to October 1765. The journal of his Corsican tour pretty certainly consisted only of rough notes which have since disappeared, and we had to make do with the historicized version which Boswell himself published in 1768. The letters for the period are copious and newsy, and we counted on them to supply the elegance which the memoranda and notes lacked. As I remember, the reviews were good, better even than those of the preceding volume, but the sale fell off drastically. The book appeared on 23 May 1955. During the remainder of the year McGraw-Hill distributed 8,839 copies but got so many of them back at the end of the year as to result in negative sales of about 300 copies in 1956. Thereafter the sales never quite reached 150 copies a year, and the total American sales for the ten years following publication were roughly 9,400 copies—good for a scholarly book but small for a trade volume. Price could have had little if anything to do with decline in sales (*Boswell's London Journal* had been published at $5; *Boswell on the Grand Tour: Italy, Corsica, and France* was priced at $5.50). The main reasons for the falling off pretty clearly were, first, that the book contained an unbroken stretch of fifty-six pages reprinted from an eighteenth-century book, and, secondly, that the prevalence of memoranda made much of the rest seem disordered and obscure to a non-scholarly reader. *Boswell on the Grand Tour: Italy, Corsica, and France* was difficult but not difficult in the approved modern way.

In the summer of 1956 Aswell left the employ of the McGraw-Hill Book Co.

and became associated with Doubleday and Co. No one played a more important role than he in the negotiations by which the Boswell papers came to Yale, and his knowledge as publisher and skill as editor were of the greatest value to us in preparing the first six volumes of our trade edition. At Heinemann's request he continued after leaving McGraw-Hill to attend meetings of the Editorial Committee. His successors, representatives of McGraw-Hill on the Committee, have been Edward Kuhn, Jr., Editor, Trade Book Department, 9 July 1956, resigning to accept appointment as Executive Vice President of the New American Library, September 1965; Frank E. Taylor, Editor-in-Chief and General Manager, Trade Book Department, 1965–70; Dan Lacy, Senior Vice President, McGraw-Hill Book Co., 1970–75; and Thomas H. Quinn, Publisher, Scholarly Books Division, McGraw-Hill Book Co., 1975—.

Boswell in Search of a Wife, 1766–1769, edited by Frank Brady and myself, was published on 15 October 1956, eighteen months after *Boswell on the Grand Tour: Italy, Corsica, and France*. Only the first volume in the series bettered that timetable, and no later volume was to come anywhere near it. *Boswell in Search of a Wife* was put together with relative ease. Though the journal for the period is badly fragmented, there is a good deal of it, portions of it rating among Boswell's most brilliant writing. Boswell's letters to Temple, 1766–69, are remarkably detailed and informative with regard to his sentimental attachments and involvements (the gardener's daughter, Mrs. Dodds, Miss Blair, "Zélide", "B.", Mary Ann Boyd, Margaret Montgomerie), and were used pervasively as the unifying and bonding element of the volume. It may have been risky to include so much matter that had been available for a century, but it seemed to us that comparatively few readers of a trade edition would be familiar with it.

Boswell in Search of a Wife reversed the downward trend and sold somewhat better than *Boswell on the Grand Tour: Italy, Corsica, and France*. McGraw-Hill sent out 9,650 copies in the first year after publication, and the American sale down to 1973, when the book went out of print, amounted to 10,610 copies. It will be remembered that *Boswell on the Grand Tour: Italy, Corsica, and France* had no translations. *Boswell in Search of a Wife* received a complete translation into French, with a Preface by René Lalou.

In a newsletter of 28 April 1958 we reported that the paperback edition of *Boswell's London Journal*, published in the New World Library, had achieved sales of about 160,000 copies. "It has been calculated that the total books in print from our project (in original editions, reprints and translations) are now 831,000."

In the autumn of 1957, the Boswell Office established connexion with one of its most intelligent and resourceful editors, a volunteer researcher who lived seven thousand miles away and never set foot in New Haven. The story is so extraordinary that I shall detach it from the general chronology and tell it all in one piece.

A Mr. N. S. Curnow (the "S" stood for Stanley) of Johannesburg, South Africa, wrote me and Frank Brady a long and well-informed letter, inquiring when the next trade volume would be published, and asking if in the mean time we could help him to acquire a microfilm of all eighteen volumes of *Private Papers*. ("I am informed that no copy . . . is available in any Reference Library in South Africa.") Recognizing a Boswellian expert in an unlikely place, I replied at length, assuring him that it was quite feasible to make him a film. We told him, however, that Liebert thought he could pick up a set of *Private Papers* itself at a price he could afford, and suggested that he inquire of Michael Papantonio, Seven Gables Bookshop, New York City. We added that the Oxford University Press had published a small edition of the *Index* to *Private Papers* and might still have a copy in stock. Curnow followed up both suggestions and got a set of *Private Papers* for $350 and an *Index* for three pounds or so. He reported the method he was following in reading the unannotated text in *Private Papers*. First, he read Horace Walpole's letters for a given year ("for 'flavour' of the times, familiarity with topical issues, etc."). Then he read Boswell's journals for that same year, "turning to the *Life of SJ* and *Letters of JB* wherever they fit into the story. Even the *Hypochondriack* essays can be read with enjoyment at the points where they were composed." Then he used the *Index* systematically to identify the persons mentioned in the text. In a subsequent letter he proposed that in our next trade volume we include an appendix on the Scottish courts of law, sending along a draft of the sort of thing he had in mind. We gratefully accepted it and printed it with little revision.

In response to a request from me that he tell us something about himself, he replied that he was a South African by birth, forty-two years old in 1958, his father Cornish, his mother Scottish. He had no academic degree of any kind. He was by profession a chartered accountant in private practice ("mainly auditing and advice to clients on . . . financial and income tax problems"). Four years before he wrote to us, he had decided not to expand his practice, but to content himself with less income and more leisure.

Although fond of the past and with a fair knowledge of English history of the 16th and 17th centuries, I had somehow neglected the 18th, always meaning to study it. . . . I in Feb. 1955 at last bought and opened Boswell's *London Journal*. Fortunate in the gift of historical imagination, I was immediately enchanted to find myself transported, by Boswell's genius, into the living London of 1762/63. As the next two Trade volumes were available by this time, I was able to read straight through to the end of 1764.

But I soon found that to appreciate Boswell fully it needed much more knowledge than I possessed of English history, personalities and general background of the period. So I proceeded to read the most important histories, memoirs, journals and letters (Walpole, F. Burney, Gibbon, Wilkes, etc.) and very soon succumbed to the charm of the 18th century.

Boswell, however, remained my greatest interest and last August *Boswell in Search of a Wife* arrived and was read with even greater relish than the earlier volumes. . . . When I had finished it, I felt it almost unbearable not to be able to continue his saga.

So having ascertained that no copy of the Isham set was to be had in any South African public library, I wrote to you in the hope that you might permit the making of a microfilm.

By September 1958 he had read every word of *Private Papers* and was planning to compile his own annotation from 1769 on, besides reducing the *Fettercairn Catalogue* to a single chronological arrangement. He read reference works systematically, and ordered and read microfilms of several of our Boswell dissertations, all the time pouring into the office annotation for future trade volumes and corrections and additions for volumes already published. He went straight though the *Index* to *Private Papers,* verifying the identifications and compiling genealogical tables. We asked him to read the proofs of both a trade and a research volume, which he was delighted to do. We made him a member of the Advisory Committee. When the reports of the various readers of the proofs of our first research volume were in hand, we sent them all to him in Johannesburg, entrusting him with the responsibility of evaluating and digesting the recommendations for change and of entering the resulting corrections.

By a letter of 4 August 1963, we learned that he had been seriously ill with a kidney infection, and he continued to report traces of illness for some time thereafter. In January 1964 he sent us what he called "a sort of private reference work"; 150 typed pages (indexed) of biographical notes on persons mentioned in Boswell's journal. The kidney infection returned in June 1964, and he reported that life had been "rather miserable for some months". He began reading and reporting on the typescript of my biography, *James Boswell, The Earlier Years, 1740–1769.* In February 1965 he was involved as passenger in "a motor smash", and sustained a concussion from which he was suffering headaches a month later. The last letter we had from him was dated 14 June 1965. A letter from an associate written at the end of the next month informed us that he had died of meningitis, I suppose alone in his bachelor apartment, "some time between Saturday night and Monday morning last" (24–26 July 1965).

I now resume the chronological narrative with the year 1958. It will be remembered that in 1949 President Seymour of Yale had funded the Boswell Editions with a grant of $50,000. Over the years this had been supplemented by about $27,000 in royalties and by generous gifts by Hilles from his salary as Bodman Professor, totalling about the same amount. After nine years of operation our supplies had begun to run low, and the Old Dominion Foundation (February 1958) granted us $10,000 a year for five years.

Boswell for the Defence, 1769–1774 was published in the week of 16 November 1959 under the editorship of William K. Wimsatt, Jr. and myself. Wimsatt had been a student of mine in two courses in the Yale Graduate School: "Theories of Poetry" and "The Boswell Papers", the latter in the academic year 1936–37. By the time we engaged in collaboration, he was Professor of English at Yale and was teaching the course in "Theories of Poetry" himself. Theory, conducted with full

philosophical rigour, gave him the greatest satisfaction, and he was given to humorous depreciation of minute historical research, calling it "leg-work in the library
stacks". But no one did it better, as I knew from his course-exercise in "The Boswell
Papers", an edition of Boswell's London Journal of 1772. He accepted my offer of
collaboration with alacrity and turned in a minutely detailed but luminous work,
having invented a method of joining the fragments of fully written journal by a
continuous narrative constructed out of many brief excerpts from letters by and to
Boswell, embedded in a narrative which paraphrased the rough notes. Cyril Connolly
said the book was "beautifully constructed".

I had great hopes for this volume, thinking that it had greater promise of large
sales than any other in the series since *Boswell's London Journal*. My reason for
thinking so was that the last third of it was held together by one deeply interesting
theme: Boswell's struggle to save from the gallows a miserable man named Reid,
who had been his first criminal client when he was called to the bar in 1766. His
concern for Reid dominates the journal from 15 July to the end of September 1774.
We had obtained a very full account of the trial from the process in the Scottish
Record Office, and Wimsatt had quoted from this material very effectively. But
for some reason I have never been able to define, the volume did little better than
Boswell on the Grand Tour: Italy, Corsica, and France. The price was $6.95, an increase
of nearly a dollar over any of the earlier volumes, but it does not seem as though
price alone could have accounted for the disappointing performance. Perhaps the
matter was too shocking and painful (Connolly, comparing the book to a musical
composition, called the concluding section "sombre"), but it does not seem that
the taste of those years generally fled from gloom. McGraw-Hill sold 5,640 copies
of *Boswell for the Defence* in the first year of its publication and 6,786 copies down
to 1976. Perhaps the trouble was simply that the public, though relishing Boswell,
did not have so large an appetite as we were assuming.

The eighth volume of Yale's trade edition, *Boswell's Journal of a Tour to the
Hebrides, 1773*, bears the copyright date 1961, but was actually published in the
week of 3 September 1962. In the trade edition it is misplaced by about a year in
the chronology of the series, coming after, not before, the part of the journal devoted
to John Reid. This misplacement was primarily and ultimately caused by the fact
that we already had on hand plates for the Viking Press edition of 1936. We had
recovered after those plates were made a considerable quantity of new manuscript
and printed matter (proofs) that would have enabled me to improve both the text
and the annotation, but it seemed to the Editorial Committee wantonly wasteful
to reset the whole book for a reading edition. If we had reset we should still have
been faced with a very difficult problem of volume division. Boswell's marriage
(25 November 1769) and John Reid's burial (23 September 1774) are obvious breaks
in narrative movement which an editor who is looking for unifying themes can
hardly ignore. There is enough journal between those two points to fill two large
volumes, but if I had decided to follow strict chronology, I should have had to put
half of Boswell's journal of the Hebridean tour in one volume and half in another,

surely an intolerable arrangement. The beginning and end of the Hebridean journal are as obvious and compelling breaks as are Boswell's marriage and the burial of John Reid. If one could set the Hebridean tour to one side, the journal of 1772, the journal of 1773 without the Hebridean tour, and the journal of 1774 to 24 September would form a unified volume. Accordingly, I left the Hebridean tour to be published in a volume by itself, and Wimsatt and I closed up the gap in *Boswell for the Defence*. After all, the Hebridean tour, being a completely isolated episode, reads about as effectively after the John Reid journal as before it.

The text and the Appendix (pp. 3–406) of Yale's edition of *Boswell's Journal of a Tour to the Hebrides* are consequently identical in every respect with the same portions of the Viking Press printing of 1936; the front matter (pp. [i]–xxviii) and everything from page 407 to page 488 were wholly written for the printing of 1962, and the index was revised to take account of new matter. The illustrations were mainly new. Since Charles H. Bennett had collaborated with me in the printing of 1936, his name properly appears on the title-page, but he had no part in the revision of 1962, in fact, had died in 1957 and is dedicatee of the revision. The new matter appears at the back of the book in a section of Additions and Corrections and in a systematic Topographical Supplement of thirty-seven pages, also in the back, in which I attempt to guide the reader to the sites and objects mentioned so far as they are still in existence. The information in this supplement I drew partly from notes I myself had made on the spot in the early summer of 1936, partly from correspondence with various helpers. In particular, Donald A. MacDonald, of Edinburgh University, spent nearly two weeks on the road for me, collecting information I lacked. It has always seemed to me that my new matter was given rather more pleasantly and usefully in these supplements than it would have been if distributed throughout the book as footnotes.

I had no notion at all how the book would be received. Viking's experience in 1936 had shown the difficulty—perhaps the impossibility—of getting the work accepted as *new* and not a mere reprint of a classic. Still, Viking had sold enough copies in 1936 to dampen sales only twenty-six years later. The price was discouraging: McGraw-Hill kept revising it upward and finally set it at $10. Some of the reviews protested at such a price for a volume that was largely a reissue. I felt myself that price had been determined more by *weight* (the book *is* big, almost 550 pages) than by actual cost of production. Immediate sales were discouraging, and the total sales to 1970 fell a little short of 4,000 copies (3,836).

Between the journal in which Boswell identified himself so recklessly with the cause of John Reid (autumn 1774) and that which announces his succession to the estate of Auchinleck (autumn 1782) stretch eight years of journal that I never could confidently pronounce to be matter for a trade edition. I found myself reading this stretch compulsively, but I could not convince myself that those who came to it without the specialist's incentive would feel a like compulsion. It seems fairly clear from the evidence of the present survey that general readers of Boswell's journal want narrative movement towards a goal or conclusion, not mere local brilliance.

The model of their taste is *Boswell's London Journal* or, as second choice, *Boswell in Search of a Wife*. The journal of the eight years from 1774 to 1782, though fragmented, is copious and contains an impressive number of passages that almost all literary critics would agree in selecting as among Boswell's most characteristic and memorable writing. But there is no forward narrative movement: the writing does not progress. It swirls and eddies so much that divisions of it can be little better than mechanical. What I am talking about is illustrated by the extreme difficulty we had in giving suitable titles to the three volumes into which the matter was finally divided. Joseph Reed and I solved the problem for the volume covering the years 1778 to 1782 in a somewhat irresponsible fashion by naming the book from an event that happens at the very end and was certainly not one that Boswell designed or aimed at. Charles Ryskamp, then Associate Professor of English at Princeton, with whom I collaborated on the ninth volume, named it *Boswell: The Ominous Years, 1774–1776*, taking a hint from my Introduction to the eleventh volume of *Private Papers*, in which I had found "slight but ominous tokens of aging" in this record of Boswell at thirty-five and thirty-six.

But as I have already indicated, this is by no means to say that *Boswell: The Ominous Years* does not contain much absorbing matter. No volume of the series after *Boswell on the Grand Tour: Germany and Switzerland* contains so much continuous fully written journal. Particular jewels are Boswell's mini-tour with Johnson to Oxford, Birmingham, Lichfield, and Ashbourne (19–29 March 1776) and Boswell's account of his interview with Mrs. Rudd. The book was published in the week of 8 April 1963, and down to 1976 McGraw-Hill had sold 4,809 copies—more than of *Boswell's Journal of a Tour to the Hebrides*, but decidedly fewer than of *Boswell for the Defence*, which in turn had sold significantly less well than *Boswell in Search of a Wife*.

The fact probably was that our "trade edition" was slipping over or had already slipped over into a "scholarly book"—the classification which would all along have been expected for an eighteenth-century text. Any one comparing *Boswell for the Defence* with *Boswell in Search of a Wife* will immediately notice an increase in the amount of annotation; in *Boswell: The Ominous Years* the annotation had certainly not decreased, and I think had increased a little more. If what I have said above about the eddying structure of these journals of the middle years is true, this is just what one would have expected. A coherent forward-straining narrative explains itself; an eddying record does not. If one uses on the matter of *Boswell: The Ominous Years* the identical philosophy of annotation one has used for *Boswell's London Journal*, one comes out with more notes and longer notes. Considered individually, Ryskamp's notes were notably taut and sparing. Some *individual* volumes of Boswell's journal will no doubt continue to attract the general reader, but the collected *set* (and not merely because of the price) will probably always be classified as "scholarly".

Our first grant of $50,000, supplemented as I have explained above,[1] enabled

---

[1] Page 216.

us to operate till 1958 at an average annual budget of less than $12,000, an extremely modest outlay in view of the immense amount of transcription performed in those years. The Old Dominion Foundation's grant of $50,000 in 1958, eked out by $27,000 from Hilles, carried us to 1965, seven more years at an even more modest rate. The Old Dominion Foundation in 1965 granted us $25,000 more.

The first five volumes of the trade edition of the journal appeared within a period of six years. The next three appeared at intervals of three, four, and seven years respectively. The general reasons for the wider spacing, apart from the increasing bulk and complexity of the annotation of the trade journal, were the demands made on my time during those years (1956–69) by my biography, *James Boswell, The Earlier Years, 1740–1769* and the first volumes of the research edition of Boswell's correspondence: *The Correspondence of James Boswell with John Johnston of Grange*, edited by Ralph S. Walker, Molson Professor of English at McGill University, and *The Correspondence . . . of James Boswell Relating to the Making of the "Life of Johnson"*, edited by Marshall Waingrow, Professor of English at the Claremont Graduate School. My biography appeared in June 1966 and the volumes of correspondence in 1966 and 1969. *James Boswell: The Earlier Years* was my own property, not a part of the Yale Editions, but I presented it to Yale before publication under a life-income agreement. Up to the present, I have returned all the income to the principal, so that the fund now stands at more than $18,000. After the death of myself and Mrs. Pottle, the income from the fund is to go towards the expenses of the Boswell Office until the Yale Editions are completed.

Walker's volume illustrates our "single correspondence" category, Waingrow's is a "subject" volume (above, p. 209). In trade volumes, as we say, "the object of the annotation has been to illuminate the documents themselves as compositions", and we do not report sources unless we quote exactly; while the annotation of the research edition "is intended to relate the documents to the various areas of scholarship which they are capable of illuminating", and we report the sources of our annotation fully. Boswell's correspondence with John Johnston is the largest of his correspondences after that with Temple and is particularly valuable for documenting Boswell's life in London and on the Continent for the period November 1762 to January 1766 (185 printed pages). Waingrow's massive volume (over 600 pages of text) shows the care and thoroughness with which Boswell collected materials from others to add to the vast store of his own Johnsoniana.

Hilles, as editor-in-chief of the correspondence, of course devoted much more time to Walker's and Waingrow's books than I did. I think I did little work in depth on either book until the stage of proofs. In Walker's volume, because of my own parallel researches, I was able to make a number of useful corrections and additions. With Waingrow my *adversaria* were mainly minute and of the nature of suggestions. The volumes were priced at $17.50 and $20 respectively. Total sales appear to be of 1,518 and 1,248 copies.

The Old Dominion Foundation's award of $25,000, made in 1965 and supplemented by personal gifts totalling $13,500 from Hilles, kept us going till 1968, when I obtained a grant of $10,000 from the National Endowment for the Humanities and Hilles added $3,500 to it. For the six years from 1969 to 1975 our funding, except for $2,000 from Hilles's friend and class-mate, W. Peyton May (Yale A.B. 1922), came entirely from within the Committee: $54,000 from Hilles and $1,000 from a research fund of my own. We were down to two salaried workers: Harriet Chidester, typist, secretary, file-clerk, and assistant editor, who had been with us since 1955, and Mrs. Pottle, whose remuneration as cataloguer was merely nominal.

In *Boswell in Extremes, 1776–1778*, 1970, I collaborated with Charles McC. Weis, Professor of English at Ohio Wesleyan University. He had been a student of mine in the Yale Graduate School, and had edited Boswell's correspondence with Sir David Dalrymple as a doctoral dissertation (1952). I admired his editorial tact and the clarity and succinctness of his notes, and altogether enjoyed working with him. The Introduction, which blends ideas and expressions from both of us, seems to me one of the better ones in the series. The title (which generally got corrupted to *Boswell in Extremis*) was mine, and was intended to point to "the polarization of [Boswell's] states of despondency and joy, . . . the stark alternation of periods of melancholia and high spirits" which I thought characteristic of the period.

The two particular jewels of this volume were Boswell's last interview with David Hume, when Hume knew himself to be dying (7 July 1776, pp. 11–15), and the Ashbourne Journal (10–27 September 1777, pp. 143–86). Of special interest to scholars was the greater part of the London Journal of 1778 (22 March to 23 May, pp. 227–354), which had been recovered from Fettercairn and consequently did not appear in *Private Papers*. This is the longest of Boswell's London Journals after that of 1762–63, which also was found at Fettercairn. We had no collection of materials on it in the Boswell Office, but (as I have remarked above) Inge Probstein had made a complete annotated edition of it in her doctoral dissertation, 1951. Since scholars had no text of it at all, we decided to print it entire, though some bits were laconic and obscure.

In the interval between 1963 and 1970, inflation and the shift from "trade" to "scholarly" classification had driven the price of our books up horrendously. *Boswell: The Ominous Years* had been priced at $8.50. *Boswell in Extremes* was priced at $15, a two hundred per cent increase since 1950. Sales to 1976 appear to have amounted to 2,188 copies.

In so summary a narration as this, I cannot pause for systematic rendering of thanks to all those who have significantly aided our venture—I think especially of several members of the Advisory Committee who are now dead—but I must pause to memorialize three men besides Curnow whose contributions to the Yale Boswell Editions were central and enduring. Charles Bennett died on 22 January 1957. As has been mentioned, he had then been for a long time a member of the editorial staff of the Yale Walpole Edition, but he worked next door to us and continued to be interested in our affairs. His name appears on a single volume of our reading edition of the journal, but his research will pervade the whole of both series. Edward C. Aswell died on 2 November 1958. He was remarkably effective in insinuating reputable principles of trade publication into scholarly minds. After he left McGraw-Hill, he continued to attend the meetings of our Editorial Committee at his own expense and at considerable inconvenience to himself. Robert Warnock died on 23 February 1967. He had retired at the age of fifty-five from his professorship at the University of Connecticut, with hope of years of happy uninterrupted work on the research edition of the volumes containing Boswell's European journal and correspondence. He died before any of his volumes had appeared, but he left his copious and accurate materials in such shape that other scholars can carry his work to completion. He and his mother left their joined estates to Yale to found a fellowship which can be awarded to scholars working on the Boswell papers at Yale until the Yale Editions are completed. And finally I must record the passing of Frederick W. Hilles, colleague, benefactor, and friend, who died on 11 December 1975. He was engaged in every aspect of the Yale editions of Boswell for the first quarter-century of their existence, and was active in establishing policy. Frank Brady, who had been appointed to the Committee 17 April 1972, succeeded him as editor-in-chief of the research edition of the correspondence. Marshall Waingrow was added to the Committee shortly after Hilles's death. Quite recently (18 May 1979) Martin Price, Thomas E. Donnelley Professor of English at Yale, was appointed a member to ensure liaison with Yale's Department of English.

Mrs. Irma S. Lustig had taken a Ph.D. degree at the University of Pennsylvania in 1963 with a dissertation dealing with Boswell's *Life of Johnson*. I first met her in 1966, when she came to New Haven to make a close study of the manuscript of the *Life*. I gave her the more attention because few of our own graduate students at Yale were then turning to the Boswell papers for subjects for dissertations, and I found her eager and deeply committed. After several meetings, I suggested that she edit one of the chronological volumes in our research edition of the correspondence. She investigated the materials for one, but decided that her interest lay rather in Boswell's journal. The Editorial Committee accordingly made her joint editor with me of the volume of the reading edition of the journal covering the years 1782–85. She applied for and was awarded a personal grant from the National Endowment for the Humanities to support her in this project. I saw her application in various stages, and was so much impressed by the intrepidity and skill with which she handled a negotiation of that sort that I told her I should have proposed making her managing editor of the Boswell Editions if we had been in funds. She strongly urged us to apply again to the NEH in more aspiring and comprehensive terms than formerly. In April and May 1974 she worked as a volunteer, drafting an application that won us an NEH award of $118,890 for the period 1 January 1975 to 31 March 1977. This enabled us to expand our salaried staff by three more members. A second application, submitted 26 April 1976, for the period 1 April

1977 to 31 March 1980, resulted in an outright grant of $148,657 and an offer to match any funding we might obtain elsewhere, dollar for dollar, up to $75,000. We raised $16,785 by an appeal through our newsletter, and the Andrew W. Mellon Foundation most generously granted us $60,000, thus capturing the entire $75,000 with something to spare. Our hope is by our next appeal to secure from some source such an endowment as will free us from the distraction and fatigue of repeated solicitation.

Dr. Lustig was elected a member of the Editorial Committee at the same time as Martin Price.

The third volume of the research series, *The Correspondence of James Boswell with Certain Members of The Club,* edited by Charles N. Fifer, Professor of English, Stanford University, was published in 1976. Like Waingrow's book a "subject" volume, it prints all Boswell's recovered correspondences with members of The Club, excepting only the correspondences with Burke, Garrick, Johnson, and Malone. (We shall publish the correspondences with Burke, Garrick, and Malone in a volume by themselves.) Twenty letters from Topham Beauçlerk to Langton which unexpectedly turned up in Boswell's papers are included for good measure and probably provide the best reading in the book. The two most interesting among Boswell's correspondents turn out to be Thomas Barnard (who has previously been strangely underdocumented) and Thomas Percy. Hilles oversaw the book in all its earlier stages, and Brady and I worked closely with the proofs. The book seems to me an admirable realization of our editorial aims for the research edition of the correspondence. Keith Walker, who reviewed it for the *Times Literary Supplement,* pronounced the annotation "beyond praise", but took us mildly to task for reprinting complete in this volume a number of letters which Waingrow had printed in whole or in part. This I think showed a misunderstanding of our method. In this case (and perhaps it will happen only in this case) two of our "subject" groupings overlapped. Among 119 persons with whom Boswell corresponded for materials for the *Life of Johnson,* 11 were members of The Club. Of the two classifications ("Club" or *"Life of Johnson"*) one must be selected as primary, as the classification under which the letter is to be printed in full and receive full annotation of the general sort the edition aims at. Clearly in this case "Club" is primary, especially for letters printed only in part by Waingrow. The "chronological" volumes will merely list letters like this, with cross-references, and the same procedure might have been followed in Waingrow's volume, though, if that had been done, the cross-references would have been to a volume that would not be published for seven years. But since Waingrow's "subject" was of the nature of a study or dissertation, it seemed unfortunate not to have all the supporting evidence within the covers of his book. In fine, if there was any extravagance in the reprinting, it should be located in Waingrow's volume, not in Fifer's. The volume has so far sold 837 copies.

The most obvious remark to make concerning *Boswell, Laird of Auchinleck, 1778–1782,* which was published in September 1977, is that it is a very big book.

Indeed it is, a full five hundred pages, not counting index. Joseph W. Reed, Professor of English at Wesleyan University, with whom I collaborated in editing it, and I wished we could find ways to make the volume slimmer, but could see no justifiable date for a conclusion before Lord Auchinleck's death, 30 August 1782, and no tolerable way of reducing farther the journal which Boswell had provided. Reed showed himself adroit in filling gaps in the journal with letters, and for the first time related the journal systematically to Boswell's essay series, *The Hypochondriack,* which Boswell was publishing monthly in the *London Magazine* during the entire period covered by this volume. As particularly fine passages Reed cites the argument between Johnson and Beauclerk over the intentions of the Rev. James Hackman in providing himself with *two* pistols (16 April 1779; the paper served as copy for the *Life of Johnson*); a jocular debate at The Club as to who should be taxed for arrears in the bill for wine (28 March 1781); a morning conversation at Beauclerk's (15 April 1779); an account of the mutiny in Edinburgh of some of the Seaforth Highlanders (22–25 September 1778); and an account of anti-Catholic riots in Edinburgh (2–3 February 1779). One of the bits likely to be most quoted is an admiring description of Boswell's social gaiety by Fanny Burney's sister Charlotte Ann, meeting him for the first time on 7 April 1781.

As has been said above, *Boswell, Laird of Auchinleck* was published in September 1977. The book was priced at $19.95. Through January 1981 McGraw-Hill had distributed 2,503 copies.

As I bring this Epilogue to a conclusion, all of the copy for Marion S. Pottle's three-volume *Catalogue of the Papers of James Boswell* has gone to the printer and a considerable portion of the work has reached the stage of galley proofs. She has been continuously engaged on this great undertaking since the late summer of 1949, besides *being* the Catalogue during all that time to all the many workers at Yale and elsewhere who wished to locate particular items or passages in the huge Boswell corpus. The *Catalogue* (which contains some six thousand entries) lists and minutes all the personal papers of James Boswell now at Yale, and selects for like notice many of the papers of earlier and later lairds of Auchinleck. The present *History* serves as introduction to the *Catalogue* and is also published separately. I have attempted to characterize my aims and method in my Prologue above.

The eleventh volume of the reading edition of the journal (twelfth of that edition as a whole) will have been published before this *History* appears. It is titled *Boswell: The Applause of the Jury, 1782–1785,* and carries the record from the death of Lord Auchinleck, 30 August 1782, to the publication of the *Journal of a Tour to the Hebrides,* 1 October 1785. The editors are Irma S. Lustig, Senior Research Associate in English, Yale University, and myself. Boswell's "Johnsoniana Tacenda" (20 April 1783) will no doubt be held to outrank anything else in the volume, but as other particular delights may be instanced the several meetings with Burke and the Johnsonian conversations of 1783, one of the longest unbroken stretches of fully recorded Johnsonian dialogue occurring anywhere in Boswell's journals. Capt. John

Inglefield's sober narration (8 May 1783) of the sinking of the *Centaur* is an obvious show-piece, as are also two extended conversations with George III (20 May and 15 June 1785). Those who relish Boswell in elliptical effervescence will treasure the record (21 April 1783) of his jaunt to Beaconsfield in the Oxford coach, accompanied by "Stoand" the architect and a charming lady's-maid, or that of Friday 13 May 1785, where he begins his day with Betsy Smith ("twice"), breakfasts with Mrs. Mary Knowles, the Quakeress, attends a Quaker meeting, sees Lunardi ascend in a balloon, tours the wards of Bedlam, dines with Dr. Scott, the admiralty and ecclesiastical lawyer, and ends the day ("intoxicated much") in St. Paul's Churchyard, singing ballads with two women in red cloaks. But it may be that these are all put in the shade by two letters of his to Temple, 6 and 20 July 1784, hitherto unpublished, which record him gloriously inflated with warm hopes of success at the English bar and as dismally deflated by the cold blasts of Edinburgh. It should however be remarked that the interest of this volume is not merely episodic. When, in early 1785, Boswell begins to plan his first Johnsonian instalment, with the *Life of Johnson* coming into view beyond it, narrative direction again appears in the record. The stream is not so copious as before, but it stops eddying and begins to move noticeably if by no means always happily towards a goal.

There will be two more volumes after *The Applause of the Jury:* one, covering the years 1785–89, also edited by Dr. Lustig and myself, and a thirteenth, edited by Frank H. Ellis, Professor of English at Smith College, with myself as collaborator, carrying the journal to the last scraps in 1795. By the time these volumes appear, we shall undoubtedly have announced one or two volumes more of the research edition of the correspondence, and perhaps also one of the research edition of the journal.

NOTES

CHAPTER I

p. 5]
"Unsigned Title-Deeds"] To Wilkes, 6 May 1766.

Ramsay's *Gentle Shepherd*] Journ. 17 Mar. 1777. The manuscript was sold as Lot 743 of Sotheby's Auchinleck Sale of 1893 (Sotheby, Wilkinson, and Hodge, *Catalogue of the Selected Portion of the Celebrated Auchinleck Library*, 23, 24, 25 June 1893), and is now in the National Library of Scotland.

Laigh Parliament House] On nearly half the days of Sept. and Oct. 1772 (Journ.). See also Journ. 24 Nov. 1775.

Registers of Baptisms] Journ. 12, 13,14, 17 Apr. 1780.

Lord Hailes] Their correspondence of the year 1777 furnishes a good illustration. See L 602–08 and C 1463–66.

Papers belonging to other people] For example, two letters from Rousseau to Thérèse Le Vasseur, and letters to Bennet Langton from Lady Diana Beauclerk, Topham Beauclerk, Sir William Blackstone, Edmund Burke, David Garrick, Sir Joshua Reynolds, Joseph Spence, and Edward Young. See C 110–12, C 115–25, C 127–36, C 153, C 682, C 1345, C 2353, C 2418–19, C 2527–28, C 3162.

p. 6]
"Archives at Auchinleck"] For example, in letters to Wilkes, 25 June 1791 and to Burke, 16 July of the same year. See also *Life* i. 13.

Dr. Kippis] See M 9:3. The Latin ("to fly on men's lips") is Virgil paraphrasing Ennius (*Georgics* iii. 9; see also Cicero, *Tusculan Disputations* I. xv. 34). Kippis's tribute to Boswell occurs in the life of Sir John Pringle which he prefixed to his edition of Pringle's *Six Discourses*, 1783 (p. lxxvii).

Sir John Hawkins] To Temple, 5 Mar. 1789.

"No more corn growing"] Journ. 17 Mar. 1776.

p. 7]
Cells, oratories] Preface to *The Excursion*.

Nothing to be secret] Journ. 4 Jan. 1776.

Publication undesirable] Journ. 31 July 1779.

Deed of entail] Disposition of Taillie of the Lands and Barrony of Auchinleck and others by Alexander Boswel Esqr. of Auchinleck, one of the Senators of the College of Justice In favours of Himself and the heirs of Taillie and Provision within mentioned. Dated 7 Aug. 1776. On 8 Mar. 1781 Lord Auchinleck and Boswell signed a modifying Deed of Declaration giving the heirs of entail greater latitude in granting leases. Reg. B. of C. and S. (Dur.) 5 Mar. 1777 and 9 July 1781. Photocopies of the originals at Yale, together with several 18th- and 19th-century manuscript copies. The Entail was printed *in extenso* as an Appendix to Sir James Boswell's Case before the Court of Session, *Boswell v. Boswell*, 1851.

p. 8]
Tutors and curators] Copy Nomination by James Boswell of Auchinleck of Tutors and Curators to his Children. Dated 4 Jan. 1780, and 12 Oct. 1791. Reg. B. of C. and S. (Dur.) 7 Aug. 1795. Photocopy at Yale.

Succeeded to the estate] Journ. 29–[30] Aug. 1782.

Provision for wife and children other than Alexander] Disposition of Locality to Mrs. Margaret Montgomerie and Settlement of Annuities on James etc. Boswell. Dated 19 Mar. 1785 and 12 Oct. 1791. Reg. B. of C. and S. (Dur.) 7 Aug. 1795. Photocopy at Yale.

Will] Last Will and Testament of James Boswell of Auchinleck. Dated 28 May 1785, with Codicil 30 May 1785, and Copy Codicil 22 Dec. 1785. Reg. B. of C. and S. (Dur.) 7 Aug. 1795. Photocopy at Yale.

p. 9]
Final codicil] Transcript, said to be of holograph, in ILT: List A. The copy in B. of C. and S. (preceding note) differs slightly in spelling, capitals, and punctuation.

p. 10]
Dilly] Journ. 18 Dec. 1784; Reg. Let. Sent 7 and 23 Dec. 1784, Received 16, 18, 20, and 25 Dec. 1784.

12 Oct. 1791] 6th and 4th nn. back.

Fondness for Dr. Johnson] Grant to Miss Veronica Boswell of £500, 3 Mar. 1795. See Journ. 15 Aug. 1773. Never registered. The holograph original is in the Hyde Collection.

p. 11]
Completely in his own hand] The nomination of tutors and the second codicil to the will (above, 8th and 5th nn. back) are registered in copies in B. of C. and S. because the holographs did not contain a clause of consent to registration, and were therefore returned to the "ingiver", Robert Boswell, W.S. (information from Sir James Fergusson, Keeper of the Records).

Book of travels] See C 2971 and C 2973; also Temple to Forbes, 27 Apr. 1796, Fettercairn Papers.

Docketing by Alexander Boswell] See C 24, C 794, C 2146, C 2497; L 1204.

Alexander Boswell to Forbes, 8 July 1795] Fettercairn Papers.

Some of Boswell's papers may never have left Auchinleck] Alexander's letter of 4 Nov. 1805 (below p. 231, 3rd n.) shows that he still had access

to a list of wines and liquors at Auchinleck in Boswell's hand dated 22 Aug. 1794 and 11 Jan. 1795 (M 168.1), but that he could not find Boswell's "Book of Company and Liquors at Auchinleck", "tho I think I remember seeing it at the time I sent off my Father's papers to Sir William Forbes". I read this to mean that he thought he had retained the latter manuscript. M 168.1, accompanied by a lawyer's memorandum, turned up in a group of Auchinleck legal papers from a lawyer's office in Ayr purchased by Yale from Lady Talbot in 1961; the "Book of Company and Liquors" (now in the Hyde Collection) was found by Isham at Malahide in 1937.

p. 12]
Forbes to Malone, 14 Aug. 1795] Original in the possession of Jonathan T. Isham; it was in his father's collection, but did not come from Malahide Castle or Fettercairn House.

Replies to Forbes] James Boswell the younger to Forbes, 2 Jan., 5 Mar. 1796; Malone to Forbes, 25 Apr. 1796, all three in the Fettercairn Papers.

p. 13]
Temple calls on Malone] Diaries of William Johnston Temple, ed. Lewis Bettany, 1929, p. 127.

Temple to Forbes, 27 Apr. 1796] This important letter in the Fettercairn Papers was not known to me in 1960. David Buchanan found it in 1968 at Fettercairn in a box of papers from Fettercairn which Professor Abbott had kept at Durham for many years. Temple met Bennet Langton in Boswell's house, Great Portland Street, London, on 10 and 11 Oct. 1795 (TA, p. 147). As was indicated above, he met Malone in London, not in October, but in July. (He was on a three-months' visit to Norton Nicholls at Blundeston, East Suffolk, and paused in London both going and coming.)

Forbes to Malone, 30 June 1796] Original in the Hyde Collection, photocopy at Yale.

p. 14]
A few days afterwards he wrote to Temple] Diaries of William Johnston Temple, ed. Lewis Bettany, 1929, p. 192.

"Ready to concur"] In the letter of 27 Apr. 1796 quoted on p. 13.

Surviving letters of Forbes and Malone] There are among the Fettercairn Papers drafts of letters from Forbes to Malone dated 22 May 1798, 20 July 1798, and 9 Mar. 1804, and letters from Malone to Forbes dated 25 Apr. 1796 (already quoted), 5 July 1798, 3 Mar. 1804, 23 Apr. 1804, 2 May 1804, and 4 May 1804. (See also above, p. 228, 12th n.) Forbes's drafts are interesting and valuable, but none of them contains any reference to the location of Boswell's papers, and we have to reconstruct what he said on this point from Malone's side of the correspondence.

"Cannot be corrected"] iv. 381 n.

Langton had informed Malone] Malone to James Boswell the younger, 28 Sept. 1808 (C 1930).

Alexander Boswell to Forbes, 5 June 1799] Fettercairn Papers.

Malone asks Forbes to search out five letters] In a letter dated 3 Mar. 1804 (Fettercairn Papers) Malone put to Forbes a query about an ambiguity in Boswell's text concerning original and copies of the famous Round Robin (*Life* iii. 83), and then asked him to consult and report on four letters of Johnson—Nos. 541, 578, 593, and 874(1) in Chapman's numbering—besides trying to locate copies of Johnson's letters to Chesterfield and to Macpherson dictated by Johnson to Boswell, and a slip of paper in Boswell's hand in which he had recorded a change in the text of *The Vanity of Human Wishes* (*Life* iii. 357–58) dictated to him by Johnson. Forbes replied immediately on 9 Mar. (scroll copy, Fettercairn Papers), answering the query about the Round Robin (this required no search), and in a postscript (not in the scroll but referred to in Malone's letter of 23 Apr.) promised to search for the papers Malone had inquired after. Receiving no further word for more than a month, Malone wrote again on 23 Apr. (Fettercairn Papers), in apprehension, as he said, that some letter of Forbes had miscarried. The portion of the *Life* concerning the Round Robin, he reported, had been printed before Forbes's letter of 9 Mar. arrived. At Forbes's convenience he would be glad to have a report on the other matters contained in his letter of 3 Mar. This letter crossed one from Forbes dated 25 Apr., which is not traced. On 2 May Malone acknowledged its receipt, apologizing for having given Forbes so much trouble, and continued to inquire after No. 541 and the papers

Boswell had failed to deposit in the British Museum and the Bodleian. My one direct quotation ("I apprehend . . . ") is from this letter. Two days later Malone wrote again asking Forbes to hunt for Chapman's No. 1041, Johnson to Lucy Porter, 2 Dec. 1784, and send it to him. He reiterated his impression that Boswell "had kept Dr. Johnson's Letters addressed to himself in a distinct parcel", but thought that the letter to Lucy Porter would probably be found "in the very place to which it properly belongs, near the end of his work". The printer, he says, is proceeding at a great rate, but if he can have the letter within a week, he will be able to make an addition to the text that he thinks would be useful. There the preserved correspondence ends. Now, if, as Malone says, the printer had passed iii. 83–86 of the fourth edition (the Round Robin) by the middle of March and was expected to reach iv. 429 (the letter to Lucy Porter) by, at latest, the middle of May, it is pretty clear that by 2 May he must already have passed iii. 142–397, the pages in which fall all three of the letters from Johnson to Boswell that Malone had been in quest of.

p. 15]
Forbes may have found some of the documents] It seems practically certain that two of the eight documents were in Forbes's possession, for Professor Abbott found at Fettercairn the letter to Lucy Porter and that to the unnamed correspondent [Dr. John Mudge: see *Life* iv. 240 and Chapman's *Letters of Johnson* No. 874(1)]. The slip bearing the correction for *The Vanity of Human Wishes* turned up at Malahide in 1940, and was probably also in Forbes's hands in 1804.

p. 16]
Boswell's two Reynoldses in London] Forbes, no doubt, after taking advice, ruled that if Alexander wanted the two Reynoldses, he would have to purchase them from the executry at an appraiser's valuation: Alexander Boswell to Forbes, 21 Oct. 1795 (Fettercairn Papers); Forbes to Malone, 30 June 1796 (a later portion of the letter quoted above, p. 13). Alexander "would not part . . . on any account" with his father's portrait (fifty guineas), but thought he could not afford the portrait of Johnson (one hundred guineas). Forbes insisted that he buy the portrait of Johnson, "which never ought to go out of his family". Alexander accordingly purchased both pictures, finally paying one hundred sixty guineas, the difference no doubt being interest from 1795 (Observations on Notes

by the Arbiter for the Younger Children of James
Boswell, 26 Oct. 1803, ILT: List B). Sir Francis
Bourgeois valued the pictures in London without
fee, and at Euphemia Boswell's suggestion received
a gold mourning-ring (To Forbes, 30 Oct. 1795;
Forbes in reply, 3 Nov. 1795, both letters in the
Fettercairn Papers).

Robert Boswell's Memorial] Memorial and
Queries for Alexander Boswell of Auchinleck, etc.,
Robert Boswell, W.S., July 1795 (ILT: List A).
Robert Boswell gives the amount of heritable debt
as £5,400, overlooking the security of £470 to the
Rev. Dr. Mitchell on the lands of Willockshill,
though it is included in a "View" of Boswell's own,
1 Jan. 1795, which he quotes. Alexander Boswell's
Memorial and Queries of Feb. 1802 (5th n. forward)
present the matter clearly.

Two eminent advocates] Answers to the
Memorial and Queries for Alexander Boswell of
Auchinleck, etc., by Robert Blair, Solicitor-General [later Dean of Faculty and Lord President], 29
July 1795; Answers, etc. by Adam Rolland, 4
Aug. 1795 (ILT: List A; Yale has 18th- or early
19th-century manuscript copies of both Answers,
McHarg No. 5). The wording of the advice as
given in my text is Blair's; Rolland's was "to avoid
a general representation of the late Mr. Boswell,
and with that view to make up titles to the he-
retable Subjects only *cum beneficio inventarii*"—
which I believe to be the same thing. Alexander
was in fact served heir to his inheritance from Boswell *cum beneficio inventarii*, which meant that he
made himself liable for the debts only up to the
value of the lands as shown in a sworn inventory.

p. 17]
Boswell's own lands sold] Memorial and
Abstract, Alexander Boswell of Auchinleck against
his Father's Creditors, 20 June 1798 (ILT: List B).
The "Scheme", of which this document principally
consists, sets the "proven value" of the properties
at £6,287.0s. 7¾d. Search in the Register House
for the process has been unsuccessful, but J. K.
Bates has gleaned most of the pertinent facts from
the General Minute Book of the Court of Session
and a law print of the case preserved in the Signet
Library (Session Papers, 399, 88). Willockshill and
the St. Andrew's Square property were withdrawn
from the sale of 21 Nov. 1798 because there was
confusion over the boundaries of the former, and
a value had to be put on Lady Auchinleck's liferent rights to the latter. Hence the second sale of
22 May 1799.

First territorial designation] See *Journal of
a Tour to the Hebrides*, 26 Aug. 1773, near the end.

Dalblair undervalued] James Paterson,
History of the Counties of Ayr and Wigton, 1863, i.
pt. 1. 201–02. Dalblair sold for the precise amount
of the "proven value" in the "Scheme" (see the last
note but one).

Balance of £2,103. 8s. 6d.] Memorial and
Queries for Alexander Boswell Esqr. of Auchinleck,
Feb. 1802 (ILT: List A).

Veronica's illness and death] James Boswell the younger to Forbes, 28 Sept. 1795; Alexander Boswell to Forbes, 18 Aug. 1795 (both in
Fettercairn Papers); *The Farington Diary*, ed. James
Greig, 2nd ed., 1922, i. 131.

Euphemia's extravagance] Euphemia Boswell to Forbes, some thirty letters written between
19 Aug. 1795 and Mar. 1804; Forbes to Euphemia
Boswell, 26 Aug., 16 Oct., 12 Dec. 1795, 10
Nov. 1800, 14 Apr. 1804; Alexander Boswell to
Forbes, ?June or July (two letters), 10 Nov. 1801,
26 Apr., 11 Nov. 1804 (all in the Fettercairn
Papers). Euphemia's letters give an historian a great
deal of trouble. Her hand is difficult, and as often
as not she omits dates.

Elizabeth's marriage] Euphemia Boswell to
Forbes, twenty-two letters, July 1798–Mar. 1804;
Forbes to Euphemia Boswell, 10 Nov. 1800; Alex-
ander Boswell to William Boswell, 6 Apr. 1796
(*C 271.1), 28 Mar. (*C 271.3), 21 Oct. 1797
(*C 271.4), c. 4 Aug. 1798 (C 271.5); Alexander
Boswell to James Boswell the younger, 9 May 1796
(C 271.2); Alexander Boswell to Forbes, seventeen
letters between July 1796 and Apr. 1804; James
Boswell the younger to Forbes, 9, 14 Jan. 1799;
Elizabeth Boswell to Forbes, ten letters between
20 July 1797 and 9 Dec. 1799. (Five of the letters,
as indicated, are at Yale; the others are all in the
Fettercairn Papers). For William Boswell see *Fac.
Adv.* Elizabeth was married on 23 Dec. 1799 at
Auchinleck House, with neither of her guardians
and neither of her brothers present. Alexander had
married Grizel Cuming a month before.

p. 18]
Forbes hopeful of a surplus] ". . . if contrary to expectation the separate funds should not
prove equal to the debts, of which, however, I

think there is not the least danger" (draft letter, Forbes to Alexander Boswell, 4 July 1795); "I am morally certain the produce of the separate property left by your father, will fully answer for paying both the debts and your Bond. Indeed, I should even hope there may be something over" (draft letter, Forbes to Veronica Boswell, 8 Aug. 1795); "I hope there is no fear that there will be effects sufficient to pay the Legacies as well as the debts" (draft letter, Forbes to Euphemia Boswell, 16 Oct. 1795). All three letters in the Fettercairn Papers.

Arbitration necessary] Forbes to Alexander Boswell, 4 July 1795; 29 Apr. 1797, 3 Jan. 1799, 2 Apr. 1804, Memorandum, c. 15 Nov. 1804; Alexander Boswell to Forbes, forty letters between 20 June 1797 and 6 Jan. 1806; Alexander Boswell to Harry Davidson, 11 Nov. 1804; Alexander Boswell to James Boswell the younger, 13 Dec. 1807 (C 271.6), 2 June 1810 (C 272.3), 5 Aug. 1810 (C 272.4); Alexander Boswell to William Boswell, 28 Mar. 1797 (*C 271.3); Euphemia Boswell to Forbes, fifteen letters between 19 June 1797 and Mar. 1804. Except as indicated by Yale *Cat.* numbers, all these letters are in Fettercairn Papers.

William Boswell] William Boswell to Forbes, 30 May 1804 (two letters); Forbes to William Boswell, 30 May 1804; Euphemia Boswell to Forbes, ?Apr. 1802 (two letters), late 1802 or early 1803, autumn 1803, Mar. 1804; Alexander Boswell to Harry Davidson, 4 Nov. 1805 (ILT: List A). Excepting the last, all these letters are in Fettercairn Papers.

Referred the case for arbitration] Submission by Alexander Boswell of Auchinleck and his Brother and Sisters. Dated 13, 18, and 22 Nov. 1802. Reg. B. of C. and S. (Mack.) 8 Feb. 1805. Photocopy at Yale. The Isham legal transcripts contain copies of more than twenty documents bearing on this submission. I have named only those that provide material for the present study. Between the dates of his first decreet and his second, Hope was appointed an ordinary Lord of Session (with the style Lord Granton) and Lord Justice Clerk; in 1811 he became Lord President.

p. 19]
Claim for younger children] Copy Memorial and Claims for the Younger Children and Executors of the deceased James Boswell of Auchinleck, 10 Jan. 1803 (ILT: List A).

Claim for Alexander] Draft Answers and Claim for Alexander Boswell of Auchinleck to the Memorial and Claim of his Brother and Sisters, 15 Feb. 1803, Lord Advocate Arbiter (ILT: List A). In this it is stated that "the whole amount of [the Biographer's] debts as pr. Sir Willm. Forbes's State was considerably above £13,000 which was more than double the value of the lands".

Interim decreet] Decreet Arbitral in a Submission by Alexander Boswell of Auchinleck and his Brother and Sisters. Dated 19 Mar. 1804. Reg. B. of C. and S. (Mack.) 19 Mar. 1804. Photocopy at Yale.

Final decreet] Decreet Arbitral in a Submission by Alexander Boswell of Auchinleck and his Brother and Sisters. Dated 7 Feb. 1805. Reg. B. of C. and S. (Mack.) 8 Feb. 1805. Photocopy at Yale.

p. 20]
Annuities] The entail of Auchinleck permitted each successive laird to burden the estate with annuities to his children other than the heir. In case there were four such children, the burden could not exceed one fourth of the free rents. The problem was, rent at what date? Boswell's Settlement was drawn on 19 Mar. 1785, his revision of the Settlement on 12 Oct. 1791, and he died on 19 May 1795. Two eminent counsel whom Alexander consulted agreed that the effective date was 19 Mar. 1785. By that reckoning, the sum of the annuities (£150 to James, £100 to each of the girls) exceeded the permitted amount and would have to be reduced to £91 and £57 respectively. Alexander, however, immediately executed a Bond of Provision making himself responsible for annuities in the full amounts, but disregarding another provision of Boswell's Settlement that the annuities were to be increased proportionally when Lady Auchinleck's death should release the rents of her locality lands. Hope ruled that the effective date was 12 Oct. 1791, and that the annuities were to be proportionally increased from the date of Lady Auchinleck's death. The annuities consequently stood currently at £211. 9*s*. 5*d*. and £140. 19*s*. 7*d*., and Alexander received a bill for £965. 14*s*. 9*d* for arrears (principal and interest).

p. 21]
Greek and Latin [books]] The copy in ILT: List A reads "Greek and Latin and Manuscripts". I supply "books" from the will.

[and] manuscripts] My emendation. The copy in ILT: List A reads "Greek and Latin manuscripts".

Hope ruled] My extract is from the interim decreet, as in the fifth note back.

David Buchanan] TA, p. 197.

p. 22]
Alexander's lawyers] Notes in Mr. Boswells Submission with his Brother and Sisters, 14 July 1803 (ILT: List B.)

Accomptant] Copy Notes by Arbiter in Boswell's Submission, 29 June 1803 (ILT: List B).

Production No. 10] Notes in the Submission between Alexander Boswell Esq. of Auchinleck and his Brother and Sisters. Edinburgh 3 Mar. 1804 (ILT: List B).

Hope's original notes] See the 2nd n. back.

New proposal] Copy Alterations by Lord Advocate—upon his Notes in Mr. Boswells Submission, Feb. 1804 (ILT: List A).

p. 23]
Valuation by sworn appraisers] Inventory and Appraisment of the Household furniture, which belonged to James Boswell of Auchinleck Esquire taken at Auchinleck house, in Ayrshire: by Alexander Colvill and William Bruce both Apprisers in Edinburgh—the 1st of July 1795. A 2.6:2.

Valuation of books] Copy Observations Mr. Boswells Executry Octr. 1805 received from David Wemyss 26 October 1805 (ILT: List B). The younger children offered Alexander these and the books in Lord Auchinleck's library in Edinburgh for £130.

Euphemia in straits again] Harry Davidson to Alexander Boswell, 26 Dec. 1804 (ILT: List B); James Boswell the younger to Forbes, 28 Jan. 1805, Fettercairn Papers; Alexander Boswell to Forbes, 14, 15, 17, c. 20 Feb. 1805, Fettercairn Papers. The two quoted bits are from Alexander's letters of 14 and 17 Feb.

p. 24]
Alexander reports] Alexander Boswell to Thomas Miller, 18 Oct. 1805 (*C 271.55).

Alexander would pay] Alexander Boswell to Forbes, 14 Feb. 1805, Fettercairn Papers.

Euphemia assigns her assets] "AND I David Wemyss Writer to the Signet Assignee of Euphemia Boswell . . . conform to trust disposition and assignation granted by her to me in trust for behoof of herself and her creditors dated twenty seventh March last" (Preamble of Assignation of Moveables and Discharge, 21 and 31 Dec. 1805). See 3rd n. forward.

The younger children propose £400] Observations Mr. Boswell's Executry [by William Boswell, endorsed by Harry Davidson] Received from David Wemyss 26 Oct. 1805; Wemyss to Davidson, 26 Oct. 1805; Davidson to Alexander Boswell, 12 Nov. 1805; Minute about Mr. Boswell's Executry 12 Novr. 1805 present Mr. W. Boswell Mr. D. Wemyss Mr. Davidson; Wemyss and W. Boswell to Davidson, 6 Dec. 1805 (all ILT: List B). Copy Alexander Boswell to Davidson, 4 Nov. 1805 (ILT: List A). "Ready to haggle" is from TA, p. 198. Alexander commented: "Never did beings forget all Decency so much as Miss B. and that poor Creature Mr. W.B. Having acted openly and to the best of my belief and conscience liberally towards the younger children this abominable business was most irksome" (ibid.). Alexander had indeed appeared spontaneously generous in refusing to question the validity of his father's will and in agreeing to pay the full amount of the annuities as set by his father (above, p. 231, 9th n.). As it turned out, however, all the lawyers found the will valid, and Hope set the annuities even higher than Alexander had.

£400 reduced to £300] Harry Davidson to Alexander Boswell, 12 Nov. 1805; Minute about Mr. Boswell's Executry, 12 Nov. 1805; David Wemyss and William Boswell to Harry Davidson, 6 Dec. 1805 (all ILT: List B).

p. 25]
Forbes obtains his discharge] Assignation and Disposition, Sir William Forbes of Pitsligo and Alexander Boswell of Auchinleck Esqr. to the said Alexander Boswell and the Younger Children of the deceased James Boswell of Auchinleck Esqr., 9 and 13 Dec. 1805 (ILT: List C).

A complete discharge] Assignation of Moveables and Discharge, Elizabeth etc. Boswells to Alexander Boswell of Auchinleck, 21 and 31 Dec. 1805 (ILT: List A). One fourth of the £300 (as of the rest of the Executry) was owing to Veronica Boswell, who had died intestate. Each of the three surviving younger children therefore received £93. 15s. and Alexander retained £18. 15s.

"The parties seem to have side-stepped"] TA, p. 200.

p. 26]
Botetourte] Mrs. Pottle remembers reading this somewhere in a letter at Yale and has felt sure that the letter was by Alexander Boswell. She has however been unable to put her hand on the document.

Relationship remote] Botetourt was an English barony, and the line of succession appears to have been all English. But the first Lord Botetourt did have some connexion with Scotland. In 1304, during the invasion of Scotland by Edward I, he was Justiciar of Galloway, Annan, and the valley of Nith.

Oppressed by her family] Alexander Boswell to Thomas Miller, 18 Oct. 1805 (*C 271.55); T. D. Boswell to Alexander Boswell, 7 June 1813 (Yale MS., Auch. II. 3415).

Malone to Euphemia] Published with permission of the Pierpont Morgan Library.

Forbes's life of Beattie published] Lond. Chron. (17–19 June 1806) xcix. 583, "This day is published. . . . "

p. 27]
"Exceptionable" and "reprehensible"] C 1305–08.

CHAPTER II

p. 28]
Woodhouselee to Alexander] "Some time ago, Sir William Forbes [the son of Boswell's executor] informed me, that among your Father's papers, some MS. collections had been found, relative to the Life and writings of Lord Kames, and which, with the consent of Mr. Malone and the late Sir William Forbes, were to be communicated to me. . . ." (C 3017.2).

Malone to James Boswell the younger] C 1930. The list of queries in this letter overlaps the one that he had sent to Forbes in 1804 (see above, pp. 14–15 and p. 229, 5th n.) but does not contain all the queries he then put to Forbes, a curious discrepancy best explained by assuming that his labours on behalf of Boswell's book, though vigorous, were always sporadic and unsystematic. This very letter confirms that judgement. In it he asked James, as he had asked Forbes, to have an eye out for the pieces Boswell had promised to send to the British Museum and the Bodleian. But this time he mentions only the letter to Macpherson and the slip giving the correction for The Vanity of Human Wishes, which he mistakenly calls "London". "I cannot recollect any other promised pieces," he goes on, "but I have a faint recollection of something being promised to be given to Pembroke College." Either he kept no copies of his letters, or he neglected to consult them.

No specimens of Johnson's handwriting] Alexander's letter is C 271.7; Johnson's overwritten message is C 1601. "Conspicuous" Johnson autographs found later at Malahide would include the fragment of his translation into English of Addison's Battle of the Pygmies and Cranes (C 1594), and several MSS. now in the Hyde Collection: "Annales"; Diary Notes 1729–34; Diary 1765–84; fragment of a translation in English of Sallust's De bello Catilinario; The Vanity of Human Wishes; fragmentary MS. of London; fragmentary MS. of Irene. Yale has a number of small Johnsonian autographs from Malahide (see C 1595, C 1597, C 1597.1, C 1598–1600, C 1602, C 1603, C 1605) which would not all be noticed unless one handled the manuscripts leaf by leaf, but it would have been odd, had they been in the papers then at Auchinleck, if Alexander had come across none of them. What happened to the documents in the Boswell-Johnson correspondence remains the prime mystery in the story of the descent of the Boswell papers. Of the more than one hundred letters and notes which Johnson is shown by Chapman's summaries (Letters SJ iii. Appendix B; Johnson, Boswell and Their Circle: Essays Presented to L. F. Powell, 1965, p. 314) to have written to Boswell only four are known to survive: 355 (fragment, Yale MS., Tinker Cat. 1281), 550.1 (a nine-word note, C 1601), 715.1 (a twenty-three word note, Hyde Collection), and 973 (Fettercairn Papers). The survival of 550.1 is clearly and easily accounted for: Boswell used it as a piece of waste paper to write journal-notes on (J 53), and it came to Isham in

1927 or 1928 from Malahide with other fragments of the journal. Chapman plausibly suggests (*Letters SJ* i. 407 n.) that 355 (a letter of introduction) survives because it was never delivered to Boswell. It was printed by G. B. Hill in his edition of Johnson's letters, 1892, being then in the possession of G. J. Campbell of Inverness, but I know nothing of its history before that. 715.1 bears a docket by Boswell indicating that he gave it to some one as a specimen of Johnson's handwriting. The Hydes purchased it from Goodspeed's *Catalogue,* April 1963, via Lew Feldman, but its provenance beyond that is unknown (note by Mary Hyde to F. A. Pottle, 15 Mar. 1979, at Yale). No. 973 was first reported by Professor C. Colleer Abbott in the Introduction (p. xvii) to his *Catalogue of Papers . . . Found at Fettercairn House,* 1936, he having been shown it by the late Lord Clinton in a portfolio containing "letters from celebrities, of various dates". Since Abbott did not find this letter himself, he did not include it in his *Catalogue,* and it was never claimed as part of the fund *in medio* in the Fettercairn litigation. (These later chapters of the narrative, unavoidably mentioned here, will be developed further on.) Though it, and other documents in the portfolio, most likely came to Fettercairn with the papers which Abbott discovered, its presence there could be otherwise accounted for. Chapman (loc. cit.) shows that Boswell's side of the correspondence consisted of not fewer than one hundred and twenty-five letters. Boswell generally kept copies of these, and Johnson caused most of the originals to be returned to him (*Life* ii. 2). Only five originals and one copy have been traced. The originals are 3 Mar. 1772 (Hyde Collection), 14 Feb. 1777 (a one-leaf fragment, L 665), 20 Sept. 1779 (L 671), 22 Nov. 1779 (Yale MS., Tinker Cat. 301), and 1 Oct. 1782 (L 673). The copy (a hasty one, with many abbreviated words, L 670) is 29 Apr. 1779. I have never heard any plausible explanation advanced for the escape of 3 Mar. 1772 from the general oblivion. 22 Nov. 1779 was sent by Johnson to Lucy Porter and never returned, but I do not know what hands it passed through before it reached Professor Tinker's. 29 Apr. 1779 has a journal-note on it, and hence was probably filed by Boswell among his journals. The other three originals all appear somehow to owe their preservation to the fact that Boswell printed no part of them in the *Life.* — Malone's apprehension that Boswell kept "all Dr. Johnson's letters to himself in one bundle" is rendered almost certain by this evidence, and it appears equally certain that Boswell also made an effort to collect and segregate both originals and copies of his side of the correspondence. I know of no certain evidence that any one has seen any of these bundles since his death. The complete oblivion into which they have fallen may well have resulted from the special pains which he took to preserve them.

p. 29]

Printed catalogue] *Bibliotheca Boswelliana. A Catalogue of the entire Library of the late James Boswell, Esq. . . . which will be Sold by Auction, by Mr. Sotheby, at his House, No. 3, Wellington Street, Strand, on Tuesday, May 24, 1825, and Nine following Days (Sunday excepted), at Twelve o'Clock. To be viewed, and Catalogues [price 3s.] had at the place of Sale.* Lots 3151–71. David Buchanan's account of this episode in the history of Boswell's papers is particularly full and useful. He gives a complete list of the Boswellian and Johnsonian lots, pp. 19–20 n. 87.

Materials for the *Life*] Ibid. Lots 3151–55, 3158, 3160, 3162–67, 3169, 3178.

Other Boswelliana in the sale] Ibid. Lots 3173, 3172, 3171.

Verses by Boswell] Douce MS. 193. See TA, pp. 21–22 and n. 94.

Letters from Boswell to Malone] James Boswell, *The Life of Samuel Johnson, LL.D., including A Journal of his Tour to the Hebrides. . . . To which are added . . . Anecdotes by Hawkins, Piozzi, Murphy, Tyers, Reynolds, Steevens, &c. and Notes by various Hands. . . . In Ten Volumes . . .* London, John Murray, 1835, x. 209–20.

Upcott's collection] See TA, p. 22 n. 95. An annotated copy of the sale catalogue at Yale (formerly Isham's property) records Upcott as purchaser of eight lots, including 3166 (manuscript prayers by Johnson), 3170 (various proof-sheets of Johnson's *Lives of the Poets* corrected in his own hand), and 3289 (replica of Reynolds's portrait of the Biographer — the picture formerly displayed in the National Portrait Gallery as Reynolds's original). Thomas Rodd, Jr., bought the eight uncatalogued bundles. Lot 3171 ("Johnsoniana, a Selection of Scraps from periodical Papers — 2. Proof Sheets of the first Edition of Boswell's Life of Johnson, corrected in Mr. Boswell's hand, with some remarkable variations; and a parcel of loose Papers, Letters, and Memoranda, relating to the

Life of Johnson"), which might well have contained the letters to Malone, was purchased by William Pickering and in 1831 was at least partially in the possession of J. L. Anderdon (J. W. Croker, ed., *The Life of Samuel Johnson . . . in five volumes*, 1831, i. xix–xx).

Scott's report on Alexander] Scott to J. W. Croker, 30 Jan. 1829 (*The Croker Papers. The Correspondence and Diaries of. . . John Wilson Croker*, ed. L. J. Jennings, 2nd ed. rev. 1885, ii. 32; same text, *The Letters of Sir Walter Scott*, ed. H. J. C. Grierson, 1932–37, xi. 116–17. The original is at Yale: see F.A. Pottle, "The Scott-Croker Correspondence in the Yale University Library", in the *Yale University Library Gazette*, Jan. 1928, ii. 33–45). Scott expresses a similar sentiment in another important letter to Croker, to be quoted later. See above, p. 41.

"I only put a cocked hat"] J. G. Lockhart, *Memoirs of the Life of Sir Walter Scott*, 2nd ed., 1839, ch. 7, i. 276.

p. 30]
Johnson's handwriting, Johnson's works] Above, p. 28; Alexander Boswell to James Boswell the younger, 5 Aug. 1810 (C 272.4).

Reason for not rehanging portrait] Alexander Boswell to James Boswell the younger, 2 June 1810 (C 272.3).

p. 31]
Alexander's pride in his father's fame] See also the boyish letters and verses that Alexander addressed to his father concerning the *Life of Johnson*: C 234, C 244–46, C 249, C 282.

p. 32]
Deaths, of Veronica, Elizabeth, James] *Scots Mag.* (1795) lvii. 682; ibid. (1814) lxxvi. 159; *Gent. Mag.* (Mar. 1822) xcii. 277–78 (month wrongly given as March).

Euphemia, 1796–1805] The period is very fully documented by letters from her to Sir William Forbes, Fettercairn Papers.

Euphemia in London] Euphemia Bte. Boswell to [   ] Wilson, ?1805 or later (*C 336); Alexander Boswell to Thomas Miller, 18 Oct. 1805 (*C 271.55); same to James Boswell the

younger, 1810–16 (C 272.3, C 272.4, C 272.5, C 272.6, C 272.8, C 274.6).

"Pecuniary aid"] James Boswell, *Boswelliana . . . with a Memoir and Annotations* by the Rev. Charles Rogers, 1874, pp. 195–96.

Newspaper paragraph] *Lond. Chron.* (13–14 Sept. 1810) cviii. 259.

Euphemia solicits pensions, gets one] Euphemia Boswell to Sir Joseph Banks, 30 May 1811 (*C 336.6); Rogers, as in second note back; Alexander Boswell to James Boswell, 1 Oct. 1810 (C 272.5): "I observe that that wretch our Sister goes on as usual. She now figures in the Newspapers as a Publick beggar"); Grace, Lady Boswell, to William Murray, 8 July 1825 (Yale MS., Talbot Inventory No. 4, p. 11); Abstract 6 July 1836 of Decreet Alexander Robert Sutherland and Mandatory against Miss Euphemia Boswell In the Summons and Action raised and pursued before the Lords of Council and Session at the instance of the said Alexander Robert Sutherland, Physician in London agt. the said Miss Euphemia Boswell Summons dated and signeted the 28th day of April 1836 (Yale MS., McHarg Papers, Bundle 5).

Euphemia's begging letters] Euphemia Bte. Boswell to Mrs. John Landseer, after Nov. 1814 (*C 337); same to Charles Burney, with annotation by Mme. d'Arblay (*C 336.7); same to the same, after 28 Sept. 1813 (two letters, *C 336.71 and *C 336.72).

"Drink the devil"] C 274.6.

Euphemia declared insane] Abstract of Decreet, as in third note back. Narrative of the Action is given above, pp. 42–43.

p. 33]
Woodhouselee's six brief extracts] F. A. Pottle, *The Literary Career of James Boswell*, 1929, 1965, 1967, pp. 271–72; Claire Lamont, "James Boswell and Alexander Fraser Tytler", *The Bibliotheck*, (1971) vi. 8–16.

Journal of a Tour to the Hebrides] 10 Nov. 1773.

Tytler sends angry letter] Journ. 18, 30 Nov. 1785; Claire Lamont (see the second note back), pp. 1–8, 16.

Forbes finds no trace of Kames material}
Claire Lamont, ibid, p. 10.

Malone to Woodhouselee} Ibid. pp. 11–12.

p. 34]
Woodhouselee to Alexander Boswell} 27
June 1808 (C 3017.2).

Alexander Boswell to Woodhouselee} Claire
Lamont, "James Boswell and Alexander Fraser
Tytler", *The Bibliotheck,* (1971) vi. 13–14.

James Boswell the younger to Wood-
houselee} Ibid. pp. 14–15.

p. 35]
Hiatus} See BP xv. 296.

Withheld leaves} M 135 pp. 32–35, 51a,
51b, 52–59, 64–67, 79, as now numbered. The
first eighteen record interviews with Kames 17
Feb., 29 Nov., 2, 3, 4, 5, 10 Dec. 1782. In p.
79 (not an interview with Kames) Boswell records
from memory his having rebuked Kames for in-
decorous behaviour at the capital trial of Mungo
Campbell, 1769.

"Private and delicate" matter} M 135 p.
35 (17 Feb. 1782); p. 64 (10 Dec. 1782).

Jean Heron} M 135 pp. 52–54 (29 Nov.
1782).

Boswell's involvement} F. A. Pottle, *James
Boswell, The Earlier Years,* 1966, pp. 77–79,
478–79.

p. 36]
Woodhouselee makes six footnotes} Claire
Lamont, "James Boswell and Alexander Fraser
Tytler", *The Bibliotheck,* (1971) vi. 15.

"Farrago"} Ibid. p. 16, Woodhouselee con-
gratulating George Home Drummond, 20 Dec.
1809, that Boswell's materials for a life of Kames
had turned out to be so inconsiderable.

Johnson's portrait} Retained draft, Lady
Boswell to William Murray, 8 July 1825 (Yale
MS., Talbot Inventory No. 4, p. 11), but David
Buchanan found it before I did (TA, pp. 14–15).
Murray is described as "the particular friend of Mr.
J. Boswell" in copy, Lady Boswell to Mr. Romanes,

8 Jan. 1827 (Yale MS., Talbot Inventory No. 6,
p. 15). David Buchanan thinks that Lady Boswell
donated the picture to James's estate, hoping that
there would be a surplus which would be paid over
to Alexander's estate, he being James's sole heir.
As I read the transaction, the sum the picture
fetched was not merged in the proceeds of James's
sale but was remitted to Lady Boswell, who, if she
followed her original plan, donated it to the fund
realized by the sale of Alexander's executry.

p. 37]
Marriage contract} Copy Ext. Contract of
Marriage Betwixt Alexander Boswell of Auchinleck
and Miss Grizel Cuming Dated 1799; Reg'd 1823.
[Date of Copy-Ext. 1852.] (A 9.3.)

p. 38]
Miller's appointment} For Boswell's *Laird
of Glenlee,* see *Lit. Car.* pp. 267–69. There is also
a copy of this piece in the Mansfield MS. in the
National Library of Scotland (Frank Miller, *The
Mansfield Manuscript,* 1935, p. 38); "I must say I
am sorry to hear, that Tam Miller is to be Lord
Justice Clerk for Scotland, it is a Shame that Such
a *Body* Sprung from Nothing, should come before
so many more worthy Personages, I dare say my
Brother John will be almost mad at this" (David
Boswell to Boswell, 29 Apr. 1766, C 474); "However I think I may now be att ease [at not being
appointed either Professor of Medicine and Chem-
istry at the University of Edinburgh or Physician
to the King in Scotland] since I have got your
Father to keep me in countenance. I may submit
to Dr. Black gaining the one and Gregory the other
in spite of all my POTENT friends, when Tom
Millar is promoted over the Senior Lord of Justiciary, and some of whose Ancestors wald not have
allowed any Miller to have eat with them etc. etc.
not to say personal merit" (Dr. John Boswell to
Boswell, 24 May 1766, C 387).

Boswell's clash with William Miller} *Lond.
Chron.* (20 Sept. 1774) xxxvi. 276; Journ. 6–18
Oct. 1774.

Word of James's death} T. D. Boswell to
William Boswell, 25 Feb. 1822 (*C 542.7).

James's will} Dated 15 Sept. 1818. Proved
by Sir Alexander Boswell, Bt., as executor, 19
Mar. 1822 (P.C.C. 123 Herschell). Photocopy at
Yale. Quoted in full, below, p. 237, 10th n.

Sir Alexander's will] Disposition and Settlement by Alexander Boswell of Auchinleck.
Dated 11 Nov. 1813, with codicils 24 Dec. 1817
and 25 Nov. 1818. Reg. B. of C. and S. 7 Aug.
1823. Photocopy at Yale.

p. 39]
Sir James advised to decline representation]
Memorial and Queries for Sir James Boswell and
Others, Apr. 1823; Answers to the Same by Mat-
thew Ross, 7 Apr. 1823 (both ILT: List C).

Creditors unite] Translation and Conveyance, John Douglas Boswell and Sir James Boswell
to the Ayrshire Banking Co., 15 and 21 Oct. 1833,
in Excerpts from Pursuer's Print of Documents,
etc., in Cause Montgomery v. Boswell (ILT: List
C). See TA, p. 206 n. 109.

Interest kept up] Proposal of Sir James
Boswell to his Father's Creditors, 8 Aug. 1828,
also in the compendium cited in the preceding
note.

Lady Boswell purchases effects] Minute of
agreement between the Dowager Lady Boswell and
Lady Boswell of Auchinleck, 1858 (TA, pp.
205–06 and nn. 108–09). The transaction was
probably conducted without written deed of sale,
and the documents cited in the two preceding notes
as well as Account between the Creditors of the
late Sir Alexander Boswell of Auchinleck and
Messrs. Tod and Romanes, in the same compendium, credit Lady Boswell only with having purchased the carriage, the library, and the furniture.
The Agreement of 1858, however, specifies purchase of the effects, and reports presentation of
"furniture library and other effects" to Sir James
Boswell. The Biographer's bequest of the library
"to the successive heirs of entail of the Barony of
Auchinleck" did not constitute an entail, but
rather gave the books in fee simple to *his* heir of
entail, with an expressed wish that that heir should
follow his example. At any rate, Hope's decree had
restricted the bequest to the Greek and Latin
books, the others having been purchased by Alexander Boswell from the estate.

Hamilton and later Jane Douglas Boswell
appointed executor] Testament dative *qua* creditor,
Commissariot of Ayr; Testament testamentary
umquhile Hamilton Douglas Boswell, Commissariot of Ayr (TA, p. 205 and n. 106).

Eight shillings in the pound] Proposal of
Sir James Boswell, as in third note back.

Assignations of all but £2,542] Sir James
Boswell to William Home, W.S., 10 Jan. 1831
(ibid.). See also TA, p. 209 n. 118.

Sir Alexander's sorting] Lady Boswell's important letter of 8 July 1825 (above, p. 36) mentions "packages" of James's effects that "came
down" to Scotland, "never were opened", and were
"returned". This makes it look as though Alexander carried back with him to Scotland certain
papers of James's and put them in his own archives;
that by his direction or otherwise more of James's
effects were packed and sent down to Auchinleck
before it became apparent that James might be
insolvent; that when this appeared, all the packages
were recalled for benefit of his creditors, and all
were returned except the parcel that Alexander
carried down himself.

Obligation of £200] "Being in health and
sound mind but warned by the many sudden deaths
which have lately taken place I hereby make my
Will bequeathing all I have in the World to my
dear Brother Alexander to dispose of as he shall
think fit but as I have borrowed two hundred
pounds belonging to James Fryer now living with
Mr. Booth Bookseller in Duke Street Portland
Place I direct that that sum which should have
remained in the 3 pr. Cent Consols when they were
at 62 may be paid to the said James Fryer out of
the proceeds of my books or other effects and the
residue if any to go to the said Alexander Boswell
(P.C.C. 123 Herschell). James's books sold for
£2,045 (sum recorded in two annotated copies of
the sale catalogue at Yale), and the residue turned
over to Sir Alexander's estate was only £547 (see
second note below).

William How, Jane Douglas Boswell]
P.C.C., Probate Act Books, Mar. 1822, Nov.
1824, Apr. 1834.

p. 40]
Balance of £547] Account Auchinleck Es-
tate personal, in Book produced by Mr. J. D.
Boswell, in Excerpts from Pursuer's Print of Doc-
uments, etc., in Cause Montgomery v. Boswell
(ILT: List C).

CHAPTER III

p. 41]

"Masses of manuscripts"] Croker to Sir Walter Scott, 28 Aug. 1829, in *Correspondence and Diaries of . . . John Wilson Croker,* ed. L. J. Jennings, 1885, ii. 38.

Croker to Scott, 16 Jan. 1830] *The Private Letter-Books of Sir Walter Scott,* ed. Wilfred Partington, 1930, p. 193.

Scott to Croker, 28 Jan. 1830] Quoted by permission of The Carl H. Pforzheimer Library.

p. 42]

"Irretrievably dispersed"] *The Life of Samuel Johnson . . . new Edition with . . . Additions and Notes* by John Wilson Croker . . . *in five Volumes,* 1831, i. xvi–xvii.

Lady Boswell concerning Euphemia] This is a further extract from the very useful letter quoted above, p. 36 in the matter of Boswell's portrait of Johnson.

p. 43]

Sutherland's suit] All from Sutherland's Action of 1836. See above, p. 235, 12th n.

Settlement of Sutherland's suit] Copy by John Bowie of letter from Thomas Smith, 4 Upper Charles Street, Westminster, to John Bowie, 4 Jan. 1837; letter, John Bowie, Edinburgh, to Sir James Boswell, 9 Jan. 1837 (both Yale MSS., McHarg Papers, Bundle 5). These letters accompany the action cited in the note immediately preceding. A document at Yale shows that in 1848 Sir James was again taken before the Court of Session, this time by his sister, Mrs. Margaret Amelia Vassall, for non-payment of the annuity of £450 a year which Sir Alexander had bound the entailed estate to pay her. As I read the document, Sir James made only partial payments from 1832 to 1836 and no payments at all from 1836 to 1848. The Court (14 Mar. 1848) ordered him to pay the full amount of arrears, with penalty, interest, expenses of process, and fee for extracting, and to continue to pay her £450 a year for life (For Sir James Boswell Bt. 1848. Complaint by James Newton, W.S. Yale MS., Talbot Inventory No. 2).

A happy ending] *Evening Chronicle,* 8 Apr. 1836; *Times,* 9 Apr. 1836; *Morning Chronicle,* 9 Apr. 1836; *Edinburgh Advertiser,* 12 Apr. 1836.

Euphemia Boswell's will]: Public Record Office, Prob. 10, 5728, X/IL 7161; Prob. 10, 5728 (E. Boswell, Sept. 1837) 7521.

p. 44]

Suning] The transcription is uncertain; possibly Saning. I have found neither name recorded elsewhere.

"Morbid oblivion"] *Life* v. 68.

p. 45]

Euphemia's death] *Times,* (9 Sept. 1837) p. 7; *Gent. Mag.* (Oct. 1837) N.S. viii. 434.

Euphemia's burial] *Registers of St. Paul's Cathedral,* Pub. of the Harleian Soc., 1899, xxvi. 192.

The undertaker] Certified Copy of an Entry of Death, 9 Apr. 1979, General Register Office, London; Application Number PAS 57273/79/F. DA 690755.

Value of Euphemia's estate] Notation in the registry of Thomas Smith's being sworn executor, 15 Sept. 1837. General Record Office, London. It will be noted that Smith was Dr. Sutherland's lawyer in the suit against Euphemia in the Court of Session.

Bruce Boswell] See the genealogical table in TA, p. 354. Thomas Alexander Boswell, as already explained, was the only son of Euphemia's uncle, T. D. Boswell.

W. G. Adam] Letters, W. G. Adam to William Adam (his father), 21 Oct. and 17 Nov. 1806, Ex Blairadam 41/1615, National Register of Archives (Scotland), HM General Register House, Edinburgh.

Rogers's memoir] James Boswell, *Boswelliana . . . with a Memoir and Annotations* by the Rev. Charles Rogers, 1874, pp. 195–96.

p. 46]

Rogers acknowledged aid] Ibid. p. xiii.

Bishop Stevens] Extract of letter, William Mackenzie to W. B. Hodgson, 2 Sept. 1843, in "Collections of the Georgia Historical Society . . . The Mackenzie Papers, Part I", ed. A. S. Britt, Jr. and Lilla M. Hawes, *Georgia Historical Quarterly,* (Winter 1972) lvi. 536–37, 580–81.

William Mackenzie] American writing about Mackenzie has generally styled him Professor, Professor of History, or Professor of Anatomy in the University of Edinburgh. The description in the text may be taken as accurate: see R. E. Wright-St. Clair, *Doctors Monro, a Medical Saga,* 1964, p.105. David Buchanan correctly styles him "a teacher of anatomy at Edinburgh University" (TA, p. 206).

Mackenzie's research] As in the last note but one, pp. 537–38.

Honorary member] William Mackenzie to I. K. Tefft, 17 Nov. 1843, ibid. pp. 538–39.

I. K. Tefft] Herringshaw's *National Library of American Biography* and A. S. Britt, Jr., *Overture to the Future at the Georgia Historical Society,* 1974, pp. 1–2.

p. 47]
Mackenzie to Tefft, 1 Feb. 1844] Printed in full in the *Georgia Historical Quarterly* (see the fifth note preceding this), pp. 539–43. My extract is an independent transcript from a photocopy. This letter (then unpublished) was called to my attention in Dec. 1971 by Professor Phinizy Spalding of the Department of History of the University of Georgia, who seems to have been the first to realize its great importance for Boswellian scholars. I should also like to thank Mrs. Lilla M. Hawes (Director) and Col. Albert S. Britt, Jr. (President) of the Georgia Historical Society for generously furnishing me and David Buchanan with photocopies of the letter in advance of their own publication.

p. 48]
Alexander Boswell to his wife, 6 Dec. 1819] Photocopy at Yale, generously furnished by Gordon P. Hoyle, Honorary Curator of the Auchinleck Boswell Museum.

p. 49]
Minute of agreement, 1858] TA, pp. 205–06 and n. 108.

David Buchanan assures me] In notes sent to me 21 Mar. 1979.

Quotation from David Buchanan] TA, p. 206.

p. 51]
"Almost ninety-one"] The *Edinburgh and Leith Post Office Directory* for 1844–45 shows that in 1844 he did have a residence in Edinburgh (17 Brown Square) and so far meets the requirement of "residing in this city".

"Twenty years younger"] I have not yet found the date of Lady Boswell's birth, and am assuming that she was of about the same age as her husband.

p. 52]
Sir James might have opened the archives] TA, pp. 208–09. Hugh Bruce Campbell's letter is at Yale (*C 741.7), a gift from Professor C. B. Tinker. It formed part of a small group of papers in a portfolio that was once the property of the editor of the Boswell-Temple letters, Sir Philip Francis. See *Lit. Car.* pp. 275–77.

Miss MacLeod] G. B. Hill, *Footsteps of Dr. Johnson (Scotland),* 1890, p. 284.

Sir James's feelings about Johnson] TA, p. 25.

"Damned Scoundrell"] Copy. Entail and Declaration by Alexander Boswell Esqr. with consent of James Boswell Esqr. his Son, Dated 8 March 1781, Regd. 9 July 1781. (A 4.5, p. 87).

p. 53]
Macaulay's review] *Edinburgh Review,* (Sept. 1831) liv. 1–38.

CHAPTER IV

p. 54]
Extremely intimate letters] *Letters of James Boswell. Addressed to the Rev. W. J. Temple. Now first published from the original MSS. With an Introduction and Notes,* 1857.

History of MSS. of Boswell-Temple letters] Manuscript notes by Sir Philip Francis for an Introduction to a second edition of the letters, which never appeared because of a disagreement with the publisher over royalties. See *Lit. Car.* pp. 275–76. The portfolio containing these notes, formerly in the collection of Professor Chauncey B. Tinker, is at Yale.

p. 55]

Lord Auchinleck's marriage contract] Contract of Marriage Betwixt Mr. Alexander Boswell And Mrs. Eupham Erskine. Dated 21 and 27 Apr. 1738 (A 4).

Father's first cousin] Copy. Destination in Entail of Auchinleck, with List of Heirs of Entail. 1836 (A 4.51).

p. 56]

Entail void] Decision handed down 31 Jan. 1852. The passage in question occurs at the bottom of p. 15 and the top of p. 16 of the crucial document: "That it shall not be in the power of any of the heirs succeeding to the Lands and Estate hereby Disponed and Resigned To Sell Allienate Impignorate or Dispone the same or any part thereof either irredeemably or under Reversion . . . ." Adam Bruce, writer, who made the fair copy from the draft of David Erskine, W.S. (Journ. 5 Aug. 1776), seems first to have written "redeemably" (exactly the wrong word), then carefully to have erased the first three letters and to have substituted "irred". If he had mentioned this erasure in the "testing clause" at the end, thus affording proof *within the instrument itself* that the erasure was present when the document was signed, it would have done no harm. The judges (eight of whom submitted written opinions) agreed that the decision was purely technical, there being abundant evidence *outside the instrument* that "irredeemably" was what the signatories intended, but they were unanimous in holding that the statute must be strictly followed (Scotland. Reports. Court of Session Cases [XIV Dunlop] 1852, pp. 378–95).

T. A. Boswell died] *Gent. Mag.* (May 1852) N.S. xxxvii. 532. *Burke's Landed Gentry,* 1846 (that is, in his lifetime), says he was born 24 Sept. 1800, but I doubt that date. If it is correct, he had an older brother who died in infancy, for T. D. Boswell, writing to Elizabeth Boswell on 7 Oct. 1799, says his "little Boy is very stout, runs about, and begins to say some words" (*C 540.3).

Sir James Boswell's will] Disposition and Settlement by Sir James Boswell of Auchinleck. Dated 25 July 1857. Reg. B. of C. and S. 8 Jan. 1858 (ILT: List C).

Lady Boswell's will] Trust Disposition and Settlement by Lady Boswell of Auchinleck. Dated

24 and 25 June and 11 July 1873. Reg. B. of C. and S. 17 Apr. 1884 (ILT: List C). Lady Boswell had bound herself to this settlement by the Prenuptial Contract of Marriage of her daughter Emily Harriet, dated 24 and 25 June 1873, Reg. B. of C. and S. 17 Apr. 1884 (ILT: List C).

p. 57]

"Immediately destroyed"] James Boswell, *Boswelliana . . . with a Memoir and Annotations* by the Rev. Charles Rogers, 1874, p. 186. Boswell's MS. is now in the Hyde Collection.

Rogers's acknowledgements] Ibid. p. xiii.

Either [Rogers] wrote very carelessly] After this passage had gone into page-proof, it occurred to me that I was perhaps underestimating the familiarity of the time with Croker's complaint. It was not a mere matter of publication in a book forty years old. Croker's Preface (1831) was reprinted only in part in the edition commonly called his second (1835; see *Lit. Car.* pp. 181–84), it did not there contain the attack on Sir James Boswell. The attack, however, reappeared in Croker's third edition (1848), an edition that was stereotyped and had many printings (1851, 1853, 1857, 1860, 1866, 1870, etc.: see *Lit. Car.* pp. 184–86). In short, the charge of rudeness and secretiveness had not been made merely once but had been reiterated. Rogers could have taken it as accepted fact.

Alexander Boswell, W.S.] He witnessed Forbes's signature to the Assignation and Disposition, 9 and 13 Dec. 1805.

p. 58]

Verse epitaph] Rogers, as in the fourth note back, p. 188.

"Burned in a mass of papers"] James Boswell, *The Life of Samuel Johnson, LL.D. . . . . The Fifth Edition,* 4 vols., 1807, iii. 391.

Commander Gould] Letter to the TLS, (27 Feb. 1930) p. 166.

Textual history] Malone probably did not read the proofs of the fifth edition, but both he and James Boswell the younger read the text of that edition carefully in preparing copy for the sixth. (See Malone's Advertisements to the third and the sixth editions.) They apparently read in their own copies, from which Malone transferred the corrections and additions to a set of unbound sheets of the fifth edition which was to serve as printer's copy. A copy of the fifth edition with manuscript corrections by Malone, now in the British Library (10854.d.3), shows no correction of "burned", but the corrections in this copy come in clumps, as though Malone had more than one working copy (information kindly furnished by David F. Foxon). The sheets from which the sixth edition was set have survived almost intact; they were formerly in the possession of Professor Frederick W. Hilles and are now in the Yale University Library. In the footnote with which we are concerned (iii. 391 of the fifth edition, iii. 393 of the sixth) the only change enjoined by Malone on the printer was to expand to "MALONE" the "M." with which the note was signed in the fifth edition. But this change shows that Malone at the very least had that footnote under his eye, and if he had it under his eye, it is odd that he let such a misprint pass. The note consists of only five lines, is the only note on the page, and "burned" stands at the end of a line.—Boswell himself, in writing to Temple on 28 Nov. 1789, spoke of "searching for papers, buried in different masses" (*Letters JB* ii. 382).

p. 59]
Hill's scoldings] *Footsteps of Dr. Johnson (Scotland)*, p. 285.

Hill's article] *Atlantic Monthly*, (Nov. 1894) lxxiv. 657–78; also in *Johnson Club Papers by Various Hands,* ed. George Whale and John Sargeaunt, 1899, pp. 51–80. My quotation is from the former source, p. 55.

p. 60]
Hill on Boswell's executors] *Footsteps,* as in the second note back.

David Buchanan chides Hill] TA, p. 31.

p. 61]
J. J. Boswell] J. J. Boswell, *History and Genealogical Tables of the Boswells,* 1906, pp. vi–vii.

David Buchanan] TA, p. 32.

Family report] Kathleen B. Mounsey, Old Post Cottage, Itchen Abbas, Winchester, Hants, to David Buchanan, 28 Apr. 1975. I unfortunately did not write to her till 28 Oct. 1977, when I was

informed by her brother that she had died. He gives me permission to quote, saying, "Whatever my sister told you in her letter is correct" (letter, John D. Mounsey, Drogo, Winchester Road, New Alresford, Hants, to F. A. Pottle, 16 Nov. 1977, at Yale).

p. 62]
J. J. Boswell's Auchinleck papers] Jasper John Boswell's papers, or many of them, are now in the Fondazione Sella, San Gerolamo, Biella, Italy, his daughter Gertrude having married an Italian gentleman, Ing. Gaudenzio Sella. The present curator, Dr. Lodovico Sella, Jasper John Boswell's great-grandson, has been prompt and courteous in aiding the Boswell Editions.

Earl of Elgin] The 11th Earl of Elgin, 15th of Kincardine, then Lord Bruce, to F. A. Pottle, 22 Feb. 1960, excerpting letters to the ninth Earl of Elgin from Sir Arthur Halkett of Pitfirrane, 29 and 30 Oct. 1886, and from Hamilton & Inches, jewellers, Edinburgh, 1 and 2 Nov. 1886. I have been unable to locate a copy of Dowell's catalogue, but Sir Arthur's first letter makes clear that there was one, and that the dressing-set was listed on p. 7. I should very much like to know whether the Auchinleck coins and medals were included in this sale: Sir Arthur says merely "some things . . . belonging to the late Sir James Boswell of Auchinleck". The pieces of the dressing-set not bought by Lord Elgin were acquired and resold by S. J. Philips of Bond Street, but Philips has no records of the purchasers. Philips bought in again one important piece of the set, a helmet-shaped ewer, in 1959, and sold it to a Dutch dealer, who resold it at The Hague Antique Dealers' Fair (letter, eleventh Earl of Elgin, then Lord Bruce, to F. A. Pottle, 2 Sept. 1960, at Yale). On 28 Apr. 1965 Lord Bruce sold at Christie's the pieces which had been in the possession of his family since 1886. Thirteen of the eighteen pieces of the set have ultimately been acquired by the Gemeentemuseum at the Hague (letter, Dr. A. Westers, keeper of the Applied Arts Dept., to F. A. Pottle, 3 Mar. 1980, at Yale).

p. 63]
Proof-sheets] This was the virtually complete set of revises now in the Hyde Collection. The fragmentary set of first proofs (1st. ed. i 1–56, 81–224), also in the Hyde Collection, was probably part of Lot 3171 of the sale of James Boswell the younger. See above, p. 29 and p. 234, 2nd n.

CHAPTER V

p. 64]
Hon. J. B. Talbot inherits pictures and books at Auchinleck] Will of Mrs. Julia Mounsey. Dated 25 Jan. 1905. Registry as in the note next following.

Cumberland Infirmary Mrs. Mounsey's residuary legatee] Will of Mrs. Julia Mounsey. Dated 17 June 1905, Codicil 24 June 1905. Proved and reg. in District Probate Registry at Carlisle, 24 Apr. 1906 (ILT: List C). Mrs. Mounsey died on 8 July 1905.

Fifth Lord Talbot arranges sale of household effects at Auchinleck] Howden and Molleson, C.A., Edinburgh, to Lord Talbot, 15 Aug. 1905 (copy in ILP, TA, p. 39, n. 157).

Dowell's sale, 17 Mar. 1906] From an inventory of documents which I have called ILT: List B (see above, p. xiii) I conclude that Lord Talbot bought all the furniture and effects at Dowell's valuation (£1,141. 5s.) and then sold at auction through Dowell the articles that he had no use for. Dowell's *Catalogue of valuable antique Furniture . . . to be sold by Auction by Mr. Dowell . . . on Saturday, 17th March 1906* (photocopy at Yale) is a miscellaneous collection, only "Andrew R. Scott" being mentioned on the title-page, but the annotated copy in the National Library of Scotland assigns ownership of forty-three lots to "Talbot". As an example of an item that had belonged to Boswell one might cite Lot 177, "Splendid old Canton gong, 21 in. dia." See Journ. 2 May 1785; *Lit. Car.* p. 249.

Thomas Drysdale's recollections] Memorandum of conversation, 16 Nov. 1937, with Thomas Drysdale, land-steward at Auchinleck from c. 1896 to c. June 1920. Typed undocketed document among the Isham legal transcripts, shown by letters to Colonel Isham from Denton Hall & Burgin, 11 Nov. 1937 and 15 Jan. 1938, to have been made by Steedman Ramage & Co. (ILT: List C).

p. 65]
Samuel Gurney's recollection] Samuel Gurney, *Isabel, Mrs. Gurney, afterwards The Lady Talbot de Malahide, 1851–1932,* 1925, p. 140. Gurney made extended visits to Auchinleck from 1905 to 1915. He wrote me (24 Jan. 1960) that his personal

recollection remained as stated in his book, and that his elder brother, Sir Hugh Gurney, and his wife had the same recollection.

Boswell's journals at Malahide by 1908] Isabel, Lady Talbot to Samuel Gurney, 1 Jan. 1915 (ibid.).

Contents of ebony cabinet in Boswell's time] On Charles Hope's inquiring whether the medals and coins had come into the family with the cabinet, the younger children replied that the cabinet did not "properly contain anything else than the Dressing Plate" (Notes by Arbiter in Boswell's Submission, 29 June 1803; Observations on Notes by the Arbiter for the younger Children, 26 Oct. 1803: ILT: List B). Besides the medals and coins (which are always referred to as the more important portion of the contents at the time of the arbitration), the following objects are specified: miniature portraits of the Biographer and of Annie Cuninghame, a seal ring, a few detached rose diamonds, some "toilets of lace work", and "sundry curiosities natural and artificial" (Alexander Boswell's Answers and Claim, 15 Feb. 1803; Assignation of Moveables, 21 and 23 Dec. 1805; Alexander Boswell to Harry Davidson, 4 Nov. 1805). The last three papers cited are in ILT: List A. The Biographer did apparently put in the cabinet certain documents that he considered show-pieces. See *Letters JB* ii. 311 and BP xviii. 290.

p. 66]
Isabel, Lady Talbot seeks advice as to publication] Samuel Gurney, *Isabel, Mrs. Gurney, afterwards The Lady Talbot de Malahide,* p. 140. David Buchanan saw Warner's reply, 8 Feb. 1907, among papers in Joyce, Lady Talbot's hands (TA, pp. 39–40 and nn. 160, 161).

p. 67]
Fifth Lord Talbot against publication] Samuel Gurney, as in the note preceding this, p. 140.

Colonel Talbot reads the journal] Col. Milo Talbot, 19 June 1930, to Joyce, Lady Talbot (TA, p. 40). The date 1908 is confirmed by Samuel Gurney, as in the second note back, p. 88. Evidence of Colonel Talbot's careful work in sorting the journal fragments into dated series appears in numerous inscriptions by him on envelopes which once contained unbound journals and journal-notes and on labels pasted on the covers of journals in notebooks. Lord Talbot's hand also appears, but much more sparingly. See J 2, J 10, J 14, J 17, J 18, J 24, J 27, J 28, J 36, J 39, J 40, J 45, J 47, J 49–51, J 54, J 57, J 67, J 70, J 77, J 86, J 88, J 96, J 98, J 102, J 116, J 117.

Murray's letter] From a typed transcript of the letter-press copy preserved in the files of John Murray, Ltd., the original having been entirely in the hand of the late Sir John Murray. Transcript furnished and permission to publish kindly granted by Sir John Murray, K.C.V.O., D.S.O.

p. 69]
"Copies of the Boswell Diaries"] 27 June 1911, also kindly transcribed for me by Sir John Murray.

Typing Agency] One blank leaf bears the impression of a stamp, "Typed by Mrs. Springett, 5 Salters Hall Court, E.C." The typescript is in many fascicles, but clearly all came from the same office.

Extensively expurgated] It accompanied the manuscripts when they were sold to Isham, and was used as printer's copy for his *Private Papers of James Boswell.* I greatly regret that I was not more vigilant to recover all of it from the printer and preserve it.

Some of the most scabrous matter] For example, the journals for 12 June 1776 to 8 May 1777. See J 49 and J 50. To be sure, Boswell veils his indecencies in Greek characters, but they would not have given anybody any trouble to decipher.

Excised matter preserved in transcript] See BP vii. 166, x. 166, and *Boswell in Search of a Wife,* beginning of 25 Mar. 1768. I found the missing leaf of the typescript in a file in Isham's house after Vol. vii. of BP had been printed. It had presumably been removed at Malahide to be destroyed and then by inadvertence strayed into some other portion of the Murray typescript. Since a good part of this transcript is now lost, my generalization in the text may seem risky. But if the typescript had been the sole source of any portion of the text of BP, I should certainly have noted the fact, as I did at vii.166 and x.166. There remains the possibility that in some place or other the typescript may originally have contained more matter than the manuscript now does and then have been trimmed with scissors to correspond with the (later) mutilated original.

I cannot trust my memory on this, but if there were such cases, it is odd that they should all have occurred in the missing portion of the typescript.

p. 70]
Fifth Lord Talbot sensitive about Boswell's journal] As above, p. 242, 10th n.

Casual Boswellian pilgrims] A. Edward Newton said he called at Auchinleck without an introduction at a time when the family was not in residence and was told by the servant who answered the bell that instructions were to admit no one to the house under pain of instant dismissal (*The Amenities of Book-Collecting,* 1918, pp. 181–84). Newton does not date his pilgrimage, and it may have been in Mrs. Mounsey's time, but I get the impression that it occurred nearer 1910. Joyce, Lady Talbot said this strictness was resorted to because things were believed to have disappeared when visitors were admitted ("History of Papers", a typed three-page document in ITC, written, I believe, in 1937 to correct certain statements made in a brochure advertising the Viking Press–William Heinemann edition of Boswell's *Journal of a Tour to the Hebrides,* 1936).

p. 71]
David Buchanan reports] TA, p. 45.

Bonded debt on Auchinleck] From a "List of heritable Bonds over the Estate of Auchinleck in Order of Ranking, showing presently existing Amount thereof" among the Isham legal transcripts (List C), undated but before 4 Mar. 1921, it appears that the bonded debt by that time had reached the enormous sum of £143,910. 10s. 2d., nearly $700,000 at the rate of exchange then obtaining.

Talbots breaking away from Auchinleck] Samuel Gurney, *Isabel, Mrs. Gurney, afterwards The Lady Talbot de Malahide,* pp. 140–41.

Sale of furniture in Auchinleck House] *Catalogue of superior modern and antique Furniture . . . to be sold by Auction by Mr. Dowell, Edinburgh, within the Mansionhouse of Auchinleck, Ayrshire, on . . . 4th and 5th April 1917* (National Library of Scotland, photocopy at Yale).

Only one MS. listed as sold] *Catalogue of valuable Books and Manuscripts, the Property of the Honble. James Boswell Talbot, of Auchinleck, Ayrshire;* [two other owners] *and other Properties . . .* Sotheby, Wilkinson, & Hodge, 29, 30, 31 Mar. 1916. The book from Lofft is Lot 19.

A good deal of clumping] These lots are totally undescribed in the catalogue but are itemized in a "Roup Roll of Household Furniture and other Effects sold at Auchinleck, Ayrshire, 4th April 1917, Alex. Dowell, Auctioneer" (ILT: List C). I should be glad to know more about the following, sold from the housekeeper's room: "Painting" (16s.), "Painting Group" (£1. 6s.), "2 Portraits" (9s.), "Painting" (18s.), "Sword" (£5).

Dowell's catalogue of books] *Catalogue of Valuable Libraries . . . including that from Auchinleck House, Ayrshire . . . to be sold by Auction by Mr. Dowell . . . on 28th, 29th and 30th May* 1917 (National Library of Scotland, photocopy at Yale). Lots 927–1062 are grouped under the heading "Library removed from Auchinleck House"; miscellaneous lots 1099–1172 are also assigned to Auchinleck in a printed note following Lot 1062 and in manuscript notes in the margin opposite those lots.

McKinlay] See *Lit. Car.* p. 134. I seem to have lost the letter itself.

Final shipment] Letters to me from Joyce, Lady Talbot de Malahide, 13 Aug. 1950 and 17 May 1958, placing the date of the final transfer in 1917. In writing to Isham on 21 Mar. 1942 (ITC) she set it in 1915, apparently inferring this from the fact that some of the papers were wrapped in newspapers of that year. Since Dowell's sales can be definitely dated in the spring of 1917, her later suggestion of 1917 seems rather more likely.

p. 72]
McCrone] McCrone refers to "Account Books" of Boswell's time still at Auchinleck, and says that he has "quite a number of his Memoranda and Letters of Instructions, but there is a considerable gap prior to his becoming laird. In fact I do not think I have anything of his prior to 1782" (to C. B. Tinker, 8 Sept. 1920). These letters of instruction sound as though they might have been Boswell's letters as laird to James Bruce, his overseer, for which we now have only the minutes (L 274–307). The well-known series to Andrew Gibb, of which many originals are now reported, did not begin till 1790, and besides seems in 1920 to have been in the possession of a descendant (*Letters JB* ii. 472 n. 2). See also ibid. i. 90 n. 1, where

Tinker gives information from a letter of T. D. Boswell to Lt. John Boswell, 11 Jan. 1766, communicated to him by McCrone from "manuscript letters at Auchinleck House"; also (ibid. i. 187 n. 2) a quotation from a letter of Lady Auchinleck to Lt. John Boswell, 22 Jan. 1765, "preserved at Auchinleck House". Tinker's source for this last was a facsimile "privately reproduced" by Dr. J. T. T. Brown of Glasgow, but it would seem to me virtually certain that Brown got access to the original through McCrone, who in his letter of 8 Sept. 1920 refers to him as "my good friend". I have never seen any of the letters mentioned in the present note, and am not even aware that they now exist.

Sale of farms at Auchinleck] Information from Messrs. Tait and Crichton, W.S., Edinburgh, kindly obtained for me by Messrs. Howden and Molleson, C.A., Edinburgh, letter dated 23 Oct. 1958.

Mansion-house of Auchinleck sold] Colonel Boswell paid £75,000 for the mansion-house, a number of farms, mineral rights, etc. The missives of sale were dated 15 July, 16 and 25 Aug., and 22 and 23 Sept. 1920; conveyance by disposition was dated 19 and 26 May 1922. The missives covered other properties which Colonel Boswell resold before the grant of a formal conveyance (Disposition in favour of John Douglas Boswell dated 19 and 26 May and recorded in the Division of the General Register of Sasines for the County of Ayr on 1 July 1922).

Hill's tribute to Adam] *Atlantic Monthly*, (Nov. 1894) lxxiv. 658; also in *Johnson Club Papers by Various Hands*, ed. George Whale and John Sargeaunt, 1899, p. 53.

p. 73]
Adam and Newton] Brief but informative sketches of R. B. Adam, second, by R. F. Metzdorf and of Newton by T. A. Adams will be found in *Grolier 75: A Biographical Retrospective*, 1959.

Enjoyed great popularity] *The Amenities of Book-Collecting*, 1918, had a sale in America of about 43,000 copies (letter to me from Little, Brown & Co. 14 Feb. 1950).

p. 74]
Carlyle's essay on Boswell] The review appeared in two instalments in *Fraser's Magazine* for

Apr. and May 1832 (v. 253–60, 379–413) and appears in Carlyle's *Critical and Miscellaneous Essays* as "Biography" and "Boswell's Life of Johnson".

p. 75]

Two replies] The anonymous communication appears no longer to be among Professor Tinker's papers, but I remember hearing him mention it. The signed one (which I have not quoted in full) bears the date and Dublin postmark 31 July 1920 and the address 19 Westland Row, Dublin. The signature is "Elsie Mahaffy late of Provosts Ho Trinity College Dublin". Miss Mahaffy died later in 1920.

p. 76]

A prompt but cryptic answer] Dated 5 Aug. 1920. Signed "James B. Talbot".

McCrone] Continuation of the letter cited in p. 244, 6th n. above.

p. 77]

Burning of Papers] Letters, T. D. Drysdale to F. A. Pottle, 15 Oct., 14 Nov., 23 Dec. 1979; 7 Feb. 1980. All at Yale.

p. 78]

David Buchanan] TA, p. 46.

p. 79]

Eveleigh Nash] "My husband . . . had been advised by Mr. Nash not to part with [the papers] until they had been published" (Lady Talbot's "personal statement" in the BBC broadcast "The Boswell Story", 12 Aug. 1951); "[Mr. Nash] advised us to find an honourable and reliable Purchaser, as to publish the papers intact could bring huge financial profit of a kind he supposed (quite correctly) my husband would not care to take; but to publish them in a worthy manner he thought would be beyond our means" (letter to me from Lady Talbot, 17 May 1958). The date of May 1925 for the conference with Nash comes from Lady Talbot's "History of Papers, Note D" (above, p. 243, 9th n.). Lord Dunedin's presence is established by a letter from Nash to Lady Talbot, 4 June 1925 (TA, p. 49 and n. 6). Nash died on 9 July 1956, and I have been unable to locate his papers.

p. 80]

Tinker goes to Malahide] Letter, C. M. Hathaway to C. B. Tinker, 29 Mar. 1950 (in Tinker papers); letter, C. B. Tinker to A. G.

Thomas, 17 Aug. 1946 (TA, p. 53); my own recollection of Tinker's oral reports.

Lady Talbot] Typed three-page narrative by C. B. Tinker prepared in the spring of 1950 for the use of Christopher Morley in writing the Preface for McGraw-Hill's edition of *Boswell's London Journal, 1762–1763*, 1950; also manuscript notes by C. B. Tinker for the same, dated 3 Apr. 1950; letter, C. B. Tinker to A. G. Thomas, 17 Aug. 1946 as in the note preceding this (TA, p. 53).

p. 81]

Two printed accounts] R. D. Altick, "The Secret of the Ebony Cabinet", in *The Scholar Adventurers*, 1950; Hamilton Basso, "The Boswell Detective Story", in *Life*, 4 Dec. 1950.

Boswellian scholars did not know] Roger Ingpen, a Boswell scholar of sorts, remarked, in a preface dated Apr. 1925 to a new printing, 1925, of his illustrated edition of the *Life of Johnson*, that the rumour of the destruction of Boswell's papers was unfounded and that Boswell's journals had survived. Ingpen's book, however, was not reviewed in the *Times Literary Supplement* till 8 Oct. 1925, p. 659, and is listed in the Fall (July–Dec. 1925) index of new publications in *Publishers' Weekly*. The passage has the look of a clumsy change made in proofs at the last possible moment.

Roberts] Account sent by him to Mrs. Donald F. Hyde, 16 Mar. 1966 (TA, pp. 61–62, p. 61 n. 52).

CHAPTER VI

p. 82]

Tinker, Newton, Rosenbach] Tinker sent Newton a postcard from Dublin, 6 July 1925: "Everything here and nothing to be touched. I have been on the rack" (quoted, TA, p. 53 from a letter in the Hyde Collection, Newton to R. B. Adam, 13 July 1925, quoting Tinker). I have no documentary evidence that Newton passed the word on to Rosenbach, but have always understood that to have been the fact. He probably did it by telephone or at a personal meeting.

Rosenbach cables] Rosenbach seems to have preserved no copy of this cablegram, and I have

not seen the copy delivered to Lord Talbot. Its
tenor and the sum offered are reported in later
letters from Lady Talbot to Isham.

Lady Talbot] From the files of the Philip
H. and A. S. W. Rosenbach Foundation.

p. 83]
Hathaway] Tinker papers at Yale.

Newton] Christopher Morley, Preface to
McGraw-Hill's edition of *Boswell's London Journal,
1762–1763*, 1950, p. xviii. Morley knew Newton
well and was an acquaintance of Isham's. He says
that Newton "next had a go at the papers. Again
the stone wall." This is probably too definite
(David Buchanan found no correspondence with
Newton at Malahide), but my term "reconnoitre"
may be acceptable.

Nesbitt] Pencilled draft or copy of cablegram in Isham's hand, without date or name of
recipient; cablegram, Nesbitt to Isham, London,
27 Feb. 1926; copy of cablegram, Isham to "Major
Nesbitt, 56 Rutland Gate, London", 28 Feb.
1926; copy of cablegram, Isham to same, 4 Mar.
1926; cablegram, "Fred" to Isham, received in
New York 6 Mar. 1926 (all ITC). Letters to me
from General Beaumont-Nesbitt, 24 Dec. 1959,
19 Jan. 1960.

Isham to Denton, Hall, & Burgin] Draft
of cablegram, Isham to "Burginhal", London, 6
Mar. 1926 (ITC).

p. 84]
Burgin to Isham] Cablegram, "Harold" to
Isham, received in New York 9 Mar. 1926; ca-
blegram, Burgin to Isham from Dublin, received
11 Mar. 1926; cablegram, "Harold" to Isham from
Dublin, received 11 Mar. 1926. All ITC.

Isham] See "Ralph Heyward Isham,
1890–1955", by Herman W. Liebert, in *Grolier*
75, 1959, pp. 233–36.

p. 85]
Newton] Letter, Newton to Isham, The
Plaza, New York, undated, IFP; letter, Newton
to Adam, 24 June 1926, Hyde Collection. Both
TA, p. 60.

Sailed on the *Olympic*] *New York Times*, (28
May 1926) p. 34a ("Col. Ralph Isham among those

booked to sail on the *Olympic* (White Star) for Cher-
bourg and Southampton shortly after midnight
that night"); Board of Trade Passenger Lists, PRO,
BT 26/828 ("Ralph Isham, *Olympic,* 1st Cl., Southampton from New York, arr'd 4 June 1926").

Talbot to Isham] Letter, Lord Talbot to
Burgin, 30 May [1926] (ITC). David Buchanan's
corresponding extract from TFP shows many textual variants. Presumably the document he used
was a retained draft.

p. 86]
"Journeys to Mecca"] Letter, Isham to Lord
Talbot, 7 June 1926 (TFP, TA, p. 60).

Talbot answered] Letter, Lord Talbot to
Isham, 10 June [1926]: "We shall be at home all
the afternoon of Tuesday June 14th and shall be
very pleased to see you, if you are able to call"
(ITC). In 1926, 14 June actually fell on Monday.
Isham made his call on 15 June (Lady Talbot's
diary, TA, p. 61).

Lord Ivor Spencer-Churchill's recommen-
dation] Letter, Lord Ivor Spencer-Churchill to Lord
Talbot, 11 June 1926 (TFP, TA, p. 60).

Journey seemed interminable] "The Boswell Story", B.B.C. broadcast by Isham, 12 Aug.
1951 (typescript at Yale, p. 18).

Roberts] Account sent to Mrs. Donald F.
Hyde, 16 Mar. 1966 (TA, pp. 61–62).

p. 87]
Roberts's meetings with Newton] S. C.
Roberts, *Adventures with Authors*, 1966, pp. 92–93.
He visited R. B. Adam at Eastertide of 1925 (ibid.
pp. 91–92).

Roberts mistaken] S. C. Roberts, *Dr. Johnson and Others*, 1958, p. 28.

Roberts offers services] Letter, Roberts to
Lord Talbot, 25 June 1926 (TFP, TA, p. 62).

Valued at £120] TA, p. 64.

"Four or five thousand"] Letter, Isham to
Lady Talbot, 5 July 1926 (TFP, TA, p. 65).

Nash] Letter, Nash to Lady Talbot, 12 July
1926 (TFP, TA, p. 65).

Lady Talbot sells Goldsmith letter] Letter, Lady Talbot to Isham, 27 July [1926] (ITC).

Goldsmith letter sent and received] Letter, Lady Talbot to Isham, 21 Aug. [1926] (ITC). Three other documents in ITC deal with Isham's payment by cheque, the dispatch of the letter, and its receipt by Isham (8 Sept. 1926).

p. 88]
Lady Talbot suggests £10,000] Letter, Lady Talbot to Isham, 30 Nov. 1926 (ITC).

Isham insists on journals] Letter, Isham to Lady Talbot, 17 Dec. 1926 (TFP, TA, p. 68).

Lady Talbot promises to price the letters] Letter, Lady Talbot to Isham, 14 Feb. 1927 (TFP, TA, p. 68).

Lady Talbot studies catalogues] Letter, Lady Talbot to R. F. Metzdorf, 16 Apr. 1960, at Yale.

Lady Talbot invites Isham to Malahide] Letter, Lady Talbot to Isham, 18 July 1927; cablegram, Lord Talbot to Isham, received in New York 2 Aug. 1927, asking if he can come 19 Aug. (ITC).

Set price per page] This conflates David Buchanan's extremely valuable description of the working lists used by Lady Talbot and Isham (TA, p. 68 n. 76) with my own recollection of what Isham told me more than fifty years ago. I seem to remember the figure of £10 a page for the miscellaneous manuscripts. In the subsequent correspondence in which Lady Talbot and Isham fixed a price for the journal (e.g. 19 Nov. 1927), she adopted £10 a page as a preliminary valuation.

£13,585] TA, p. 68; bill of sale, Lord Talbot to Isham, 21 Aug. 1927, at Yale.

p. 89]
Ashbourne Journal] See J 52.

Ashbourne Journal delivered] Four documents in ITC, 9 Sept. to 19 Nov. 1927, deal with this transaction. The packet containing the Ashbourne Journal was personally delivered at Claridge's by an agent of the Royal Bank of Ireland, Dublin.

"She was my mistress"] My recollection of Tinker's own oral report to me and others.

p. 90]
"I preferred"] Also my recollection. For a similar sentiment see Tinker's letter to A. G. Thomas, 17 Aug. 1946, as quoted in TA, p. 71.

Lawrence] Letter, Lawrence to Isham, 22 Nov. 1927 (IFP, TA, p. 71).

Scott engaged] Obituary essay by Isham on Scott, *Sat. Rev. Lit.* (24 Aug. 1929) vi. 74.

p. 91]
Geoffrey Scott] Meryle Secrest's biography, now in hand, will fill a long-felt need. Her useful sketch, "Golden boy, king of mopers" (*Harvard Magazine,* July–Aug. 1980, lxxxii, no. 6, 41–44) appeared after my text had gone to the printer.

Isham's description] As in the second note back.

Iris Origo] Iris Origo, *Images and Shadows,* 1970, p. 103.

p. 92]
Haslam] Letter, W. H. Haslam to David Buchanan, 9 Oct. 1975, photocopy at Yale. I have also drawn on a typed four-page memorandum, "Geoffrey Scott", sent by Haslam to David Buchanan.

p. 93]
Isham pushes Lady Talbot] Letter, Isham to Lady Talbot, 26 Sept. 1927; same to the same, 28 Oct. 1927; cable, unrecorded, but mentioned in the letter next cited; letter, Lady Talbot to Isham, 19 Nov. 1927 (TFP, all TA, p. 77).

Journal sent, price £20,000] Letter, Lady Talbot to Isham, 21 Nov. 1927; same to the same, 28 Nov. 1927; Isham to Lady Talbot, 19 Dec. 1927 (all ITC); same to the same, 30 Nov. 1927 (TFP, TA, p. 78).

Isham asks deferment of half the price, requests title to all Boswell's papers owned by Talbot] Letter, Isham to Lady Talbot, 19 Dec. 1927 (ITC).

Isham denied deferment; if any more journal turned up, to have it free] Letter, Lady Talbot to Isham, 4 Jan. 1927 (ITC).

Isham's purchases of real estate] Letter, Newton to Adam, 9 Nov. 1927 (Hyde Collection, TA, p. 79 n. 115).

Newton on Isham's publishing venture] (TA, p. 81).

Isham's earlier attempt to get Newton and Rosenbach to go halves] (TA, p. 60 and n. 44).

p. 94]
Van Alen] TA, p. 79 and n. 116.

Ostensible offer of papers to Rosenbach] Edwin Wolf and J. F. Fleming, *Rosenbach, a Biography,* 1960, pp. 276–77.

Swann's appraisal] Ibid. (" . . . the figures, which totaled almost a million and three-quarter dollars"). I have lost my note identifying the source of the precise figure, but assume that I got it either from ITC or the files of the Philip H. and A. S. W. Rosenbach Foundation. I think however that, huge as Isham's asking price of Sept. 1927 was, it did not go the length of Swann's appraisal, which was made after Isham had acquired the journals, i.e. after Jan. 1928.

CHAPTER VII

p. 96]
Murray transcript] "I had to undertake [the task of censoring] with no help beyond the typescript you have, and which, made over twenty years ago, roughly suggested the ideas of the men then engaged on work on the M.S.S." (letter, Lady Talbot to Isham, 15 Apr. 1930, ITC); "We deleted some passages, keeping as near as possible to the deletions that had been made in the typewritten copy which had been submitted to Sir John Murray" (B.B.C. broadcast, "The Boswell Story", 12 Aug. 1951, p. 20; letter, Lady Talbot to F. A. Pottle, 14 Jan. 1960: both at Yale).

p. 97]
Lady Talbot employs a secretary] The secretary afterwards worked for V. Sackville-West. V. Sackville-West, who gave a lecture at Yale in 1933, told me about her then. In 1958, at my request, she enabled me to put some questions to the secretary by post (letter, F. A. Pottle to V.

Sackville-West, 6 May 1958; letter, V. Sackville-West to F. A. Pottle, 15 May 1958: both at Yale).

Blue-black ink] "I am sure the same ink was used at Malahide generation after generation. Large stone bottles of 'Stephen Blue Black Ink' from which all inkstands were filled up by a servant" (letter, Lady Talbot to F. A. Pottle, 14 Jan. 1960, at Yale).

p. 98]
Three versions] David Buchanan provides useful texts of all three versions, TA, pp. 335, 336, 337–38.

Absence of certain details suspicious] For detailed newspaper reports of this storm, see *Earlier Years,* p. 527.

p. 99]
Lady Talbot denies destroying any papers] "That I burnt and destroyed papers is absolutely untrue" (B.B.C. broadcast, "The Boswell Story", 12 Aug. 1951, p. 20).

Lady Talbot very tired] "Since Colonel Isham is so sure that he himself has seen her burn one particular paper in Boswell's Journal, she feels this must be the case, and . . . she would prefer to qualify her denial by telling you that if Colonel Isham tells her he saw her burn one page of the Journal, she presumes she did so, though she has no recollection of doing it herself.—When Colonel Isham stayed here in 1927, he and Lady Talbot worked so hard at the papers that I think Lady Talbot was tired enough to do almost anything and forget she had done it" (typed transcript in ITC of a portion of a letter, I do not know by whom written or to whom addressed).

Lady Talbot certain that she destroyed nothing in her general review of the journal] Letter, Lady Talbot to F. A. Pottle, 17 May 1958, at Yale. David Buchanan's extract (TA, p. 338) from this letter ("I cannot tell you what happened to 'the many leaves which were removed'. I did not remove them and I did not burn them. I most emphatically deny that I burned any papers") is misleading, the printer having failed to indicate by an ellipsis that over two hundred words have been omitted between the second and third sentences. The omitted passage is much in the tone of that quoted in the note preceding this: "I do not however want Colonel Isham's word brought into dispute now. When he and I went through the papers I became very tired, and he had a good deal to drink. There were many papers of no Boswell value, and much was pushed aside. Perhaps I burned something." The third sentence of Buchanan's extract properly runs, "But I do most emphatically deny that I burned any papers while preparing the papers to send over to him."

Earlier Years] Page 277.

p. 101]
Free will on the carpet] Journ. 29 Aug. 1764.

p. 102]
Charming picture of Scott] *Sat. Rev. Lit.* (24 Aug. 1929) vi. 74.

Sales to Rosenbach] Collect telegram, The Rosenbach Company to Isham, 3 May 1933 (IFP). See above, p. 94. The telegram also lists the final sale, 3 Dec. 1928, of the five-page "Paper Apart" from the manuscript of the *Life of Johnson* and the two letters from Boswell to his wife ($8,000).

Bruce letters lost] Letter, Arthur Swann to Isham, 27 June 1928 (IFP). Photocopy sent to me by David Buchanan.

p. 103]
Glowing reviews] Reviewed by F. A. Pottle in *Sat. Rev. Lit.* (16 Feb. 1929) v. 677–78.

Scott changes residence] Information from Mrs. Ray Slater Blakeman (formerly Mrs. James B. Murphy).

Scott a burden on Mrs. Isham] TA, p. 85.

p. 104]
Scott's invested funds] Letter, Scott to W. H. Haslam, undated but written from Glen Head. Original at Yale by gift of Haslam.

Scott said to be "loveless"] "He slowly gave up. In 1927 [actually 1926] he and Sybil were divorced, and, loveless, he spent the last years of his life in New York, where he edited Boswell's papers. . . . Vita had not been kind to Geoffrey—she had smashed his life and finally wrecked his marriage—but what part does kindness play in love? For him their pledge had been cut in granite;

for her it had been written in chalk on slate" (*Portrait of a Marriage,* 1973, p. 200).

A gifted woman] Mrs. Muriel Draper, whose address in 1928 appears to have been 24 East Fortieth St., New York City, interior decorator by profession, amateur of music and literature, author of avant-garde poems and *Music at Midnight,* 1929, a best-selling memoir of life in the musical and literary circles of Florence and London, 1909–14. "Best known as a patron of artists . . . and a hostess who combined social glitter with bohemia" (New York *Herald Tribune,* 27 Aug. 1952, p. 22). In later years she visited the Soviet Union and Spain and identified herself strongly with various organizations reported to be Communist front. Scott's "last attachment" was revealed in the *Listener,* 27 Dec. 1973, p. 887, by Mrs. Marguerite Harris, formerly Ross, Scott's secretary during his first year of work at Glen Head, who wrote to correct Nigel Nicolson. (See the note preceding this.) On 23 Mar. 1975, at the Department of Oral History of Columbia University, the late Professor James L. Clifford and his wife Virginia arranged for the recording of a three-hour interview with Mrs. Harris, in which they questioned her minutely about the Isham ménage, Scott's appearance and behaviour, and her own work on the papers. Mrs. Harris has kindly given me a transcript of this tape to use as I see fit. She reports Scott's deep emotional involvement with Mrs. Draper, his "pacing the lanes waiting for the postman to bring her letter", and admits to having "peeked" into a letter of hers that Scott left lying on his desk. Mrs. Draper preserved twenty-six letters and five telegrams from Scott, and left them with her other papers to Yale University. She died on 26 Aug. 1952.

p. 105]
Asking price of $30,000] Letter, Catherine McCarthy of Harcourt, Brace & World to F. A. Pottle, 17 Jan. 1961, at Yale. So far as I know, no part of it ever was written. In June 1929 I was shown by Isham at his home in Glen Head typescript of what appeared to be a chapter by Scott for a life of Boswell, but Isham told me (I think correctly) that it was the introduction for the volume in the English Men of Letters series, written before Scott had seen any of Isham's manuscripts. See above, p. 92.

Scott's contract with Isham] Memorandum of Agreement between Isham and Scott, 20 May 1929, photocopy at Yale.

Cordial and intimate letters] Letter, Scott to Isham, from S.S. *California,* undated, but clearly written on first day of sailing from New York, which was 25 May 1929; postal showing Boswell vault, Auchinleck, Scott to Isham, posted at Chesham, Bucks, 10 June 1929; letter, Scott to Isham, from 8, Hanover Terrace, Regent's Park, N.W., 4 July 1929. All at Yale.

p. 106]
Excursions to Auchinleck and Crawley Grange] Last two items in note preceding this.

Scott's death] Letter, Melvin H. Loos to Dr. James B. Murphy, 20 Aug. 1929; *New York Times,* (15 Aug. 1929) p. 23c. Loos wrongly reported the date as 13 Aug.

Article by Isham] 24 Aug. 1929, p. 74.

Scott's obsequies] "Geoffrey Scott", by W. H. Haslam, accompanying letter, Haslam to David Buchanan, 9 Oct. 1975. Buchanan kindly furnished me with a photocopy. The ceremony at New College was held on 7 Oct. 1930 (printed invitation accompanying Scott's letters to Mrs. Draper, at Yale).

Outlook] 18, 25 Sept., 2, 9, 16, 23 Oct. 1929 (vol. 153, nos. 3–8).

F. A. Pottle in touch with Isham] Letter, Pottle to Isham, 12 Sept. 1926 (IFP, TA, p. 89 n. 3).

p. 107]
Scott to Pottle] Quoted in the printed Announcement sent to subscribers to *Private Papers.* The original was presented to me by Arthur Mallet, Scott's executor.

Rudge my paymaster] Helen Cohan, Scott's secretary during 1929 and continuing as mine, was soon after also put on Rudge's payroll.

p. 108]
My contract with Isham] Memorandum of Agreement between Isham, Pottle, and Rudge, 1 Oct. 1929, at Yale.

CHAPTER VIII

p. 109]
Scott's suppressions] Scott suppressed two considerable passages: he omitted 112 words in the journal entry for 26 May 1764 and 74 at the end of the journal entry for 11 Oct. 1764 (BP ii. 129, iv. 128). He acknowledged the former by asterisks; the latter, which was probably inked by Boswell himself, he made silently. *Boswell in Holland* and *Boswell on the Grand Tour: Germany and Switzerland* give the full text.

p. 110]
Isham's settlement with Scott's heirs] W. H. Haslam, "Geoffrey Scott", accompanying letter from him to David Buchanan, 9 Oct. 1975, photocopy kindly furnished me by Buchanan. The settlement was $22,500 plus legal costs of $1,022.60 (General Release, Melville H. Cane to Isham, 16 June 1931, at Yale; bill of legal costs in IFP, TA, p. 91 n. 15).

Van Alen becomes joint owner] TA, pp. 93–94.

Lady Talbot charges breach of faith] Letter, Lady Talbot to Isham, 27 Sept. 1929 (TFP, TA, p. 83).

Isham's promise to respect Lady Talbot's censorship] Letter, Isham to Lady Talbot (TFP). Copy at Yale made at Abbeylea, 21 May 1961, by R. F. Metzdorf.

p. 111]
Lady Talbot's letters assume Isham's acceptance of censorship] Letter, Lady Talbot to Isham, 9 Dec. 1927 (ITC).

Isham expresses approval of a policy of censorship] Letter, Isham to Lady Talbot, 7 Dec. 1927 (ITC).

"One possible decision"] TA, p. 83.

Lady Talbot's suppressions unworkable] Letter, Isham to Lady Talbot, 28 Jan. 1930 (ITC).

The croquet-box discovery] Letter, Lady Talbot to Isham, 15 Apr. 1930 (ITC).

p. 112]
"Clip. A marker which may be clasped on a particular hoop to indicate it" (OED). The word was Lady Talbot's.

Isham interested, short of funds] Letter, Isham to Lady Talbot, 6 May 1930 (ITC).

Negotiations with Doubleday] TA, pp. 75, 80. My knowledge of the negotiations with Doubleday comes entirely from David Buchanan. He cites only the general source, "Correspondence in IFP".

p. 113]
Contract with Viking] Agreement between Isham and the Viking Press, Inc., 1 May 1930, at Yale.

Advances from Viking and Heinemann] As in note preceding this; also Agreement between Isham and William Heinemann, Ltd., dated 1930 (IFP, TA, pp. 94–95).

Proceeds from sale] £2,696. 10s. less commission (letter, Sotheby Parke Bernet & Co. to Mrs. Rachel McClellan, 25 Apr. 1978, at Yale).

Lady Talbot's reports] All ITC.

Isham fails in plea to get the *Hebrides* MS. free] Referred to by Lady Talbot in letter to Isham, 17 Sept. 1930; Lady Talbot wrote again on 17 Oct. 1930 (both ITC).

Negotiations over croquet-box papers] Letter, Isham to Lady Talbot, 21 July 1930; letter, Lady Talbot to Isham, 27 July 1930; letter, same to the same, reporting a transatlantic telephone conversation, 17 Sept. 1930; letter, same to the same, 17 Oct. 1930 (TFP, TA, pp. 96–97).

p. 114]
Costs of *Private Papers* vols. 1–9] IFP, TA, p. 98 n. 39.

"Black Tuesday"] The document is actually dated 1 October, but I remember that it had been awaiting Isham's signature for some time. The signing took place in the late afternoon. Isham was unusually abstracted, indeed appeared to be in a state of shock. Cane expressed sympathy, which I had to ask him to explain. I then learned that the bottom had dropped out of the stock market.

p. 115]
Arrangement with Guinzburg] Agreement between Isham and the Viking Press, 18 Oct. 1930 (IFP, TA, p. 98).

Isham's Glen Head Property] Letter, Newton to Adam, 9 Nov. 1927 (Hyde Collection, TA, p. 79 n. 115).

p. 116]
Further loan from Van Alen] Memorandum of Agreement between Isham and Van Alen, Feb. 1931 (IFP, TA, pp. 97–98).

"Latter half of 1930"] Letter, David Buchanan to F. A. Pottle, 18 Jan. 1978, at Yale.

p. 117]
"Expense, profit . . . "] Margaret B. Evans, in *Sat. Rev. Lit.* (25 July 1931) viii. 15.

p. 118]
Volumes sent to the dump] TA, pp. 109–10.

CHAPTER IX

p. 120]
"Property of a Lady"] Cable, Isham to Lord Talbot, 20 May 1932; letter, Lord Talbot to Isham, 20 May 1932 (TFP, TA, p. 103). Isham also sent a cable to C. G. des Graz of Sotheby & Co. and received both a cable and a letter in reply, all of the same date (ITC).

Identity of the "Lady"] TA, p. 104. I have seen among papers at Yale in 1978 a letter or telegram which I cannot now put my hand on saying that the "Lady" was either "Lawrence" or "Eliott". David Buchanan gives only a general reference to Scheuer (ibid. n. 65).

p. 121]
Mrs. Lawrence Eliott] Dora Flournoy Hopkins Eliott (Dowager Lady Eliott of Stobs) and Sir Arthur Eliott, Bt. of Stobs, *The Elliots*, 1974, pp. 105–07, 109–11; TA, Table IV, p. 355.

Willison portrait of Boswell] See C. B. Tinker and F. A. Pottle, *A New Portrait of James Boswell*, 1927.

Blanche as sole trustee] *The Elliots*, as in the second note back, pp. 109–15.

p. 122]
An important letter, 6 Dec. 1819] It contains a passage (the only one known to me) that would seem to confirm Mackenzie's report that Thomas Alexander Boswell "made an unsuitable marriage". See above, pp. 48–49.

p. 123]
"Preoccupation with the Boswell papers"]
TA, p. 99.

Isham's trust income] TA, p. 107 n. 75.

"The Isham slaughter"] Letter, Newton to
R. W. Chapman, 31 May 1933 (TA, p. 107).

Sold for $12] *The Renowned Library of Lt.-
Col. Ralph H. Isham*, American Art Association,
Anderson Galleries, 4 May 1933, Lot No. 10, p.
2. Marked copy at Yale.

Isham on radio, lectures] TA, p. 107.

$2,000 and the rest of the manuscripts]
TA, p. 108.

p. 124]
No popular edition until *Private Papers*
completed] Memorandum of Agreement signed by
Isham, Scott, and Rudge, 22 Dec. 1927, at Yale.

Trust account] "My idea about the handling of the money is this. I shall place it in a
Special Account in the banking house of Harris,
Upham & Company, 11 Wall Street, New York
City. I shall invest it and any interest or profit
from such investment I shall withdraw from the
Special Account; the principal to remain intact.
For your eventual benefit, should there be any loss
of the principal, I agree to replace it, and I shall
also instruct Harris, Upham, & Company to replace any such loss out of my regular account with
them. I believe this gives you as full protection as
you could wish" (Isham to F. A. Pottle, 18 June
1935. The third and fourth sentences should of
course be punctuated". . . to remain intact for
your eventual benefit. Should there be . . . .").
The release, which Isham sent me to sign and
return to W. E. Rudge, Inc., is dated 6 June 1935.
The second and last paragraph reads: "Colonel Isham having given me assurance of his willingness
to ensure me this protection in another way, satisfactory to me, I hereby release the firm of William
Edwin Rudge from all further responsibility to me
under that contract, and instruct you to turn the
money over to Colonel Isham" (both documents
in my personal file).

p. 125]
A new contract] Agreement between Isham
and the Viking Press, 10 Feb. 1936, at Yale.

p. 126]
Oxford Press] TA, p. 110, n. 99. David
Buchanan reports that by this arrangement the total cost to Isham of printing and binding 607 copies
of the book was £208. 3s. Even with Bennett's
stipend and mine added, the books cost Isham less
than $6 apiece—surely a bargain.

Hasty scribble] One of the full-page illustrations of TA: see p. 114.

Forbes and The Club] In DNB and elsewhere Forbes is erroneously credited with mem-
bership in The Club, no doubt because he served
as clerk for the famous Round Robin addressed to
Dr. Johnson on the subject of Goldsmith's epitaph.
Eight of the signatories of that document were, or
later became, members of The Club, but the occasion, as Forbes himself reported, was a dinner
at Sir Joshua Reynolds's (*Life* iii. 82–83).

p. 127]
A quantity of papers by or about Beattie]
Unless otherwise specified, everything that follows
till I give further notice is taken from, or based
on, Professor Claude Colleer Abbott's Introduction
(pp. xiii–xxvii) to his *Catalogue of Papers . . . Found
at Fettercairn House . . . 1930–1931*, 1936.

p. 128]
The Spalding Club's publications] *The Jac-
obite Cess Roll for the County of Aberdeen in 1715*,
Third Spalding Club, 1932; *The Valuation of the
County of Aberdeen for the Year 1667*, Third Spalding
Club, 1933. The latter is "printed from the orig-
inal manuscript (now at Fettercairn House) by per-
mission of Lord Clinton".

Apology to Abbott] I have not generally
called attention to places where I have corrected
the history of the papers I published in 1950, but
I should like to have a correction noted here. I
seriously misread (or under-read) Abbott's Introduction when I said that he went to Fettercairn
"hoping to find certain missing portions of the
manuscript of Forbes's *Life of James Beattie*", and
my misreading did the more harm by being picked
up and repeated in various accounts of wide circulation: Hamilton Basso's article in *Life* (4 Dec.
1950) and *Reader's Digest* (March 1951), Christopher Morley's Preface to McGraw-Hill's edition of
Boswell's London Journal, 1762–1763, 1950, and
the Publisher's, Note to William Heinemann's
edition of the same book. What I should have said

was that Abbott went to Fettercairn expecting to find Sir William Forbes's private papers, and hoping to find among them Boswell's letters to Forbes.

p. 129]

Abbott takes important papers to Aberdeen] I cease here to base the narrative on Abbott's Introduction. See above, the third note back.

Abbott's assistants] Besides Miss Davidson, his "chief helper", Abbott names two students at Aberdeen who gave him extensive assistance as "scribe" and in copying and indexing: A. D. Adam and Alexander Macdonald (Fettercairn *Cat.* p. x).

CHAPTER X

p. 130]

Negotiations with Milford] From this point until further notice, I base my narrative partly on TA, pp. 130–42, which in turn is based partly on "Fettercairn Papers", a five-page typed memorandum prepared in 1962 for David Buchanan from the files of the Clarendon Press by D. M. Davin, then Assistant Secretary, and partly on a twelve-page typescript, "The Devil Answers Even in Engines: R. W. Chapman and the Fettercairn Papers", which Davin, then Publisher of the Academic Division of the Oxford University Press, used as the basis of a talk at the Johnson Club in Mar. 1977. The latter typescript was sent me by Davin himself.

p. 133]

For five years] From this point I cease to draw on TA, pp. 130–42 and the typescript Davin sent to me (see preceding note) except as specifically stated.

p. 134]

"To see what happened"] Davin's typescript sent to me; TA, p. 132.

"Might not suffer"] TA, p. 132.

p. 135]

Four thousand hours] TA, p. 135 n. 52.

A card he could not play] TA, pp. 137–38 and n. 63.

"Clear that . . . ownership should be settled"] From a sheaf of comments he sent to me after reading the typescript of this History as it stood in 1961.

Abbott said to have wanted secrecy ended] TA, p. 138.

p. 136]

Isham "a pirate"] Reported to me orally by Chapman at Oxford in 1936.

"Humbly . . . grateful"] TA, pp. 138–39.

p. 137]

". . . from being broken up"] This and the two direct quotations following are quoted as I remember them from our conversation of 1936.

p. 138]

"unable to use"] TA, p. 140.

CHAPTER XI

p. 141]

Isham sails] Typed draft of cable in ITC. The *New York Times* for 21 Mar. 1936, p. 35, gives the date and hour of sailing, and the *New York Times* of 28 Mar. 1936, p. 18, the destination and hour of arrival: Plymouth, 6:00 a.m.

p. 142]

Not to be back before the end of May] Letter dated 30 Mar. 1936 (TFP, TA, p. 147).

Isham offers cooperation] Reported in a letter from Robinson to Lady Talbot, 1 Apr. 1936 (TFP, TA, pp. 147–48).

Isham comes home] Ibid. Robinson, in the letter just cited, says Isham plans to return to America. He was presumably there when he wrote the letter of 17 Apr., next mentioned.

Talbot should present his claim] Letter, Isham to Messrs. A. J. & A. Robinson, 17 Apr. 1936 (IFP, TA, p. 151).

Talbot decides to put in a claim] Letter, J. M. Howden to Lord Talbot, 13 Mar. 1936; letter, Sir Gilbert Eliott to Lady Talbot, 21 Mar. 1936 (both TFP, TA, p. 148); letter, Scott Moncrieff & Trail to E. M. Wedderburn, 30 Mar. 1936 (in Steedman Ramage & Co.'s papers, ibid.); Extract Decree of the Court of Session in Favour of E. M. Wedderburn, dated 27 Mar. and extracted 27 Apr. 1936 (ibid.).

p. 143]

Talbot claims] Letter, Scott Moncrieff & Trail to Wedderburn, 17 Sept. 1936 (Steedman Ramage & Co.'s papers, TA, p. 152).

Lady Talbot decides that Elizabeth's descendants have the best moral claim] Letter, Lady Talbot to Sir Gilbert Eliott, 7 Oct. 1936; letter, C. E. Cumberlege Ware to Lady Talbot, 30 Oct. 1936; letter, Lady Talbot to C. E. Cumberlege Ware, 30 Oct. 1936; letters between Lady Talbot and Robinson (all TFP, TA, pp. 151–53).

p. 144]

Isham comes to Dublin, opposes claim of Elizabeth Boswell's descendants] Letter, Lady Talbot to C. E. Cumberlege Ware, 30 Oct. 1936 (TFP, TA, p. 143 and n. 45).

Lady Talbot wants to keep Isham a friend] Letter, Lady Talbot to Robinson, 30 Nov. 1936 (ibid.).

Talbot assigns his claim to Isham] Letter, Lady Talbot to Sir Gilbert Eliott, 21 Apr. 1937 (TFP, TA, p. 154).

Cumberlege Ware] Letter, Lady Talbot to C. E. Cumberlege Ware, 30 Oct. 1936; letter, Lady Talbot to Isham, 9 Nov. 1936 (both TFP, ibid.).

p. 145]

E. P. Buchanan engaged; conference in London] Memorandum by Thackrah, 3 Nov. 1936 (TA, p. 155–56); Note of Conference with E. P. Buchanan and Thackrah, 14, Pall Mall, London, 6 Jan. 1937 (Steedman Ramage & Co.'s papers, TA, p. 160).

Sales of the new *Hebrides* in U.S.A.] My recollection of what I was told at the time at the Viking Press office.

Sales in Britain] Letter, N. M. Viney for William Heinemann, Ltd., to Rachel E. McClellan, 6 Mar. 1978, at Yale.

Agreements with Viking] Letter, Guinzburg to Isham, 18 Dec. 1936; Isham's docket on the same, 18 Dec. 1936 (both IFP, TA, p. 144).

p. 146]

Alistair Tayler] *Clan Chattan . . . Journal of the Clan Chattan Association,* No. 4 (1937) pp. 99–100. An appreciation of Tayler in the London *Times,* (17 Nov. 1937) p. 10b, refers to this address and says that Tayler "mentioned that in one house he had lighted on a collection of letters from James Boswell".

p. 147]

Conference in London] See above, the fifth note back.

p. 148]

Isham waits Lady Talbot's return] Steedman Ramage & Co.'s papers, TA, pp. 160–61.

Isham again at Malahide] TA, p. 161. Thackrah telephoned to Steedman Ramage & Co. on Friday 12 Mar. saying that Isham was going to Ireland "that week-end" (Steedman Ramage & Co.'s papers, ibid. n. 83).

Isham finds more Boswell papers] Lord Talbot mentioned the dispatch-box in his letter to the *Times.* See below, p.149. TA, pp. 162–63. Yale has lists establishing the date of acquisition of all papers permanently added to the Isham Collection after the printing of the *Isham Catalogue.* TA reports all items sold by Isham. For example, he afterwards sold the diary of Johnson and the Book of Company to Donald and Mary Hyde (ibid. nn. 87, 88).

Isham sails home] TA, p. 163.

p. 149]

Irresponsible stories of Isham's find] Correspondence between E. P. Buchanan and Thackrah and press cuttings in Steedman Ramage & Co.'s papers (TA, p. 164).

Isham tries to get the Talbots to say that he found the dispatch-box in the kitchen] Letter, Lady Talbot to R. F. Metzdorf, 16 Apr. 1960, at Yale.

Isham's yarn about the Grant to Veronica] I indeed reported in a learned article that he had found the paper himself: "Notes on the Importance of Private Legal Documents for the Writing of Biography and Literary History", *Proceedings of the American Philosophical Society,* (Aug. 1962) cvi. 329–30.

E. P. Buchanan collects evidence] TA, p. 165 (sources listed nn. 97, 98).

Claims lodged] Interlocutors of Lord Stevenson, 17 Mar. and 8 May 1937 (Steedman Ramage & Co.'s papers, TA, p. 166). See also TA, pp. 154–55.

p. 150]
Isham assists with evidence, returns home] Steedman Ramage & Co.'s papers, TA, p. 167.

I help Isham's case] TA, p. 160.

Isham marries for the third time] *New York Times,* (2 Nov. 1938) p. 20. *Burke's Peerage,* 1953. She died in 1972 (Debrett).

Cable to me] Pencilled text of cable delivered by telephone to me at Davenport College, Yale. The student who took the message over the telephone got the name of the bride as "Vest Countess Churchill" (my personal file).

Court directs claims to be printed] Interlocutors of Lord Stevenson, 23 June 1937, and of Lord Robertson, 7 July 1937 (TA, p. 167).

p. 151]
Lady Boswell's purchase of furniture and library at Auchinleck] He did not find the crucial document. See below, p. 256, 10th n.

Lady Boswell's will] Disposition and Settlement by Dame Grace Cuming or Boswell, 5 Apr. 1860 (TA, pp. 167–68).

Will of James Boswell the younger] See p. 236, last n.

E. P. Buchanan's systematic readings] TA, p. 168.

Isham notifies the Cumberland Infirmary] Memorandum as to points dealt with at Consultation with Counsel, 21 Sept. 1937; letter, E. P. Buchanan to E. M. Wedderburn, 20 Oct. 1937; the solicitors for the Infirmary reported 9 Nov.

1937 that they were lodging a claim (all Steedman Ramage & Co.'s papers, TA, pp. 169–70).

Seemingly endless delays] Letter, E. P. Buchanan to Thackrah, 24 Sept. 1937 (Steedman Ramage & Co.'s papers, TA, p. 170); Interlocutor of Lord Stevenson, 13 Oct. 1937 (ibid.).

Date extended] Interlocutors of Lord Stevenson, 10 Nov. 1937, 8 Dec. 1937, 5 Jan. 1938, 2 Feb. 1938, 2 Mar. 1938, 23 Mar. 1938, 4 May 1938 (TA, pp. 170–72).

Isham in Europe] Letter, Thackrah to E. P. Buchanan, 11 Nov. 1937: "Colonel Isham telephoned to us yesterday morning to inform us that he had arrived in England and was intending to spend the winter in Europe" (Steedman Ramage & Co.'s papers, TA, p. 170); letter, David Buchanan to F. A. Pottle, 18 April 1978, at Yale.

Isham in Edinburgh] Letter, David Buchanan, cited in the note preceding this.

E. P. Buchanan researches Mrs. Mounsey] TA, p. 169.

p. 152]
Mrs. Vassall] Mrs. Vassall had died without issue so far back as 1890. Her settlements had left the bulk of her estate to three trustees for the paying of certain legacies and annuities, one of which was to a grand-nephew and another to a grand-niece. The trustee had power to elect successors (there were in fact three trustees still acting), and would have had legal title to claim in Mrs. Vassall's name (Mrs. Vassall's Settlements, 19 Apr. 1889, 14 Mar. 1890, 4 Apr. 1890, Scottish Record Office RD5/1890/vol. 2314).

Mrs. Hailey claims] Letter, E. M. Wedderburn's solicitors to E. P. Buchanan, 15 Feb. 1939 (TA, p. 171). Mrs. Hailey claimed as great-granddaughter of Boswell's youngest daughter, Elizabeth. Elizabeth died in 1814, leaving three sons (Robert Cramond, James Paoli, Bruce) and one daughter (Elizabeth Margaret Montgomerie). Robert Cramond and James Paoli both died young and unmarried in 1821 and 1820 respectively. William Boswell died in 1841. Of Elizabeth's children, this left Bruce, who never married and died in 1855 (*Gent. Mag.* Dec. 1855, ii. 669), and Elizabeth Margaret Montgomerie, who married John Williams, had a daughter Elizabeth Anne

Williams, whom she outlived, and died after 1871. Elizabeth Anne Williams, who died in 1871, married the Rev. Charles Cumberlege and left four children: Charles Edward Cumberlege Ware, Mrs. Edith Marriot, Mrs. Elizabeth Hailey, and Miss Katharine Augusta Cumberlege (TA, Table III, p. 354). Miss Katharine Augusta Cumberlege died 21 Feb. 1936 (TA, p. 152 n. 41), just before the discovery of the Fettercairn papers was announced. See above, p. 143.

Isham appears in Edinburgh] Letter, E. P. Buchanan to Isham, 13·Apr. 1938 (Steedman Ramage & Co.'s papers, TA, p. 215).

Record closed] Interlocutor of Lord Keith, 11 May 1938 (TA, p. 173).

Date of 12 July 1938 set] TA, p. 173.

Isham buys out Mrs. Vassall's trustees] TA, pp. 218–19.

"Dictated the presentation of his case"] TA, p. 215.

p. 153]
Fettercairn Cause decided] TA, pp. 219–20.

CHAPTER XII

p. 154]
Clinton's case] Closed Record in Action of Multiplepoinding and Exoneration . . . Ernest Maclagan Wedderburn . . . against . . . Lord Clinton and Others, Defenders, 11 May 1938. (Scottish Record Office: Unextracted Process 1785 of 1950, photocopy at Yale.)

Isham's case] Ibid. pp. 13–20.

p. 155]
Papers passed to Sir James from his mother, she having purchased the library of Auchinleck House] It would have been much more cogent to argue that the papers passed to Sir James by gift of his mother, she having purchased the whole effects of Auchinleck House. See above, p. 237, 5th n. Isham's lawyers, however, found proof only that Lady Boswell purchased the carriage, the library, and the furniture. David Buchanan turned up the crucial document only years after the decision of

the Fettercairn Cause (TA, pp. 205–06 and nn. 108, 109).

Case of Mrs. Vassall's trustees] Ibid. pp. 20–24.

Case of the Cumberland Infirmary] Ibid. pp. 24–28.

Mrs. Hailey's claim] Ibid. pp. 28–30. The line of descent is given above, p. 255, last n. No wills were found for Elizabeth Boswell and her husband William Boswell, and it was assumed that both of them died intestate. Mrs. Hailey's lawyers did not investigate the bearing of possible testamentary dispositions by Robert Cramond Boswell and James Paoli Boswell, indeed, did not list them at all, but claimed one half of Elizabeth's share for Mrs. Williams, assuming apparently that the other half may have gone to the one son they list but do not name, Bruce Boswell. The lawyers also made no attempt to establish whether Elizabeth's family succeeded to any further share of the papers on the death of Euphemia. From Mrs. Williams on, the lawyers were able to present testamentary evidence. She divided her residuary estate between Mrs. Hailey and Miss Katharine A. Cumberlege; Miss Cumberlege left everything to Mrs. Hailey. Mrs. Hailey's lawyers simply did not have time to make proper research. One thing they *did* establish was that C. E. Cumberlege Ware (at one time Lady Talbot's favourite candidate: above, p. 144) had no right to any property which might have been Elizabeth Boswell's.

Mrs. Vassall's case not pleaded] TA, p. 219.

Claims of Lord Clinton and Mrs. Hailey dismissed] Typed copy of Lord Stevenson's opinion in the hands of Messrs. Mackenzie and Kermack, W. S., Edinburgh, solicitors for the Judicial Factor and Lord Clinton. Photocopy at Yale. See also *The Scotsman*, 13 July and 20 Aug. 1938. Abridged text of the opinion in TA, pp. 223–25.

p. 156]
Lord Stevenson's judgement] Ibid.

p. 157]
David Buchanan] Page 47 of typewritten comments sent to me in the spring of 1979.

Deed of renunciation] "I do hereby renounce the right and privilege of entering heir of line or in general to the said deceased Sir Alexander Boswell my father, with all benefit or advantage that might accrue to me from such entry" (Renunciation by Sir James Boswell . . . to be heir to the deceased Sir Alexander Boswell, his father. Dated 22 Oct. 1831. Reg. B. of C. and S. 10 Dec. 1832. ILT: List B).

p. 158]
"I am confident"] TA, p. 210 n. 121; p. 54 of David Buchanan's notes referred to in the last note but one.

"It is very difficult"] Ibid. p. 44.

p. 159]
Agreement to delay action] "MESSAGE FROM EDINBURGH by 'Phone 5.45 p.m. 2/12/38. Lord Clinton's Solicitors will do everything to delay the hearing until R. H. I's return. Decision of costs to be given in January. Decision on division to be held up until the end of February" (IFC). I take this to be a message received by Denton Hall & Burgin in London and reported to Isham by post or cable after he had sailed. David Buchanan says he returned to the United States "in late November", and Isham himself gives the month as November in a letter of the following March (TA, pp. 227, 231).

Isham explores possibility of sale to a university] TA, pp. 226–27.

Hearing set, Isham not disposed to attend] TA, pp. 235–36 and nn. 55, 56, 57.

Abbott intimates intention of claiming, Isham goes to Edinburgh] TA, pp. 227–28, 231, 236 and n. 44.

p. 160]
Consequences of Abbott's threat] TA, p. 229.

Hearing postponed] TA, p. 236 and nn. 57, 59, 60, 62, 63.

Isham attempts to come to terms with the Infirmary] TA, pp. 230–35.

Offer and counter-offer] TA, p. 235.

Isham goes home] TA, p. 236.

Lord Stevenson available, Isham non-committal] TA, pp. 237–38.

Three cables] 1 May 1940, 7 Jan. 1941, June 1941 (Steedman Ramage & Co.'s papers, TA, pp. 240, 245, 246 and nn. 6, 25, 33).

Index to *Private Papers* published] *Publishers' Weekly*, (31 July 1937) cxxxii. 337.

p. 161]
"Lying out their fees"] TA, p. 247.

Yale needed a definite figure] TA, pp. 239–40.

Offer from the Cumberland Infirmary] Cable, Isham to E. P. Buchanan, 1 May 1940; letter, E. P. Buchanan to Isham, 15 July 1940 (both in Steedman Ramage & Co.'s papers, TA, p. 240).

Van Alen] TA, pp. 93, 98, 240.

Cryptic communication from Burgin] Cable, Burgin to Isham, 10 Jan. 1941 (IFP, TA, p. 240).

Three months] It was dated 17 Oct. 1940 (TFP); Burgin posted it to Isham with a covering letter dated 15 Jan. 1941 (IFP, TA, p. 241).

Exchange with Burgin] Isham cabled on 10 Jan. 1941, Burgin sent an answering cable on 12 Jan. 1941 (IFP, TA, p. 241).

Lady Talbot's report] Letter, Lady Talbot to Burgin, 17 Oct. 1940, copied without date in letter, Burgin to Isham, 15 Jan. 1941; letters, Lady Talbot to Isham, 21 Mar. and 4 June 1942 (all ITC); letter, Lady Talbot to Pottle, 13 Aug. 1950, at Yale. In her letter of 17 Oct. 1940 Lady Talbot said that the second case was "full of m.s.s. previous to the Biographer", in that of 4 June 1942, that the papers in that case were "all MSS. of Sir Alexander". I believe they were of both sorts, as stated in the text. For another discrepancy, see the note following this.

p. 162]
1917] In a later letter (4 June 1942, printed in full, TA, pp. 248–49) she said the newspapers were of the year 1915.

p. 163]
Isham instructs Burgin to claim the new
papers] Cable night letter, Isham to Burgin, 21
Jan. 1941 (ITC).

Burgin had not waited] Cable, Burgin to
A. J. & A. Robinson (Talbot's Dublin solicitors),
14 Jan. 1941; letter, same to same, 15 Jan. 1941
(TFP, TA, p. 244); cable night letter, Burgin and
E. P. Buchanan to Isham, 8 Feb. 1941 (ITC).

Talbot's solicitors repudiate claim] Letter,
A. J. & A. Robinson to Denton Hall & Burgin,
30 Jan. 1941 (Steedman Ramage & Co.'s papers,
TA, p. 244).

Action would have to be taken in Eire]
Letter, Burgin to E. P. Buchanan, 29 Jan. 1941;
letter, E. P. Buchanan to Burgin, 5 Feb. 1941
(both in Steedman Ramage & Co.'s papers, TA,
pp. 244–45).

Lawyers tell Isham he has no enforceable
claim] Memorandum of conference in Steedman
Ramage & Co.'s papers, TA, p. 245. Wardlaw
Burnet died unexpectedly a few days later (ibid.
n. 24; *Fac. Adv.*, p. 25).

Isham asks for firm figure from Cumberland
Infirmary] Cable, Isham to E. P. Buchanan, 7 Jan.
1941 (Steedman Ramage & Co.'s papers, TA, p.
245).

"An unfortunate decision"] Letter, J. & J.
Galletly to Steedman Ramage & Co., received 17
Jan. 1941 (Steedman Ramage & Co.'s Business
Ledger, TA, p. 245).

Tinker had reported] Letter, Tinker to R.
B. Adam, 9 Nov. 1925 (Hyde Collection, TA, p.
53). He reported the same thing in other accounts
of his visit to Malahide, e.g. in a written statement
he made for Christopher Morley in 1950.

p. 164]
Lady Talbot had no memory of it] TA, p.
241 n. 16. When Lady Talbot, in the spring of
1960, read the typescript of the present History
as it then stood, she expressed shocked disbelief
of Tinker's report of being told in 1925 that there
were still two unopened cases of Boswell papers at
Malahide: "Lower down on *page 57* it says I said
I knew of two unopened cases of papers. There
were papers other than those in the ebony cabinet,

I probably mentioned them, they were shown soon
afterwards to Colonel Isham. But the words put
into my mouth by Professor Tinker sound as if I
already knew of the two cases found in 1940, and
I did not know about them until they were found
in 1940" (letter, Lady Talbot to Robert Metzdorf,
16 Apr. 1960, at Yale).

A nominal figure] Letter, Isham to Lady
Talbot, 5 Mar. 1942 (ITC).

Charge of ill-usage] Letter, Lady Talbot to
Isham, 21 Mar. 1942 (TFP, TA, p. 247).

She told Spingarn] Letter, Lady Talbot to
Spingarn, 24 Apr. 1942 (TFP, TA, p. 247). In
this very long letter of instructions, Lady Talbot
gave a detailed account of her dealings with Isham
from 1926. The letter therefore constitutes an important source, and is several times cited by David
Buchanan as "Spingarn Letter". He gives a brief
biographical notice of Spingarn, TA, p. 247 n. 41.

More friendly terms] Letter, Isham to Lady
Talbot, 7 May 1942; letter, Lady Talbot to Isham,
4 June 1942 (both TFP, TA, pp. 248–49).

p. 165]
His daughter] Samantha Isham Gulden
died on 21 July 1941 at the age of twenty-six (*New
York Times*, 22 July 1941, p. 20). She left two
children.

Van Alen] Letter, Van Alen to Isham, 25
Feb. 1942; same to the same, 7 Oct. 1942 (both
IFP, TA, p. 250).

Isham reopens negotiations with E. P.
Buchanan] Letter, Isham to E. P. Buchanan, 7
Mar. 1945; letter, Steedman Ramage & Co. to
Isham, 11 Apr. 1945 (both in Steedman Ramage
& Co.'s papers, TA, p. 251).

Burgin died] 16 Aug. 1945 (*Times*, 17
Aug. 1945, p. 7d).

p. 166]
Chapman granted access in Edinburgh]
Letter, Chapman to Isham, 25 Sept. 1945; same
to the same, 21 Nov. 1945; same to the same, 21
Mar. 1946; same to the same, 28 May 1946; same
to the same, 22 June 1946 (all IFP, TA, p. 265);
letter, Isham to Pottle, 19 Oct. 1945; letter, Pottle
to Isham, 21 Dec. 1945 (both in my private file).

Johnson letters sent to the Bodleian for Chapman] Letter, Mackenzie & Kermack to Steedman Ramage & Co., 20 Dec. 1946 (Steedman Ramage & Co.'s papers, TA, p. 265).

To Lady Talbot and to the Cumberland Infirmary] Letter, Isham to Lady Talbot, 19 Oct. 1945 (TFP); letter, Isham to trustees of Cumberland Infirmary, 19 Oct. 1945 (Steedman Ramage & Co.'s papers, TA, pp. 251–52).

Guinzburg and Isham] Letter, Pottle to Isham, 24 Nov. 1945 (IFP); same letter to Guinzburg, same date. I advised against publication until Isham should at least have obtained the important London Journal of 1762–63 in the Fettercairn hoard.

p. 167]
Proposal and counter-proposal] Letter, Lady Talbot to Isham, 24 Oct. 1945; letter, Isham to Lady Talbot, 17 Jan. 1946; letter, Lady Talbot to Isham, 24 Jan. 1946; letter, Isham to Lady Talbot, 13 Feb. 1946 (all ITC); letter, Pottle to Lady Talbot, 25 Mar. 1946 (TFP, TA, p. 252).

Lady Talbot accepts offer of £2,000] Letter, Spingarn to Lady Talbot, 28 Feb. 1946; letter, Lady Talbot to Spingarn, 5 Mar. 1946 (both TFP, TA, p. 253). The fragments of journal were posted 15 Mar. 1946: Lady Talbot to Isham of that date (ITC).

Down to £1,750] Letter, Spingarn to Lady Talbot, 21 Mar. 1946; letter, Lady Talbot to Spingarn, undated; letter, Spingarn to Lady Talbot, 23 May 1946; letter, Lady Talbot to Spingarn, 31 May 1946; letter, Spingarn to Lady Talbot, 7 June 1946; Agreement, 1 Aug. 1946, between Lord Talbot and Isham (all TFP, TA, pp. 253–55).

David Buchanan] TA, p. 253.

CHAPTER XIII

p. 168]
Sale of *Private Papers*] IFP, TA, p. 255 and n. 75.

p. 169]
Isham sells the Hydes a manuscript] Letter, Isham to Hyde, 20 Aug. 1946 (in possession of Mrs. Donald F. Hyde; TA, pp. 255–56).

p. 170]
Stable-loft papers arrive] TA, p. 256 from "a lengthy correspondence on the subject in IFP and TFP"; letter, Isham to Thackrah, 17 Oct. 1946 (IFP).

Papers held up at Boston] Elizabeth Kay, "The First American Birthday for Dr. Johnson", in *Four Oaks Farm,* ed. Gabriel Austin, privately printed, Somerville, New Jersey, 1967, pp. 96–98 (TA, pp. 256–57).

"Documents of all kinds"] TA, p. 259. My enumeration of the major items also follows Buchanan's useful summary (ibid. pp. 258–59).

David Nichol Smith] David Nichol Smith Memorial Seminar, Canberra, 1966, *Studies in the Eighteenth Century,* ed. R. F. Brissenden, 1968, pp. 15–16.

p. 171]
I miss the party at Four Oaks Farm] From this point to the end of the first paragraph on p. 174, I follow closely two memoranda that I wrote in the early autumn of 1947 for the late James T. Babb, Librarian of Yale, and the late Edgar S. Furniss, Dean of the Graduate School at Yale, respectively.

I visit Isham in New York] It was shortly before 11 Oct. 1946. Letter, Babb to Isham of that date (my private file).

p. 172]
Isham's announced policy] "I feel exactly as you do about Chapman. Permission should be given him to publish the Johnson letters, and for my part I shall grant it gladly" (letter, Isham to Pottle, 19 Oct. 1945, my private file).

I expected a friendly reply] He encouraged me to: "I appreciate your long and informative letter of November 22nd which is most helpful. First of all, I want to assure you that Colonel Isham has no desire to be other than completely friendly with you about the entire matter. . . . Colonel Isham's primary desire is to see that the papers are available to scholars. Yet you so well know he has a valuable property interest which he must protect. It is important to reconcile these two considerations at the present time, which I believe to be both proper and possible" (letter, Hyde to Pottle, 26 Nov. 1946, my private file).

Early in April] Probably about 12 Apr. I wrote to Hyde on 17 Apr. summarizing the things I wanted to talk about, and he replied on 22 Apr. He again avoided saying anything that would imply that the "scholarly effort" I was trying to get instructions for was work that Isham had hired me to do. But he again ended on a friendly note: "I feel confident that it all can be worked out to everyone's satisfaction."

p. 173]

Correcting some things] I wrote twice, 2 and 12 May, as Hyde's reply indicates. Probably the letter of 2 May was merely a brief note covering the copy of the contract, that of 12 May an extended statement. I have copy of neither. Both may have been manuscript.

p. 174]

Isham writes directly to the Cumberland Infirmary] Letter, Isham to trustees of Cumberland Infirmary, 19 Oct. 1945 (Steedman Ramage & Co.'s papers, TA p. 251–52).

Trustees ask £2,250] Letter, T. D. Harston (the Infirmary's solicitor) to Isham, 11 Jan. 1946 (Steedman Ramage & Co.'s papers, TA, p. 262).

E. P. Buchanan back at work] Letter, E. P. Buchanan to Isham, 4 Jan. 1946 (Steedman Ramage & Co.'s papers, TA, p. 262).

Negotiations turned over to E. P. Buchanan] Letter, Isham to E. P. Buchanan, 6 Feb. 1946; letter, Isham to Harston, 14 Feb. 1946 (Steedman Ramage & Co.'s papers, TA, p. 262).

Cumberland Infirmary might be nationalized] Letter, Thackrah to Isham, 23 May 1946 (Steedman Ramage & Co.'s papers, TA, p. 262).

Thackrah gets conditional assurance] Letter, Isham to E. P. Buchanan, 12 Apr. 1946; letter, E. P. Buchanan to Isham, 24 Apr. 1946 (both in Steedman Ramage & Co.'s papers); correspondence with Thackrah in Steedman Ramage & Co.'s papers, TA, p. 263.

p. 175]

E. P. Buchanan requests £2,700] Letter, J. & R. A. Robertson to Steedman Ramage & Co., 10 Oct. 1946; letter, Isham to Thackrah, 15 Nov. 1946; letter, Isham to E. P. Buchanan, 26 Nov. 1946; cable, Isham to E. P. Buchanan, 9 Dec.

1946 (all in Steedman Ramage & Co.'s papers, TA, p. 263).

Isham gets a loan of $12,000] Letter, Hyde to Isham, 7 Jan. 1947 (IFP); other correspondence in IFP; promissory notes in IFP, TA, p. 264.

Papers properly Clinton's to be sorted out] Letter, Steedman Ramage & Co. to J. & J. Galletly, 15 Dec. 1946; same to the same, 21 Jan. 1947; letter, J. & J. Galletly to Steedman Ramage & Co., 27 Jan. 1947 (all in Steedman Ramage & Co.'s papers, TA, p. 265).

Dr. C. A. Malcolm engaged] Letter, Steedman Ramage & Co. to Malcolm, 28 Jan. 1947; report by Malcolm, 28 Feb. 1947; letter, Steedman Ramage & Co. to J. & J. Galletly, 21 Mar. 1947 (all in Steedman Ramage & Co.'s papers, TA, pp. 266–68).

Settlement with Infirmary completed] Letter, E. G. M. Fletcher of Denton Hall & Burgin to E. P. Buchanan, 14 Feb. 1947 (Steedman Ramage & Co.'s papers); other correspondence in Steedman Ramage & Co.'s papers (TA, p. 268).

E. P. Buchanan's proposed strategy: £2,500 needed] Letter, E. P. Buchanan to Isham, 11 Aug. 1947; "Estimate of approximate costs" (both in Steedman Ramage & Co.'s papers, TA, p. 268).

p. 176]

Hyde finds me in the wrong] Letter, Hyde to Pottle, 21 May 1947 (my personal file).

Willingness to consider concessions] Letter, Pottle to Hyde, 24 May 1947 (my private file).

p. 177]

Hyde declares the contract broken] Letter, Hyde to Pottle, 23 June 1947 (my private file).

A letter of quiet protest] Letter, Pottle to Isham. The retained draft in my private file bears only the date July 1947.

p. 178]

Heyward Isham and the Hydes see the Fettercairn papers] Letter, Mackenzie & Kermack to Steedman Ramage & Co., 25 July 1947; E. P. Buchanan to Isham, 18 Sept. 1947 (both, with other correspondence, in Steedman Ramage & Co.'s papers, TA, p. 269).

Isham sells manuscripts to Hydes] Letter, Hyde to Isham, 4 Feb. 1948; letter, R. J. Barry to Isham, 10 Nov. 1947; formal letters between Isham and Mr. and Mrs. Hyde, 12 Mar. 1948 (all IFP); cable, Isham to E. P. Buchanan, 9 Mar. 1948 (Steedman Ramage & Co.'s papers, TA, pp. 269–70).

Isham impatient for delivery] Cable, Isham to E. P. Buchanan, 14 May 1948 (Steedman Ramage & Co.'s papers, TA, pp. 270–71).

David Buchanan's summary] TA, p. 271.

Death-duties] Cable, E. P. Buchanan to Isham, 15 May 1948; letter, E. P. Buchanan to Isham, 22 May 1948; letter by Estate Duty Office to Mackenzie & Kermack, 28 May 1948 (all in Steedman Ramage & Co.'s papers, TA, pp. 271–72).

p. 179]
Violent cable] Draft in Heyward Isham's hand in IFP; photocopy furnished me by David Buchanan.

Transatlantic telephone call] E. P. Buchanan reported this telephone call in a letter to Hyde, 7 July 1948 (Steedman Ramage & Co.'s papers, TA, p. 272).

Terse and angry cable from Isham] Cable, Isham to E. P. Buchanan, 29 June 1948 (Steedman Ramage & Co.'s papers, TA, p. 272).

Mysterious cable from Isham] Cable, Isham to E. P. Buchanan, 29 June 1948 (Steedman Ramage & Co.'s papers, TA, pp. 272–73).

p. 180]
E. P. Buchanan's generous offer] Cable night letter, E. P. Buchanan to Isham, 1 July 1948 (IFC).

Isham gratefully accepts] Cable night letter, Isham to E. P. Buchanan, 3 July 1948 (Steedman Ramage & Co.'s papers, photocopy furnished me by David Buchanan).

Death-duties paid] Cable, E. P. Buchanan to Isham, 5 July 1948 (copy in Steedman Ramage & Co.'s papers, TA, p. 273).

Hydes and Heyward Isham] Information furnished to David Buchanan by Mary Hyde, confirmed by her journal (TA, p. 273).

Bills paid, papers packed] Steedman Ramage & Co.'s papers, TA, p. 273.

Final interlocutor] David Buchanan prints it in full, TA, p. 274 n. 167.

Papers go on the *Queen Mary*] TA, p. 275; information furnished to David Buchanan by Mary Hyde, confirmed by her journal; fifteen documents in IFC, including the export licence and copy of Lord Sorn's interlocutor.

Abbott does not file suit] All the final arrangements were shadowed by fear that Abbott would hold everything up by bringing suit, but Isham had guessed right: if Abbott had been planning to go to law, he would have done it sooner. In 1961 or thereabouts Abbott wrote for this History a long note, part of which, I think, should be published: "When started, the *Catalogue* was a record of papers I was to edit or superintend as general editor. It had, of course, to be finished even when litigation made everything doubtful. The legal action was only possible so quickly because the *Catalogue* was ready. It was used as the authoritative record of all the documents that were in question. Without it there must have been great delay and considerable expense in preparing a suitable record. It was vaguely understood that if the findings were against Lord Clinton, the Fettercairn papers would bear some of my expenses. I was therefore advised to consult an agent, who recommended a claim against the adjudged owners or owner of the papers. Counsel's opinion was nicely balanced. The claim seemed, and still seems, to me both just and reasonable. On first consulting my agent I had made clear that I had no intention of becoming part of a contested suit, and I named to him a modest sum for expenses beyond which I was not prepared to go. It should be sufficient, I thought, to register my claim effectively."

CHAPTER XIV

p. 182]
Invitation] David Buchanan reproduces this invitation as an illustration, TA, p. 278.

Loan repaid, releases] All these releases are at Yale.

Brandt and Brandt, Heinemann, Van Alen] TA, p. 287.

Guinzburg] TA, pp. 285–86.

p. 183]
"Pottle must have felt hurt"] TA, p. 285.

p. 184]
Isham said to be weary] Ibid.

David Buchanan's list] TA, pp. 346–48. The number is only approximate, for some of Buchanan's "items" are in fact "lots":e.g. item 2, which consists of 119 letters by Johnson.

p. 185]
Agreement signed] Memorandum of Agreement . . . between R. H. Isham . . . and Yale University, 28 June 1949, at Yale. Buchanan lists the retained pieces, TA, pp. 342–44.

Closing in New Haven] Deed of Sale, R. H. Isham to Yale University, 22 July 1949, at Yale; Mrs. Hyde's diary, Tues. 19, Wed. 20 July 1949 (TA, pp. 290–93); letter, Isham to E. P. Buchanan, 30 Aug. 1949 (Steedman Ramage & Co.'s papers, TA, p. 293). Mrs. Hyde's engagement calendar shows that her diary was misdated by two days (letter, Mary Hyde to F. A. Pottle, 8 Jan. 1980, at Yale).

Isham authorized to buy remaining portion of MS. of *Life*] Letter, F. W. Hilles and H. W. Liebert to Isham, 6 Mar. 1950, confirming terms apparently agreed on verbally some time before (Hyde's legal papers, TA, p. 294).

Isham offers £8,000] Letter, Isham to Spingarn, 15 Dec. 1949 (IFP, TA, p. 295).

Lady Talbot accepts] Letter, Spingarn to Lady Talbot, 11 May 1950 (TFP, TA, p. 295).

Isham asks Hydes to go to Ireland] "Remarks" by Hyde at the annual Johnson dinner, Grolier Club, 18 Sept. 1950 (TA, pp. 295–96).

p. 186]
Lady Talbot has some oddments] Letter, Lady Talbot to Hyde, 18 May 1950 (IFP, TA, p. 296).

Isham pays £10,500] Letter, Hyde to Isham, 2 June 1950 (IFP, TA, p. 300).

Isham sells to Yale for $51,650] Bill of Sale and Assignment by . . . R. H. Isham to Yale

University, 25 July 1950; Memorandum of Agreement . . . between Yale University . . . and McGraw-Hill Book Company, 28 July 1950. Both at Yale. McGraw-Hill paid one third, the Old Dominion Foundation two thirds. The correspondence with the Old Dominion Foundation is undoubtedly at Yale, but I have not consulted it.

Lord Talbot's jocularity misunderstood] "Any papers I may have told a story about finding during a house party had been previously discovered in my predecessor's lifetime. I was no doubt being facetious, as I sometimes am" (seventh Lord Talbot to R. F. Metzdorf, 24 July 1960, at Yale).

p. 187]
Isham sends papers bearing on *London Journal*] I find no documentation of this in the files of the Boswell Office, but can personally vouch for all of it except the precise month "June". The transaction was probably made by telephone and personal delivery of the papers by common friend.

EPILOGUE THE FIRST

p. 188]
Fifteen documents given by the Hydes] Marion S. Pottle's pencilled inventory (Yale); Messrs. Hodgson's *Catalogue* (No. 10 of 1951–52), at Yale.

£12] Information furnished by Mrs. Donald F. Hyde. The Hydes retained at least one piece from the lot: the letter of William Upcott, 4 June 1825, mentioned in the description.

p. 189]
S. C. Roberts informs Yale of sixty Boswell letters] Letter, S. C. Roberts to F. A. Pottle, 22 June 1953; letter, same to the same, 8 July 1953. Both at Yale.

Alexander Bruce Roxburgh] Destination in the Entail of Auchinleck (A 4.51); Jasper John Boswell's unpublished second volume of the *Boswell History* (photocopy at Yale); *Burke's Landed Gentry*, 1937, "Boswell, formerly of Auchinleck"; letter, D. R. Boswell to F. A. Pottle, 5 Mar. 1979; *Times,* 18 Mar. 1953 (10b), 27 Aug. 1977 (16b); *Who Was Who*, 1951–60.

Cost of £300] Letter, R. F. Metzdorf to Comptroller, Yale, 25 Jan. 1954; letter, R. F.

Metzdorf to Mrs. Edith Roxburgh, 25 Jan. 1954; letter, R. F. Metzdorf to S. C. Roberts, 25 Jan. 1954; letter, Edith Roxburgh to F. W. Hilles, 12 Feb. 1954. All at Yale.

Roberts reports the incident] *TLS*, (1 Jan. 1954) liii. 16; letter, R. F. Metzdorf to S. C. Roberts, 25 Jan. 1954, at Yale.

Roberts given one letter] This letter (30 July 1792) was sold at Sotheby's (Lot 301) on 14 Mar. 1979, and was purchased for Yale on the Tinker fund.

p. 190]
Liebert gives Auchinleck "writes"] Marion S. Pottle's pencilled inventory, at Yale.

More "writes" from Stonehill] Ibid.

August 1955] Ibid.

p. 191]
In 1953 I visit Lord Crawford] Letter, Lord Crawford to F. A. Pottle, 19 July 1953; letter, same to the same, 22 July 1953; notes of mine written on verso of the latter. All at Yale.

Letters between the Hon. Andrew Erskine and James Boswell, Esq.] See *Lit. Car.* pp. 19–21.

Letters at first not for sale] Letter, Lord Crawford to F. A. Pottle, 20 Aug. 1953; letter, F. A. Pottle to Mrs. Anstruther, 16 Oct. 1953; letter, Mrs. Anstruther to F. A. Pottle, 19 Oct. 1953; letter, same to the same, 2 Nov. 1953. All at Yale.

Sir Ralph Anstruther consents to sell] Letter, Sir Ralph Anstruther to F. A. Pottle, 3 May 1954; letter, F. A. Pottle to Sir Ralph Anstruther, 17 May 1954; letter, F. A. Pottle to Lord Crawford, 17 Nov. 1954; letter, Lord Crawford to F. A. Pottle, 24 Nov. 1954; letter, F. A. Pottle to Lord Crawford, 6 Dec. 1954; letter, Sir Ralph Anstruther to F. A. Pottle, 1 Jan. 1955; letter, F. A. Pottle to Sir Ralph Anstruther, 11 Mar. 1955; letter, Sir Ralph Anstruther to F. A. Pottle, 15 Apr. 1955; letter, F. A. Pottle to Sir Ralph Anstruther, 21 Apr. 1955. All at Yale.

William Beattie] Letter, R. F. Metzdorf to Sir Ralph Anstruther, 2 June 1955; letter, Mrs. Anstruther to R. F. Metzdorf, 9 June 1955; letter,

same to the same, 28 June 1955; letter, same to the same, 9 July 1955. All at Yale.

Letters arrived at Yale] Letter, R. F. Metzdorf to Mrs. Anstruther, 15 Aug. 1955, at Yale.

Cumberlege informs Yale of Miss Hailey's letters] Typed list, "The Boswell letters belonging to Miss Elma Hailey", with attached pencilled memorandum by Marion S. Pottle of conversation with R. L. Purdy, at Yale.

p. 192]
"Family Oath"] BP i. 162–63 (facsimile).

Elma Hailey, Boswell's great-great-great-granddaughter] See Table III, TA, p. 354.

Metzdorf to see Cumberlege] Letter, Geoffrey Cumberlege to R. F. Metzdorf, 13 June 1956, at Yale.

Letters acquired for Yale] "Tuesday I am to see Cumberlege and will close the deal on the things Mrs. Hailey offered us" (letter, R. F. Metzdorf to F. A. Pottle, 4 Oct. 1956, at Yale).

Yale pays Mrs. Hailey $80] Yale Univ. Treasurer's Office, Request for cheque, 22 Oct. 1956, at Yale.

Documents received by Yale] Marion S. Pottle's pencilled inventory, at Yale.

Milo Talbot, seventh Lord Talbot] TA, p. 295.

Lady Talbot living at Mount Shannon] TA, p. 296.

p. 193]
Milo, Lord Talbot corrects report about "new new" papers] Letter, Rose M. Talbot to R. F. Metzdorf, 3 Mar. 1958; letter, R. F. Metzdorf to Rose M. Talbot, 17 Apr. 1958. Both at Yale. The "report" came from Hyde (above, p. 186). Lord Talbot did not give us a correction in writing until after he had been able to discuss the matter with him (letter, F. A. Pottle to Lord Talbot, 14 Mar. 1960; letter, R. F. Metzdorf to Lord Talbot, 12 May 1960; letter, Lord Talbot to F. A. Pottle, 7 June 1960; letter, Lord Talbot to R. F. Metzdorf, 24 July 1960: all at Yale).

We offer to sort and inventory papers still at Malahide] Letter, R. F. Metzdorf to Lord Talbot, 9 Nov. 1959, at Yale, a carbon copy inquiring about the earlier papers, but making no offer to put them in order. Either a letter from Metzdorf to Talbot is missing, or (more probably) Metzdorf made the offer in a manuscript addition to the letter sent.

Lord Talbot sends tattered papers] Letter, Lord Talbot to R. F. Metzdorf, 28 Nov. 1959; letter, same to the same, 24 July 1960. Both at Yale.

Papers brought to New York] Letter, R. F. Metzdorf to Lord Talbot, 8 Aug. 1960, at Yale.

Rotted papers vetted] Letter, R. F. Metzdorf to Lord Talbot, 24 Aug. 1960, at Yale.

Inventory made] Marion S. Pottle, "Analysis of Boswell Material Sent by Lord Talbot de Malahide" (revision of list of 8 Aug. 1960, with additions, at Yale).

p. 194]
Bits recovered from 1769] J 20, J 20.1, J 22.

Also from 1773, 1779] J 26, J 33, J 33.1, J 63.1, J 64.

Lt. John Boswell's diary] C 404.1.

Sketch of flower by Veronica] P 25.

Missing leaves] Lg 43, M 85.3, M 135.

We ask Talbot his price] Letter, F. A. Pottle to R. F. Metzdorf, 17 Aug. 1960; letter, R. F. Metzdorf to F. A. Pottle, 24 Aug. 1960; letter, R. F. Metzdorf to Lord Talbot, 24 Aug. 1960. All at Yale.

Talbot asks for a figure, Barry appraises at $2,000 to $2,500] Letter, Lord Talbot to R. F. Metzdorf, 27 Aug. 1960; letter, same to the same, 28 Feb. 1961. Both at Yale.

We tactfully suggest that Talbot give Yale the papers, he postpones discussion] Letter, R. F. Metzdorf to Lord Talbot, 20 Mar. 1961; letter, Lord Talbot to R. F. Metzdorf, 28 Mar. 1961. Both at Yale.

Talbot gives Yale the tattered papers, wishes to retain one piece for display] Letter, R. F. Metzdorf to F. A. Pottle, F. W. Hilles, and H. W. Liebert, 20 May 1961, at Yale. He puts marks of quotation around "by carelessness . . . negligence", indicating, I assume, that the words were Lord Talbot's.

We agree] Letter, F. A. Pottle to Lord Talbot, 31 May 1961, at Yale.

p. 195]
Talbot wishes to send early and later papers to Yale for sorting and appraisal] Letter, as in the last note but one.

Metzdorf goes to Abbeylea] Letter, R. F. Metzdorf to Harriet Chidester, 21 May 1961, at Yale.

Purse and wedding ring] These articles and others were named in Schedule B of the Instrument of Sale of the Isham papers to Yale, 22 July 1949, at Yale.

Auchinleck House in a bad way] Letter, Mrs. J. P. D. Boswell to R. F. Metzdorf, 4 July 1957; letter, R. F. Metzdorf to Mrs. J. P. D. Boswell, 8 July 1957; letter, Mrs. J. P. D. Boswell to R. F. Metzdorf, 22 Jan. 1960; letter, same to the same, 29 Aug. 1960 (all at Yale); personal visit to Auchinleck, 1964.

Lady Talbot wished to make a contribution] Letter, R. F. Metzdorf to F. A. Pottle, 25 May 1961; letter, Lady Talbot to F. A. Pottle, 28 May 1961. Both at Yale.

Lady Talbot has another residue] Letter, Lady Talbot to F. A. Pottle, 28 May 1961, at Yale.

p. 196]
Lady Talbot thought *Hebrides* proofs unbound sheets] Letter, Lady Talbot to F. A. Pottle, 2 Mar. 1951, at Yale.

A hundred letters] Marion S. Pottle's "Summary of 'Abbeylea' Material", at Yale.

My personal favourite] L 1236.9.

Broadsides and separates] P 4, P 29 (8 items), P 54, P 95, P 96, P 132, P 136, P 163.

One previously recovered] P 102.

Metzdorf advises sale of duplicates by auction, sale of some items to the Hydes] Letter, R. F. Metzdorf to F. A. Pottle, 15 June 1961, at Yale; TA, p. 309. The clear Johnsonian item was eight proof pages of *Taxation no Tyranny;* a questionable one was nineteen cancel leaves for the second or third edition of the *Life of Johnson.*

p. 197]
"Mr. Metzdorf . . . got through more work"] Letter, Lady Talbot to F. A. Pottle, 28 May 1961, at Yale.

Metzdorf allowed to examine Auchinleck legal papers at Ayr] Letter, Lady Talbot as in the note preceding this; TA, p. 309.

Boswell papers remain at Auchinleck] Letter, J. P. D. Boswell to R. F. Metzdorf, 30 Sept. 1959, at Yale.

Lady Talbot waived claim] Letter, R. F. Metzdorf to Boswell Editorial Committee, 28 May 1961, reporting a meeting in Edinburgh, 26 May 1961, with the Boswells' lawyer, the Hon. D. A. Balfour. At Yale.

A trunk-full of estate papers] Letter, R. F. Metzdorf to Mrs. J. P. D. Boswell, 10 Oct. 1960, at Yale.

Metzdorf searches and appraises papers at Auchinleck] Letter, R. F. Metzdorf to Harriet Chidester, 21 May 1961; letter, R. F. Metzdorf to Boswell Editorial Committee, 28 May 1961. Both at Yale.

Metzdorf's formula] Letter, R. F. Metzdorf to F. A. Pottle, 7 July 1961, at Yale. Metzdorf's appraisal seems to have been £1,700.

Yale purchases estate papers at Auchinleck] Letter, F. A. Pottle to J. P. D. Boswell, 7 June 1961, at Yale.

p. 198]
We ask Metzdorf to bring back papers from Auchinleck and Abbeylea] Letter, R. F. Metzdorf to F. A. Pottle, 29 May 1961, at Yale.

Metzdorf gets Lady Talbot's consent] Letter, R. F. Metzdorf to H. W. Liebert, 14 June 1961, at Yale.

Metzdorf to sort legal papers at Auchinleck] Ibid.

From Auchinleck to Dublin] Letter, R. F. Metzdorf to F. A. Pottle, 15 June 1961, at Yale.

To Abbeylea] Letter, R. F. Metzdorf to H. W. Liebert, 14 June 1961; letter, R. F. Metzdorf to F. A. Pottle, 15 June 1961, both at Yale. Metzdorf wrote hasty manuscript letters on successive days with a good deal of repetition. I have made up this paragraph partly from one version, partly from the other.

Metzdorf not met at customs] Letter, R. F. Metzdorf to F. A. Pottle, 30 June 1961, at Yale.

Lady Talbot sets price of £10,000] Letter, Lady Talbot to H. W. Liebert, 30 June 1961, at Yale.

$34,750 estimated for purchase and photocopying] Letter, H. W. Liebert to Ernest Brooks, Jr., President, Old Dominion Foundation, 17 Oct. 1961, at Yale.

p. 199]
Metzdorf suggests appeal to Old Dominion Foundation and McGraw-Hill] Letter, R. F. Metzdorf to the Boswell Editorial Committee, 28 May 1961, at Yale.

Old Dominion Fund makes gift of $23,000] Letter, Ernest Brooks, Jr. to H. W. Liebert, 3 Nov. 1961, at Yale.

McGraw-Hill makes an advance of $10,900 against royalties] Letter, Helen E. Crawford (secretary to Edward Kuhn, Jr., Editor, McGraw-Hill, and McGraw-Hill's representative on the Editorial Committee) to F. A. Pottle, 5 Mar. 1962, enclosing a cheque for $10,900 "in payment of McGraw-Hill's share of the purchase of new acquisitions for the Boswell collection" (at Yale). I find no other correspondence: the matter was probably negotiated with Kuhn at a meeting of the Editorial Committee. Our royalty statements after Mar. 1962 show that the sum was treated as an advance.

Parke-Bernet sells a number of Lady Talbot's printed pieces] Letter, as in the 20th note back; Parke-Bernet Galleries, *First Editions Illuminated Manuscripts Letters of Presidents Other MSS.*

and Books . . . Public Auction . . . Oct. 3 and 4, 1961. Lady Talbot's lots ("British Collector") were Nos. 276–80, 282–84, 332, 355, 356, 434, and 466. All but lots 276 and 282 were bought for the Hyde Collection (TA, p. 309).

H.T.F. Cahoon brings over three suitcases of papers] TA, pp. 310–11. Letter, H.T.F. Cahoon to F. A. Pottle, 2 May 1979, at Yale. See also the second note below.

Auchinleck papers recovered from Sandgate] TA, pp. 311–12; letter, R. F. Metzdorf to H. W. Liebert, 11 June 1962, at Yale.

p. 200]
Metzdorf brings over the remainder of Talbot's parcels] Letter, Metzdorf to Liebert, as in the note preceding this: there seems to be some uncertainty as to how the shipment was divided. Five suitcases and a carton arrived at Yale. Cahoon took over three. Metzdorf on 11 June thought he would be bringing two.

Five suitcases and a carton of Talbot papers brought to Yale] I do not find record of who did this. Perhaps personnel of the Yale Library staff.

Yale declines Garallan papers, offers £300 for two Auchinleck lots] Letter, H. W. Liebert to J. P. D. Boswell, 21 June 1961, at Yale.

J. P. D. Boswell finds offer unacceptable] Letter, J. P. D. Boswell to H. W. Liebert, 30 July 1962, at Yale.

Yale offers £400 for one lot and £100 for the other] Letter, H. W. Liebert to J. P. D. Boswell, 9 Aug. 1962, at Yale.

J. P. D. Boswell accepts offer for first lot, sends it over by Prof. and Mrs. Hankins] Letter, Patricia S. Boswell to H. W. Liebert, 24 Aug. [1962]; receipt signed by J. E. Hankins, 22 Aug. 1962. Both at Yale.

Cheque ordered 3 Oct. 1962] Letter, Harriet Chidester to Yale Univ. Treasurer's Office, 11 Oct. 1962, at Yale.

J. P. D. Boswell offers to send Lot 2 to Yale for study and appraisal] Letter, Patricia S. Boswell to H. W. Liebert, as in the last note but one.

Yale approves arrangement] Letter, H. W. Liebert to Mrs. J. P. D. Boswell, 31 Aug. 1962, at Yale.

Talbot considers Yale's offer too small] Letter, F. A. Pottle to Lord Talbot, 28 Jan. 1964; letter, Lord Talbot to F. A. Pottle, 24 May 1964; letter, H. W. Liebert to Lord Talbot, 28 July 1964; letter, Lord Talbot to H. W. Liebert, 16 Sept. 1964. All at Yale.

Talbot finds seventeen more Boswell items] Last item cited in the note preceding this.

p. 201]
Yale proposes to divide the purchase between Liebert and Yale] Letter, H. W. Liebert to Lord Talbot, 8 Oct. 1964, at Yale.

Talbot accepts, asks that sum be paid toward the purchase of *Curtis's Botanical Magazine*] Letter, same to the same, 28 Dec. 1964; memorandum, H. W. Liebert to F. A. Pottle, c. 20 Apr. 1979, based on Talbot file and records of Rare Book Committee, Beinecke Library. Both at Yale.

Suitable set of *Curtis's* found] Last item in the note preceding this.

Mrs. Pottle and I again at Auchinleck] Letter, Patricia Boswell to F. A. Pottle, 18 May [1964], at Yale.

J. P. D. Boswell dies] Letter, Patricia Boswell to F. A. Pottle, 13 June 1966, at Yale.

We propose that R. C. Cole bring back Auchinleck papers] Letter, F. A. Pottle to Mrs. J. P. D. Boswell, 1 May 1968, at Yale.

p. 202]
Auchinleck papers not located in 1968] Letter, R. C. Cole to F. A. Pottle, 28 July 1968, at Yale.

"The *Palladia* of our Family"] Letter, Boswell to Robert Boswell, 21 May 1789 (*L 223).

David Buchanan arranges sale of the "Palladia" to Yale] TA, pp. 317–18.

Death of Lady Talbot] *Times,* 8 July 1980.

EPILOGUE THE SECOND

p. 203]
President Seymour grants the project $50,000] Appendix A, p. 15, Grant Application to the National Endowment for the Humanities, 6 May 1974, at Yale.

Editorial Committee approved] Memorandum of Agreement, 22 July 1949, Agreement H, at Yale.

A research and a reading edition] "A[swell] suggested that publication proceed on the assumption that two editions would be published, a trade edition containing everything possibly of popular interest, and also a complete research edition, but pointed out that this operating assumption would have to be confirmed by his colleagues" (Minutes, first meeting of the Editorial Committee, 23 Aug. 1949, at Yale). The minutes of the second meeting, Aswell present, contain no specific report of confirmation, but the publication of "popular" and "scholarly" editions was discussed as policy agreed upon, and the style "Yale Editions of the Private Papers of James Boswell" was proposed (ibid. 20 Sept. 1949, at Yale).

Policy of research edition] General Editorial Note, p. [viii]; Textual Note, pp. xlvii–xlviii, *The Correspondence of James Boswell and John Johnston of Grange,* ed. Ralph S. Walker, 1966. The details of policy were worked out during the preparation of this volume, mainly by F. W. Hilles, but I think were not fully and systematically stated till copy was prepared for these Notes.

p. 204]
Policy of reading edition] General Editorial Note, as in the note preceding this; *Boswell's London Journal,* ed. F. A. Pottle, 1950, pp. 35–36.

Contents of first volume] "The question of the contents of the first volume of the YBP was discussed. It was agreed that the 62–63 journal would be published first. P[ottle] raised the question of prefacing the journal of the harvest jaunt; H[illes] and L[iebert] supported his view that it should be included if possible in view of its earlier date and its continuous relationship to the 62–63 journal. . . . A[swell] said he had not read the harvest journal and would do so before expressing a view." (Minutes, 23 Aug. 1949). The minutes

of the next meeting (20 Sept. 1949) do not record Aswell's strong advice to ignore the journal before 15 Nov. 1762, but I remember his arguments clearly. He said that, if there seemed to be a call for it later, McGraw-Hill would include the journal of the harvest jaunt as a bonus in the last volume of the reading edition of the journal.

p. 205]
Selection of editor] Abbott was in New Haven at the time of the second meeting of the Editorial Committee. "Discussing the role of Abbott, the committee agreed that there were several things he might do. L[iebert] reported his talk with Abbott indicating he wanted to edit the 63 journal, the Boswell-Temple letters, and/or the Boswell-Forbes letters. It was agreed he could not do the first, that we would offer him the second, and that we would probably have to depend on him for the third in any event" (Minutes of the Editorial Committee, 20 Sept. 1949, at Yale).

Sunday Times] 15, 22, 29 Oct., 5, 12, 19, 26 Nov., 3 Dec. 1950.

Omnibook Magazine] Mar. 1951.

Sales of *Boswell's London Journal*] Newsletter to the Advisory Committee, signed F. A. Pottle, 17 Oct. 1950, summarizing correspondence in the Boswell Office, at Yale.

p. 206]
Reprints, translations] Newsletter to the Advisory Committee, signed R. F. Metzdorf, 19 Jan. 1953, summarizing correspondence in the Boswell Office, at Yale.

Managing editor appointed] Patricia B. Wells, Memorandum of Employment, Personnel Director's Office, Yale, 21 Sept. 1950; Newsletter, F. A. Pottle to Members of the Advisory Committee, 17 Oct. 1950. Both at Yale.

Stenographer and typist] Newsletter, as in the note preceding this.

Mrs. Wells] Patricia B. Wells, Memorandum of Employment, Personnel Director's Office, Yale, 25 May 1951; letter, Patricia Wells to F. A. Pottle, 24 Apr. 1952. Both at Yale.

p. 207]
R. F. Metzdorf appointed] Newsletter, R. F. Metzdorf to Members of the Advisory Committee, 19 Jan. 1953, at Yale.

R. F. Metzdorf, career summary] Above, p. 194; letter, R. F. Metzdorf to Frank Brady, 17 July 1961, at Yale.

Iola S. Haverstick] Iola S. Haverstick, Yale Univ. Recommendations, 2 Oct. 1961, 28 Feb. 1962, at Yale.

B. F. Houston] Letter, B. F. Houston to Harriet Chidester, dated only "Saturday", clearly towards the end of June 1962; Benjamin Franklin Houston, Yale Univ. Personnel Profile, 31 Jan. 1969. Both at Yale.

Mrs. Helen Cooper] Helen A. Cooper, Yale Univ. Personnel Profiles, 11 Feb. 1969, 30 June 1970, at Yale.

Dr. Irma S. Lustig] Newsletter, Irma S. Lustig and F. A. Pottle to Members of the Advisory Committee and Others, 20 June 1975, at Yale.

p. 208]
Royalties, *Boswell's London Journal*] McGraw-Hill royalty reports, including payments from Heinemann, 1950 and 1951, at Yale.

Hilles on half-time teaching] Newsletter to the Advisory Committee, signed F. A. Pottle, 17 Oct. 1950, summarizing correspondence in the Boswell Office, at Yale.

p. 210]
Date of publication of *Boswell in Holland*] *Publishers' Weekly.*

Geoffrey Scott's publication of Holland material] *Zélide . . . Inviolable Plan . . . and Other Papers,* 1929 (BP ii).

Boswell in Holland serialized, selections printed] *Atlantic Monthly,* (Apr. 1952) clxxxix. 34–43; *Daily Mail,* (28, 29, 30 Apr., 1, 2, 5, 6, 7, 8, 9, 12, 13 May 1952).

Sales of *Boswell in Holland*] Newsletter to the Advisory Committee, signed R. F. Metzdorf,

19 Jan. 1953, summarizing correspondence in the Boswell Office, at Yale.

p. 211]
Review in *TLS*] 13 June 1952, p. 388.

Sat. Rev. Lit. prints pre-publication extracts from *Portraits*] 11 Oct. 1952, xxxv. 20–21, 30; 15 Nov. 1952, xxxv. 11–12, 35–37.

Sales of *Portraits*] McGraw-Hill's royalty reports, including payments from Heinemann, at Yale.

p. 212]
Date of publication of *Boswell on the Grand Tour: Germany and Switzerland*] *Publishers' Weekly.*

Selections from *Boswell on the Grand Tour: Germany and Switzerland*] Newsletter to the Advisory Committee, etc., 8 Jan. 1954, at Yale.

Times Literary Supplement] 30 Oct. 1953, p. 694.

p. 213]
Date of publication of *Boswell on the Grand Tour: Italy, Corsica, and France*] Newsletter to the Advisory Committee, etc., 2 Feb. 1956, at Yale.

Sales of *Boswell on the Grand Tour: Italy, Corsica, and France*] McGraw-Hill's royalty reports, at Yale.

Aswell leaves McGraw-Hill] Letter, H. W. Liebert to F. A. Pottle, 25 June 1956, reporting a telephone conversation with Aswell on the previous evening, at Yale.

p. 214]
Aswell continues to represent Heinemann on Editorial Committee] Personal recollection; Aswell file, 30 Aug. 1956 to 23 July 1958, at Yale.

Edward Kuhn, Jr.] As in the second note back; letter, Harold W. McGraw, Jr., to F. A. Pottle, 15 Oct. 1965, at Yale.

Frank E. Taylor] Letter, Harold W. McGraw, Jr. to F. A. Pottle, 15 Oct. 1965, at Yale.

Dan Lacy] Newsletter to the Members of the Advisory Committee, etc., 20 June 1975, at Yale.

T. H. Quinn] Letter, Irma S. Lustig to T. H. Quinn, 20 May 1975, at Yale.

Publication date of *Boswell in Search of a Wife*] *Publishers' Weekly*.

Sales of *Boswell in Search of a Wife*] Appendix E, p. 29, Yale Boswell Editions Grant Application to the National Endowment for the Humanities, 26 Apr. 1976, at Yale.

Paperback sales of *Boswell's London Journal*] Newsletter to the Members of the Advisory Committee, etc., 28 April 1958, at Yale.

Inquiry from N. S. Curnow] Letter, N. S. Curnow to F. Brady and F. A. Pottle, 3 Nov. 1957, at Yale.

p. 215]
We reply] Letter, F. A. Pottle to N. S. Curnow, 18 Nov. 1957, at Yale.

Curnow acquires *Private Papers* and *Index*] Letter, N. S. Curnow to F. A. Pottle, 10 May 1958; letter, same to the same, 28 Nov. 1957. Both at Yale.

Curnow's method of reading] First letter cited in the note preceding this.

A subsequent letter] Letter, N. S. Curnow to F. A. Pottle, 17 June 1958, at Yale.

Curnow tells us about himself] Ibid.; letter, same to the same, 11 Dec. 1962, at Yale.

p. 216]
Reads through *Private Papers*, makes chronological arrangement of Fettercairn *Catalogue*] Letter, N. S. Curnow to F. A. Pottle, 27 Sept. 1958, at Yale.

Orders microfilms of dissertations, sends annotations and corrections] Letter, N. S. Curnow to F. A. Pottle, 14 Feb. 1959; letter, same to the same, 3 June 1959; letter, R. F. Metzdorf to N. S. Curnow, 21 June 1959; letter, N. S. Curnow to R. F. Metzdorf, 14 Feb. 1960. All at Yale.

Verifies *Index* to *Private Papers*, compiles genealogical tables] Letter, N. S. Curnow to F. A. Pottle, 6 July 1961; letter, same to the same, 11 Feb. 1962. Both at Yale.

We ask him to read proofs] Letter, Harriet Chidester to N. S. Curnow, 5 Oct. 1961; N. S. Curnow to H. Chidester, 10 Oct. 1961; letter, F. A. Pottle to N. S. Curnow, 17 Sept. 1962; letter, N. S. Curnow to F. A. Pottle, 21 Sept. 1962. All at Yale.

We appoint him member of the Advisory Committee] Letter, F. A. Pottle to N. S. Curnow, 29 Oct. 1962; letter, N. S. Curnow to F. A. Pottle, 6 Nov. 1962. Both at Yale.

We put him in charge of revision of the first research volume] Ibid.

Curnow reports a kidney infection] Letter, N. S. Curnow to F. A. Pottle, 4 Aug. 1963; letter, same to the same, 15 Sept. 1963; letter, N. S. Curnow to B. F. Houston, 1 Oct. 1963. All at Yale.

Sends 150 typed pages of biographical notes] Letter, N. S. Curnow to F. A. Pottle, 20 Jan. 1964, at Yale.

Kidney infection returns] Letter, N. S. Curnow to B. F. Houston, 31 Oct. 1964, at Yale.

Begins reporting on typescript of *James Boswell, the Earlier Years*] Letter, N. S. Curnow to F. A. Pottle, 18 Jan. 1965; letter, same to the same, 18 Feb. 1965. Both at Yale.

In "a motor smash", suffers concussion] Letter, N. S. Curnow to F. A. Pottle, 15 Mar. 1965; letter, same to the same, 24 Mar. 1965. Both at Yale.

Dies of meningitis] Letter, W. R. Schaerer to F. A. Pottle, 31 July 1965, at Yale.

Second grant from Old Dominion Foundation] Appendix A, p. 15, Grant Application to the National Endowment for the Humanities, 6 May 1974, at Yale.

Boswell for the Defence published] *Publishers' Weekly*.

p. 217]
Cyril Connolly] *New Yorker,* (30 Jan. 1960) xxxv. 99.

Sales of *Boswell for the Defence*] McGraw-Hill royalty reports; Appendix E, p. 29, Grant Application to the National Endowment for the Humanities, 26 Apr. 1976. Both at Yale.

Date of publication of *Boswell's Journal of a Tour to the Hebrides*] *Publishers' Weekly.*

p. 218]
Sales of *Boswell's Journal of a Tour to the Hebrides*] As in the last note but one.

p. 219]
Publication of *Boswell: The Ominous Years*] *Publishers' Weekly.*

Sales of *Boswell: The Ominous Years*] As in the fourth note back.

p. 220]
The Old Dominion Foundation awards us $25,000 more] Appendix A, p. 15, Grant Application to the National Endowment for the Humanities, 6 May 1974, at Yale.

James Boswell, The Earlier Years published] *Publishers' Weekly.*

"The object of the annotation"] "General Editorial Note", p. [vi] of vol. 1 of *The Yale Editions of the Private Papers of James Boswell* (Research Edition) and of succeeding volumes.

Sales of vols. 1 and 2 of research series] McGraw-Hill's royalty reports, including payments from Heinemann, at Yale.

p. 221]
Grant of $10,000 from NEH] Appendix A, p. 15, Grant Application to the National Endowment for the Humanities, 6 May 1974, at Yale.

Funding 1969–75] Ibid.

"Periods of melancholia and high spirits"] Page ix.

Sales of *Boswell in Extremes*] As in the fourth note back.

Death of Charles Bennett] Alumni records, Yale.

p. 222]
Death of Edward C. Aswell] *New York Times,* 6 Nov. 1958.

Death of Robert Warnock] Alumni records, Yale.

Death of Frederick W. Hilles] *New York Times,* 12 Dec. 1975.

Frank Brady appointed to Editorial Committee] Letter, Kingman Brewster to Frank Brady, 17 Apr. 1972, at Yale.

Marshall Waingrow appointed to Editorial Committee] Letter, F. A. Pottle to Kingman Brewster, 27 Feb. 1976, asking him to confirm the appointment, at Yale.

Martin Price appointed to Editorial Committee] Letter, A. Bartlett Giamatti to Frank Brady, 18 May 1979, at Yale.

NEH award, 1 Jan. 1975 to 31 Mar. 1977] Newsletter of the Boswell Office, 1 Oct. 1976, at Yale.

NEH award, 1 Apr. 1977 to 31 Mar. 1980] Newsletter of the Boswell Office, May 1979, at Yale.

p. 223]
Irma S. Lustig appointed to Editorial Committee] As in third note back.

Times Literary Supplement] 13 Aug. 1976, no. 3,883, p. 1007.

Sales of third volume of the research series] McGraw-Hill's royalty reports, including payments from Heinemann, at Yale.

Boswell, Laird of Auchinleck published] *Publishers' Weekly.*

p. 224]
Sales of *Boswell, Laird of Auchinleck*] As in the last note but one.

INDEX

Noblemen, Lords of Session, and their wives are entered under their titles. Maiden names of married women are supplied in parentheses. Titles of books are listed under the names of the authors. Under personal names, references to letters are grouped at the end of other subentries, followed by titles of works. The following abbreviations are used: D. (Duke), M. (Marquess), E. (Earl), V. (Viscount), B. (Baron), Bt. (Baronet), W.S. (Writer to the Signet), JB (James Boswell), SJ (Samuel Johnson). Informal style (Grace Boswell, Joyce Talbot) has been used in the analysis for two often repeated names.